LOST FEDERATIONS

THE UNOFFICIAL
UNMADE HISTORY OF
STAR TREK

A.J. BLACK

POLARIS
PUBLISHING

This edition first published in 2022 by

POLARIS PUBLISHING LTD
c/o Aberdein Considine
2nd Floor, Elder House
Multrees Walk
Edinburgh
EH1 3DX

www.polarispublishing.com

Text copyright © A.J. Black, 2023

ISBN: 9781915359117
eBook ISBN: 9781915359124

The right of A.J. Black to be identified as the author of this work has been asserted by him in accordance with the Copyright, Designs and Patents Act 1988.

All rights reserved. No part of this publication may be reproduced, stored or transmitted in any form, or by any means electronic, mechanical, photocopying, recording or otherwise, without the express written permission of the publisher.

The views expressed in this book do not necessarily reflect the views, opinions or policies of Polaris Publishing Ltd (Company No. SC401508) (Polaris), nor those of any persons, organisations or commercial partners connected with the same (Connected Persons). Any opinions, advice, statements, services, offers, or other information or content expressed by third parties are not those of Polaris or any Connected Persons but those of the third parties. For the avoidance of doubt, neither Polaris nor any Connected Persons assume any responsibility or duty of care whether contractual, delictual or on any other basis towards any person in respect of any such matter and accept no liability for any loss or damage caused by any such matter in this book.

This is an unofficial publication. All material contained within is for critical purposes.

Every effort has been made to trace copyright holders and obtain their permission for the use of copyright material. The publisher apologises for any errors or omissions and would be grateful if notified of any corrections that should be incorporated in future reprints or editions of this book.

British Library Cataloguing-in-Publication Data
A catalogue record for this book is available on request from the British Library.

Designed and typeset by Polaris Publishing, Edinburgh
Printed in Great Britain by MBM Print, East Kilbride

For every writer of *Star Trek*.
You gave us the final frontier.

Thanks to Ronald D. Moore and Andre Bormanis for sharing lost stories, and their time. Thanks to Peter Burns for his ongoing support, and to Jonathan Melville for helping me improve the work. And thanks to my wife Steph, endlessly supporting me as I boldly go.

CONTENTS

Prologue: Secret Histories   1

1: Star Trek Is . . .   7

2: The Man of Tomorrow   23

3: These Were Almost the Voyages: *The Original Series*   41

4: The Motion Pictures: Part I   67

5: The Lost Years: Phase II   98

6: Where No One Had Gone Before: *The Next Generation*   128

7: The First and Final Adventures: *The Final Frontier* and *The Undiscovered Country*   162

8: The Rifleman in Space: *Deep Space Nine*   181

9: Damn Fine Cups of Coffee: *Voyager*   208

10: The Motion Pictures: Part II   239

11: The Beginning: *Enterprise*   270

12: Uncharted Frontiers: The Animated, Video-Game and Live-Action Pitches   291

13: The Motion Pictures: Part III   313

14: Strange New Shows: The Age of *Discovery*   342

Epilogue: Where No Franchise Has Gone Before   357

Bibliography   361

PROLOGUE

SECRET HISTORIES

LATE IN THE sixth season of the second *Star Trek* spin-off series, *Deep Space Nine*, a startling revelation takes place.

In the episode 'Inquisition', after the station's chief medical officer Dr Julian Bashir is accused of being a spy and interrogated by a sinister Starfleet Intelligence officer named Luther Sloan, amidst a devastating galactic war the United Federation of Planets are facing, we, Bashir and the rest of the crew discover that Sloan in truth works for Section-31, a black operations intelligence unit within Starfleet who have existed for over two centuries, secretly as part of the Federation's founding charter.

It was, and indeed remains despite subsequent series including *Star Trek: Enterprise* and *Star Trek: Discovery* expanding on the Section-31 mythos, a deeply controversial concept within the franchise Gene Roddenberry created in the mid-1960s because, ostensibly, it operates directly in contradiction to the future historicity of what we understand to *be Star Trek*. It suggests lurking beneath *Star Trek*'s veneer of openness, hope and a belief in the triumphant power of the human condition lies a cynical foundation of fear, anxiety and falsehood. It suggests a secret history we might never entirely appreciate.

This feels relevant as a touchstone because, while the creation and establishment of *Star Trek* since the original pilot episode, 'The Cage', first aired in 1965, has been well documented over half a century, there has long existed if not a secret then without question an *alternate* history to the story of a series that began as a quirky addition to a bright, colourful canon of 1960s American television and grew into one of the world's most dominant, recognisable intellectual properties and franchises.

'The Cage' itself, of course, became something of a lost artefact in *Star Trek* history. Roddenberry's first attempt at bringing his concept of future humans exploring the galaxy and 'boldly going' where no one had gone before on the USS *Enterprise*, featured Jeffrey Hunter as Captain Christopher Pike and an entirely different crew around Leonard Nimoy's Mr Spock. It was rejected by studio NBC for several reasons, as Roddenberry explained: "The reason they turned it down was that it was too cerebral and there wasn't enough action and adventure. 'The Cage' didn't end with a chase and a right cross to the jaw, the way all manly films were supposed to end. There were no female leads then – women in those days were just set dressing."

NBC sought to have Roddenberry remove the soon-to-be-iconic character of Spock – as his pointy ears and demeanour were considered somewhat 'satanic' – and replace his future wife Majel Barrett as Number One, the measured, intelligent second-in-command to Pike. Given the rare opportunity to shoot a second pilot, Roddenberry refused on the former but relented on the latter. Spock and Number One were conceptually melded for 'The Man Trap', the newly filmed pilot that replaced Pike (as Hunter rejected the chance to return) with William Shatner's Captain James T. Kirk and a whole new crew. The rest, as we know, is history.

'The Cage', however, was never broadcast at the time. Portions of the episode were inserted into 'The Menagerie', a two-part story in *Star Trek: The Original Series* which explored Spock's relationship to Kirk and the earlier crew of the *Enterprise*, thereby making events of 'The Cage' canonical in *Star Trek* history. The original pilot did not re-emerge for two decades, until an early VHS release in 1986, crafted from a 16mm black-and-white print Roddenberry held. It was combined with the original print, a print earlier cut apart to fashion 'The Menagerie', before a year later the full colourised version was pieced together and 'The Cage' was finally broadcast late in 1988 as part of a tie-in with the new, and successful, sequel series *Star Trek: The Next Generation*.

It is now, thankfully, in wide circulation thanks to the age of Blu-Ray and 4K box sets, not to mention streaming services, and has rightly taken its place as the Rosetta Stone of *Star Trek*. Pike was revived by J. J. Abrams in his 2009 *Star Trek* reboot film, while sequel series *Star Trek: Discovery* revived both Pike and Number One for an extended arc that reintroduced a younger Spock, served as a sequel to 'The Cage' and prequel to 'The Menagerie', and set in motion storylines that would lead to *Star Trek: Strange New Worlds*, with Anson Mount's Pike and Rebecca Romjin's Number One as main characters in their own *Enterprise*-set prequel to *The Original Series*.

What the story of 'The Cage' demonstrates, nonetheless, is how easily *Star Trek*'s narrative can fall prey to what scholars have described as 'the unmade', or as noted professor of unmade studies James Fenwick terms it, 'unproduction studies': "The unmade seems to be an integral part of how the media industries work. One reason for this is because of the nature of the creative process: ideas mutate and evolve, stories and scripts are developed and redeveloped, revised, and edited, to the point they become wholly new ideas and stories unrecognisable from the original idea. Draft one of a script will likely be very different to the final draft of the script. However, beyond this particular aspect of the creative process, there is clearly an expectation amongst producers and screenwriters that most projects will never be produced, particularly if they become stuck in 'development hell', a process in which a project (not necessarily even a screenplay, but maybe just a film title, a planned adaptation or an elevator pitch) becomes trapped in a perpetual cycle of creation and revision for many years and usually leads to it eventually being abandoned, or even just left in a purgatory state."

Many of these states can be attributed to a range of projects across the history of *Star Trek*, from the mid-1960s when *The Original Series* was first in production through to the 21st-century era of cinematic and televised *Star Trek*. Some were simply ideas, such as Roddenberry's 'The Cattlemen'. Some were fully developed scripts, such as the original draft of what became the *Original Series* episode 'Assignment: Earth'. Some were turned later into book or comic series adaptations. Some made it as far as pre-production before collapsing in on themselves, in the case of 1970s *Original Series* adaptation movie *Planet of the Titans*. Some were inches away from going into full production, as was the case with Roddenberry's first intended sequel series *Star Trek: Phase II*. Some are almost mythical. Many have been discussed and explored over the decades by a range of writers and scholars fascinated as much by the *Star Trek* that never made it to the screen as the *Star Trek* that we have fallen in love with across numerous generations.

This is *Star Trek* that fits Fenwick's 'unproduction studies' mould of "exploring a shadowy archival world where little makes sense within the framework of existing canonical film history", or in this case film, TV and computer gaming history, given *Star Trek*'s trans-media reach particularly since the 1990s.

Canon has always meant a great deal to audiences who have engaged with *Star Trek* over the last half-century and more, the idea of a consistent world of constant universal in-world history that subsequent narratives pay attention to and respect. For instance, the placement of *Discovery* within the 23rd century *Star Trek* timeline was deliberate; set a decade before *The Original Series*, it allowed the series to explore events – such as a Federation-Klingon war mentioned in an *Original Series* episode – in the same era without contradicting what came before but would be set, from a narrative perspective, later. Audiences learning that Spock had a human sister, Michael Burnham, raised on Vulcan by his parents, raised canonical eyebrows given earlier *Star Trek* productions – albeit set later – made no suggestion of this in Spock's backstory. This was for a very good reason – *Discovery*, nor Burnham, had been invented yet.

The origin of 'canon' in fictional terms, given the term applies to numerous ongoing fictional universes outside of *Star Trek*, is sourced directly from the Biblical canon – the set of religious texts considered scripture, as opposed to the Apocrypha, or non-canonical texts. It is a rigorous application of structure and chronology that comes, ostensibly, from the higher power behind such events. Thereby the term was first applied to fiction by Sir Arthur Conan Doyle in the 19th century for his Sherlock Holmes adventures, and Roddenberry would later exist as the God-like arbiter of what was and was not considered canonical *Star Trek* storytelling, as his assistant Richard Arnold declared in 1991: "As long as Gene Roddenberry is involved in it, he is the final word on what is *Star Trek* . . . And when he says that the books, and the games, and the comics and everything else, are not gospel, but are only additional *Star Trek* based on his *Star Trek* but not part of the actual *Star Trek* universe that he created . . . they're just, you know, kinda fun to keep you occupied between episodes and between movies, whatever . . . but he does not want that to be considered to be sources of information for writers, working on this show, he doesn't want it to be considered part of the canon by anybody working on any other projects."

Roddenberry as arbiter naturally changed after his passing in 1991. Rick Berman, one of his primary producers on the second era of *Star*

Trek from 1987 onwards, nominally became the authority – Peter to Roddenberry's Christ, to continue the tortured Biblical analogy – alongside numerous denominated head writers who steered the direction of many of the spin-off and sequel series to come: Michael Piller, Ira Steven Behr, Jeri Taylor, Brannon Braga, etc. Following the end of that era in 2005, the torch passed through Bad Robot Productions and J. J. Abrams' stable of creatives to the modern era steward under Paramount-CBS – Alex Kurtzman, who at the time of writing serves as the latest chief creative figure, alongside numerous studio executives and consultants, deciding the nature of canonical *Star Trek*.

By the 2020s, and the ever-evolving trans-media landscape of modern intellectual property, this no longer simply covers what we see on screen. Books, games, comics and other applications are now assuming, if not a full canon status, then a quasi-canonical position within the *Star Trek* framework. Kurtzman even legitimised the long assumed non-canonical *The Animated Series*, which ran from 1972–1973, produced by Roddenberry and featuring most of the original cast, by including references to elements of that series that had never featured in *Star Trek* anywhere else. This was after Roddenberry decades earlier had 'de-canonised' it within his own deific definition of *Star Trek*. The nature of canon is likely to consistently evolve as *Star Trek* itself does.

If, therefore, so-called 'unmade *Star Trek*', by the very nature of never coming to pass on screen or indeed in any other format, cannot be considered as canon, it must by definition fall into the bracket of Fenwick's 'shadow world'; a secret history, explored to varying degrees over the years, which points the way toward an entirely different, potential canonical story for *Star Trek* and, in part, the history of science fiction on television and in cinema itself. While perhaps lacking the all-consuming cultural dominance in the late 1970s as George Lucas' *Star Wars* achieved in cinematic terms, *Star Trek* stands as one of the defining cultural artefacts of the mid-20th century in how it shaped American social, political and cultural trends amidst two decades of significant national tumult.

Nichelle Nichols, who played a trend-setting black television character in the *Enterprise*'s Lieutenant Uhura, tells a story that underlines this reach from when she attended an NAACP fundraiser in the late 1960s and was told a big fan of the show wanted to meet her: "I thought it was a Trekkie, and so I said, 'Sure.' I looked across the room, and there was Dr Martin Luther King walking towards me with this big grin on his face.

He reached out to me and said, 'Yes, Ms. Nichols, I am your greatest fan.' He said that *Star Trek* was the only show that he, and his wife Coretta, would allow their three little children to stay up and watch. [She told King about her plans to leave the series.] I never got to tell him why, because he said, 'You can't. You're part of history.'"

History might have played out very differently had, for example, 'The Cage' been accepted by NBC and the series progressed from there. On the bridge of Pike's *Enterprise*, there was no Uhura and no Nichelle Nichols, indeed there was no black officer on the bridge pointing the way on American television, during the powder keg era of Civil Rights, for black representation in an idealised future.

This book, in part, will seek to understand how history and culture might have been altered had the secret, or at least often under-reported story of the 'unmade' *Star Trek* future, ended up coming to pass. How might Roddenberry have pushed the needle in the national conversation about animal rights in the 1960s had he made an intended feature film called 'The Cattlemen'? Might *Star Trek* had achieved the same cinematic science-fiction dominance in the 1970s if 'Planet of the Titans' had come to be, and how might that have affected the post-American New Wave transformation of the auteur filmmaker into what became the high-concept, blockbuster, franchise-driven Hollywood landscape that still exists today? Would the advent of serialised television have been prefigured by unrealised long-form attempts at storytelling on established, formulaic *Star Trek* series such as *Voyager* or *Enterprise*?

The history of unmade *Star Trek* is not simply the story of untold wonders but larger unrealised possibilities that might have shaped trends, the fate of actors who subsequently became iconic and the reach and appreciation of a television series which, perhaps like no other in television history, has reflected and continues to reflect our hopes, our anxieties and our beliefs, across transformations in rights and freedoms, through wars and genocides, and giant leaps for man, woman and those who are not defined by gender. As Ira Steven Behr said: "The theory I've always heard says that when the western died, science fiction filled the gap. We could not dream in the past anymore, so we started to dream in the future."

Star Trek helps us dream. And *Lost Federations*, this book, hopes to dream again of what almost was, what could have been and what we can only imagine. Let's see what's out there . . .

ONE

STAR TREK IS . . .

'A ONE-HOUR dramatic television series. Action-Adventure-Science Fiction. The first such concept with strong central lead characters plus other continuing regulars.'

In March 1964, two years before the first season of *Star Trek* arrived on the airwaves, Roddenberry put the finishing touches on an initial 'bible' for the series he intended to use to pitch the show. It was called 'Star Trek Is . . .' and it contained what stands as the original documented intention for what became *Star Trek*. The quote above stands as the first description he ever gave of what he intended *Star Trek* to be.

One of the first people to read it was Dorothy Fontana, Roddenberry's secretary at the time who would later go on to pen some of *Star Trek*'s finest episodes and rank as a pioneer of female science-fiction writing for television under her pen name D. C. Fontana: "There was nothing like it on television at that time. It had lots of possibilities and you could see the stories. They'd begin to pop into your mind automatically."

Roddenberry's initial pitch contains characters and concepts that would surface in the eventual series, but others have passed into deeper *Star Trek* lore. His original name for the ship that was immortalised as the USS *Enterprise* was the SS *Yorktown*, with a naval moniker that more deliberately evoked the Hornblower influences, a name borrowed both from a Second World War aircraft carrier and the decisive final battle of the American War of Independence at the end of the 18th century (the

USS *Yorktown* would later be referenced in Art Wallace's 'Obsession' in the second season; appear, briefly, captained by tennis pro Vijay Amitraj in *Star Trek IV: The Voyage Home*, and serve as the name of a gigantic space colony in 2016's *Star Trek Beyond*). The SS *Yorktown* was designated as a 'United Space Ship', a large, bulky cruiser with a crew of several hundred designed to embark on the aforementioned five-year mission.

Star Trek staff writer John D. F. Black explained the thinking behind this: "There was a reason for it being five years. Sure, the Navy – and this, in a sense, was the U.S. Navy in space – will send you on a tour of duty, but not for five years. Truth is Gene was hoping the show would last five years! If you could get five seasons done, you were assured a long run in syndication."

So much for those plans! Roddenberry nonetheless had visions of a show designed to have the science-fiction grandeur of the classic 1956 film *Forbidden Planet*, itself based on William Shakespeare's *The Tempest*, but he was also inspired by *Space Cadet*, a late-1940s pulp novel by Robert A. Heinlein, one of the seminal American science-fiction authors of the mid-20th century: "Space Cadet is a very humane book. It deals with not only the problems of science – about space travel and technology and so on – but of the need we have to act in a conscious responsible manner with all this technology . . ."

His original assemblage of characters retained facets, and in some places names, that continued into 'The Cage' and the series beyond. The *Yorktown*'s original, intended commander was one Captain Robert April, described by Roddenberry in the document as "Colorfully complex, capable of action and decision which can verge on the heroic – but who lives a continual battle with self-doubt and the loneliness of command." April was a name Roddenberry had used before in a two-parter he wrote for the Western series *Have Gun, Will Travel*, which ran for over 200 episodes over six seasons between 1957 and 1963, where April was a prison chaplain. For 'The Cage', he was later re-named and re-tooled into Captain Christopher Pike, and then for the series, of course, Captain James T. Kirk, but April remained a part of deeper *Star Trek* lore.

After *The Original Series*, April first appeared in animated form in the final episode of *The Animated Series*. In 'The Counter-Clock Incident', he is described as the original commander of the *Enterprise* for a five-year mission in the 2240s, a decade before Pike and two decades before Kirk, suggesting the mission planned in 'Star Trek Is . . .' *did* indeed take place. 'The Counter-Clock Incident' presents April as a distinguished, older white Admiral with white hair, but the canonical status of *The Animated Series* remains disputed to this day. Elements of the show have been incorporated in the 2017-onwards era of the franchise, yet simultaneously counteracted, with April a good example of that fact.

As of writing, the most recent spin-off series, *Strange New Worlds*, which focuses on Pike's own five-year mission in the 2250s before 'The Cage', includes Admiral Robert April as a character, only he is a black man. *Discovery*'s Season 2 premiere, 'Brother', establishes that Pike was April's first officer and inherited command of the *Enterprise* from him, further cementing that Roddenberry's initial, intended five-year mission took place. Several of the crew in 'Star Trek Is . . .' described around April, also, carried over into future projects.

Roddenberry lists April's second-in-command as 'Number One' as early as the 1964 pitch document, describing her as: "a mysterious female, slim and dark, expressionless, cool, one of those women who will always look the same between years 20 and 50 . . . is probably Robert April's superior in detailed knowledge of the multiple equipment systems, departments and crew members aboard the vessel." Be in no doubt that he was describing Majel Barrett, an actress who he met and cast in an episode of *The Lieutenant* and, despite him being married at the time with children, became his mistress. Barrett went on to become the 'First Lady of *Star Trek*' when she married Roddenberry, immortalised as the voice of the Starfleet computer system in the 1980s era onwards, the comedic and flirtatious Lwaxana Troi in *The Next Generation* and *Deep Space Nine*, and especially as the original incarnation of the mysterious Number One in 'The Cage'. The role would be inherited by Rebecca Romijn in *Strange New Worlds* and given the canonical name, Una Chin-Riley (her forename christened in honour of *Star Trek* novelist Una McCormack).

The document also named the ship's chief medical officer as Dr Philip Boyce, given the nickname 'Bones', "humorously cynical . . . enjoys his own weaknesses; [and is] the Captain's only real confidant . . . considers himself the only realist aboard, measures each new landing in terms of relative annoyance, rather than excitement". This sure sounds like the Bones we would come to know and love! Roddenberry knew DeForest Kelley, who would ultimately play Dr Leonard 'Bones' McCoy in the series (though not 'The Cage') after they made a TV pilot called *333 Montgomery Street* together and he was always the first choice for *Star Trek*'s famously irascible MD.

Moreover, the document describes a South American navigator called Jose Ortegas, with a fiery Latin temperament, a man "painfully aware of the historical repute of Latins as lovers – and is in danger of failing this ambition on a cosmic scale". Though he was eventually loosely adapted into a lieutenant called Jose Tyler (played by Peter Duryea) who appeared only in 'The Cage', the name was partly adopted for the character of Erica Ortegas (played by Melissa Navia) in *Strange New Worlds*, also a navigator and equally possessed of a similar fiery temperament.

It also lists the captain's yeoman as a woman called Colt who "serves as Robert April's secretary, reporter, bookkeeper, and undoubtedly wishes she could also serve him in more personal departments. She is not dumb; she is very female, disturbingly so." As a descriptor, this has arguably dated poorly since the early 1960s – and with one hand in Roddenberry giving Number One a sense of modern agency, the other takes away – but it suggests the intention to have a beautiful female in April's thrall to satisfy more of a romantic audience demographic, and arguably she serves as the template for Grace Lee Whitney's recurring crew member Janice Rand in the series and several big-screen adventures.

The only character to survive the document largely intact is Mr Spock, described here as 'First Lieutenant' and right-hand man to the captain, not to mention generally taking care of the ship's functions. Though he suggests the first view of him can be frightening with "a face so heavy-lidded and satanic you might also expect him to have a forked tail". He describes him as "probably half-Martian, he has a slightly reddish complexion and semi-pointed ears". On first blush, though this suggests Roddenberry had in mind the idea of Spock being half-alien from the very beginning, the satanic description and complexion suggests a more devilish, perhaps even trickster character in line with the alien creatures *Star Trek* would often encounter during Roddenberry's involvement, such as Trelane or later Q.

However, Roddenberry also adds "but strangely, Mr Spock's quiet temperament is in dramatic contrast to his satanic look", which hints at the stoic ocean of Vulcan calm he will develop into via 'The Cage' and eventually arrive fully formed with the series. Roddenberry describes him as April's physical and emotional equal, with a "cat-like curiosity over anything the slightest 'alien'", with the suggestion being that the triumvirate which will become central to *Star Trek* – that of Kirk, Spock and Bones – would have existed in this initial five-year mission with April, Spock and Number One.

Roddenberry in his document, having established the *Yorktown* and the initial crew, opened a wide timeframe for when the series would be set, before settling on the middle of the 23rd century: "The time is 'somewhere in the future'. It could be 1995 or 2995. In other words, close enough to our own time for our continuing characters to be fully identifiable as people like us, but far enough into the future for galaxy travel to be thoroughly established."

He goes on to discuss the make-up of the *Yorktown* as a vessel, and from a production standpoint how the sets involved could be utilised. Drawing from the Blair General Hospital setting used by Dr Kildare in Dodge City, in the Western series *Gunsmoke*, Roddenberry suggests the *Yorktown* be established as a vessel where the camera can rove, intercepting main, secondary or guest characters as a means of telling the story. "The interior construction is utilitarian rather than exotic with a few appropriate indications of advanced controls and instruments. There are galleys, recreation rooms, a library, a hospital unit, and scientific laboratories, in addition to expected items such as the bridge, communication room and crew quarters with a slight naval flavour."

This sounds not too dissimilar to the eventual production design of the *Enterprise*, if perhaps less colourful, and was no doubt partly adapted for the 2001 prequel series, *Star Trek: Enterprise*, featuring the NX-01 *Enterprise* almost a century before *The Original Series* took place.

Roddenberry also discusses how infrequently an entire story could take place on the *Yorktown* itself: "Such as the tale of a strange 'intelligence' which has made its way aboard and is working to take over the minds of certain crewmen. Or the transportation of a person or a material which poses a mounting jeopardy to the ship and our characters."

Already, stories are forming around the *Yorktown* and the characters Roddenberry was developing, and his pitch would contain a great deal more in this manner of thinking.

*

A key factor to Roddenberry's development of the world of *Star Trek* and the early narratives he suggested was the idea of the 'parallel worlds' concept, whereby he intended for the *Yorktown* to visit 'Class M' planets with a similar level of social and evolutionary development as Earth, which he admits is in part a production concern: "The 'Parallel World' concept makes production practical via the use of available 'Earth' casting, sets, locations, costuming, and it means simply that our stories deal with plant and animal life, plus people, quite similar to that on Earth." At the same time, this is a deliberate attempt by Roddenberry to retain the core idea that *Star Trek* will tell relatable *human* stories within a science-fiction framework, however far into the galaxy April and his crew will explore.

The document came armed with numerous episode concepts that both hinted at exciting possible *Star Trek* stories to come, stories that would form facets of episodes we know and remember, but also adventures that we can perhaps wonder if Robert April and his five-year mission experienced. Roddenberry's first idea, 'The Next Cage', appropriately formed the basis of the very first produced episode of *Star Trek*: "The desperation of our series lead, caged and on exhibition like an animal, then offered a mate."

Whether this was always intended as Roddenberry's introduction to his world is open for debate, but what would have been a striking introduction to Captain April was certainly adapted for Jeffrey Hunter's earlier discussed Captain Pike in 'The Cage'. It is a wonder, however, that the title 'The Next Cage' was never appropriated for a sequel.

'The Day Charlie Became God' ended up split into two early Season 1 episodes, 'Where No Man Has Gone Before' – the first filmed episode of *The Original Series* – and 'Charlie X': "The accidental occurrence of infinite power to do all things, in the hands of a very finite man." Roddenberry dives straight into the 'parallel worlds' idea with 'President Capone': "A parallel world, Chicago ten years after Al Capone won and imposed gangland statutes upon the nation." This served as the basis for Season 2 romp 'A Piece of the Action', albeit going through numerous interesting conceptual development phases as we will learn more about later.

'To Skin a Tyrannosaurus' is the first indication of *Star Trek*'s consistent interest in the devolution of mankind: "A modern man reduced to a sling and a club in a world 1,000,000 BC." No doubt partially inspired by the original 1940 Victor Mature-starring adventure *One Million B.C.* (which will memorably be remade in 1966 as *One Million Years B.C.* with pin-up Raquel Welch in a loincloth), it would inspire the Season 3 episode 'All Our Yesterdays', which sees Spock falling in love with an ancient female 'ice age' resident of the dying planet Sarpeidon. *The Next Generation*, *Voyager* and *Enterprise* will also explore man being reduced to baser instincts more directly in, specifically, Season 7 episode 'Genesis', Season 2 episode 'Threshold', and Season 3 episode 'Extinction'.

Shooting for comedy in 'The Women', Roddenberry describes: "Duplicating a page from the 'Old West'; hanky-panky aboard with a cargo of women destined for a far-off colony." This will ultimately end up parlayed into the early Season 1 episode 'Mudd's Women', featuring the introduction of swashbuckling pirate and con-man Harry Mudd (more on him later), but also sowed the seeds of 'The Perfect Mate' in Season 5 of *The Next Generation*, which struck rather a different tone.

'The Coming' ventures into religious waters: "Alien people in an alien society, but something disturbingly familiar about the quiet dignity of one who is being condemned to crucifixion." Roddenberry's ultimate approach to religion in *Star Trek* is rather atheist in nature, though he remains fascinated by the conceptual idea of Christianity, and he will offer an early parallel of a Christian society in Season 2 episode 'Bread and Circuses'. We will return to his approach to the idea of God and worship when discussing the development of *Star Trek*'s feature film legacy.

He describes 'The Perfect World' as the *Yorktown* finding a civilisation like that of Earth in 1964, making good use of the 'parallel worlds' format, "but with some unusual exceptions – seeming perfect order, no crime, no social problems, no hunger or disease, a place of charming and completely adjusted people. In fact, so pleasant and well-ordered that something has to be wrong." A common *Star Trek* refrain, discovering a society with a dark secret, and subsequently "Robert April is seized and subjected to incredible police barbarism, even more shocking by its contrast. Only slowly does it become apparent that our wanderers have stumbled upon an example similar to the novel '1984', but with all the rough edges removed, i.e, completely efficient, also completely despotic communism carried to the extreme."

Roddenberry here seems to be reacting to the police brutality he would have been witnessing in American society as burgeoning Civil Rights movements clashed with police and authority in events such as the Freedom Rides of 1961, and just a year earlier the March on Washington saw Martin Luther King deliver his immortal "I have a dream" speech to hundreds of thousands of activists. More acutely, Roddenberry is anxious about the long-term effect of Communism, long demonised in American society following the rise of the Soviet Union after The Second World War, and his reference to George Orwell's seminal 1948 text *1984*, which concerned a totalitarian future Britain, suggests the writer wished to discuss his anxiety about how undiluted socialism, and assumed utopian life, can lead to fascist brutality. These ideas would filter down into Season 1's memorable 'The Return of the Archons' and the sentient, dictatorial computer Landru.

'Mr Socrates' was an idea eventually adapted for Season 3 episode 'The Savage Curtain', described as "the most unusual world in the universe, a society secretly in a telepathic contact with the earth for centuries, selecting and duplicating in intelligent, lifelike form, the most unusual intellects produced in mankind's history". He cites the potential use of Julius Caesar, Napoleon, Florence Nightingale, Genghis Khan, Thomas Jefferson and even Adolf Hitler, all living in the same community. "What at first seems like pure fantasy to the *Star Trek* principles, suddenly becomes a very real and very deadly game as they begin to realise this is a form of 'Roman Colosseum', that the participants are 'Gladiators', the stakes are life and death, and the games are about to begin."

This is the first written example of *Star Trek*'s fascination with the ancient world and specific periods of cultural human history but 'The Savage Curtain' – which Roddenberry co-wrote with Arthur Heinemann – avoids using all of these examples and instead broadens the range beyond great human figures (in this episode particularly Abraham Lincoln) to include established icons of established alien cultures – the Vulcan philosopher Surak or foundational Klingon warrior Kahless, for example, both in the myth-making of those cultures akin to religious figures. Nonetheless, the basic elements of 'Mr Socrates' lie in 'The Savage Curtain'.

Roddenberry seeks in his next tale, 'The Stranger', to invoke a different sub-genre altogether – horror. "After taking off from a planet, the S. S. Yorktown proceeds toward another planet in the same solar system. Not until then does it become apparent that an alien intelligence has made its way aboard with the aim of taking over the minds of key crew members, its purpose to use our cruiser to attack a rival civilisation on the other planet. Actually a 'horror' tale, we emphasise the subtleness of this attack on intelligence, reaching a point where mutual suspicion is endangering the entire ship."

Though never a series that would engage in blood, gore and jump scares, *Star Trek* was never afraid to indulge in a more chilling horror story, often involving alien possession. 'Day of the Dove' in the third season has elements of this kind of tale, as an incorporeal alien intelligence pits the *Enterprise* crew against Klingon commander Kang and his forces, though trace elements can be found in *The Next Generation* Season 5 episode 'Conundrum', and two outings in *Deep Space Nine* – Season 1's 'Dramatis Personae' and Season 3's 'The Adversary', which shares primary DNA with Ridley Scott's *Alien*.

Roddenberry includes an episode called 'The Man Trap', better known as one of the earliest episodes of the first season and indeed the first episode of *Star Trek* ever broadcast. In that episode, Captain Kirk and the *Enterprise* crew face a strange, alien salt monster who stalks the corridors of the ship murdering people. Roddenberry's initial pitch for an episode of the same name ends up resembling a story closer to what would become Season 1's 'Shore Leave'. "A desert trek story, taking members of our band from one point on a planet to another. But what appears to be a pleasant, totally earth like and harmless world, rapidly develops into a hundred miles of fear and suspicions as Captain April and crew begin to encounter strange apparitions. Actually more than apparitions, these are wish-fulfilment traps which become as real as flesh and blood . . . The traps become increasingly subtle to the point where our crew nearly destroys itself out of a total inability to separate the reality they must have from the apparition which will destroy them."

'Camelot Revisited' could be considered something of an attempt at light comedy. "A planet of Hermes II, an incredible social order which is thoroughly modern in many respects but retains the knighthood, armour and other trappings similar to our Middle Ages. A touch of 'A Connecticut Yankee in King Arthur's Court', as our star wanderers stop briefly to investigate and then become increasingly embroiled in a web of archaic social practices, finally reaching the point where they too are engaged in lance and sword play to preserve their own skins."

The mention there of Mark Twain's best-known work from 1889 is the giveaway. Twain – who would later appear in several episodes of *The Next Generation* played memorably by Jerry Hardin – wrote his time travel story as a satire on feudalism and monarchy, caricaturing notions of Romantic chivalry. *The Next Generation* evokes this itself in 'Qpid' during its fourth season, when omnipotent trickster Q traps Captain Picard and his crew in a Robin Hood fantasy. *Star Trek* in later years, thanks to the holodeck in no small part, successfully manages to place characters inside historical scenarios without the need for the 'parallel worlds' concept, and 'Camelot Revisited' also evokes *Voyager*'s Season 1 episode 'Heroes and

Demons', which uses Ensign Harry Kim's holo-program to explore the Beowulf legend.

Little is given for '100 A. B.' beyond its alternate title, perhaps invoking 1963's recent *Dr Strangelove*. "Or, 'A Century After the Bomb' – a terrifying parallel as we examine what might be our own world a few decades after an atomic holocaust."

Roddenberry completed this pitch just months after the assassination of President John F. Kennedy and eighteen months after the Cuban Missile Crisis. As we will see in his work on 'Assignment: Earth' a few years later, atomic anxiety was a key factor in his storytelling on *Star Trek*, and more broadly the notion of civilisations destroying themselves. *Strange New Worlds*' self-titled first episode, almost sixty years hence, will begin with a similar parallel world on the brink of civil war and the use of weapons of mass destruction, with the episode very openly paralleling the breakdown of 2020s American democracy with those events. Decades on, *Star Trek* still worries for the future.

'Kentucky, Kentucky' gives us an early indication of Roddenberry's thought process on the Klingons, a version of whom will later appear in similar fashion in Season 1 episode 'Errand of Mercy', which essentially utilises the same plot. "An earth colony on a planet in the Sirius group is visited by the S. S. Yorktown fifty years after colonisation. An attack by Viking-like savages has destroyed and scattered the colonists, reducing them to a 'frontier' log-fort life. Unwilling to risk the S. S. Yorktown, Captain Robert April attempts, with a small band, to regroup and lead the colonists in defence."

'Errand of Mercy' adds the powerful alien entities known as the Organians in what by 1967 had mutated into one of several Vietnam War allegories *Star Trek* would embark upon, but Roddenberry here seems actively looking to channel the spirit of the Alamo and, again, as with references to the *Yorktown*, connect *Star Trek*'s future with America's mythologised, revolutionary past.

Roddenberry suggests what could be the first mooted two-part story in *Star Trek* history in 'Reason' and 'Reason II'. The first is described as "In the Isaac IV group, a world where intelligent life has died, leaving a perfectly functioning robot society. Long speculative problem on earth, this requires investigation and analysis, even at the risk of the Cruiser's reconnaissance party pretending to be robots themselves. Can a robot be capable of emotional feeling? Can it be capable of reasoning in human terms? What happens when an efficient robot society discovers alien flesh and blood spies in its midst?"

While there are some similarities with what will become the Season 2 episode, 'I, Mudd', which brings back Harry Mudd ruling a planet of female androids, 'Reason' more specifically sees Roddenberry musing on concepts that will fascinate him across his time working on *Star Trek* and culminate in the character of Data, the android crewman seeking to understand his own humanity and perhaps achieve a level of sentience.

The second part, 'Reason II', picks up on these questions: "An extension, possibly the second part of the previous tale, portraying the struggle of the last human survivors, aided by our Cruiser's reconnaissance party, outmatched and relatively defenceless as they attempt to reseize possession of their planet. Can a man, rugged and miserable, still be master?" What intrigues about this second episode is that it feels like the opposite side of the coin, in that Roddenberry is less interested in a conventional two-part story telling a narrative filled with tension and stakes, and rather wants to approach his interest in that world from a human perspective after exploring the 'alien' perspective of artificial life. In that respect, 'Reason' as a double episode might have been a fascinating approach to a bigger storyline, and perhaps more of a rounded and satisfying one than 'The Menagerie', *Star Trek*'s actual first two-part story, created simply to reconcile and canonise events of 'The Cage' after the fact.

'A Matter of Choice' is described by Roddenberry as "a starring vehicle for Captain Robert M. April," called it "another entrapment story, i.e., a planet in which the intelligent life has achieved no great material success but instead, has learned the power to live and relive over and over again in different ways, any portion of their past life they choose". April in this story is "presented with the chance to do those certain things all over again".

A powerful character study in the making for whoever played April, no doubt allowing the recesses of his persona to be fully explored and learn more about him. Hints of this linger in 'Tapestry', from *The Next Generation* Season 6, one of the series' acclaimed episodes where Picard, via the magic of Q, is transported back to his youth and a violent incident as a much less tempered man that almost resulted in his death. Such tales became ubiquitous in episodic science fiction and fantasy in the decades to come.

Roddenberry then suggests a love story, 'The Radiant One': "The passion of a crew member for an angelic female on a 'Garden of Eden' planet – the one hitch being her chemistry includes radium in lethal quantity. The man who became her lover would live six weeks to six months, no longer." It is unknown which male crew member might have become embroiled in such a narrative from the pitch. Ortegas perhaps, given his backstory of Latin lover heritage? To have him faced with a choice between love and death would have been interesting. Braver would have been to make this a showcase for Number One, especially given the word association in the title, although it is unlikely an example of LGBTQ storytelling would have passed NBC censors at this point in television.

There are nonetheless shades of this storyline in Season 3's 'That Which Survives', where a ghostly, beautiful woman on the surface of a planet threatens the crew of the *Enterprise*, and the memorable 'The Way to Eden' in the same season, not just thanks to the Edenic references but the idea of a deadly force awaiting those who find such a paradise.

'The Trader' is the early example of what would become quite an overused trope in *The Original Series*: "Satunii, a planet of incredible oriental splendour mercilessly ruled as emperor by a space trader turned renegade. Like a visit to the court of Genghis Khan." Roddenberry certainly had a fascination with the murderous Mongol warlord, utilising him in replicated fashion ultimately in the aforementioned 'The Savage Curtain', but more broadly this pitch evokes the previously discussed Harry Mudd and 'I, Mudd', not to mention several different examples across the series where the *Enterprise* crew visited planets where a traveller had established themselves as a leader and created problems – 'Bread and Circuses', 'Patterns of Force', 'The Omega Glory', and so on.

The next story, 'A Question of Cannibalism', we shall return to in a later chapter as it forms the basis of a fascinating, unformed feature-film concept, but Roddenberry then enters *The Twilight Zone* territory with 'The Mirror': "Near collision with another Yorktown on an exact opposite course. Not only is it the same cruiser, it is manned by exactly the same crew. Could you face yourself after discovering survival depends upon killing yourself?"

Star Trek became very enamoured of the doppelgänger concept across the entirety of the franchise's run, but we certainly see elements of this in 'The Enemy Within', a Season 1 episode where a transporter accident creates two Kirk's – one good, one evil. 'Mirror, Mirror', instigating an entire, franchise-spanning sub-genre of episodes called the Mirror

Universe, creates a pulp, vicious alternate reality with the majority of the *Enterprise* crew hamming it up as sinister doubles. On a more scientific level, *Voyager* later provides multiple versions of the same ship and crew facing each other down in Season 1's 'Parallax' and Season 2's 'Deadlock'. Roddenberry was already here considering how he could explore the conceptual dualities of the self, 'The Mirror' sounding like a pitched game of chicken in space.

'Torx' very much foreshadows the plot of *The Motion Picture*, which we will return to in more detail in a forthcoming chapter: "The first major menace comes to Earth. An alien intelligence, claiming to be pure thought and no body, which 'devours' intelligence, leaving behind a helpless idiot. Near starvation for eons, it has been frantically seeking precisely the type of 'food' the Earth could supply in quantity."

This of course also recalls Season 2's 'The Changeling', itself an episodic prototype of *Star Trek: The Motion Picture*, where the *Enterprise* encounters Nomad, an ancient probe from the earliest days of human space travel, which has mutated into a powerful machine that sterilises populations that fail to live up to its standards of perfection. V'Ger, in *The Motion Picture*, ends up seeking 'the Creator', adding a Biblical notion that both 'The Changeling' and 'Torx' avoids.

'Torx' also foreshadows Galactus, one of the greatest villains in Marvel comics lore; a cosmic entity who consumes planets to sustain his life force. The fact he didn't make his debut in *Fantastic Four* until 1966 puts paid to any suggestion Roddenberry borrowed the idea from Stan Lee and Jack Kirby's work, however. It perhaps also, on a more evocative level, presages Roddenberry's creation of the Borg in *The Next Generation*, in terms of an existential threat to humankind that assimilates human consciousness to 'feed' its broader collective. We will see this, initially, realised profoundly in two-part Season 3 episode 'The Best of Both Worlds'.

'The Pet Shop' sounds quite a surreal take on the 'parallel worlds' concept: "Exactly duplicating St Louis, 1910, a city where women are so completely the masters that men have the status of pets. Something of a satire on 'people and dogs', this story shows men treated in that fashion, caged in kennels, others clothed and perfumed and treated as lapdogs, as long as they continue to fawn, appreciate and selflessly love." Roddenberry here is attempting to provide a level of commentary on gender roles long before they were a potent source of discussion, nodding at the earliest beginnings of an amorphous nuclear family during the post-war boom era for America, where over the next several decades women would move out of the kitchen and homestead into careers of their own. 'The Pet Shop' takes this idea to a heightened degree in a 'historical' context that no doubt would have yielded unusual, if not comedic, overtones.

He gets to explore the concept of a female-dominated society later in *The Next Generation*'s Season 1 episode 'Angel One', and beforehand in his 1972 pilot TV movie *Planet Earth*, but long after his passing *Enterprise* explores the idea of men becoming subservient due to powerful Orion slave girl pheromones in Season 4 episode 'Bound'.

Roddenberry might well have courted controversy with 'Kongo', a tale we shall return to in a later discussion of 'A Portrait in Black and White', an episode of *The Original Series* that came close to being produced, in which he strays into the thorny issue of race and slavery.

'The Venus Planet', however, sees Roddenberry back in safer territory: "The social evolution process here is centered on love – and the very human male members of our crew find what seems the ultimate in amorous wish-fulfilment in the perfectly developed arts of this place of incredibly beautiful women. Until they begin to wonder what happened to all the men there." In some ways, this recalls 'The Radiant One', in the sense of Roddenberry being intrigued, repeatedly, in the idea of a beguiling female presence that ultimately spells death and danger to male crewmen, in what could be seen as a rather suspicious and regressive view on potent female sexuality – a rebuke of a developing age of growing sexual agency among young women in Western society.

This will be explored in cartoon form in *The Animated Series* first season episode 'The Lorelai Signal', in which the *Enterprise* crew run aground of a planet filled with women who dominate the minds of the male crew members, forcing Uhura – as the only woman close to command – to save the day. The idea is a play on the mythological Sirens of Greek legend and is again employed as far down the line as *Voyager*'s Season 3 episode 'Favorite Son', where Harry Kim is beguiled by the female member of a planet who attempt to convince him he is biologically one of their species.

The final proposed episode in the pitch document is 'Infection', which might sound akin to the classic 'killer virus' tale, but ventures in a different direction: "A female crew member discovered to be pregnant, and the growing realisation it could be the larvae of an alien, using her body like some insects plant their eggs in other living insects." At first glance, this recalls the body horror of later science-fiction films such as

Alien, which fuses motherhood and birth with the ultimate terror of extraterrestrial replication, but Roddenberry is unlikely to have turned this episode into such a ghoulish example. It sounds like a potential showcase for Yeoman Colt in a way that 'The Child' ended up being for Deanna Troi in *The Next Generation*'s second season, albeit ending up a very different take on the 'suddenly pregnant' idea, one we will explore in more detail in a later chapter.

All these intended plots and character tales, many of which as we have seen would inspire classic – and not so classic – *Star Trek* episodes to come, are an example of how rich, even in the development phase, the concept of this series was, and how many voyages Roddenberry had in his mind to tell.

*

The story of how *Star Trek* came to be has filled many a volume.

Roddenberry pitched the document around Hollywood, to MGM especially, but he received little to no interest until he entered the orbit of Desilu, a production company owned by the married duo of Lucille Ball (one of America's most beloved comediennes of the era thanks to her hit 1950s series, *I Love Lucy*) and her husband Desi Arnaz (the name of their company being a fusion of their first names).

Desilu had a long association with CBS and produced numerous other hit series over the years, including *The Untouchables* (set in 1930s Prohibition Chicago, much like Roddenberry's above 'President Capone' idea) and later *Mission: Impossible*. Desilu brought in experienced television executives Oscar Katz and Herb Solow to help Roddenberry sell the pitch, which CBS passed on as they had well known 1960s series *Lost in Space* in production and considered Irwin Allen the only science-fiction purveyor in town.

Then they took the idea to NBC, pitched it utilising examples such as *Gunsmoke* and *Wagon Train* (which famously led to the description of *Star Trek* as "*Wagon Train* to the stars . . ."), and provided three-episode concepts, based on several in the initial pitch, for the network to consider as a pilot. One was 'The Cage', the second was called 'Visit to Paradise', which was renamed from the original title of 'The Perfect World' as described above, and which one Roddenberry biographer, Joel Engel, described as "the first of what would be several *Star Trek* episodes in which man searches for God, finds Him, debunks Him, and lives more happily afterward – or kills Him off metaphorically, thus improving mankind's well-being".

The third was 'The Women', which named the character we could later know as Harcourt Fenton Mudd in 'Mudd's Women', as Harry Patton, plying the trade of 'wiving settlers' aka galactic prostitution. Perhaps aware that a story about a rejection of conformity and authority, or a sex farce, were not the best options for a series opener, NBC chose the strange illusion and hypnotism of 'The Cage' and the rest is history.

Money was put up to finance 'Where No Man Has Gone Before', at which point numerous revised drafts of the pitch – which became the 'Writers Bible' – ultimately blossomed into the fully formed series we know and love. Captain Robert April and his nascent crew vanished into history, into lore, dare one suggest even myth, destined as stories and lives – in that incarnation – never to be seen on screen. Not even the *Yorktown* as a name of the ship in question survived the metamorphosis into what we know *Star Trek* to be.

Before *Star Trek*, however, Roddenberry's career was more successful and varied than people might imagine. And those successes factored into what would become his first attempt at a spin-off series from the show that would cement him in storytelling legend . . .

TWO

THE MAN OF TOMORROW

BEFORE, DURING AND after Gene Roddenberry's development of *Star Trek*, he developed numerous pilot scripts and indeed produced episodes for series that, unlike *Star Trek*, never entered development or failed to proceed to series. Many of them contain connectives to his most famous creation, displaying evidence of how he carried everything from ideas to names into his fictional 23rd century.

His first attempt, *The Wild Blue*, which he described to Bill Dozier, head of the production company Screen Gems as an adventure story involving "quiet, ordinary and identifiable men caught up in the extraordinary background furnished by this most romantic, bizarre and flavour-filled backwash of World War II", featured several key character names that would be carried through into *Star Trek* ship commanders: Pike, the name of his first *Enterprise* captain; Jellicoe, who would become an antagonistic, authoritarian Starfleet captain who briefly commands *Enterprise* in *The Next Generation* two-parter 'Chain of Command'; and James. T. Irvine, the first two initials later given to Captain Kirk. His second attempt, *333 Montgomery*, which cast eventual Dr Leonard McCoy, DeForest Kelley, as a lawyer, ended up with a different script and name in *Defiance County*, though it never went to series.

After success with *The Lieutenant*, about William Tiberius (a middle name he would also borrow for Kirk) Rice, a second lieutenant platoon leader at Camp Pendleton in a drama that focused on the US Marine Corps during the peace of the Cold War, which ran for one season of twenty-nine episodes and featured several eventual *Star Trek* alumni including Leonard Nimoy and Nichelle Nichols, Roddenberry focused his attention on *Star Trek*. His input on the show he created began to wane during the second season of a series that, while a modest success, was nowhere near the cultural behemoth it would become across the 1970s and particularly in the decades beyond. He turned his attention first to *Police Story*, a procedural crime story in the vein of *The Lieutenant*, producing yet another unsuccessful pilot script in 1967 that eventually was turned into a solo TV movie.

While Roddenberry's attention strayed elsewhere in the second season, *Star Trek* faced numerous difficulties while under the strong creative stewardship of Gene L. Coon, who *Star Trek* scholars widely attribute as being one of the unsung storytelling heroes of *The Original Series*. Though new cast members were being added, with Kelley becoming a regular and Walter Koenig arriving as Pavel Chekov, the budget on *Star Trek* was depreciating week on week as comedy legend Lucille Ball, whose production company she built with husband Desi Arnaz took a chance on products such as *Star Trek* and *Mission: Impossible*, both destined to become iconic products of the 1960s, were forced to sell to Paramount thanks to rising deficits. They were losing upwards of fifteen thousand dollars per episode (a huge sum by today's comparison) and battled a concerned board, worried about haemorrhaging money, but it was ultimately too late. Six months later, *Star Trek* was playing globally and raking in cash, which turned out to be the great irony.

To compound the stresses and difficulties on *Star Trek* around this period, Coon – who had been a significant steadying hand on the tiller – opted to leave the production staff. Roddenberry was at this point writing the script for a Robin Hood TV pilot that he was paid for but would never be commissioned. Coon's replacement was John Meredyth Lucas, with whom Roddenberry was happier as he had grown concerned that under Coon's direction the series had relied more on lighter stories and comedic tales. Roddenberry wanted a level of dramatic intensity back and considered Lucas the right man to do it.

Lucas' very first episode produced for the second season was 'Obsession', in which Captain Kirk confronted a deadly cloud entity which years before, when he was a lieutenant on the USS *Farragut*, killed a crew member he knew. The story was designed, purposefully, to give Shatner's protagonist more of a driven narrative than the show had provided him for a while. The writer Lucas worked with on a producer-level to write 'Obsession' was one Art Wallace, best known as one of the creative forces behind the supernatural soap opera *Dark Shadows* and whose resumé on television went back to the 1940s and some of the foundational examples of the form in America.

Wallace recounted to Starlog how the episode came to be: "Gene and I were having dinner one night, and then it came to me that it wouldn't be a bad idea to do a version of *Moby Dic*k, which became Obsession. I just substituted the cloud for the great white whale."

Though replete with high-minded ambitions, 'Obsession' was not considered an example of a great episode of *The Original Series*. *Moby Dick* would be better evoked three decades later with *Next Generation*-movie *Star Trek: First Contact* and Captain Jean-Luc Picard's battle against the Borg. Moreover, many considered *Star Trek*, in the recent Coon era, to have covered the same ground with 'The Doomsday Machine', which aired just seven episodes earlier. It helped signal what many inside and outside of *Star Trek* feared was coming: cancellation.

Star Trek in the 1960s seemed to live in the constant shadow of termination by network NBC, especially after the difficulties in getting the show commissioned following struggles over 'The Cage', developing a second pilot, cast changes, the expense needed for futuristic sets and alien planets, and just how Roddenberry's series pushed from a creative perspective into allegory that challenged societal preconceptions at a time of fervent, rapid change. Those who had fallen for the show were already incredibly protective over losing Kirk, Spock and the crew of the *Enterprise* and so began a massive letter writing campaign by committed audience members to save the series.

Elyse Rosenstein, an early organiser of *Star Trek* conventions that began to take off during and especially after the series ended, described the effect: "Do you realize how many pieces of mail NBC eventually received on *Star Trek*? They usually got about fifty thousand for the year on everything, but the *Star Trek* campaign generated one million letters. They were handling the mail with shovels – they didn't know what to do with it. Their policy was to answer everything, even if it was a form letter, and a million pieces of mail is a lot of money. So they made an unprecedented on-air announcement that they were not cancelling the show and that it would be back in the fall."

Quite whether NBC received that many letters is part of *Star Trek* mythology, but the fan response was, in part, enough to move the needle on giving *Star Trek* what would be a third and final season, unable as it was to avoid a final cancellation a year later in 1969. By the end of the second season, Roddenberry had once again asserted greater control over the series, following the failure of *Police Story*, but had grown convinced that cancellation was imminent. He was unprepared for the fan response, one he actively supported, but he also was preparing for another pilot he was convinced would be a sure bet for the 1968–1969 season as a replacement for *Star Trek*.

He didn't know it yet, but he was preparing the ground for what would become 'Assignment: Earth', as indeed was another man in his orbit: Art Wallace.

*

Although it has been conventional wisdom since certainly the 1980s to expect a season of television to conclude with a finale that places the main characters in life-changing situations and even leaves audiences on a 'cliffhanger', the halfway point in a story they are desperate to see the conclusion of, this was far from the case in 1960s storytelling, and indeed in *Star Trek*.

The first season ended with the grandiose-sounding 'Operation: Annihilate!', a story which in fact saw Spock infected with an amoeba virus. The third season ended with what would be the final ever episode of the show, 'Turnabout Intruder', which was a rather anticlimactic body swap episode revolving around Kirk and a sinister doctor, Janice Lester. In neither instance did *Star Trek* end a season with a story that contained any significant narrative or character development, but rather a story that could have been placed anywhere in the season overall. The same was true of the second season finale, albeit with a slight twist.

'Assignment: Earth' begins in rather unconventional fashion with the USS *Enterprise* having travelled back to the year 1968 (the same year the episode aired) for what Kirk describes as a mission of "historical research" that involves "monitoring Earth communications to find out how our planet survived desperate problems" in that same year. Though a method of time travel is given, the same "light-speed breakaway factor" that would memorably be used almost two decades later in the fourth big screen adventure *The Voyage Home*, Starfleet officers travelling through time would increasingly be considered a dangerous and near taboo action as the franchise progressed. Here, the reason is throwaway and never truly explained.

When looking at the episode from a production perspective, the reason becomes very clear. 'Assignment: Earth' was intended as the 'back-door' pilot for the first planned spin-off series in *Star Trek* history.

Before we get to that, it serves to break down the constituent elements of 'Assignment: Earth' as an episode, which will help us understand the wider context of the story and where it sits within *Star Trek* lore. Having returned to 1968, the *Enterprise* immediately encounters Gary Seven, a mysterious human man in a business suit with transporter technology, whose return to Earth from an unknown planet (unknown, he claims, even to Starfleet in the 23rd century), is intercepted by the ship and crew. He carries with him an expressive pet cat, Isis, and claims that if Kirk interferes with his work on Earth then "you'll change history. You'll destroy the Earth and probably yourselves, too." Seven's attempt to escape, proving impervious even to Spock's all-encompassing neck pinch, frames him as a strange and potentially dangerous enemy as the episode begins.

'Assignment: Earth' very quickly positions itself as a *Star Trek* episode built on a deep sense of cultural and political unease. 1960s *Star Trek* is riven with such concerns which manifest in all kinds of episodes – take 'Errand of Mercy' or 'A Private Little War' and how they grapple with broader ideas about the conflict in Vietnam. 'Assignment: Earth' has a deep-rooted fear, ultimately, of nuclear annihilation and the ever-present threat of a Third World War, but it also proves strangely prophetic about the world the crew of the *Enterprise* have returned in time to study. As Spock notes: "There will be an important assassination today, an equally dangerous government coup in Asia, and, this could be highly critical, the launching of an orbital nuclear warhead platform by the United States countering a similar launch by other powers."

The episode aired on 29 March 1968. Just six days later, Martin Luther King Jr (who had so influenced Nichelle Nichols as the show came on air) was shot dead on a balcony in Memphis, Tennessee, one of two 'important' assassinations that would rock 1968 (the other, just two months later, would be Robert F. Kennedy, the senator brother of the also assassinated and already legendary President John F. Kennedy). Though not Asia, and more specifically the Middle East, the 17 July Revolution in

Iraq would see a bloodless coup in which the Arab socialist Ba'ath Party – led by a young Saddam Hussein – would come to power and create a dangerous regime that would destabilise the region for 35 years.

In what is perhaps the strangest coincidence with Spock's words, on the same day as King's death, the Apollo 6 Saturn V unmanned rocket was launched and due to technical failure veered off course, in a mirror of Seven's attempts to prevent the launch of an American nuclear weapons platform into Earth's orbit. Kirk states at the end of the episode that the ultimate donation of the warhead was not "generally revealed" to the public at the time, thereby ensuring the *Enterprise*'s involvement in history was part of the natural flow of time, it could be theorised that Seven's sabotage and the Saturn V events are one and the same; the episode even uses launch footage of the earlier Apollo 4 mission as part of the story. Just another example of how *Star Trek* works, especially in time travel stories, to combine real-world history with its own future arcanum and create a canonical 'secret history' to Earth's past.

Spock mentions "other powers" when describing the rationale behind the United States launching such a platform to maintain the "balance of power" and while the country is never named, he is quite clearly referencing the Soviet Union. If the late 1960s were not quite the height of post-Second World War, fall of the Iron Curtain, sabre-rattling rhetoric of the atomic test-ridden 1950s, then the Cold War remained in full and active swing, with Vietnam a key proxy staging post for the ambitions of the superpowers. In the real world, no such nuclear weapons platform was ever built but on many occasions during the conflict, in projects such as the infamous 'Star Wars' or 'Brilliant Pebbles', the idea of a missile defence shield protecting America was well-discussed and almost implemented. The episode, therefore, actively tapped into the fear of the nuclear annihilation that might result from such a possibility.

'Assignment: Earth' frames the narrative, in a way no previous *Star Trek* episode – even those such as 'City on the Edge of Forever' or 'Tomorrow Is Yesterday', which dabbled in time travel – ever did, in how it relegates much of the principal cast to guest star status. Barely any of the main cast outside of William Shatner and Leonard Nimoy feature and even they, for much of the episode, play second fiddle to the establishment of Gary Seven as the main character of the story. The actor cast in the role, Robert Lansing, even gets his guest star credit placed in the main credits of the episode – something never before and never again repeated in the series. The inference is clear: Gary Seven is being primed throughout as a protagonist.

Lansing, however, already by this point established as a successful stage and screen actor, known best as a taciturn brigadier on a successful Second World War military drama called *12 O'Clock High*, was reluctant at the idea of appearing in what increasingly became known as 'genre television': "At the time, Gene was a good friend, but I was a New York snob actor, come out to Hollywood. Many folks in my self-perceived position didn't do *Star Trek* because it was considered a kid's show, or a young show at any rate. Gene said, 'I'm writing this for you and we can play with it. It might be a series.' He said, 'Well, you don't have to, but just do this one thing for me.' So, I did. It was a damn good script and a lot of fun."

Close to middle-aged, with a gruff exterior and handsome features that veered on the craggy in the wrong light, Lansing's Seven was very clearly designed in the mould of another famous '00' Seven in James Bond, who in 1968 had by now over the last half a decade been immortalised as one of the biggest cultural breakout sensations of the 1960s, as had Sean Connery, the man who was in the process of ceding the role of 007 after 1967's *You Only Live Twice*. Nonetheless, Seven is cool, calm, sharp-suited and suave, even if his gadget 'servo' and magical computer accoutrements, in hindsight, place him just as readily in the orbit of the Doctor from Britain's quirky science-fiction hit of the same decade, *Doctor Who*. Seven is portrayed as a distinctly American approach to those two very definably British, if altogether different, heroic archetypes.

'Assignment: Earth' primes Seven, ultimately, as a rather remote hero of the story. He claims himself to be a 'supervisor', sent by a mysterious alien race, who monitors specific 'agents' – two of whom have gone missing from their base in New York. As he describes in a fidelity test to the Beta-5 sentient computer in the base: "Agents are male and female, descendants of human ancestors taken from Earth approximately six thousand years ago. They're the product of generations of training for this mission. Problem. Earth technology and science have progressed faster than political and social knowledge. Purpose of mission. To prevent Earth's civilisation from destroying itself before it can mature into a peaceful society."

Seven is therefore a man with knowledge of the universe around him, of extraterrestrial life, as considers himself a steward against the better nature of man. Much like the Doctor, he is on one level unknowable, hence why

'Assignment: Earth' brings in a female counterpoint in Roberta Lincoln (played by Teri Garr, better known to future generations as Phoebe's kooky mother in 90s sitcom *Friends*), a woman employed by the missing agents who initially treats Seven with suspicion as a mysterious agent of a government agency, such as the FBI or the CIA. She is, theoretically, the audience's window into the narrative, positioned as a sympathetic part of the 'hippie' generation now in full force protesting war and seeking love: "I want to believe you. I do. I know this world needs help. That's why some of my generation are kind of crazy and rebels, you know. We wonder if we're going to be alive when we're thirty."

Ultimately, Seven by the end of the episode is vindicated. Kirk trusts him enough to let him detonate an American nuclear warhead rapidly heading for, as Sulu puts it confusingly, "the Euro-Asian continent" (he probably means Russia). A Third World War is for now averted and Spock optimistically claims the records show that the near miss "resulted in a new and stronger international agreement against the use of such weapons". Roberta begins to place her trust and faith in him, despite Seven remaining a man of mystery. And Spock predicts, in almost meta-fashion, "Captain, we could say that Mister Seven and Miss Lincoln have some interesting experiences in store for them."

The *Enterprise* returns to the 23rd century, leaving the door open for not simply another 'Assignment: Earth' episode but rather, 'Assignment: Earth' the TV show.

Yet in truth, 'Assignment: Earth' the series had been conceived some time before this episode aired, and almost came to be. It would remain the closest audiences ever came to seeing the adventures of Gary Seven, Roberta Lincoln and Isis again.

*

Art Wallace had been writing for television since the medium truly came into being during the 1940s, in the wake of the Second World War.

He penned episodes of nascent anthology series such as *Studio One* or *Kraft Television Theater* and dabbled in Second World War adventure with *Combat* and science-fiction with *Tom Corbett, Space Cadet*. His career, to some extent, mirrored Roddenberry in how he quietly helped to shape the early television drama landscape, especially when he became involved in one of the bigger genre hits of the 1960s, *Dark Shadows*.

A Gothic soap opera that ran into the early 1970s and boasted a remarkable 1200+ episodes by the time it concluded, *Dark Shadows* revolved around the supernatural Collins family in Maine and popular vampire Barnabus as it threw a brace of paranormal characters and creations into a melting pot that was melodramatic but equally dramatic, comedic and influential, spawning numerous sequels and remakes, including a largely unsuccessful Johnny Depp-starring reboot from Tim Burton in 2012.

While the series was created by Dan Curtis, based on a dream he had experienced, Wallace was the creative talent behind the throne, developing the initial series and creating the show bible which laid foundations for what the series would be. By the time Wallace came to *Star Trek* and contributed to 'Obsession', he was therefore a talented creative force in his own right separate from Roddenberry who had, before him, developed one of the seminal genre TV series of the 1960s.

Come 1968, and Wallace and Roddenberry both, it seems, were circling around similar ideas based around their influences and interests at the time: "Assignment: Earth is interesting in a sense, because I had gone to Paramount and pitched a series idea to them. They had said that Gene Roddenberry had come up with a very similar idea. So I saw Gene and we decided to pool the idea, which was about a man from tomorrow who takes care of the present on Earth. That was intended to be the pilot, although it was never made into a series. It was a good pilot and it's a shame, because I think if they had done it as a series with just Gary Seven, it would have been a very successful show."

Roddenberry, convinced *Star Trek*'s days were numbered, saw an opportunity to capitalise on the boom in not just science fiction across the 1960s but also 'spy-fi', the intersection between established espionage in cinema and television (such as the Patrick McGoohan-led *Danger Man*, which itself gave way to the iconoclastic *The Prisoner* later that decade) and elaborate, colourful science fiction. He discussed this in a letter he wrote to NBC executive Herb Schlosser: "Today's audience more and more seeks escape and identification with 'larger than life' characters. Ordinary people are getting hemmed in by an increasingly complex and frightening world and the viewer finds that identification and escape are possible only through characters who have unusual strength and abilities. Example: 'I Spy', 'Mission Impossible', 'Harper', 'Our Man Flint', James Bond; and we find the same factor in comedies such as 'Bewitched', 'Get Smart' and others."

Mission: Impossible, a franchise in the modern day with almost as much continued cultural traction as *Star Trek* thanks to the highly successful Tom Cruise-fronted film series launched in 1996, also came from the Desilu stable and was roughly a contemporary of *Star Trek*'s original run, while the James Bond film series – thanks in part to Connery's iconic performance in the role – became *the* cinematic cultural phenomenon of the decade, tapping into the emergent youthful counter-culture rocking the Western world. *Star Trek*, at the time, did not have the same zeitgeist-baiting traction, hence its eventual cancellation, but Roddenberry certainly understood the growing audience predilection for the 'superhero', the charming vanguard against global threats.

This too factored into many of Roddenberry's anxieties about political and social change, anxieties which often bled into *Star Trek*'s allegorical storytelling. In the same letter to Schlosser, he conveyed his intention to make that a prime part of 'Assignment: Earth''s brief, to not shy away from those reflections: "The late 1960s and 70s are the most critical Earth is likely ever to face. Our audience, from housewife to college draftee to scientist, knows this and personally identifies. A public figure was quoted recently as saying – 'I am only half joking when I say I pray every night that somewhere on earth there are visitors from an advanced race who can help earth out of its growing dilemma'. If you don't think *that* possibility (or hope) isn't on a lot of average audience minds, consider the recurring waves of 'flying saucer visitor' stories that flood the newspapers every month or so."

Roddenberry would end up utilising elements of the quote he cites in his letter in 1974, after the cancellation of *Star Trek*, on his TV movie *The Questor Tapes*. The film starred Robert Foxworth (who would decades later appear in *Deep Space Nine* in a memorable guest role) as Questor, an android with a wiped memory who seeks to understand where he comes from. The failure of 'Assignment: Earth' as a pitch fuelled the script that he wrote with Coon, in which Questor discovers he is one of numerous androids created by 'Masters' from before human history who were created to protect mankind. He is told by Vaslovik, a fellow android played by Lew Ayres: "We protect, but we do not interfere. Man must make his own way. We guide him – but always without his knowledge."

Questor is, essentially, a version of the Gary Seven archetype Roddenberry intended for 'Assignment: Earth' the series, albeit one who combines Mr Spock's detached reasoning with the robotic nature Roddenberry would later import into Data, a key member of the main ensemble of *The Next Generation* from 1987 onwards, and even influence Odo, the shapeshifting security chief in *Deep Space Nine* played by René Auberjonois who, for several initial seasons, sought answers as to where he came from. *The Questor Tape*s was intended to be a thirteen-part series in which Questor would aid and protect humanity in stand-alone stories but, like numerous TV movies Roddenberry produced throughout the 1970s with series intentions – such as *Genesis II*, *Spectre*, *Planet Earth* and so on – it was never picked up to series.

Returning to the Schlosser pitch, Roddenberry gave a precis about his belief that Gary Seven, his weekly series, could find "the sparks of Armageddon and extinguish them before the blaze engulfs us", making clear the nature of the stories and threats the character might face: "It may be a large story, as in our pilot, or it may be as small a story as saving a highly necessary young scientist, who is about to wreck his life and career and deprive the world of something vital he must offer. The 'enemy' can be the Mafia, a greedy politician, an overly eager agent operating inside the Kremlin, or an honest mistake about to be made by a powerful Senate Committee. It can be a university bacteriological experiment about to go awry, it can be, in fact, any action-adventure about almost any interesting subject in almost any place."

With this remit, Roddenberry is determined not to pigeon-hole 'Assignment: Earth' into one specific sub-genre of storytelling and, much like *Star Trek* had the freedom within the structures of a starship exploring the galaxy to tell a range of stories in different registers and on alternating canvases, 'Assignment: Earth' is pitched with the DNA not just of James Bond or *Mission: Impossible* but also *Doctor Who*, as mentioned earlier; a mysterious protector of Earth, a man of partly alien origin, in scenarios battling a range of existential threats from a wide variety of sources with a loyal companion or two at his side.

Roddenberry is keen to stress to Schlosser, however, that 'Assignment: Earth' is not intended to be science fiction in the vein of *Star Trek*: ". . . if you mean by that strange planets, exotic alien and science-oriented stories. Our time is today, our locales contemporary, our action-adventure takes place in recognisable story areas. Yes, it is science-fiction, if you mean that by imaginative stories, lots of exciting gimmicks and devices and extraordinary challenges to an extraordinary man."

The modus operandi Roddenberry intended with 'Assignment: Earth' was clear. He intended to tell stories an audience could relate to, in the

1960s, by utilising an extraordinary figure. Perhaps with *Star Trek*'s probable cancellation imminent, Roddenberry did not believe audiences saw in the adventures of the *Enterprise* a world they recognised, even despite the fact it used science fiction as a mirror to reflect the issues of the 1960s with aspirational but largely very human and *humane* characters. He had no idea the legacy *Star Trek* would have at this point. It was, in 1967, just another series he had created and one, seemingly, not destined for a long shelf life.

And so, he wrote a script for what would be the 'Assignment: Earth' pilot, some time before Art Wallace would craft it into the episode that brought the curtain down on *Star Trek*'s second season. It gives us a window into a series that might, had history unfolded differently, taken *Star Trek*'s place, and turned Gary Seven and Roberta Lincoln into creations as iconic as Captain Kirk and Mr Spock.

*

The pilot script for 'Assignment: Earth' is dated 14 November 1966 and consists of just three acts as an intended half-hour format, unlike the 45–50 minute run time of *Star Trek*. It runs, as a result, to 47 pages with Roddenberry credited as sole writer.

He opens with a teaser that would have served to not just introduce the concept of the series week in week out, but also serve as a preview of the events in the episode to come set to Seven stepping into his gaseous transporter chamber. This was a common refrain in numerous escapist 1960s TV series, such as clips behind the burning fuse of the *Mission: Impossible* credits or the snapshots of action after the immortal 5 . . . 4 . . . 3 . . . 2 . . . 1 at the beginning of Gerry Anderson's *Thunderbirds*. In each episode of 'Assignment: Earth', a narrator would have voiced the following: "In the hands of this one man . . . could rest the future of all mankind. His name . . . Gary Seven . . . born in the year 2319 AD. The only survivor of Earth's attempt to send a man back through time to today. Assignment . . . fight an enemy who is already here, trying to destroy us. If he fails . . . there'll be no tomorrow!"

This backstory for Seven immediately differs from that of Robert Lansing's version in *Star Trek*. Here Seven is a time traveller from Earth's future as opposed to, as Seven suggests in the later episode, the agent of a mysterious alien race or organisation who plucks humans from antiquity to serve them. J. Michael Straczynski would later adopt a similar concept, in more sinister fashion, for the agents of the deadly Shadows in his magnum opus *Babylon-5* in the 1990s, but here Seven's backstory more closely recalls that of *Quantum Leap*'s Sam Beckett (played in the late 1980s by future *Enterprise* Captain, Scott Bakula), only Seven never becomes unstuck in time.

Where Roddenberry's script here does match *Star Trek*'s depiction is in Seven's genesis at the behest of an alien force. The produced episode never names them and presents them as benevolent extraterrestrials attempting to help Earth's progress, whereas in this script, Seven is one numerous agents sent back by the sinister Omegans. They are described as warlike and satanic-looking, continuing Roddenberry's interest in depicting Biblical evil through science-fiction tropes, given how Spock was devised to have devil features.

After humanity lands on the Moon in 1967 (just two short years before the real space flight), they expand into the stars before, in the 24th century, the Omegans encounter humanity and choose to try and destroy them from within by sending agents back to the 1960s, here the critical time period in Earth's history, with the intention to change Earth's past by eliminating "the statesmen of tomorrow, corrupt the parents of a future educator, destroy a key scientist, corrupt, weaken, destroy . . . until Earth has no tomorrow!". This would have been communicated, fairy-tale fashion, by cycling through a tome labelled Earth History 1967 through AD 2300.

The script then introduces us to Roberta 'Bobbi' Hornblower, 20 years old and described as "a mixture of wacky teenager and self-assured young lady", who arrives at 'The 7 Agency' in New York to meet with the still-unseen Gary Seven. The nomenclature of her surname serves as a perhaps intentional wink to *Star Trek*, which was described by Roddenberry himself as "Hornblower in space", referencing the 19th-century C. S. Forrester naval adventures that provided inspiration for the voyages of the *Enterprise*. This was presumably dropped in the episode and replaced by Lincoln out of a concern it would have been too pointed a referential in-joke.

Bobbi serves as the audience's entry point to the world of 'Assignment: Earth' in a manner the *Star Trek* episode, having to serve two masters, never quite successfully pulls off. The scene as written unfolds similarly to that filmed with Teri Garr in the role; Bobbi finds various objects that are technologically advanced in nature (a servo pen, X-ray glasses that see through solid objects, a voice-activated typewriter). She does recount the strangely serendipitous (and quite dark) events that led her to applying for the job of Seven's secretary, namely seeing a woman who intended to apply crushed to death by masonry and leaving behind details of the job and address she intended to apply for. Roddenberry suggests fate, or perhaps more of a sinister hand, led Bobbi into Seven's orbit.

She meets the strange black cat wearing a jewelled necklace, who we will know as Isis, before Seven materialises via the shimmering transporter inside his vault. He is immediately in the James Bond mould – handsome, charming, funny, debonair (albeit with an intended modern suit with traces of alien metallic fibre, no doubt intended to reflect his slightly alien nature). Seven claims he is the fourteenth agent on Bobbi's trail, referring to her as an agent called 3y3, but the rest were killed. Bobbi has no idea what he means.

This roughly follows the interactions we see in the filmed episode, with the difference being that Seven in that story believes Roberta found him due to her having a level of future significance, whereas in this pilot script, Seven believes Bobbi to be agent 3y3 who was supposed to replace the original Roberta Hornblower, who history records died in a freak accident being crushed by marble. In truth, 3y3 was the woman Bobbi saw die and has now stumbled into a world beyond the comprehension Seven believes she has.

Another change lies in the use of the cat, Isis. In this original script, Isis has a partner cat in Harth. She is still described as a beautiful, exotic woman (who we will see in *Star Trek* played by April Tatro, a credit only discovered as recently as 2019 by noted *Star Trek* historian Larry Nemecek), but Harth is described as a "Count Dracula figure", sallow-faced in human form. They are both described as "Omegan agents" and across the script their intentions are far more hostile than that of Isis in the episode. She is presented as Seven's feline companion by that point whereas here she and Harth actively serve as antagonists across much of the episode.

Roddenberry's script differs in having a mysterious package delivered containing an explosive device that almost kills Seven and Bobbi (she only protected by the metallic polymers in his suit that soak up the explosion), before Seven uses his servo to turn back time (with a span of up to thirty minutes) and removes all trace of the fire and destruction that burned his office. The first act ends as Seven takes Bobbi through the transporter to his apartment for a change of clothes.

The second act begins with Bobbi still distrustful about Seven's claims he is from the distant future. Roddenberry here employs time travel as an emotional plot in a manner he often enjoyed in certain *Star Trek* episodes previously mentioned, such as 'City on the Edge of Forever'. Seven tells her that her best friend Cynthia will marry a man called Eddie Norris, which Bobbi disbelieves, and only later in the act do we learn that Eddie is, in fact, Bobbi's boyfriend, but he is also indeed having an affair with Cynthia. As Harth and Isis recruit Lieutenant Brenner, a local police officer suspicious generally of Seven, to arrest him for counterfeiting, Harth offers Bobbi a devilish pact – if she helps him, he will "destroy" Eddie for her, after his ultimate betrayal.

The final act, Harth leans into the Dracula overtones by attempting to put a spell on Bobbi and cloud her mind. "What a lovely one of us you'll make," he purrs. Bobbi manages to shake off his advances and Isis presents herself to the imprisoned Seven as, seemingly, a friend. She offers to help him kill Harth and for them to escape at any time. "And which one of us would own the other, Isis?" Seven asks, not taking the bait. Meanwhile, in a clear attempt at levity which would potentially have taken away from the dramatic stakes of the episode, Bobbi's attempts to escape Harth lead her bouncing through the transporter to different places in comic effect – the office of a Senator, a men's steam room, the heart of the Kremlin. Seven, escaping police custody (his suit absorbing Brenner's bullets as he tries to shoot him), rescues Bobbi from the transporter leading her into the Omegan headquarters on Earth and the clutches of Harth and Isis.

The episode ends with Seven, in rather sinister fashion, scaring away a visiting Eddie, looking for Bobbi, and lying about someone coming to visit her. The police are happy Seven was innocent, Bobbi is working for him, and their partnership seems established, though Seven still seems troubled by the fact Bobbi is not the agent he believed he was working with. The episode ends with him musing: "Well, I can't kill the girl simply because she was supposed to die. And since I do need a secretary, she doesn't contaminate history . . . (suddenly irritated). And it's totally ridiculous for a man to be talking to himself. Even in this century!"

None of this survives into the filmed 'Assignment: Earth' episode, which must balance Kirk and Spock's presence with the bigger stakes of possible nuclear Armageddon that Seven seeks to avert, leaving little time for Roberta's introduction, but it is possible these storylines could well have emerged had the pilot gone to series. Bobbi, or Roberta, might have ended up with a boyfriend who factors into the plot. Isis no doubt would have been fleshed out as a character with perhaps unclear intentions. Harth would likely have emerged as a recurring villain and, almost certainly, the Omegans as a threat would have deepened, even if Roddenberry has kept their alien nature largely off screen.

One factor Roddenberry took issue with when pitching the idea to Schlosser was the similarity of 'Assignment: Earth' with *The Invaders*, a series by Larry Cohen that ran for two seasons in 1967–1968 and starred Roy Thinnes as David Vincent, a man who discovers evidence of Earth's infiltration by an invading alien race – disguising themselves as humans and infiltrating Earth's institutions – and his efforts to stymie their invasion plans, even while official organisations and the public refuse to believe him. A cross between the ongoing, one-man-against-the-system narrative of the highly popular 1960s series *The Fugitive* and the paranoid thrills of 1950s B-movie *Invasion of the Body Snatchers*, *The Invaders* didn't last as long as *Star Trek* and lacked the same legacy, but did go on to inspire the 1990s revival of alien conspiracy thrillers, in no small part the biggest series of that decade, *The X-Files*, in which Thinnes even appeared as a shapeshifting alien himself.

Roddenberry, however, was no fan of the Quinn Martin Productions show: "QM Productions made a basic error in their most important ingredient of the show – they picked the wrong villain. One-dimensional 'bad guys from outer space' make for one-dimensional stories. Every successful dramatist should know that the only villain capable of supporting the main episodes of a television show is *man himself*. The list of man's possible villainies is endless, an extraordinary collection of vices, weaknesses, creeds, jealousies, hatreds . . . you name it. There has never been a successful novel, screenplay, stage production or television series using any theme but *man against man, or man against himself*."

In this declaration, Roddenberry establishes that he would have wished for 'Assignment: Earth' to eschew the reliance on alien villains (despite the key presence of two shapeshifting alien felines in the pilot script!) and see Gary Seven exploring man's capability for self-destruction. In the wake of the height of the nuclear age, just a few years after the Cuban Missile Crisis brought humanity closer to Armageddon before or arguably since, would the series have added to the mission Roddenberry began with *Star Trek*, not to explore new worlds but reflect post-war Western society? Or would it have challenged the notion that *Star Trek* was able to tell such stories precisely because they served as allegory set in a supposedly fantastical future?

Would 'Assignment: Earth' been as successful in grounding Gary Seven as a darker reflection of the superheroes the 1960s had become so enthralled by?

Audiences of the 1960s were destined never to find out.

NBC passed on the concept before Roddenberry had the chance to further flesh out the first draft pilot script and following the 'backdoor pilot' Art Wallace adapted and integrated with Roddenberry into *Star Trek*. Wallace passed away in 1994 after a long career but he never wrote for *Star Trek* again after 'Assignment: Earth' and arguably never recaptured the heights of the projects he worked on during the 1960s. The resulting episode that concluded Season 2 was certainly Roddenberry's last conscious attempt to get 'Assignment: Earth' made. Sets had been built and some have suggested it was the most expensive outing of *Star Trek* ever made, by virtue of being designed in lavish fashion for an entirely different project and ultimately ending up retrofitted for the adventures of the *Enterprise*.

Moreover, Roddenberry's fears of cancellation were unfounded – for now at least. *Star Trek* was renewed in 1967 for a third season after a co-ordinated letter-writing campaign by devoted fans, not that Roddenberry himself would have a great deal of input directly in what became *Star Trek*'s final year.

*

Gary Seven and Roberta Lincoln were never seen on screen again but, in deeper *Star Trek* lore, their narrative continued.

In the decades following *The Original Series*, an entire apocrypha arose separate to the episodic canon and continuity that saw the lost or dropped story threads from *Star Trek* history picked up by a litany of novelists, comic-book artists and video-game producers, a trend that continues into the modern day, albeit to a lesser degree as multi-platform continuity is now more closely connected and maintained in an era of corporatised intellectual property.

Nonetheless, in 1998, Greg Cox revived the characters for his original work, 'Assignment: Eternity', which saw Seven and Roberta travel to the future and join the crew of the *Enterprise* on a mission into the heart of the dangerous Romulan Empire. Cox later incorporates them into the second volume of his novels, *The Rise and Fall of Khan Noonien Singh*, released in 2001 and 2002, which depicts *Star Trek*'s most legendary antagonist – best known from the episode 'Space Seed' and movie sequel *Star Trek II: The Wrath of Khan* – as a younger man in the 1990s on Earth, embroiled in a secretive global conflict called the Eugenics Wars. Later, in 2005, writer John Byrne revived 'Assignment: Earth' as a six-part IDW Publishing comic series intended to serve as a version of the show Roddenberry planned to make, seeing Seven and Roberta become embroiled in the Vietnam War, President Nixon's visit to China, and events leading into the 1970s.

There are other appearances in non-canonical form which suggest that for a generation of writers who came after Roddenberry, and long after *The Original Series*, interest in the mystery of Gary Seven and his mission on Earth has never faded. Though 'Assignment: Earth' has never been considered one of *Star Trek*'s greatest episodes, it arguably is the series' one true example from the 1960s of attempting to use the adventures of the *Enterprise* as a platform to launch a spin-off series that held true, albeit in a different and perhaps more grounded fashion, to the principles of Roddenberry's approach to storytelling – to explore the human condition, to capture man's conflict with himself and nature, at a time when around him society, culture and politics were febrile and unpredictable.

'Assignment: Earth' could have ended up one of the signature pieces of thoughtful escapism of the 1960s had NBC taken the same kind of chance on it that it took on *Star Trek*.

It is, however, just one of many alternate possibilities that stemmed from *Star Trek* in the 1960s. Next, let us turn to the adventures of Captain Kirk and his crew that, for whatever reason, were never made. These were *almost* the voyages . . .

THREE

THESE WERE ALMOST THE VOYAGES: *THE ORIGINAL SERIES*

"YOU STAR TREK fans have fought the 'good fight', but the show has been cancelled and there's nothing to be done now."

These were the words of a newspaper columnist for *The Palm Beach Coast* in July of 1969, some six months after the news came down from NBC. The five-year mission was over in three. In February of that year, after production on a third season that almost didn't itself happen, wrapped early in January, *Star Trek* had officially been cancelled. And no amount of letter-writing campaigns were going to save it this time.

Seventy-nine episodes of the series had aired since 1969. Some were almost immediately recognised as classic episodes of both 1960s and more broadly science-fiction storytelling. Others, less so. As enjoyable as the unforgettable cast always were in their roles, many episodes of *The Original Series* played the middle. Gene Roddenberry, Gene L. Coon, John Meredyth Lucas, Fred Freiberger and many of the writers who came and went on *Star Trek* parlayed a myriad assortment of vibrant and fascinating concepts into the series, even if some worked better on the page than the screen.

Many such concepts, however, never got that far. Some came close to being shot. Some were written and fell by the wayside. Some were never more than ideas, certain of them fleshed out more than others. All, across three seasons of storytelling, suggest a rich seam of science-fiction stories that remain the vestige of the unmade; adventures for the crew of the USS *Enterprise* that could have been, some of them tantalisingly original, unique and could have sent the series spiralling into vivid new directions.

*

As mentioned in an earlier chapter, 'The Cage' – *Star Trek*'s original 1965 pilot episode – was rejected and unseen for decades following the premiere of the show that did emerge. NBC described it as "too cerebral", yet they did eventually offer to produce a second pilot episode, with one or two key conditions.

The budget would be half the size, given the *Enterprise* sets had already been constructed, with costs more in line with the standard budget of an NBC drama series. They also requested cast changes. Jeffrey Hunter refused under any circumstances to play Pike again and would pass away in an accident at just 42 years old in 1969. Roddenberry decided not to bring back actor John Hoyt, who played Dr Phil Boyce – the *Enterprise*'s chief medical officer – in 'The Cage'; an aged, acerbic man as described in Roddenberry's 'Star Trek Is . . .' pitch and a forerunner to Dr McCoy.

In the end, the only character and cast member to survive the cull was Mr Spock, aka Leonard Nimoy, and as Roddenberry described: "The network told me to get rid of Number One, the woman first lieutenant, and also to get rid of 'the Martian fellow.' I knew I couldn't keep both, so I gave the stoicism of the female officer to Spock, and married the actress who played Number One. Thank God it wasn't the other way around."

While in terms of gender roles and progressive attitudes toward women on screen, the ditching of Number One – a commanding female presence, to be replaced by the more servile and at times anonymous Uhura – was unfortunate, retaining Spock would turn out to be one of Roddenberry's shrewdest moves. Majel Barrett was compensated with the lesser but still fan favourite role of Nurse Christine Chapel in the series, a semi-regular character who, like Number One, was eventually transformed into a major player in 2022's *Strange New Worlds* series.

NBC nonetheless authorised three scripts that would form the basis of the second pilot, with Roddenberry drafting in Samuel Peeples, who had been an instrumental force in helping him develop 'The Cage', to write a treatment known as 'ST-2' – which became the basis of 'Where

No Man Has Gone Before', the pilot NBC eventually chose. The second concept, called 'ST-3', was Roddenberry's and he chose 'The Omega Glory', an action story that eventually was developed into a Season 2 story; a parable on a 'parallel world' about a society ravaged by nuclear war and the clash between a Western cultural group and the remnants of a Communist society.

The third script was intended for Stephen Kandel, who had previously sold the concept for a science-fiction pilot called 'Stranger in Our Midst', which as Kandel recalled, "dealt with a UFO carrying refugees from another world. They were undocumented aliens – immigrants. And the problem – the thing that made it interesting to Gene, I think – was they had different strengths and weaknesses than human beings, but they were able to blend in to our culture."

Roddenberry liked the idea and they worked together on an intended third pilot episode pitch called 'Warrior World', which as Kandel described, "was about a planet where combat created a sort of a regency existence. The crew of the *Enterprise* found itself caught up in this highly hierarchal villagerized [sic] world where everybody was excessively polite because a breach in manners would lead to deadly combat. The problem was not to offend and thereby create an interstellar incident. But, of course, they did offend and this led to a great deal of individual combat."

The idea sounds a combination of the Klingon warrior code and that of the Samurai, though Roddenberry wasn't altogether enthused by the concept, writing to Kandel: "An interesting outline, certainly full of action, but perhaps weighed too heavy in the direction of a feudal-Roman world and a bit too lightly in story and motivated character."

Though Kandel did attempt to develop the idea further, Roddenberry decided to switch him to redevelop 'The Women', one of the initial rejected pilots, but this too was again rejected before it was incorporated into the series that they eventually green-lit, on which Kandel had a writing credit.

So began the true five-year mission, or so they hoped at the time. 'Where No Man Has Gone Before', in which the *Enterprise* is flung toward the Galactic Barrier by the god-like delusions of Starfleet officer turned super-being Gary Mitchell, set a template for many such adventures to come, even if it did not end up the first episode aired on television.

That mission would contain, right from the beginning of the first season, a litany of possibilities and discarded concepts, ideas and in some cases simply titles, for stories that never materialised.

*

Each conceptual episode followed the format when pitching to NBC of being designed 'ST' and the intended number in terms of production, with an assortment of writers venturing concepts for what, at the time, remained an early vision of the *Star Trek* template the first season would lay down.

ST-10 was named 'The Machine That Went Too Far' and would have been penned by A. E. Van Vogt, a celebrated science-fiction writer of the era in line with many other known and published authors who successfully produced a script for the show, such as Richard Matheson, Theodore Sturgeon and Harlan Ellison. Celebrated as a major influence on the work of the better-known Philip K. Dick, van Vogt's work certainly had an influence on the formation of *Star Trek*, with his tales collected in his work 'The Voyage of the Space Beagle' sit among the first science-fiction works to display a militaristic crew exploring the galaxy, and surely served as inspirational fodder for Roddenberry in devising his show.

He carried some cache, however, within *Star Trek* as it worked to earn its stripes. This tale, concerning an android who seeks to assume control of the *Enterprise*, will later get more than one repeat attempt to make it work in stories such as 'Machines Are Bette', but van Vogt's style generally was on the strange side often for *Star Trek*.

This trend of employing known science-fiction writers did not carry through into future eras of *Star Trek* in quite the same fashion, perhaps due to the rigours of producing many hours of television swiftly on a budget, but van Vogt's presence is perhaps an indicator of how much of an impact writers in this genre made on television and cinema, and how much prestige they carried in comparison to future decades.

George Clayton Johnson, a veteran writer on *The Twilight Zone*, worked on ST-11, which was titled 'Chicago II'. Taken from the original 'Star Trek Is . . .' pitch where Roddenberry described an episode called 'President Capone', it was a 'parallel world' story set on a world that duplicated 1920s Chicago. Roddenberry, however, didn't feel Johnson's work on the story was yielding successful fruit, as he wrote John D. F. Black: "I feel this story lacks action. There is a lot of background and a lot of soul searching, but not much happening . . . While well-written, and makes me want to keep him authoring for us, it has too many points of similarities with other tales we've put to work. Therefore, rather than lose him . . . he and I are making a simple switch of stories."

Said assignment turned out to be 'The Man Trap', which held the honour of being the first broadcast episode of *Star Trek* on television. 'Chicago II' would eventually find its way into existence as the memorable Season 2 tale 'A Piece of the Action', which served as the inspiration for a potential feature film in the late 2010s from none other than Quentin Tarantino. More on that much later.

'Alien Spirit' was the title of the intended ST-15, a concept from award-winning writer Norman Katkov, best known for his work on *Wanted: Dead or Alive*, a Western series that ran on CBS from 1958 to 1961 and starred no less than future screen icon Steve McQueen, and *Ben Casey*, an ABC medical drama which ran from 1961 to 1965. Katkov based his treatment on a 1958 science-fiction B-movie called *It: The Terror from Beyond Space*, directed by Edward L. Cahn and written by Jerome Bixby, who went on to pen four episodes of *Star Trek* across all three seasons.

A direct inspiration on Dan O'Bannon, one of the screenwriters of Ridley Scott's *Alien* in 1979, Cahn's film centred around a mission to Mars to discover the fate of an earlier spacecraft sent there. Only one survivor is found in the wreckage, the ship's commander, who informs them a Martian creature killed the crew. It ends up boarding their rocket, stalking them on the return voyage to Earth. As described: "Katkov changed the rocket to the starship *Enterprise* and then opted for an invisible beast, capable of trashing rooms and tossing crewmembers through the air."

It was deemed by Roddenberry too expensive and potentially too frightening to air on television at the time, but it suggests science fiction was steadily heading toward the intersection with horror it would eventually fully embrace with *Alien*, John Carpenter's *The Thing* and many such films, often playing on 1950s or earlier stories, into the 1980s and beyond. Future series in the *Star Trek* franchise too would indulge such episodes.

'Journey to Reolite' was the intended ST-20, to be penned by Alfred Brenner, who had also written for *Ben Casey* and numerous series across the 1950s and 1960s, including fare such as *One Step Beyond*, an anthology series of paranormal, folklore and horror tales that was a contemporary of *The Twilight Zone*. The story sees Captain Kirk transporting Hugo, the brash leader of the planet Acrid to a peace summit on the neighbouring titular world of Reolite. His species are militaristic while the Reolites are democratic and peace-loving, but Hugo and Galatea, his mistress, have a 'life-giving drug' to pass on to the Reolites as a peace offering, one that also serves as an aphrodisiac.

Robert Justman, an associate producer on the show at the time, wrote to Roddenberry and Black about his concerns regarding the story: "Gentlemen: I find one really interesting idea in this story treatment. And that is of 'The Galatea Syndrome' – the thought of having a very beautiful, seductive, and highly unsophisticated female creature on board the *Enterprise* – free to work her wiles – a most engrossing sort of situation. Most everything else in the outline bothers me. Kirk does not act like Kirk; he is subject to sudden rages and also to weaknesses of the flesh that would panic NBC right out of its skull."

Justman's appreciation of the Galatea aspect speaks again, as mentioned in an earlier chapter, to the largely all-male writing staff employed on *The Original Series* (D. C. Fontana being the lone exception) and their acceptance of the sexualised female trope. Roddenberry certainly remained keen on such a story and, while Brenner's approach was avoided, these ideas would feed into John Meredyth Lucas' third season episode 'Elaan of Troyius', in which the *Enterprise* transports the spoiled princess Elaan to a betrothal designed to end an interstellar war between two species.

Justman and Black both had issues regarding ST-22, 'Return to Eden', which was given two drafts by a writer called Alvin Boretz, a prolific and award-winning writer on radio with an estimated thousand script credits to his name once his career was all said and done. One of the more popular series he wrote for in the 1960s was *The Defenders*, a courtroom drama about father and son defence attorneys that ran on CBS.

Roddenberry described the story to Dave Kaufman of *Daily Variety*: "We have a story going to a planet with automated people, where it is so perfected there is no crime, no hunger, no illness, no choice, the climate is always the same. But the people are like zombies, it's a computerized society. They find what is Utopia for such a society is sterile."

He added also in a memo to Justman around the same time: "[A] shore leave story in which the accumulated boredoms, fatigues, dissentions, male needs, etc., come to a head with our continuing characters . . . The shore leave planet will have something of a Shangri-La aspect with many temptations . . . 'Eden' is a trap, a sort of death. When mankind, or a particular man stops growing, he begins dying."

Boretz's script accentuates another fear prevalent in *Star Trek*, that of the danger of a Utopian society. It evokes H. G. Wells' anxieties about the future in *The Time Machine* (adapted not long before *Star Trek* in 1960 memorably for cinema by George Pal), where a Utopian race of regressed children come under threat from cave-dwelling troglodytes.

'Return to Eden' suggests a tale where the *Enterprise* crew are threatened by such a slow death, one where 'perfection' leads to apathy and ultimately decay. Shangri-La references a fictional, mystical city as described in James Hilton's well-known 1933 novel, *Lost Horizon*, later adapted into a film by Frank Capra, and the title recalls the concept of a Biblical, Edenic paradise where, in theory, humans can find eternal solace. This concept worries that such an idea is a fallacy and even evokes 'Shore Leave', another Season 1 episode, where the crew face danger in what appears to be an idyllic setting.

Justman and Black hated the idea and Boretz's script was canned, but some of these ideas later filtered into 'The Return of the Archons', which was not long from entering production.

ST-25 was titled 'Rites to Fertility' and was the first of two attempts at getting an episode on air from Robert Sheckley, a Hugo and Nebula award-nominated science-fiction writer whose novels and short stories were considered absurdist and unpredictable, which no doubt accounts for his unusual initial pitch for a story which would see a crewman transforming into a vegetable (of the plant kind) following an accident.

As described: "Worse, what is happening to him happens to others and the *Enterprise* becomes a plague ship filled with walking, talking foliage. Spock, who appears to be immune, beams down to a nearby planet in search of answers and, hopefully, a cure. Once there, he encounters a primitive Indian-like race that worships the trees and longs for the day when they can become one with their gods and to root among the forest. They are reluctant to share information as to how the crew can counteract the changing of flesh to soft wood until Spock explains to them, "Earth people do not consider turning into a plant to be an acceptable form of immortality."

The second attempt from Sheckley lay in ST-27, 'Sisters in Space', where the *Enterprise* discovers the wreckage of its sister ship, the SS *Saratoga* (a name borrowed eventually as a briefly seen starship at the beginning of *The Voyage Home*), where Kirk and an away team discover cages that contained living specimens of captured alien species. One such alien creature has escaped, and they discover not only destroyed the ship and crew but stalks the halls, picking off *Enterprise* crewmen, hard to detect through having a transparent, chameleonic nature.

Much like the aforementioned 'Alien Spirit', it was a forebear of *Alien*, not to mention *Deep Space Nine*'s own take on that iconic picture in 'The Adversary', it was nonetheless deemed – as Sheckley's previous effort would have been – too expensive, as Black claimed, but also he seemed to doubt the writer's abilities in pulling it off: "As a premise, the lost and drifting *Enterprise*-class space vessel holds promise – when it has a monster aboard . . . The question is, is Sheckley the writer to do it? From this version of this yarn, the question is a genuine question . . . I'm not sure at all."

ST-28 remains one of the most controversial proposed episodes in *Star Trek* history, based on Roddenberry's earlier idea 'Kongo' from the 'Star Trek Is . . .' pitch document.

Written by Barry Trivers, in exchange for doing a rewrite for Roddenberry on the produced 'The Conscience of the King', 'Portrait in Black and White' would have been another example of the 'parallel Earth' concept, this time resembling the slave-driven plantations of the American South, but here with white slaves traded by black owners in a cultural reversal.

Justman was perhaps understandably weary of the idea, as he wrote to Coon: "Since Gene Roddenberry assigned it, I assume that this story is what he was after . . . Personally speaking, I am not sure about this property. There is more here than meets the eye. Allegories are fine and the allegoric cause as depicted in this show is naturally very close to many people's hearts. Certainly it is to mine. However, I wonder if we aren't starting to lose sight of the fact that we are supposedly making an 'entertainment' show."

Trivers went away to work on a second draft, which Justman remained equally as uncertain about: "We have several problems in this proposed outline . . . [including] a reference to sending a young girl to a 'breeding farm' – which I think NBC would strike immediately – [and] quite a lot of bloodshed indicated. We may have a lot of beautiful words and philosophies here [but] can we afford to spend pages on preaching? . . . Isn't a Negro Lincoln really a bit much? . . . I would suggest that this present draft be submitted to NBC immediately, prior to ordering a script. I am afraid that this allegorical treatment will get resentment from all sides if it is ever shown on the air."

Justman also voiced concerns about the expense, once again, of recreating the American South, and worried yet another 'parallel Earth' story idea would lead audiences to tune out. Roddenberry, nevertheless, had his heart set on the idea, fighting back for the concept. NBC did, indeed, turn the idea down with a brusque: "We believe that this story does *not* fit into the *Star Trek* concept."

Roddenberry remained undeterred, refusing to let go of the core idea: "What we want to emphasize is not the political conflict, but the melodrama of Kirk captured . . . thrown into physical jeopardy . . . emotionally moved to act and react . . . the advancing armies . . . the strangeness of Kirk being considered and treated like an inferior, etc."

Justman wrote to Coon, who was mounting an attempt to rescue Trivers' draft: "This piece will have to be totally overhauled . . . restructured, rewritten. Dialogue is 'unspeakable'. Mostly I strongly object to the Negro masters and the slaves using minstrel show accents and pronunciations. A Southern accent might be all right, but I think we should go for as straight a speech patterns as we can get so as not to insult the intelligence of our actors and our audience."

Coon tried but in vain – NBC remained staunch in their refusal to air such an idea, perhaps wisely given the febrile national mood regarding Civil Rights of the 1960s, though as a counterpoint it might have stoked a broader conversation about the morality and legacy of slavery that could have contributed the discourse of the era in a profound manner.

George Clayton Johnson returned for ST-29, 'Rock-A-Bye Baby and Die', describing the story thus: "The ship in space, hurtling toward Minerva – a planet: To pick up two ruthless criminals. They have been judged criminally deranged and must be taken to a hospital planet. Several persons have been badly wounded apprehending the two and a starship doctor is needed. Abruptly, a glowing speck on the view screens, swift, radiant, headed toward the ship on a collision course. Evasive action. The speck follows. Pressor beams. Phaser weapons. All fail to destroy the tiny hunk of matter. All hands brace for impact. The ship rocks savagely as the tiny sock of matter hits it. Close on the communications console: a switch flips up on its own accord. All hands react to a strange sound that reverberates throughout the ship. The sound of a baby squalling!"

His concept would have found no actual baby but rather evidence that the ship itself lives: "The glowing speck of matter was an entity, a soul – trying to be born – to become – to exist. It found a host – the complex circuitry of the ship. There seems to be no way to separate the entity from the ship. To Mr Spock it is a scientific marvel. To Kirk it is a responsibility – something to take back to Earth for the experts to examine. To Dr McCoy it is a nuisance – something that stands between himself and his patients on Minerva. To Uhura, the ship is frightening. Her switchboard is the baby's voice. The crying disturbs her. Kirk puts Spock and Scott to work to locate the offending circuits. Spock's advice: Save the ship at any cost. The complication: There is evidence that the 'baby' is growing at an accelerated rate. In the first five minutes the ship had apparently aged one year. It is beginning to explore its body and environment – working doors, the propulsion system. It is developing an awareness of itself."

Johnson's idea was rejected as being "too fantastical", Coon believing it better suited to *The Twilight Zone* that the writer had previously penned for, which frustrated Johnson. He bought back the rights to the tale and subsequently chose never to pitch again to *Star Trek*. 'Rock-A-Bye Baby and Die' was never developed in any other medium.

'The Squaw', ST-31, was a potentially fascinating examination of cultural myth and appropriation by Shimon Wincelberg.

Picking up space debris from a ship called starship *Pioneer XIX*, lost sixty years earlier, Spock leads a search for survivors on nearby planets and discovers a race of 'savage Vulcans', who capture him. He is befriended by the 'squaw' of the title, Missie. Kirk and a team mount a rescue mission and are attacked by descendants of the Pioneer, living in a western-style town called Fort Antrim, modelled after a book called *Astounding Western Romances* one of the original *Pioneer* survivors had – pulp schlock considered a 'Bible' by the settlers.

Kirk and Spock learn the Vulcans were originally peaceful until the *Pioneer* descendants came to believe, thanks to the book, that the aliens were savages, creating hostilities over decades which saw the Vulcans become that which the humans believed them to be. Missie prevents Spock being killed as a 'half breed' before Kirk manages to rescue him and they make their escape.

Wincelberg ended up falling out with Roddenberry after he rewrote 'Dagger of the Mind' and, following several completed drafts, nothing came of 'The Squaw', again to the relief of Justman given the proposed cost involved. It would nonetheless hold a legacy in future *Star Trek* episodes such as 'The Royale', in *The Next Generation*, where a poor paperback novel serves as the basis of a civilisation, and *Enterprise*'s 'North Star', a similar tale of Captain Archer and his crew finding a 19th-century Old West settlement in the middle of the strange Delphic Expanse.

As well as the marked 'ST' production episodes that came closer to fruition, unsolicited story pitches also arrived on *Star Trek*'s doorstep.

Philip Jose Farmer, the prodigious pulp novelist behind the expansive *Wold Newton* universe of stories, pitched 'Mere Shadows' in March 1966, in which the rescued woman of a prospecting ship falls in love with Kirk and, after he rebuffs her (which doesn't sound much like Tiberius . . .), she takes over engineering and hurtles the *Enterprise* through space so fast it breaks "the skin of the universe" and enters a spacial void.

Though that was deemed too expensive, with elements later surfacing in 'Is There No Truth in Beauty?', Farmer later pitched 'Image of the Beast' which sees an *Enterprise* team transport down into the wreck of a vast alien spacecraft amidst a huge desert on an empty planet. On investigating, Kirk and his team start hallucinating and suffer memory loss, discovering telepathic aliens have implanted devices in their skulls to communicate with them. Though Farmer never sold the concept, he did reuse the title later for an erotic science-fiction novel, though with a much different plot.

He also pitched 'The Uncoiler', in which the *Enterprise* responds to a distress call from a seemingly uninhabited world, only to find an old man living inside a jungle in the wreck of his spacecraft near an ancient city, in which they find the idol worshipped by the long-dead race who lived there. The old man won't be rescued unless Kirk allows him to take the idol with him.

As in 'Image of the Beast', once the idol is on the ship, they begin to experience amnesia and find the aliens – the Zaltots – have transferred their minds into the idol. It used the man to get onto the *Enterprise* as a means of escaping and living through others. They are described as "electronic vampires" who Kirk and Spock manage to defeat by recording information designed to exorcise the aliens from their minds before the Zaltots possess them for good.

This concept Black liked and paid for, though later agreed with Roddenberry that it didn't work. Farmer had one last attempt with a story called 'The Rebels Unthawed', but it had too many similarities to the in-production 'Space Seed', as indeed did a pitched story by Robert Bloch called 'Sleeping Beauty', which saw a 21st-century gangster revived by the *Enterprise* crew after putting himself in suspended animation to avoid prosecution. It sounds, in retrospect, more *Demolition Man* than *Star Trek*.

One factor that emerges from Farmer's failed attempts to write for *Star Trek* is that he visualised the series in science-fiction horror terms, seeking to bring an almost-Lovecraftian sensibility of wonder and terror to the nascent universe. It is disappointing he wasn't given the chance to present that vision on the show.

Another writer, amidst many who unsuccessfully lobbied stories, was William Shatner himself, who claimed he had written three potential *Star Trek* scripts and sought the chance to write an episode. One treatment of a Shatner story survives from April 1966 called 'The Web of Death'.

It sees the *Enterprise* encounter another intended sister ship, the USS *Momentous*, in orbit around a planet. An away team investigates the ship and finds no crew but their uniforms, all draped around the vessel. No food remains and holes have been made in the hull. Shatner's story ultimately reveals the cause – a gigantic, hungry space spider.

It might come as little surprise that Shatner's story was never commissioned, nor did he write for *Star Trek* on the small screen. The big screen, however? That's a story for later . . .

*

As the second season of *The Original Series* beckoned, numerous hold-over stories planned for development in the first year, again sporting the 'ST' moniker.

Paul Schneider, after penning 'Balance of Terror' and 'The Squire of Gothos', returned for ST-40 with 'Tomorrow the Universe', pitched in December 1966, which sees a Federation maverick visit a 'parallel Earth' where he founds a philosophy in a circa 1930 society identical to Nazism, with him as the Hitler figure. It was designed as a backup for 'City on the Edge of Forever' in case that script foundered and subsequently wasn't picked up, but Nazis in *Star Trek* cast a long shadow, not least in the similar concept eventually developed into 'Patterns of Force' from Meredyth Lucas – which Schneider considered so suspiciously familiar, he filed a complaint to the Writers Guild of America.

Speaking of Nazis, one of the strangest and what easily would have been one of *Star Trek*'s most controversial episodes, was pitched in April 1966 called 'Hitler's Father'.

An outline, from an unknown source, reads thus: "A physicist aboard the *Enterprise* has been doing experiments with time warps – materialises a human being from the late 19th century aboard the ship. It turns out to be Adolph [sp] Hitler's father. His name: Alois Schicklgruber – a man who in the near future will sire a son who will turn out to be the scourge of humanity. The problem: should he be sterilised before he is returned to his proper time? Sterilisation – a favourite weapon of the Nazis. A Jewish geneticist is aboard the *Enterprise*. Schicklgruber is a warm, wonderful, humanitarian man. A ship historian aboard – knows the story – that Schicklgruber died young – when his son was only a child – had nothing to do with the shaping of the monster-to-be."

Quite apart from the questionable sensitivity of suggesting Hitler's father was the precise opposite of his son, the idea moves away from allegory into direct confrontation with historical, philosophical ideas that science fiction has long played around with, especially the idea of whether killing Hitler in his crib would have prevented the Second World War and the Holocaust. *Star Trek* was undoubtedly wise in not pursuing this concept further.

ST-55 was called 'The Orchid People', written by Catherine Turner and John Collier, the latter of whom had penned numerous science-fiction novels and contributed to both *Alfred Hitchcock Presents* and *The Twilight Zone*.

Their story sees the *Enterprise* answer the distress call of a planet Spock says holds legends of "beautiful visitors" who trapped weaker visitors into never leaving. They rescue such beautiful people known as the 'Orchid People' of the title and, once aboard, the two men and one woman begin to beguile the crew, though strangely they never gaze upon each other. Their race died because their species fed off the weaker energy of those around them, with the three intending to use Kirk and his crew as food.

Similarities to 'The Man Trap' were considered but the concept was bought, though Collier and Turner later relocated to Europe and the script was never developed further, despite DC Fontana voicing her support for the creepiness of the script. *Star Trek* would play with the idea of 'sirens' in subsequent episodes and indeed spin-off series, such as *The Animated Series* episode 'The Lorelai Signal'.

A. G. van Vogt, author behind the undeveloped Season 1 story, 'The Machines That Went Too Far', decided to retool his concept for a tale called 'Machines Are Better' on learning *Star Trek* had been recommissioned for a new series.

His tale saw Kirk lead an away team to an unexplored planet, discovering a building containing a non-functional android called 'Number Two', who has been feuding with another android called 'Number One'. Spock is recruited to help mediate between the androids, before Number One – who moves faster than the eye – seizes the *Enterprise*.

While several of the writing staff debated the use of van Vogt's story, which Roddenberry bought on two occasions, NBC executive Stan Robertson rejected it, citing concerns: "Captain Kirk is portrayed as being indecisive, unmotivated, more of a 'traffic cop' than a participant. Mr Spock is shown as being illogical, even though the author keeps reminding us of his logic, and [shows] more [emotion on the] surface than we have portrayed the highly introspective Vulcan."

Van Vogt nonetheless continued pitching concepts before settling on what became ST-61, 'The Search for Eternity', in which following everyone on the *Enterprise* blacking out with memory loss, Starfleet accuse Kirk of destroying a planet called Palada II. Evidence points to the *Enterprise* having fired on the planet, which causes tensions between the uncertain Kirk, and Spock and McCoy, both of whom come to believe Kirk ordered it. A Starfleet admiral arrests Kirk and has him sentenced to death by firing squad, meted out by Kirk's own crewmates. They ultimately end up shooting the admiral, having pretended to mutiny, as the admiral reveals himself to be 'The Rull', a snake-like alien, whose race – boasting powers of illusion – tricked the *Enterprise* crew as part of an invasion plan.

Naturally, several of the *Star Trek* writing team took issue with elements of van Vogt's script, as Fontana wrote to Coon: "I find it difficult to believe a Star Fleet Admiral would under any circumstances address a starship captain as 'you rat,' unless, of course, said Star Fleet Admiral is portrayed by James Cagney . . . I feel we have shot another $655 on a totally unusable story . . ."

Van Vogt's attempt to write a voyage for the *Enterprise* crew would continue in the third season, as we shall see further in this chapter.

One of the most interesting in-development outings for the second season was 'Shol', ST-64, written by Darlene Hartman, a young female writer who was a fan of *Star Trek* and had penned several spec-scripts, of most interest to the writers being 'Shun-daki', in which she killed Spock's parents Sarek and Amanda. She pitched another idea called 'Krail', in May 1967, which the staff deemed too like 'Operation: Annihilate'.

Nonetheless, Roddenberry and Coon saw enough promise in Hartman to take her under their wing and begin a mentoring process, which ultimately led to them rewriting her treatment of 'Shol', in which the *Enterprise* discovers the peaceful Alpha Cygnus 12, believed to hold the source of the Biblical Garden of Eden. Kirk and his crew find a society devoted to art and culture, but they are devoid of soul, seeking death to become one with their God, Shol. Everyone over the age of 40 has already been 'absorbed' by God. Uhura and Chekov themselves suffer this fate (despite probably not being middle-aged at the time!) and, as McCoy races to save their minds, Kirk and Spock hunt Shol, learning it is a network of telepathic communities which, if destroyed, will destroy everyone connected – including Uhura and Chekov.

Spock ends up being absorbed by Shol, with his Vulcan mind powers allowing him to retain individuality, and he allows those trapped to return to their bodies. The outline then adds: "The rising ethereal sound of Shol rises higher, to a frightening pitch, and it begins to be shot through with blackness. It throbs, advances, retreats . . . and the Cygeans present begin to scream, to cry. The balance of Shol is obviously destroyed . . . there is a great mournful sound . . . and then a sound of a million sobbing voices have begun to wail all at the same time . . . and Shol fades, and fades . . ."

A strange after-effect of the returned crew is the sense that they have returned to a lesser existence, and being part of Shol made them feel more alive: "Spock is shaken, moved as he has never been moved before . . . His words are totally inadequate . . . to have dreamed, and wake with a sense of utter loss, knowing only that you had dreamed . . . to have been extended across the universe, limitless, without end . . . to realize with a sudden infallible clarity that all of the ancient beliefs had been right, and yet, in a real sense, wrong, too . . . 'I knew, Jim,' he says, trying to get it across. 'I knew and I saw and I was' . . . but he, like the others, cannot find the words. What he does feel is intense guilt, for it was his mental discipline which threw Shol out of balance, and then destroyed the entity. He asks Kirk, 'Do you know what it was you destroyed? Do you have any idea?'"

One of the trapped natives, a 13-year-old girl, is described approaching Kirk: "Tears running down her face, staring at him, alone, sad, a tiny figure. 'What will we do,' she asks. 'Where will we go? Why are we here now?' There is no answer, now. There never was. A sobered, strangely subdued group transport back to the ship . . . And does Kirk know what he had destroyed? He nods his head, feeling the awe of it, the tragedy of it, run through him . . . Paradise, Heaven, Nirvana . . . the eternal, the unending, the ground without beginning or end . . . and Man touched it, and it is gone. We carry that primal curse with us, don't we? For such a long time. Across the galaxy, never knowing what it is we are hunting for. And then we find it, and we destroy it, and continue our search. A terrible, cosmic joke, and somewhere God laughs . . . and it echoes down the corridors of stars, endlessly, eternally . . . and always unreachable."

Roddenberry and Coon, perhaps somewhat buoyantly, believed they had *Star Trek*'s version of *2001: A Space Odyssey*, the film of which by Stanley Kubrick would arrive just a year later, on their hands in 'Shol', defending concerns from the network and engaging Hartman in delivering a draft in the summer of 1967.

'Shol' came very close to being produced, though Coon himself grew unsure on the marketability of such a thoughtful and philosophical script, and by the time Hartman's second draft would be developed, he had been replaced by Meredyth Lucas in one of *Star Trek*'s numerous producing shuffles. He was discouraged from taking 'Shol' on by Fontana and Hartman, who both had their doubts.

It didn't mean the end of Hartman's immediate association with Roddenberry or the franchise, however. They exchanged ideas about a possible *Star Trek* spin-off series called 'Hopeship', built around a hospital in Federation space run by Dr M'Benga, a character who appeared in two *Original Series* episodes and later as a main player in *Strange New Worlds*. Though 'Hopeship' never sadly materialised, Hartman did develop a *Star Trek*-like novel run, called the 'Einai series', with one book based around her 'Krail' outline and another the 'Hopeship' concept. 'Shol', however, remains perhaps one of the great, unproduced *Original Series* episodes of the 1960s.

Speaking earlier of John Meredyth Lucas, he attempted to mount ST-68, 'The Lost Star', writing two drafts in June of 1967.

The idea saw the *Enterprise* struck by a force field blocking an entire solar system from outsiders, ending up severely damaged in penetrating it and seeking supplies and materials on a planet populated by primitive slaves of a race called the Old Ones. They left long ago but return to punish rule breakers as part of their plan to keep the society on the planet degenerate. When several of the crew, in mining for materials, are killed, Kirk learns from Spock – via a mind meld with a native called Kollos – that the Old Ones are fake and the people are descendants of an advanced civilisation, with an elite concealing the truth about their past for fear knowledge of it will lead to their race's destruction.

Meredyth Lucas' story then would have seen Spock telepathically link with Kollos as she suspects the *Enterprise* poses a threat, eventually using the powers of her mind to open a tunnel in space allowing the ship to leave, as Kirk and Spock wonder if she will bring positive change to her race or not. It was, as many of the rejected scripts were, deemed too expensive but also lacking in enough action and dramatic impetus to sustain an hour of television.

Norman Spinrad, who had developed 'The Doomsday Machine', developed ST-69, 'He Walked Among Us', which strongly evoked elements of the script Meredyth Lucas – after failing to mount 'The Lost Star' – moved on to pen in 'Patterns of Force', albeit without the Nazi aspect.

The script sees the *Enterprise* discover the planet Jugal has come under the thrall of Dr Theodore Bayne, a Federation scientist, who has interfered in an alien culture and is determined to develop its society with greater efficiency. The Jugal natives have come to see Bayne as a God-figure whose sudden disappearance would see two major power brokers, King Kaneb and High Priest Lokar, vie for supremacy and trigger a devastating war. Kirk seeks a solution and discovers that Kaneb was the one who rescued Bayne when his ship crashed and knows who he really is, intending to use him to his own ends.

Spinrad commented on development of the idea: "It began with Gene Roddenberry. Gene says, 'Milton Berle wants to do a show and we've got this set which we'd like to use – it's this exterior set which is something like a semi-primitive village with overgrown weeds and shit – so why don't you go drive down there to the Desilu backlot and take a look at it and see what you can come up with.' And they had this Prime Directive – the idea that you're not supposed to interfere with the culture of a less advanced civilization on another planet. So I came up with the idea of a guy who goes there and he's violated the Prime Directive, so they've got to get him out of there and do it in a way that they aren't violating the Directive themselves. And that was the genesis of the thing."

Kirk ends up using Kaneb's information to convince Bayne he has done more harm than good on Jugal and gets him to leave, not before helping broker a lasting peace between Kaneb and Lokar as joint rulers.

Numerous writers on staff did not believe Spinrad's script was strong enough to carry off the concept, and the writer attests that Coon ended up developing a funnier rewrite that was worse, as a means of coaxing Milton Berle – one of America's best-loved and successful comedians of the time known colloquially as 'Uncle Miltie' – on to the show, though Berle reputedly wanted to play presumably Bayne in a serious role. Despite this, it did nonetheless come the closest of all *The Original Series* ideas to enter production in the second season, only narrowly missing out on being made.

The final second season concept was ST-77, 'Pandora's Box', which made it through two drafts by writer Daniel Aubrey.

The *Enterprise* would have discovered strange rock creatures on an asteroid that was intended to mount a Federation outpost, creatures who feed on plutonium and end up killing several crewmen as they try to eat a portable nuclear generator. This gives them enhanced powers, including transporting to the *Enterprise*, which they terrorise looking for more power to consume. Kirk wants to trap and destroy them, but Spock believes their energy can be harnessed and seeks to communicate with them.

It was considered too derivative of both 'The Man Trap' and 'The Devil in the Dark' from the previous season, the latter written by Coon who, having unsuccessfully tried to steer multiple concepts to the screen during this season, grew increasingly disillusioned with his role on the show, and the consistent rebuke of his writing from producers such as Justman in particular. He would soon leave the series in the hands of John Meredyth Lucas as a troubled and, ultimately, final third season beckoned.

It too would be a season littered with unmade ideas that *Star Trek* would leave to the imagination.

*

As the somewhat embattled *Star Trek*, rescued from the jaws of cancellation through the indefatigable support of the burgeoning fanbase, prepped the third season, Roddenberry was determined not to repeat mistakes of the past. Immediately, numerous story concepts were bought with the intent of getting them into production, but numerous ended up morphing into entirely different episodes that did make it to air.

Fontana had four story concepts that were quickly snapped up. 'Survival' (ST-82) concerned an automated planetary defence system protecting a long-dead race and ultimately morphed into the produced episode 'That Which Survives'. 'Van Vogt's Robots' (ST-83) saw her attempt to have a third run at A. G. van Vogt's 'The Machine That Went Too Far', which much like those attempts curried little success. 'Ears' (ST-84) evoked a recent major diplomatic incident, the capture of a naval intelligence spy ship the USS *Pueblo* by the North Koreans, and was developed ultimately into 'The *Enterprise* Incident'. It was her first pitch that remains, perhaps, the most fascinating.

ST-81 was called 'Joanna' and would have brought McCoy's youthful daughter of the same name to the *Enterprise*, where she would have romanced Kirk. It was an idea Fontana had wanted to do for some time and DeForest Kelley had added flesh to this aspect of McCoy's backstory: "The common thought was, of course, that [McCoy] had a very unhappy marriage, divorced, with a daughter whose name was Joanna. But he's a Southerner, out of the South, and, I think, [he] just was such an unhappy guy that he joined the service and decided he would abandon what practice he had."

Fontana expanded on this in her concept: "McCoy, soon after the divorce, entered the space service. He has provided for Joanna, but due to the demands of the service, has seen her very seldom as she was growing up . . . In the course of the story, Kirk will find himself drawn to Joanna, and she is – naturally – attracted to him. This situation will turn our usually competent and amiable Doctor into a fiercely protective father – a situation meant to create a note of humor as well as conflict. After never seeing much of her father, Joanna might begin to resent McCoy's sudden fatherliness, especially if it threatens a deepening relationship with Kirk. Kirk, too, would probably be first amused and then irritated by McCoy's changed attitude. All of which would play large hell with the smooth operation of both the medical and command departments of the U.S.S. *Enterprise*."

'Joanna' ended up developing into 'The Way of Eden', a late third season episode that revolved around 'hippie culture' that was prevalent in the United States in the late 1960s, with Fontana's original story seeing Joanna part of a band led by Dr Sevrin, an ex-computer programmer who is seeking Nirvana, a planet that rejects technology and the Federation and holds a peace-loving species. Kirk considers it a myth started a century ago, but Sevrin is determined for him and his followers to find it.

The resulting plot of 'The Way to Eden' bears similarities but, crucially, the character of Joanna is excised and replaced by Irina, the Russian ex-girlfriend of Chekov, thereby transferring the romantic angle of Fontana's idea to the Monkees-evoking Walter Koenig and away from Shatner, with the added concern among the writers and NBC that they did not want to overtly portray McCoy as older than Kirk, which they considered him having an adult daughter would do. Fontana would shortly, following this succession of frustrating writing assignments, herself leave the writing staff as Coon had earlier done.

Roddenberry subsequently bought concepts from Meredyth Lucas, who along with Fred Freiberger had operational show-running responsibility of the series for a spell. ST-86, 'Helen of Troyius', a space-bound remake of *The Taming of the Shrew* by William Shakespeare, ultimately became the produced episode 'Elaan of Troyius', but ST-85 'The Godhead' would be a story he worked on before being diverted to script 'That Which Survives', following Fontana's departure after her 'Survival' outline.

In this tale, the crew of the *Enterprise* discover a civilisation who sought immortality by abandoning their bodies and uniting their consciousness into a single mind called 'Ehdom' aka the Godhead. Ehdom becomes increasingly powerful and seeks to expand as he gathers more knowledge, growing ever madder. Kirk ends up seducing a native female who has not succumbed her mind to Ehdom and helps him try and defeat the super-being, who begins attempting to gain control of the *Enterprise* computer, forcing Kirk to consider blowing the ship up to stop him.

Staff writers considered Meredyth Lucas' story to have pilfered from previous episodes too heavily, in particular 'By Any Other Name' and 'Who Mourns for Adonais?' Expected to be a cerebral effort, concerns mounted that it would lack enough action to entertain audiences. Meredyth Lucas wrote three drafts but none of them got far enough to make it into production.

Numerous stories failed to even get beyond titles but do point toward pulpy, adventure-based narratives that they might have become. ST-89 'Japan Triumphant' and ST-90 'One Million B.C.' both were intended to be contributions by Coon, despite him leaving operational control of the series, but Freiberger vetoed them. Both suggest time-travel stories, the first perhaps seeing the *Enterprise* visiting an alternate, post-Second World War history where Japan emerged as victors (evoking Philip K. Dick's later novel, *The Man in the High Castle*), and the latter perhaps taking Kirk and company back to the prehistoric era, no doubt inspired by the Raquel Welch-starring B-movie *One Million Years B.C.* from 1966.

Theodore Sturgeon, who had penned 'Shore Leave' and 'Amok Time' in the first and second seasons, developed a concept that carried through from the second year called 'The Joy Machine', ST-67, which many considered to be the most thoughtful and cerebral concept *Star Trek* would ever have produced during the 1960s. It was the rare example of a script producers such as Justman and NBC as a network knew would be expensive but seriously considered making happen.

Originally named 'The Root of Evil', Sturgeon's story sees the *Enterprise* arrive at the planet Timshel, from where 'nobody ever returns', as Kirk searches for his ex-fiancee Danielle du Molin, who decamped to the planet for work. The crew find a civilisation entirely involved in hard, forced labour, with their reward being time with the 'Joy Machine', a device that stimulates brain pleasure and causes addiction in the brain to the point a person's driving purpose is to work hard to access more of it. Kirk learns Danielle too is an addict of the device and works against Marouk, the only citizen on the planet not addicted, who believes if freed the society would destroy themselves.

A second draft saw Sturgeon make Spock addicted to the device after Roddenberry raised concerns the main cast were too passive, despite the powerful idea in play that resonated with growing concerns in American society around drug addiction. The same concerns remained and Freiberger gave Meyer Dolinsky, who had penned 'Plato's Stepchildren' (famous or infamous for the interracial kiss between Shatner and Nichelle Nichols), the chance to provide a rewrite. Timshel was renamed Nirva, now described as a "convalescent planet", where Scotty (not Kirk) comes to find his lost love, Lisa Crofts, who becomes the Marouk antagonist and the head of a medical sanatorium where *Enterprise* crewmen now become addicted to the Joy Machine.

That idea, despite being briefly earmarked for Shatner to direct, never came to pass following rewrites, so Sturgeon went to work on ST-94 – 'Shore Leave II', a sequel to his first season outing, which was itself quite unusual given *The Original Series* had never revisited a plot or storyline across all three seasons, with its only two-part episode, 'The Menagerie', the result of production necessity, and the only exception being the return of Roger C. Carmel's villainous pirate Harry Mudd in more than one episode.

Little is known of Sturgeon's narrative but his glacial pace as a writer in part put paid to the concept, though the idea of a 'Shore Leave' follow-up did resurface in *The Animated Series* as 'Once Upon a Planet' several years later.

Mudd was also planned to reappear for a third episode, developed by Stephen Kandel, who had written the previous outings 'Mudd's Women' and 'I, Mudd', with a story he devised called 'Deep Mudd'. This would have been a direct sequel to the previous Mudd outing, as Kandel describes: "'Deep Mudd' involves Mudd's escape from that world, after he tricked these particular robots into revealing to him the location of a cache of scientific equipment and weaponry left by their makers. Suddenly Mudd found himself with very, very advanced armament, which he used to bribe a group of pirates into helping him escape. The problem was, of course, that he could control neither the weapons nor the real heavies he was supposed to be in control of, the pirates. They tangled with the *Enterprise*, on a planet with a surface of molten, viscous mud. And it went on from there. That was basically it: bailing Harry Mudd out of his own problems, getting control of this weaponry they couldn't destroy, and sending it into a sun."

Sadly, Mudd's return failed to materialise due to Carmel's unavailability, nor was Roddenberry that enthused by the idea. Mudd did eventually reappear in *The Animated Series* and, many decades hence, in the form of Rainn Wilson, in the first season of *Discovery*, depicting the character before the events of 'Mudd's Women'.

There was also, briefly, an idea to develop a spin-off during the late 1960s focused on Mudd, which Carmel discovered at a party Roddenberry threw following the cancellation of *The Original Series*: "Gene said, 'It's a shame that series thing for you never worked out.' I said, 'What series thing?' He said, 'Oh, didn't you know!? Well, after the successful Harry Mudd episodes [in TOS], NBC wanted to know if I would develop a spin-off series for you starring the Harry Mudd character. A space pirate, intergalactic con-man kind of thing.' 'My God, Gene, I didn't know anything about that! What happened?' He said, 'Well, the artists didn't have enough time to develop it.' And of course, you couldn't blame Gene, he didn't want to let somebody take it off in a direction he didn't approve of. Since he didn't have time to handle it all, the Mudd series project died. But it was a real blow to me, because that was the first time I had heard of it. But what a great chance that would have been for me to star in my own spin-off series."

As 'Shore Leave' was reprised in *The Animated Series*, so too was ST-95 'Bem', from David Gerrold, which saw the titular character, an alien ambassador, engage in practical jokes while travelling on the *Enterprise*, in an adventure that would have seen the crew visit a prehistoric planet filled with cavemen. Bem could also replicate himself into two separate beings and was a 'mini-colony' of a person. Gerrold sketched out what he imagined Bem to look like, believing two midgets – one on the shoulders of the other – could play the character!

Despite these eccentricities, 'Bem' nonetheless was designed to reflect the ongoing debates around civil rights at the tail end of the 1960s, with Gerrold intending Spock to serve as the unlikely *Enterprise* crew member who turned out to hold prejudice against the alien ambassador. An initial story outline saw Bem part of a group of scientists who the *Enterprise* couriers to observe a supernova in the Zeta Omicron system, a group led by Dr Isaacson (designed as a tribute to science-fiction author Isaac Asimov). Bem would have played practical jokes on Spock but ends up saving him with multiple detachable limbs when Spock is irradiated by the supernova. Gerrold's story focused on cultural differences by revealing Bem's efforts were because he believed he would gain acceptance by Spock playing a practical joke back on him.

A later draft more directly involved Bem in issues on a planet in the system, Zeta Beta II, as he sabotages a mission to learn whether the cavemen, ape creatures on the planet were civilised. He would have convinced the *Enterprise* crew that Kirk and Spock, who he trapped on the planet, were dead, as the primitives came to see Kirk as a God figure. Bem would have ultimately been revealed as a 'psycho-sociologist' conducting an experiment on human nature and left the audience wondering if his actions had helped the civilisation create tools or weapons with their newfound discoveries through Kirk as a God-avatar.

Freiberger disliked Gerrold's idea (also vetoing his plans for a second episode featuring *Star Trek*'s infamous Tribbles) as he didn't see *Star Trek* in comedic terms, which Fontana agreed with: "He was rather humorless. He was a very straightforward person who had mostly been involved with action-type shows. I think that he didn't necessarily get the colors of *Star Trek* – that we could have humor; that we could have pathos; that we could have humanity – not just bang, bang action . . . I was just never sure that Fred Freiberger got the concept. He certainly didn't get the flavor, because we did so many different kinds of stories, involving humor and strong themes, and sad themes, and love themes. And, for him, my perception was that he saw it just as action-adventure/science-fiction. That was it."

'Bem' as a result failed to be produced for *The Original Series*, ultimately serving as an unusual entry to *The Animated Series*, with its greatest claim to fame perhaps being the first story to christen Kirk's middle name as 'Tiberius'.

ST-100 was named 'Beware of Gryphons Bearing Gifts', developed by David P. Harmon, who had written 'The Deadly Years' and contributed to 'A Piece of the Action'. His story sees the *Enterprise* losing power in unexplored space it is mapping and lands on a planet, where a giant cat looks in on the bridge before Kirk and Spock are transported to a room where a beautiful woman reveals they are on the planet Gryphon, and she proceeds to guide them as they learn the *Enterprise* has been entirely shrunk and miniaturised as part of her seemingly God-like power.

The Gryphons are bent on helping races reach their natural potential but do this at points in disturbing ways, such as torturing *Enterprise* crewmen as they seek to discover races' flaws. Kirk escapes, carries the *Enterprise* and escapes the cat, helping the ship fly away and return to normal size before they all beam away and escape the Gryphons. It was a story by Harmon that had similarities with several episodes *Star Trek* had previously developed, such as 'Catspaw', 'Arena' and 'The Squire of Gothos'. Roddenberry was baffled that Freiberger considered it good enough to purchase a story concept, though Justman defended the initial idea.

'The Beast' was the name of ST-102, developed by Marc Daniels who had previously directed several earlier episodes of the show. Kirk would have used a shuttle to reach a planet filled with 'summium', a mineral that was a futuristic substitute for gold in richness, encountering a guardian of the deposit called The Beast. As he fights the guardians, his crewmen betray him and steal the summium, with the *Enterprise* just rescuing him in time, though he is under the psychological clutches of The Beast. It takes 'ESPER' (the code for someone skilled in extra-sensory perception), anthropology officer Janet Matthews, to communicate with The Beast, who eventually returns to his guardian role after releasing Kirk.

Though Daniels would later contribute to *The Animated Series*, his concept failed to gain traction and he clashed with Freiberger over the direction of 'Spock's Brain', one of *The Original Series*' strangest episodes, at which point he departed the series. 'The Beast' never saw the light of day.

Freiberger assigned ST-109, 'The Aurorals', to former *Gunsmoke* writer Frank Paris, a story in which the *Enterprise* is sent to the planet Auroral after they request to join the Federation. The ship becomes trapped in space on arrival and Kirk, Spock and Bones are transported to the planet by the aliens who want to make them breed with their females to return a sense of individualism to their culture, which has grown stale. They develop android copies of the trio who they send back to the *Enterprise*, while the real versions are forced to wear telepathic devices by the Aurorals, lest they be preserved in laboratories for future study.

On the *Enterprise*, the crew grow suspicious of who we know to be android copies and Scotty ends up leading a mutiny against the trio of officers, while on the planet – as the *Enterprise* heads back to Auroral for war – Kirk attempts to convince the Aurorals that they can find the cultural diversity they seek by joining the Federation peacefully.

Though the core idea could have explored the issue of diversity in an intriguing way, Robertson at NBC was not keen on using doppelgängers while Freiberger considered the story too like previous outings, such as 'What Little Girls Are Made Of?' which featured an android version of Kirk.

The final unmade *Original Series* episode, ST-114, had perhaps the fitting title of 'The Foreseeable Future', developed by Jean Lisette Aroeste, who had written 'Is There No Truth in Beauty?'

The *Enterprise* heads to the planet Baran, threatening to engage in civil war, which the Federation is concerned could lead their mineral-rich world open to Klingon domination in the future. Kirk, Spock, McCoy and Chekov meet with the Baran leader, but his daughter Amilla reveals Baran people can predict the future and their arrival was 'pre-logged', with them seeing the reality of a war with a neighbouring planet called Parva in their future. Amilla also sees herself dying the next day with Kirk, having had a premonition that if she ever met him, they would die. All of Baran society live in constant fear that they know their fate, but Kirk manages to convince them, through Amilla, that they can change their own personal destiny, thereby avoiding the fate she saw for them both.

Freiberger liked this concept, as did Justman, but the former eventually steered Aroeste toward another idea she had called 'A Handful of Dust', which ultimately morphed into one of the final episodes of the series, 'All Our Yesterdays'. 'The Foreseeable Future' remained unmade but the core idea certainly had a prophetic power of its own. *The Original Series* was about to face its own unassailable fate, one not even Captain Kirk could talk anyone out of: cancellation.

Yet while the adventures of the USS *Enterprise* were no more on the small screen, the aspiration for a broader canvas for the future of *Star Trek* remained a possibility.

The human adventure was just beginning . . .

FOUR

THE MOTION PICTURES (PART I)

THOUGH IT TOOK a decade following the cancellation of *The Original Series* for a movie version of *Star Trek* to see the light of day, the concept of bringing back Captain Kirk and the crew of the *Enterprise* had been mooted as early as 1967. It was during the shooting of the second season of the show that DeForest Kelley, Gene Roddenberry and producer Gregg Peters discussed the idea of a motion picture, with Kelley later remembering: "That far back, we thought, what a terrific thing that would be. Had we done it, God knows what might have been the result of it. It was much later that *2001* and *Star Wars* came along. We were all ahead of our time in the thinking, even then [. . .]"

Stanley Kubrick's *2001: A Space Odyssey* emerged during the filming of *The Original Series*, arriving in 1968 and spellbinding audiences with a combination of high-concept science-fiction, philosophy and religious imagery. *Star Wars*, imagined by George Lucas and delivered to audiences long after *Star Trek*'s cancellation, came from the other end of the spectrum; a revival of adventure series rooted in myth-making fantasy tropes placed in a science-fiction paradigm.

Both would undoubtedly influence production of *The Motion Picture*, released in 1979. Neither originated from the small screen, which at the time arguably hampered the potential of it coming to bear, as Kelley attested: "We kicked the idea about off and on and then it was kicked out the window; 'Who would ever think of making a motion picture out of a television show?'"

Many, in truth, was the answer to Kelley's rhetorical question, not least of whom Roddenberry himself.

*

In late August-early September 1968, as production of ultimately the final season of *Star Trek* was taking place, Gene Roddenberry attended the 26th 'Worldcon', otherwise known as the World Science Fiction Convention, in Berkeley, California, an assemblage of fans and science-fiction writers which had been running consistently since 1939, even during the Second World War.

As writer Garfield Reeves-Stevens recounted, Roddenberry spoke to a highly enthusiastic crowd and discussed the possibility of taking *Star Trek* to a bigger canvas: " . . . he said that he was talking to Paramount about making a feature film version of *Star Trek* that would tell the story of how Kirk, Spock and McCoy met at the Academy".

The most famous triumvirate of the franchise in their youth would be an unrealised storyline for many decades to come, until becoming a reality (in a different form) early in the 21st century, and it is absolutely a thread we will return to and further unspool in a later chapter, but this serves as the first discussed concept during *The Original Series* run of what a feature film could look like.

Following the end of the live action series, and in advance of *The Animated Series* during the early 1970s, Roddenberry claimed later in the decade that following the cancellation he struggled in how he was perceived as a writer: "They said 'You're a science-fiction type.' I said 'Hey, wait a minute, I used to write Westerns; I wrote police stories.' And they said 'No, you're now science-fiction.' I don't feel bitter about that. That's the way Hollywood is, and that's the way mediocre people think."

Roddenberry defiantly attempted, at first, to move on to different pastures. Under the auspices of *Star Trek* producer Herb Solow, he wrote and produced for MGM the sexploitation picture *Pretty Maids All in a Row*, released in 1971 starring, amongst others, Rock Hudson, Telly Savalas and Angie Dickinson, and directed by Roger Vadim, best known for the 60s bubble-gum science-fiction oddity *Barbarella* and his marriage to the film's star, Jane Fonda. The film flopped significantly, and

Roddenberry turned his energies back to where he had experienced the greatest success to date: television.

Nevertheless, as Roddenberry moved on to develop other projects a remarkable thing was happening to the little science-fiction show that could. Thanks in no small part to syndicated networks across the United States showing the series regularly, not necessarily in order, *Star Trek* began to gain a cultural shelf life unbidden to many similar kitsch 1960s series. *Star Trek* wasn't simply appealing to existing fans who watched originally, it was sweeping up new devotees.

Show magazine reported around the time: "Surprisingly enough, the show's following is growing even though it is not on the NBC web anymore. The reason is that local stations have been buying all three seasons of it at a phenomenal rate – and at a phenomenal rental fee."

The same year that Roddenberry went back to work, 1972, the first official *Star Trek* convention took place – following numerous fan gatherings and events during the late 1960s – at the Statler Hilton hotel in New York, drawing thousands of fans, who were beginning to adopt the collective moniker of 'Trekkies' or 'Trekkers', all of whom came together to share their adoration of the show. A 16mm print of 'The Cage' was shown, art shows and costume contests took place, and guest speakers included Majel Barrett, D. C. Fontana and Roddenberry himself.

He remarked in a 1972 interview on the longevity of *Star Trek* following the series' cancellation: "I think the thing people dug was that *Star Trek* was one show that was optimistic about the future. Kids today are growing up at a time when people are saying there is no tomorrow, that it may all be over in 20 years. *Star Trek* said there is a tomorrow and that it can be as challenging and as exciting as the past. It said there are things to be done, places to be explored, that things are not at a standstill."

Roddenberry understood that the passion *Star Trek* engendered in the audience was undimmed and there remained a desire to see the crew of the *Enterprise* continue, in some form, their five-year mission. He too, even despite his ongoing frustration with how NBC had ended the series, saw a future in *Star Trek* on a theatrical basis: "My own feeling is not to go back into television. I'd like to have a series of *Star Trek* features in the theatres, like *Planet of the Apes* has done. The statistics show there's a ready-made audience of at least three million who would go to a *Star Trek* feature."

Amidst his television work, Roddenberry therefore, in 1973, solicited Solow with the express purpose of pitching, finally, a *Star Trek* motion picture to Paramount. His pitch concerned a story that he first developed almost a decade earlier, as part of the 'Star Trek Is . . .' brief documented earlier in this chapter: an intended episode known as 'A Question of Cannibalism'.

In the original pitch document, designed for the crew of Robert April and the *Yorktown*, the idea ran as such: "Visiting the earth colony on Regulus, April's sortie party became aware that the cow-like creatures raised on the ranches there are actually intelligent beings. But the colonists, who have built their empire largely on the capture and sale of this meat, rebel at the attempt to free their 'cattle'." Updated to fit the crew of the *Enterprise*, Roddenberry intended to name the movie version of this idea 'The Cattlemen'. Kirk, Spock and the crew would learn that despite the cruelty of the humans processing them as lesser creatures, this was actually part of their natural life-cycle, as they would lay eggs after being consumed and consume their hosts into alien beings themselves.

Solow took the idea to Frank Yablans, President of Paramount, a studio who certainly saw the potential of reviving *Star Trek*, especially on a theatrical level. Solow, nonetheless, had doubts about the chosen storyline for such a big canvas: "It did not foreshadow an enjoyable night at the movies," he was quoted as saying, suggesting audiences might prefer a rip-roaring yarn to bring them out of their homes. Yablans did not seem to share these concerns, believing the film could gross at least $30 million at the box office, a significant sum of money in the early 1970s.

Although the plot of 'The Cattlemen' was darker than many episodes of 60s *Star Trek* and leaned toward dystopia, this was certainly a current trend in American cinema of the early to mid-1970s. Aside from the aforementioned *Planet of the Apes* franchise, which continued to successfully churn out sequels, pictures such as *Westworld*, *Silent Running*, *The Omega Man* (also starring *Apes*-protagonist Charlton Heston), were striking a chord with audiences. If Yablans could not quite foresee the next *Star Wars* game changer, he understood *Star Trek*'s return in this vein had strong potential to engage audiences.

The stars seemed aligned except for one factor: Roddenberry himself. Greed overcame his desire to bring *Star Trek* back. He sought $100,000 just for the script, the same amount he had been paid to also produce *Pretty Maids All in a Row*, which Yablans was aware had flopped. While nobody wanted to upset the *Star Trek* fanbase by making a movie without him, equally Paramount were not prepared to pay Roddenberry such a figure without him being a bankable box-office property. Solow was incensed and never worked with Roddenberry again. Roddenberry suggested Paramount had ulterior motives for refusing to green light a film or new live action episodes in 1973 linked to the series' syndication success: "Now that's what is holding up any further talks about the new live episodes. The people at NBC have come to the point of being ready to put up the money for a new pilot – a two-hour film – but the brass at Paramount are reluctant to take it. They say that if they produce new shows, the old ones won't be worth the high rental fees they are charging and the demand will drop off. So we're stalemated again."

Whatever the ultimate reason the deal never happened, 'The Cattlemen' fell apart, never even adapted as a concept for the intended *Phase II* series or *The Next Generation*; quite rare given how many ideas from the initial 'Star Trek Is . . .' pitch and subsequent episodes during *The Original Series* that were never made did end up being repurposed further down the line. It would no doubt have been a challenging story with a strong moral central core, exploring the exploitation of animal species, the line between sentience and non-sentience, and the darker corners of humanity's carnivorous nature. Not perhaps a breezy night at the pictures but a tale rooted in the kind of allegory *Star Trek* on television had given us week on week during the series' run.

Star Trek did end up returning for *The Animated Series,* but Roddenberry had not given up on bringing the crew of the *Enterprise* to theatres. That journey was only just beginning.

*

Over the next couple of years, as *The Animated Series* came and went, as did Roddenberry's other television projects, persistent talk remained of both a *Star Trek* feature film and a revived series of episodes, both of which Paramount were keen to invest in.

A Piece of the Action magazine reported how by early 1975, Roddenberry was developing a script: "He has been thinking about bringing people up to date on the past history of the *Enterprise*, showing how it was built in space, and how each character became part of the *Enterprise* crew; also something more on the mating cycle of Vulcans – whether or not it would be strictly every seven years or Spock's human blood would alter it."

Lots of rumours were circulating in the media landscape at this point. Paramount reportedly wanted ten cameo appearances by name actors, causing fans to worry that the ancillary main cast – actors such as James Doohan, Nichelle Nichols and George Takei – could be squeezed out to make room for 'guest stars'. Anxieties floated around that characters might even be recast from their 1960s versions, including a wild and unfounded bit of gossip that Leonard Nimoy would be thrown out and Spock recast with none other than screen idol Robert Redford!

Ultimately, Roddenberry's cinematic aspirations also were serving as a backdoor mechanism to try and revive the series again on television: "I didn't know if we could resuscitate it as a feature or a series. I guess the feature may enable us to get the series back on the air if it shows a good box office return to our 'friends' at the networks." And if it did get back on the air, "I can tell you that I won't see it as a series of hour shows. I would expect the magnitude to be that of a series of Movies of the Week . . . a 90-minute or two-hour mini-series like *Columbo*. The old hour format is not suitable anymore."

This defiant refusal to conscience the same format as *The Original Series* would wane as development first of *Phase II* became a reality, then some years later *The Next Generation* came to bear. Roddenberry nonetheless visualised both a possible big screen theatrical approach to *Star Trek* and the popular 'television movie' style that had become increasingly popular during the 1970s. Examples such as Steven Spielberg's debut feature *Duel*, in 1971, began life as a TV movie before gaining an international theatrical release. The lines were in some cases blurred.

In July 1975, Paramount rejected a completed draft for Roddenberry's *Star Trek* feature, which contained many of the composite elements that would ultimately appear in *The Motion Picture*. We will discuss this in more detail in the next chapter.

Plans initially were to have it in theatres during 1976. Roddenberry remained steadfast that the film would honour the spirit of the series, as he communicated through his writing partner Susan Sackett: "I have made a commitment to the fans and to myself that when we make a *Star Trek* movie, it will be *Star Trek*. This means that I'm waiting for a guarantee that in producing the motion picture, I can exercise the same kind of creative supervision that I exercised in creating and producing the television show . . . I want some guarantee that we will not end up with something like Captain Kirk Meets Godzilla, and if that delays the movie for the time being, I hope *Star Trek* fans will agree with my stand."

As 1976 dawned, numerous treatments were developed by Roddenberry in line with other writers. Jon Povill developed a draft centred around Spock, evoking the plot of perhaps the strongest episode of *The Animated Series*, 'Yesteryear', whereby an 'energy shimmer' erases all memory of Spock in people's minds and over 200 years of human contact with the Vulcans. This was rejected, with concerns the narrative – seemingly now steering away from Roddenberry's initial tussle with a version of the Almighty – lacked the scope necessary for a big screen adventure.

Povill also contributed a draft which concerned time travel and evoked the classic *Original Series* outing 'City on the Edge of Forever', as described by Judith and Garfield Reeves-Stevens, "involving an alternate timeline created when Scotty introduces advanced technology and computers to the Earth in 1937. This results in a future in which humans are enslaved by a central computer, and in which the Federation and Starfleet never existed. The *Enterprise* must travel back in time to find Scotty, and then try to undo what he has done. In the end, Kirk and the others are aided by a 'plasma entity' that is really an advanced stage of humanity from the alternate timeline."

Acclaimed science-fiction scribe Harlan Ellison described the mindset of Paramount in the regard to drafts, and how they were flitting from idea to idea, in discussing a draft he had worked on: "Roddenberry called me in – you know, he was really desperate to call me in . . . we came in and we thought up an idea. Paramount keeps saying to them, no matter what plot they offer, it's not big enough, it's not big enough. In one of them we destroyed the universe, we thought that was big enough – no, it wasn't big enough. I have a meeting with the guy from Paramount, the guy who's the liaison, he's the interface between the great powers . . . we get a story, it's a super-duper story, Gene and I work it out and it's all solid. So in comes this tumtum from the head office, and he's going to listen to it. We explain the whole thing to him. It's complex but it's fascinating, it goes back to the dawn of time and parallel species that grew up with humankind, and so on. When we get all done, he sits there and he goes, 'Hmmm. You know, I was reading von Däniken, and y'know the Mayan calendar is the same as our calendar. Why don't you put in some Mayans?' We said, 'Um, Mayans?' 'Yeah, why don't you put in some Mayans? That's terrific!' We tried to explain to him that there were no Mayans at the dawn of time. He didn't understand that."

1976 also saw the 10th anniversary of *Star Trek* since the series had launched, with the fandom seeking ways to celebrate such a moment. Magazines such as *Star Trek Today* kept the flame of 'Star Trek II' alive, with Jim Meadows describing in print details of the draft from a year earlier: "The script, by all reports, took place after the *Enterprise*'s five-year mission, with the show regulars in different walks of life (Kirk holding down a military desk job, McCoy as a veterinarian, etc.). The plot involved bringing the regulars back together in a newer and bigger starship to battle a creature that claimed to be God. That, evidently, was the script Paramount turned down last summer."

Despite the absence of a concrete draft or clear vision for the film, with writers coming and going in places, Paramount's intention was to make the film ideally for 1977. Contracts were being signed with actors. Directors were being mooted or even perhaps approached, big names of the so-called 'American New Hollywood' such as Francis Ford Coppola, William Friedkin and Steven Spielberg, all of whom in recent years made seminal examples of cinema that would rank among some of the best pictures of the 20th century. None, if approached, were interested in 'Star Trek II'.

Then came along one director who, aside from Robert Wise who eventually was corralled to make *The Motion Picture*, edged closest to bringing the first *Star Trek* movie into being.

His name was Philip Kaufman. The film he almost made was *Star Trek: Planet of the Titans*.

*

You can probably picture the scene, as immortalised in cinema history. Donald Sutherland, on a San Francisco city street, pointing and shrieking, mouth agape, a veritable Wilhelm Scream committed to celluloid and a chilling reminder, at the climax of 1978's *Invasion of the Body Snatchers*, that the so-called 'Pod People' – extraterrestrial invaders who take the form of unaware sleeping humans – remain among us.

This remains one of Philip Kaufman's best-known contributions as a director who emerged at the tail end of Hollywood's Golden Age, producing his first picture – *Goldstein* – in 1964, before moving through the counterculture scene of the 1960s and contributing to pictures as the New Hollywood transformed into a high-concept, box-office driven landscape such as Clint Eastwood's *The Outlaw Josey Wales* and Spielberg's iconic *Raiders of the Lost Ark* (the former as scriptwriter, the latter working on story). He would adapt and direct *The Right Stuff* in 1983, about trainee American astronauts, that gained a Best Picture nomination at the Academy Awards.

Much of this was to come but Kaufman, pointedly, was already an acclaimed screenwriter and director before he entered the orbit of 'Star Trek II' in 1976, in much the same way as Robert Wise would be when he eventually secured the position, albeit Wise having a greater connection to an older Hollywood. Kaufman, approached on the basis of Roddenberry being a fan of his pictures, such as his Western *The Great Minnesota Raid* (1972), was not a devoted 'Trekkie' and only had a casual sense of the show as an audience member, but as he related to Sackett, he understood the scale needed for such a cinematic translation: "In the feature we've got to remember that it's going to be up there on a big, huge screen and people in a sense are going to be inside the movie rather than looking at it on a small tube, and there's a big difference as to how people respond in a theatre. They want to see more atmosphere, they want to see more backgrounds and so forth. On a television screen you can cut to a close-up and it really fills the screen – you can go back and forth, close-up to close-up. In a theatre that technique generally doesn't work quite that well. You have to use close-ups, but people want a sense of place, a sense of mood and atmosphere."

By the end of 1976, with Kaufman established now in the director's chair, Roddenberry hired Chris Bryant and Allan Scott, a British writing team, to work with him in penning the 'Star Trek II' script. They were best known for adapting Daphne du Maurier's short story *Don't Look Now* into a celebrated and haunting 1973 picture by Nicolas Roeg (in another Kaufman connection, starring Donald Sutherland), which at the time gave them a great deal of cache, especially in the eyes of Paramount executive Jerry Isenberg who brought them in, as Scott related: "We came out and met with him and Gene. We talked about the project, and I think the only thing we agreed on at the time was that if we were going to make *Star Trek* as a motion picture, we should try and go forward, as it were, from the television series. Take it into another realm, if you like. Another dimension. To that end we were talking quite excitedly about a distinguished film director, and Phil Kaufman's name came up. We all thought that was a wonderful idea, and we met with him. Phil is a great enthusiast and very knowledgeable about science fiction."

With writers in place, Kaufman began his process with Roddenberry: "I met with Gene and I looked at episodes with him and we talked about all sorts of things. Somehow through the whole process, I must say, Gene always wanted to go back to his script, that he always wanted to really just do another episode with a little more money. Paramount wasn't interested in that, because they'd already turned it down. But in the process of working with Jerry and Gene, we got them to commit to a ten-million-dollar movie, which was a good amount of money in those days."

Meanwhile, Bryant and Scott – who uprooted from England to Los Angeles to work on the film – studied the 1960s series, watched science-fiction films (despite not having too heavy a grounding in the genre) and began working on a story. Sackett discussed their process: "Often during a strained writing session, the air would suddenly explode with raucous laughter, their door would burst open, and Allan, the more outgoing of the two, would charge out, his blue eyes dancing with mischief, to tell his latest joke or pun – he was very big on puns – to anyone within earshot. To relieve the tensions of the constant writing pressures, they played with toys, did magic tricks, and wrote funny memos [. . .] [that] often jokingly used other people's names [as the sender]."

Kaufman himself had in mind the kind of fusion of adventure and philosophy that had driven Kubrick's aforementioned already legendary foray into science fiction: "Whatever the requirements of sixties television were, they were really lacking in a visual quality and in all those things that a feature film in science fiction needed to have. I felt that those elements were in there, if properly thought out and expanded, and could be a fantastic event. We knew what the feature films in science fiction had been prior to this: *2001: A Space Odyssey*, *Planet of the Apes*, a few of these things that were wondrous adventures."

Bryant and Scott delivered a treatment for their proposed movie, titled *Planet of the Titans*, which was submitted in October 1976 and accepted by Paramount, with the go-ahead to develop a full script draft.

The plot saw the *Enterprise* investigating the disappearance of a ship called the USS *Da Vinci*, during which Kirk is struck by an electromagnetic wave that alters his behaviour and he leaves the ship in a shuttle. Three years go by, Spock has retired and returned to Vulcan, and a new *Enterprise* captain in Gregory Westlake brings him aboard as they find, in the area Kirk disappeared, a planet previously hidden which holds a race known as the Titans, a mythical and powerful people whose planet is steadily being drawn into a black hole. The Klingons are on the horizon, looking to conquer the planet, as Spock looks for Kirk on the surface and finds a bearded, bedraggled captain who has been living there all this time and the world is inhabited by the Cygnans, a race who destroyed the Titans. The *Enterprise* is seized by the Cygnans, with either Kirk or Westlake steering the ship into the black hole to destroy them, as the planet too is sucked in. The Cygnans are destroyed but the black hole deposits the ship above Earth during the Palaeolithic era, whereby the crew teach early primitive man to make fire, a Promethean effort that sparks into life human progress and existence – suggesting the hidden Titans planet was, somehow, Earth from the beginning.

There is, in this draft, a notable absence of Kirk for much of the story, which was the result of several factors. Isenberg was vocal about how what he believed was the core of *Star Trek* lay elsewhere, discussing this with Kaufman. "We sat in a room and he basically talked to us about the *Star Trek* audience and who the characters are, who the most important characters are, and who is the center of *Star Trek* and it's Spock. You can take any other character out of that series and the series is the same. Even Kirk. You just replace him with another captain. But Spock is the center of that series. That character represents the essence of what that show is about."

Two earlier, pre-Kaufman treatments certainly influenced elements of this story. John D. F. Black proposed a tale in which the *Enterprise* attempted to prevent the universe being destroyed by a black hole, though much like Jon Povill's earlier stories, this was bizarrely written off by Paramount as not being "big enough". Robert Silverberg also developed a tale revolving around the *Enterprise* battling aliens over the possession of an advanced, ancient civilisation. Paramount equally didn't want to know, but Roddenberry clearly appreciated aspects of these storylines. Whether they were coincidental or supplied to Bryant and Scott for their treatment is unknown.

Returning to the absence of Kirk in *Planet of the Titans*, another factor lay in the availability of William Shatner. Though it would be Leonard Nimoy who, ultimately, proved the hardest to convince in returning to the franchise, Shatner by 1976 was out of contract to star in the movie. Roddenberry was unhappy with the absence of Kirk in the treatment, more so than Kaufman, which Scott described: "Without any ill feeling on any part, it became clear to us that there was a divergence of view of how the movie should be made between Gene and Phil. I think Gene was quite right in sticking by not so much the specifics of *Star Trek*, but the general ethics of it. I think Phil was more interested in exploring a wider range of science-fiction stories, and yet nonetheless staying faithful to *Star Trek*. There was definitely a tugging on the two sides between them. One of the reasons it took us so long to come up with a story was because things like that would change. If we came up with some aspects that pleased Gene, they often didn't please Phil and vice versa. We were kind of piggies in the middle."

Kaufman had his own view on Roddenberry: "Gene was a great guy, but it was a little bit of the Alec Guinness syndrome in *Bridge on the River Kwai*. He built a bridge and he didn't want to be rescued and he couldn't see anything other than what he wanted it to be. I thought science fiction should go forward and I thought that the order was to go boldly where no man has gone before, but Roddenberry wanted to go back."

Once Paramount had approved the Bryant/Scott treatment, a deal had been made with Shatner, which as a result saw him given a revised and updated role in the script draft that built on the treatment. Silverberg's throwback on the Titans being a technologically advanced, albeit ancient race was part of the mix, and in an unusual move – certainly against the vaunted 'Prime Directive' of the Federation so beloved in the 90s era of *Star Trek* – Kirk and the crew are revealed as the 'Titans' of historical and mythical human legend, seemingly rewriting time itself, or creating a pre-destination paradox. Jean-Luc Picard, one senses, would have had none of it.

Scott remembers: "The ending involved primitive man on Earth, and I guess Spock or the crew of the *Enterprise* inadvertently introduced primitive man to the concept of fire. As they accelerated away, we realize that they were therefore giving birth to civilization as we know it. I also know that eventually we got to a stage where we more or less didn't have a story that everybody could agree on and we were in very short time of our delivery date. Chris and I decided that the best thing we could do was take all the information we had absorbed from everybody, sit down, and hammer something out. In fact, we first did a fifteen- or twenty-page story in a three-day time period. I guess amendments were made to that in light of Gene's and Phil's recommendations, but already we were at a stage by then that the situation was desperate if we were going to make the movie according to the schedule that was given to us."

Kaufman also had designs on an actor to play the main Klingon antagonist, who would have gone down in history as an incredible contribution to the *Star Trek* mythos: Japanese actor Toshiro Mifune, best known for his role in several Akira Kurosawa pictures in the 1950s: "I had loved the power of those Kurosawa movies and *The Seven Samurai*. If any country other than America had a sense of science fiction, it was Japan. Toshiro Mifune up against Spock would have been a great piece of casting. There would have been a couple of scenes between the two of them, emotion versus Spock's logical mind shield, trying to close things off, and having humor play between them. Leonard is a funny guy and the idea was not to break the mold of Star Trek, but to introduce it to a bigger audience around the world."

It is interesting to note at this stage just how much crossover there was developing between *Planet of the Titans* and the forthcoming *Star Wars*. George Lucas had initial designs on Mifune to play Obi-Wan Kenobi in a film heavily indebted to Kurosawa and *Seven Samurai*. Kaufman sought a similar fusion of myth and science fiction as Lucas would bring to *Star Wars*, albeit in different ways. And the script was being written, Kaufman and Isenberg were already soliciting names who were seeped and would seep into creative cinematic legend to work on the film, including master production designer Ken Adam – who had scaled incredible heights on a succession of James Bond productions alone, including *You Only Live Twice*'s vast volcano lair in 1968 – and Ralph McQuarrie, having recently provided what would become iconic designs for *Star Wars*, who was drafted in to provide conceptual designs for a refitted starship *Enterprise*, one that would have evoked but differed significantly from the 1960s-era vessel.

Adam came in before McQuarrie, who was brought on after the Bryant/Scott draft was submitted. Kaufman describes the intended ambition behind the production design: "The opening shot, for example, was going to duplicate the original bridge of the *Enterprise*, which you only saw one side of on television. We were finally showing you the reverse of that – Kirk walking from off-camera and swinging around and showing you this eleven-story ship that was beneath them, with 430 people working. Hence the big stage at Pinewood. We needed that to construct something of the awesomeness of that spectacle."

Adam created numerous designs intended for the film that included a geometric chamber where Spock would have a vision of his own death, a giant crystalline 'space brain', various *Enterprise* interiors, including a hangar deck and an 'open' saucer interior with tubes connecting various platforms – a design he later replicated for Hugo Drax's space station interior in Bond film *Moonraker*, released in 1979. He also worked with McQuarrie on designing a refitted *Enterprise* following a battle which almost destroys it.

Kaufman recalls the mood at the time around these names and the approaching uncertainty of *Star Wars* itself: "Ken Adam and I became good friends, and we had that sense of making *Star Trek* a big event with this sense of wonder and visuals. I got to know Ralph McQuarrie through George Lucas, and Ralph came aboard and started designing things. I went to London scouting with Ken Adam, looking for locations. They were going to pull the plug on *Star Wars*. Fox and all the people in London were laughing at what a disaster it was. George and his producer, Gary Kurtz, had gone on with the last couple of days with cameras to hastily try and piece together what they knew they needed to finish the movie. So there was this mood out there that *Star Wars* was going to be a disaster. I knew otherwise; I had seen what George was doing and had been to what became ILM in the Valley and had spoken to George about that when we were working on the story for the first *Raiders of the Lost Ark* together. It was a sense of storytelling of what science fiction could be that George was into. That was brilliant and excited me. I'd been in touch with him while he was shooting *Star Wars*, and I think George possibly had tried to get the rights to *Star Trek* prior to his doing *Star Wars*. I knew there was something great there. Times were crying out for good science fiction. Spielberg was also developing *Close Encounters* at that time, but Paramount didn't really know what they had. It was to Roddenberry's credit that he and the fan base had convinced them that a movie could be made, albeit on the cheap, and I didn't want to do that, nor did Jerry."

The script was submitted in March of 1977, by which point a fan frenzy existed at the growing reality of *Star Trek*'s revival as a movie. Bryant and Scott were even invited to conventions, soliciting Roddenberry on advice on how to survive the experience. Then came a twist in the tale – Paramount rejected the script. Bryant and Scott understood theirs would be the first of several rewrites, as per film production generally, but the consensus lay in Scott's comments above that too many tweaks and concessions had taken place within the script to give it the necessary coherence. The writers departed back for England and while Roddenberry, aware *Star Trek* had a specific style and tempo that *Planet of the Titans* had perhaps struggled to capture, sought a committee of writers to get the script into shape, in the end a rewrite was developed by a committee of one: Kaufman.

For some time, much of his version of *Planet of the Titans* was shrouded in secrecy and mystery as he sought to move away from the Bryant and Scott draft, taking the story further in the direction of Spock and Mifune's intended Klingon warrior: "It was an adventure through a black hole into the future and the past, and there were more relationships really developed beyond just the crew relationships. Kirk was to have an important role but not the center. The center was Spock, a Klingon, a woman parapsychologist who was trying to treat Spock's insanity [he had gotten caught in his pon farr cycles], and there was going to be sex, which the sixties series never had, but we were here at the end of the seventies and we're in a world where great movies were being made and the times were really ripe for expanding your mind."

He expanded on this later for *Starburst*: "Well, it was a mystery. An *Enterprise* mystery – the crew of the *Enterprise* had disappeared and only Spock was left. Only Spock had a memory hidden deep in his mind as to what had gone wrong. Spock filled with shame. Returns to Vulcan. Large Vulcan sequences. A woman arrives who is going to explore his mind and take him on an adventure through time and space, to beginnings and endings. It was really a love story exploring Spock's human and in-human sides."

The plot of Kaufman's treatment was delivered in May of 1977. The plot saw the *Enterprise* rescuing survivors of a planet destroyed by a black hole at the end of the initial five-year mission, after which Spock intends to leave Starfleet and return to Vulcan. A Klingon attack, led by a commander impressed by Spock, and strange effects from the black hole that cause Kirk and Spock to have flashes of the past and future, lead Spock into violent actions he later can't remember. On arriving at a starbase, he meets Dr Riva, who helps Spock investigate before he and the Klingon leave for Vulcan, the latter believing he is bound to Spock through visions of a dark beast in the black hole, now heading straight for Earth. Strange feelings in the *Enterprise* crew draw Kirk to Stonehenge where they find a connection to the Titans and eventually come together with Spock and the Klingon to face down the black hole. The *Enterprise* is sucked into the phenomenon and into a bizarre journey which leads them to encounter the Last Man, a creature at the heart of the black hole, and a non-corporeal descendant of humanity from far into the future.

Kaufman's proposed film – heavily influenced by the work of author Olaf Stapledon and his novels *First and Last Men* and *Star Maker* –

would have been a unique and at points bizarre concoction of imagery, symbolism, adventure and special-effects one wonders how technology at the time would have successfully managed to conceive – psychedelic space sequences, giant spider-creatures, strange alien ape creatures, weird landscapes, even a separated *Enterprise* saucer section sequence that would not be achieved ultimately until 'Encounter at Farpoint', the two-part pilot of *The Next Generation* a decade later.

Kaufman was open about how different it would have been from what came before: "My version was really built around Leonard Nimoy as Spock and Toshiro Mifune as his Klingon nemesis . . . My idea was to make it less 'cult-ish', and more of an adult movie, dealing with sexuality and wonders rather than oddness; a big science fiction movie, filled with all kinds of questions, particularly about the nature of Spock's [duality] – exploring his humanity and what humanness was. To have Spock and Mifune's character tripping out in outer space. I'm sure the fans would have been upset, but I felt it could really open up a new type of science fiction."

Povill later went into more specific detail as he argued *Planet of the Titans* lacked the spirit of the franchise: "[Kafuman] had Kirk and the crew battling these ugly creatures that zap you and rob the serotonin out of your brain and take your intellectual abilities. The idea was that these creatures were the inheritors of this incredible Foundation Three technology. This planet had been the home of the Titans with capacities far beyond anything human – like V'Ger's planet in the final script we did shoot, in a sense. After the race of Titans had died of attrition, these people had come and taken over the planet but had become corrupted by its tremendous power. They were huge, ugly, spider-like things, and, in the Kaufman version, eventually Kirk stabs them with a sword from underneath, and this is how he gets rid of them. As you can gather from this, *Star Trek* was not there at all."

In this sense, Kaufman was the first example of a filmmaker adopting the *Star Trek* franchise with the intention of transforming it through his lens as an auteur, jettisoning the established tropes and conventions of the franchise itself. This would often cause anxiety with fans and in most cases contributed to a project's undoing. Kaufman and *Planet of the Titans* were no exception.

He later recalled: "I still remember the night when I was getting very close, I was then writing and I stayed up all night, but I knew I had a great story. I remember how shaky I was trying to stand up from my writing table and I called Rose, my wife, and I said, 'I've got it, I really know this story,' and right then the phone rang. It was Jerry Isenberg saying the project's been canceled. I said, 'What do you mean?' and he said, 'They said there's no future in science fiction,' which is the greatest line: there is no future in science fiction. They just canceled it, they never saw my treatment, nobody read it. I still have it, but that was the end of the project. Barry Diller was going to start another network and go back to TV and said, 'Let's just do what Gene Roddenberry was pushing for,' which was that same stuff, which I found passé and kind of clunky. Now, people are coming back to TV, but back then everything was the world of features, which was the only way you could make a movie like *2001*."

This was 8 May 1977, just two weeks before *Star Wars* would open in theatres and allay the concerns among studio executives that Lucas' revival of adventure and fantasy not seen in decades would crash and burn. "That could have been us!" voiced Paramount President Michael Eisner on seeing *Star Wars'* demolition of the box office.

Kaufman would later attribute the cancellation of *Planet of the Titans* to the success of *Star Wars*, despite Paramount pulling the plug before they knew Lucas' film would be a hit. Others suggested the project was canned because it both felt too distant from the *Star Trek* fans knew, and that audiences would struggle to accept another major science-fiction picture in the slipstream of *Star Wars*. No one, ultimately, can be quite sure how successful *Planet of the Titans* would have been. Kaufman's ambitions to evoke Kubrick, the psychedelia of the 1960s and the broad visual scope of the cinema screen might have either felt old hat in the wake of *Star Wars* or could well have aligned with more cerebral science-fiction sensations such as *Close Encounters of the Third Kind*, which was also released in 1977 from Steven Spielberg.

It would likely have steered *Star Trek* into an altogether different direction, although as Isenberg claims, few eyes were looking ahead long term at this stage: "We weren't thinking, this is a franchise and we're going to do eight movies, we were thinking we would make one good movie. *Star Wars* launched as a franchise and nowadays you look back and think that everything is a franchise. What we would have ended up doing is a version that was essentially *Star Trek*, but not the *Star Trek* that was the series, because we would have focused on Spock and his conflict and being human and what being human is. And that's really what 80 percent of the *Star Trek* episodes are dealing with: being human. We were not trying to perpetuate the *Star Trek* franchise at that time. No one was."

By 1979, when *The Motion Picture* was released under Robert Wise's direction, and after even more drafts through Roddenberry (as chronicled in the next chapter), while almost none of Kaufman or Bryant and Scott's story ideas remained, their vision for a cerebral *Star Trek* adventure in debt to *2001: A Space Odyssey*, and counter to the adventure fantasy of *Star Wars*, would very much be in evidence.

Indeed, a longer legacy of *Planet of the Titans* equally exists with the *Star Trek* franchise on a design level. *The Next Generation* would import ship designs into the Wolf 359 starship graveyard in 1989's 'The Best of Both Worlds', as would *Star Trek III: The Search for Spock* docked in a starbase. McQuarrie's designs for an asteroid dock would appear in 2004 in *Enterprise* episode 'In a Mirror, Darkly'. And most famously, Bryan Fuller would be heavily inspired by McQuarrie's updated *Enterprise* designs for the USS *Discovery* in 2017's *Discovery*, the series that after a twelve-year hiatus from television reignited the flame of *Star Trek* in the 21st century.

Not just as the most fascinating *Star Trek* motion picture never made, *Planet of the Titans* continues to live on in *Star Trek* to this day.

*

Although Paramount were frustrated compared to the cost of marketing, the large amounts of capital spent on production over numerous years, and fan expectations, by the success of *The Motion Picture*, a success it was. It remains the biggest *Star Trek* movie in terms of box office, over forty years on, adjusted for inflation, and was only beaten in ticket sales by 2009's reboot *Star Trek*. A sequel was, therefore, inevitable.

The Wrath of Khan, released in 1982, very swiftly became a fan favourite and critical darling, considered decades on by many as still the greatest *Star Trek* film ever made to date. Nicholas Meyer's resulting film was not, however, originally the plan. Roddenberry had reputedly not loved the choice of Robert Wise as director of *The Motion Picture* and wanted, with the sequel, to steer the narrative more specifically in his own direction. "We know a little bit more about how to use *Trek* in motion pictures. The second run in anything is easier. If you've ever played golf, the second try you can always sink the putt. It's the first shot at the hole . . . The sequel story is much more intra-crew, intra-character. It has many more of the difficult decisions that Kirk always had in the TV episodes, decisions about morality and ideals. It's good *Star Trek*. It would have made a good three-parter on the TV show – if I'd had the money to do it."

Roddenberry's treatment for what was known, confusingly, as 'Star Trek III' – given the 'Star Trek II' moniker on what would become *The Motion Picture*, was submitted in May of 1980. The plot concerned the USS *Enterprise* returning to Earth only to discover, through a survivor of some kind of disaster, that history has been changed by Klingon meddling with the Guardian of Forever, the ancient being from 1960's classic episode 'City on the Edge of Forever'. The Federation, as a result, no longer exists, the Earth instead inhabited by a strange race of 'protohumans'. For some reason, conveniently, anyone travelling at warp at the time is affected, hence why the *Enterprise* and her crew still exist. Visiting what was once Starfleet Headquarters, Spock's mother Amanda is raped by protohumans while his father Sarek sacrifices himself so Kirk and Spock can travel back in time, via the Guardian, to stop the Klingons, who sent a small ship through to 1960s Earth. The *Enterprise* follows, mistaken for a U-2 spy plane as it crashes, damaged, in Canada. The incident, in 1963, subsequently means President John F. Kennedy never travels to Dealey Plaza in Dallas on the fateful November day he was famously assassinated and ends up coming face to face with Kirk in the Oval Office. The *Enterprise* repairs the timeline, with JFK now alive and a new wife for McCoy in tow who returns to the 23rd century with them.

Susan Sackett remembers the development of the idea well: "This wasn't as hokey as it may sound. There were sensitive moments, even tender scenes with well-developed characters and well thought out science-fiction concepts. Having given the story his all, Gene optimistically awaited a 'go' from Paramount to begin writing the screenplay [. . .] He [. . .] steadfastly believed Paramount would give it a thumbs up. This time he would produce a Star Trek movie his way, not like the last one, a film written by a committee and out of control. He would do it on time and on budget. His hopes were high."

The story is a fascinating concept, riven with many of Roddenberry's well-worn obsessions that came up time and time again in *The Original Series* – time travel, the *Enterprise* coming into contact with 1960s military forces, the fusion of human history with Starfleet crew, the Klingons as Machiavellian antagonists, and the return of characters beloved by fans, such as the Guardian or Sarek and Amanda, memorably portrayed by Mark Lenard and Jane Wyatt in 'Journey to Babel'. The presence of JFK loomed large over 1960s fiction, the tendrils of the social and political anxiety that spread through American culture following his death factoring into *Star Trek*'s allegorical storytelling. James T. Kirk has been compared to John F. Kennedy, in more ways than just their middle letter marked name; the attractive, young, liberal-minded leader with a girl in every port. The idea of Roddenberry bringing together two icons of the 1960s, real and fictional, is a tantalising one.

Critic Scott Mantz elaborated on elements of the plot: "After the Klingons go back in time to ruin humanity's future, the *Enterprise* goes back to stop that from happening. But they make things worse by accidentally revealing themselves to Earth's inhabitants, and the problems keep snowballing from there. The biggest snowball is that the *Enterprise* has materialized in November of 1963, just days before President Kennedy's assassination in Dallas, and in effect prevented this turning point of the 20th century. So now the *Enterprise* will have to go back in time again even further, but not before Kirk has a heated exchange with Kennedy, who is then beamed aboard the ship. While there is certainly a cool factor in seeing Kirk encounter another U.S. President after Lincoln in 'The Savage Curtain', there's no power to the punch at the end the way 'City on the Edge of Forever' had, and it ends up being a pointless, emotionally un-involving voyage."

As a story, elements of it foreshadow *Star Trek* cinematic adventures to come too. *Star Trek: First Contact* in 1996, albeit with a future *Enterprise* crew, travel back in time when the Borg similarly eradicate Starfleet through a similar historical hinge point akin to JFK's assassination. *The Voyage Home* a decade earlier in 1996, with Roddenberry's original crew, places our Starfleet misfits in a 'modern' San Francisco, replete with cultural clashes, a brush with suspicious military forces, not to mention a beautiful love interest who leaves her time to head into the future. Tendrils of Roddenberry's ideas here, whether coincidentally or by design, appear in the future history of *Star Trek*'s movie franchise, even after his death.

Reports indicated that the plot would have seen Spock revealed as the infamous 'lone gunman' on the grassy knoll in Dallas who spawned a thousand conspiracy theories across the rest of the 20th century, though Susan Sackett remembers it somewhat differently: "Somebody thought it had something to do with they had to kill Kennedy, which was not true.

It happened around that time in history. As with Edith Keeler, they had to allow history to unfold the way it was meant to unfold, and that was the involvement with the Kennedy thing. I really don't know why they didn't do it. It was a damn good story."

Producer Harve Bennett, hired to develop what became *The Wrath of Khan*, remembers Roddenberry's devotion to the idea: "Gene opposed every one of the *Star Trek* films on the grounds that they were not good Trek. He now takes credit for having been the spiritual father of the best one, *Star Trek IV*, because he had told us to do a time-travel story. The fact is we had rejected a time-travel story about coming back to try and stop the assassination of Jack Kennedy, and that story, for good reason, was thrown out years before because it, like going to see God in *Star Trek V*, was a story with an impossible pre-conclusion. You knew that even Kirk couldn't stop that, and if he did, how would we explain that now? And why is Jackie married to Onassis? And on and on, and we said, 'No, we don't want to do that story.' He flooded everybody with reprints of that thing, which he had written, God knows when, and he fought tooth and nail right down to the $110 million domestic gross, and he said, 'Well, I told them to do time travel in the first place.'

One of the key reasons why this proposed treatment was never made lay in the fact that Paramount were increasingly weary of Roddenberry's input in the movie franchise, and not just down to some of the questionable suggestions within the plot for 'Star Trek III', with fans threatening never to watch the franchise again if Spock was indeed revealed to be the shooter in Dallas, 1963.

Eddie Egan, a publicist on *The Wrath of Khan*, remembers this: "There was a version written which was more or less the ending of 'The City on the Edge of Forever', but instead of Kirk suddenly stopping McCoy from grabbing Joan Collins's character, something happened in Dealey Plaza and some aberration in time was causing things not to occur correctly. Spock appeared behind the fence and fired the shot and everything returns to normal. Of course, the attitude of the studio was mostly just horror; that you can't make a movie like that. Their thoughts about Gene were 'It's just in bad taste and we don't like you, anyway, so go away.'"

With the continuing belief that *The Motion Picture* underperformed, Roddenberry was 'kicked upstairs' on the second *Star Trek* movie and made 'executive consultant', which was another term for having an office and approval over scripts but zero creative input. This was, however, the one thing Roddenberry actually craved, less enamoured of the technical and business decisions that came from making a motion picture, ones Bennett seemed rather more at ease with when he was brought in to steer the ship.

"Gene is frequently a historical revisionist, and he uses a phrase that is difficult for anybody else to refute: 'That is not *Star Trek*.' When a man of his eminence and his position says that, especially in my early days, I didn't want to go against the church. But the fact of the matter is he uses that phrase whenever he chooses to . . . When I signed on, the phrase that was in my mind, and that I've used a lot, is that the franchise was a beached whale and it was my task to resurrect it, to give it CPR and to return to the central thing that had made people so loyal to the series for decades."

Though Roddenberry would have plenty of access to *The Wrath of Khan* during production, the film was steered by Bennett, fellow producer Robert Sallin and eventual writer/director Nicholas Meyer, though before he entered the picture, Bennett and Sallin were developing concepts once they had settled on a fact that would carry through to the eventual, produced movie: Khan Noonien Singh, so memorably essayed by Ricardo Montalban in 'Space Seed', would return. The film might not see a return of Sarek and Amanda, the Guardian of Forever or feature time travel, but it would connect back to the 1960s directly in a manner Roddenberry no doubt appreciated.

Some months after Paramount rejected Roddenberry's 'Star Trek III', Bennett developed an outline and later a script – with Jack Sowards – submitted in November of 1980 and called 'The War of the Generations'. The plot differs significantly from *The Wrath of Khan* but retains many of the central ideas present in Meyer's movie, as Admiral Kirk resumes command of the *Enterprise* to rescue an old flame called Diana on a distant Federation planet, where the youth in its society are being engineered into rebellion by an enigmatic 'Teacher'. He discovers his son, David, is connected to the rebels and that the 'Teacher' is none other than Khan, who now is capable of significant psychic abilities that allow him to bring forth illusions, akin to the Talosians in 'The Cage', discussed in an earlier chapter. He seeks to steal a starship and use it to destroy the Federation. It was the first of several drafts Sowards would develop and, crucially, contains the first instance of Spock being killed – as would memorably happen at the end of *The Wrath of Khan* – with here the character killed in what Kirk considers a 'meaningless death' trying to shut down a damaged warp engine.

Meyer reflects on this: "The story that I was told about the death of Spock was that Leonard, having been disenchanted with the first motion picture, wasn't eager to do any more *Star Trek* and that as a way of enticing him or exciting his interest was Harve Bennett promising him a great death scene. That's all I know. I have to say at this point I have no memory after all these years of any of these five other scripts of Star Trek II. I remember two things: I think one script had people singing "Happy Birthday" to Spock in Vulcan. And I remember that there was a simulator sequence in one of the scripts. I don't remember how Spock died in anything. He probably always died somewhere near the end. My idea was to have him die in the first scene."

A second treatment saw Sowards flesh out elements as contributing factors toward the finished film started to take shape. He turned Diana into Janet Wallace, a love interest as played by Sarah Marshall in *The Original Series* second season episode 'The Deadly Years', whose son David Wallace would become Kirk's son. Sowards also creates Saavik, here a male Vulcan first officer on the *Enterprise* and, presumably, a swift Spock replacement. He introduces characters such as Commander Terrell (later played memorably by Paul Winfield) and the USS *Reliant*, plus a weapon of mass destruction called Omega coveted by Khan.

A full first draft, submitted in February of 1981 by Sowards, was named 'The Omega System', incorporating many of these ideas. Khan's wife Marla McGivers, a former *Enterprise* crewman played by Madlyn Rhue in 'Space Seed' who falls in love with Khan and joins him in exile, is present. A later April 1981 draft, 'The Genesis Project', sees Sowards rename the weapon to the more well-known Genesis Device. Wallace is swapped out for a new character, Carol Baxter, with her son still named David. Marla is still alive with Khan, also still capable of projecting mind illusions, and here Spock survives until midway through the film where he dies. By now, Khan is seeking vengeance against Kirk rather than domination of the Federation, with Kirk experiencing a midlife crisis as he meets his lost love and son. Through these drafts, the shape of *The Wrath of Khan* steadily hovered into view.

Aside from the first use of 'Generations' in a *Star Trek* movie (or television) title, Bennett and Sowards' plot, much like Roddenberry's concept, evokes ideas to come. Khan's agenda is reminiscent of Sybok's manipulations in *Star Trek V: The Final Frontier* as he seeks to steal a starship, whereas Khan's seizure of the *Reliant* in *The Wrath of Khan* is arguably more opportunistic. In *Star Trek Nemesis*, rebel leader Shinzon, having seized control of Romulus, will manipulate the arrival of an *Enterprise* as part of a plot to destroy the Federation. These are concepts that will ripple across *Star Trek*'s movie franchise as subsequent writers seek to create action-driven storylines filled with danger and threat, in a far cry from *The Motion Picture*'s more sedate, philosophical journey.

This was by no means the final draft, however. Bennett sought numerous writers to develop fresh drafts, including Samuel Peeples, who retained all of Sowards' work besides Khan, replacing them with a pair of villains called Sojin and Moray. His July 1981 draft entitled 'Worlds That Never Were', also saw Spock – having been killed off – imparting knowledge from beyond the grave to Kirk and Bones, akin to Obi-Wan Kenobi as a 'Force ghost' in *Star Wars*. Robert Sallin was blunt about all of these efforts: "Neither the Jack Sowards or Samuel Peeples script worked. It felt like television. It felt like a long television episode, and I didn't believe that the underlying humanity and the relationships between the people were very strong. There was a lot of intergalactic weirdness in the scripts which I felt was defeating."

When Meyer was eventually hired, following his critically appreciated work on films such as Sherlock Holmes story *The Seven Per-Cent Solution* and Jack the Ripper science-fiction tale *Time After Time*, he ended up with a mountainous task in a short time frame – to make narrative sense out of drafts inside of which contained the DNA of *The Wrath of Khan*: "Harve said he was going to send me draft five of the script, and I woke up one day and said, 'What happened to that script?' It never showed up. I called Harve and he was sort of embarrassed and said, 'I can't send it to you. I don't like it. It's not good. And it's 178 pages.' I said send it anyway and he sent it. I didn't know what I was reading and I said, 'Well, what about draft four?' And he said, 'It's just five different attempts to get a different *Star Trek* movie.' So I said to send them all. This van shows up and there were all these scripts and even though I read very slowly, I read all these different scripts – and along the way a dim idea had begun to percolate through me. Philosophically, I said that I was simply going to take these characters more seriously and more literally than anyone has ever taken them before."

Meyer did just that. *The Wrath of Khan* was not the hit *The Motion*

Picture was, but it was made for almost three times less money and retains a cultural shelf life, and fan adoration, unlike little else in *Star Trek*.

And to think... instead, *Spock* might have shot JFK.

*

One day after *The Wrath of Khan* premiered, Paramount gave a third *Star Trek* cinematic adventure the green light, with Harve Bennett – having successfully wrestled a lower-budget success out of the franchise which had creatively revitalised it – remaining the steward.

Yet at the same time, in response to the critical reaction to Montalban's ferociously enjoyable reappearance as Khan, a spin-off project was mooted called 'Star Trek: Prison Planet', as discussed by Eddie Egan: "And it was to deal with what happened after the Botany Bay crashed on Ceti Alpha V, and before the *Reliant* got there in *The Wrath of Khan*. It was completely designed as a vehicle for Ricardo Montalban, and it was supervised by Harve. But then the decision was made to focus exclusively on Star Trek III instead."

As we will see in a later chapter, Meyer too would toy with telling the origin story of Khan many years later, to date only covered in non-canonical terms via Greg Cox's aforementioned 'The Eugenics Wars' books. Nor would it be the last appearance of Khan in the story of *Star Trek*. Following *The Wrath of Khan*, however, with *Star Trek* reborn for a new audience in a new decade, the follow-up movie was the priority and, inevitably, the story would focus on the major plot thread left open at the end of the film – the fate of the deceased Spock, his body left on the Edenic, newly formed planet Genesis.

Bennett describes the process: "I had to make a story out of the following 'givens'. One, there is a casket on a planet that has been created by the reformation of life forces, and life has been created from death. Two, 'There are always possibilities.' Three, before he died, Spock said, 'Remember.' Remember what? The puzzle was solved so easily that I think seventeen other people could have written the script to Star Trek III. If you end a film with a Genesis Device that can, in one poof create life where there was lifelessness, you have created an enormous story device that cannot be ignored."

Submitted in September of 1982, Bennett's treatment was called 'Return to Genesis', which sees a multitude of elements, with only some surviving through to the eventual film, *Star Trek III: The Search for Spock*. In this treatment, the Romulans are drafted in as villains rather than the Klingons, coming to Genesis to mine dilithium, until their soldiers start being killed by a reborn, feral Spock, whose rapid ageing is connected to the planet itself. The villain would have been a Romulan commander in the manner of the unnamed, cunning antagonist in *The Original Series* episode that introduced them, 'Balance of Terror'. Sulu (rather than Kirk in the eventual film) would steal the *Enterprise* to mastermind a rescue mission for Spock, a potential romance emerges between Kirk and Saavik as the latter confesses her love for him, while the Vulcans – horrified at the creation of the Genesis Device by the Federation – attempt to secede, which sees Kirk and the *Enterprise* travel to Vulcan to face them down.

Egan adds another factor: "There was a version of the story that had a very prominent role for Spock's brother, who somehow ended up on the *Enterprise* and is part of the voyage back to Vulcan to bring Spock's body back. That was eventually dropped, but I don't know whether that actually led later to the character of Sybok in Star Trek V, but he was certainly a big part of the script in the earliest versions."

One can only speculate as to whether the role of Sarek, eventually revived for *The Search for Spock* as the figure who puts Kirk on the quest to save Spock's 'katra', was originally designed for a heretofore unknown brother, but such possibilities are tantalising. The central driving force of *The Search for Spock* hinged on whether Nimoy would return as the character, with whom he had enjoyed a difficult relationship over the previous decade, struggling perhaps with the realisation that Spock would be his legacy. Having enjoyed working on *The Wrath of Khan*, despite his 'death', Nimoy was keen to play the character again and, while appearing in the climactic scene of the film, Bennett at his request also installed him as director – the first example of a performer taking the reins of a *Star Trek* project, later to be followed by Shatner, *The Next Generation* co-star Jonathan Frakes, and a litany of *Star Trek* actors on television in ensuing decades.

Nimoy had an uncredited role in the growing development of the film's plot: "The only time there was any conflict about the movie's content happened during pre-production, when I said I was satisfied with the final script and was ready to start shooting. The executives had some reservations about ending the picture on Vulcan. I felt, very, very strongly about that final sequence. I wanted to end the film by bringing Spock to Vulcan and going through the ritual. I believed it would work, and that the audience would enjoy it. Not being so familiar with *Star Trek*, the executives didn't understand what that sequence would mean to the audience. They were worried about it, and tried to convince me to substitute a different ending. They wanted to end with the dramatic escape from the Genesis planet, getting Kirk and Spock on board the Klingon Bird of Prey, reviving Spock in the sick bay, doing a little tag scene and going home."

In the end, Nimoy got his way. *The Search for Spock* revived the character who, for many, simply *was Star Trek*. Could the franchise survive without him?

*

After the film's success, Nimoy very quickly retained the director's chair for the fourth *Star Trek* picture, with him given greater creative autonomy than *The Search for Spock*, the direction of which had largely been dictated by how *The Wrath of Khan* ended. Now, there were, as Spock would like to say, possibilities . . .

"We decided early on that we wanted to do a time-travel story. When I say 'we,' I'm talking about Harve Bennett and I. We were asked by the studio to come up with a story, and our very first conversation was about doing time travel, which we both agreed was a good idea. We also felt that we should lighten up. The picture should be fun in comparison to the previous three."

The intention to provide the crew with a problem they could only solve by travelling into the past was key in the minds of Nimoy, Bennett and producer Ralph Winter, who came on board during *The Search for Spock*, a problem as Bennett said "which can only be solved by something that's now gone; extinct . . . We experimented with a lot of different ideas on the subject, including the idea that certain crafts and techniques might be lost by the 23rd century."

Nimoy initially considered a future epidemic that could only be cured by the now-destroyed Earth's rainforests in the future: "But the depiction of thousands of sick and dying people seemed rather gruesome for our light-hearted film, and the thought of our crew taking a 600-year round trip just to bring back a snail darter wasn't all that thrilling!" What began to take shape was the narrative Nimoy's team eventually delivered, that of a space probe returning to Earth to communicate with a species – in this case, the humpback whale – ran to extinction before the 23rd century.

Nimoy solicited Daniel Petrie Jr, the writer of recent action hit *Beverly Hills Cop* to write a draft, but then came a huge, unexpected twist in the tale and, arguably, the most intriguing 'what if' piece of *Star Trek* casting in the history of the franchise: Eddie Murphy, star of *Beverly Hills Cop*, wanted to be in the film: "I'm a Trekkie. I've always loved Star Trek and have wanted to do one of the films. I wanted to be in *Star Trek* and that's where they got the idea of coming back in time to Earth in 1986."

In 1984, at the point what would become *Star Trek IV: The Voyage Home* was being conceived, Murphy was one of the biggest stars in Hollywood. A fast-talking comedian, rising out of the shadow of particularly Richard Pryor, Murphy made a very youthful transition to cinematic stardom in Walter Hill's 1982 action thriller *48 Hrs*, before a year later John Landis' celebrated comedy *Trading Places*. Then came Axel Foley in *Beverly Hills Cop*, a role so tethered to his career he revisited it after three decades in the 2020s, and Murphy was firmly on the A-list. He didn't need *Star Trek*, a series well vested in strong, even sometime legendary character actors, but never movie megastars.

Steve Meerson, who wrote a draft of the script alongside Peter Krikes, remembers the intention for Murphy in the film: "Eddie Murphy was going to play a college professor who taught English, but a professor who we probably all had in the sixties or seventies, who's a little bit wacky and believes in extraterrestrials. Every Wednesday, he would open up his class to a discussion and the room would light up with conversation."

Krikes adds: "He would play whale songs, and it was the whale songs he played in the classroom that the ship locked on to. That was in the first draft we wrote, but the second draft was different. After you write a first draft of anything, once the director, the cast, and the producers come aboard, everything changes, and not necessarily for the better. But the tone was pretty much a reflection of what was in the movie. For example, there was a scene where the Eddie Murphy character was trying to convince the Catherine Hicks character that aliens do exist on Earth. In the first draft, Hicks was a newswoman and there was a marine biologist as well. Gillian Taylor was ultimately a marriage of about three characters. Murphy believed in aliens and saw them beam into his classroom."

Meerson continues: "It was the boy who cried wolf. No one would ever believe him, so he took it upon himself to follow the crew, and in one scene, he lifted a phaser from Kirk, took it back to the newswoman and said, 'See, they really do exist.' And she says, 'What's this?' and casts the gun aside, accidentally activating it. The phaser lands on the floor and her cat jumps off the couch. We follow her to her bedroom and she goes to sleep. The cat keeps phasing things out of the apartment by hitting the phaser, and when she wakes up, she sees that all the furniture is gone."

Murphy certainly intended to make this his next project, coming in for development meetings as Bennett remembers: "Now, the meeting with Eddie Murphy was a little bizarre. He had a separate meeting with Leonard. Leonard said, 'He's a little strange in a room.' So he came in with two guys, good-looking guys, and they were all in black leather. [We] told Eddie this story and he thought about it for a while and he said, 'It's good. Let me see a script,' and walked out. We sat there and thought, 'Wouldn't it be terrific to have Eddie in this movie?' Later, the studio started getting very anxious for a very good reason. Here you have a franchise called *Star Trek* and it performs in a certain wonderful way. Here you have a franchise called Eddie Murphy and it performs in an even bigger way. Why not take them together and form one franchise? Bad economics, because you are probably diminishing by compositing. So the studio was resistant to it, but Eddie has a certain amount of clout, and he said that he hadn't decided whether he wanted to do it or not, and so much of the development of the story was with the very distinct possibility that Eddie Murphy was in it."

Nimoy was just as understandably cautious at bringing such a well-known star into the franchise, aware that Paramount studio head Jeffrey Katzenberg had described it as "either the best or worst idea in the world". He was honest with Murphy: "I told him that Harve and I would be discussing story ideas, and that we'd take his request very seriously. But I also told him, 'Eddie, we like you, and you like us. You know if it's announced that you're in our movie, there'll be some sharp-shooting sceptics waiting to gun us all down if it doesn't work well. My feeling is that your part has to be terrific – or non-existent, because we don't want to hurt your career, and I know you don't want to hurt ours'. 'Then keep in touch,' Eddie said 'Let me know how your story ideas are progressing.' I agreed, because that way, either side could get off the train if it wasn't tracking well."

There existed a clear conflict between the prestige and prominence Murphy in a *Star Trek* movie would give the series and the reality of his presence overshadowing the entire film. Much of the *Star Trek* cast were unhappy at the prospect, worried they would not get much of a look-in under his star power. Meerson and Krikes, later replaced by *The Wrath of Khan* writer/director Nicholas Meyer, who wrote the majority of the Earth-bound 1986 sequences in San Francisco, claimed that once Murphy decided not to make the film, most of the narrative beats they established remained: "If you look at our script and the movie you saw, basically everything is still there, like Eddie Murphy going to meet the aliens in the park to bring them gifts, and he runs into the invisible ship . . . which is what Catherine Hicks did when she ran into the park to find Kirk. The structure really is exactly the same. Also, she grabbed Kirk's waist and is beamed aboard the Bird of Prey with him. In the script, Murphy says good-bye to Kirk who starts to beam out, then grabs him by the ankles and is transported aboard. He goes back to the 23rd century and salutes Kirk when they get the *Enterprise-A*. You know when Spock nerve-pinches the guy on the bus? In our draft, that took place in an underground subway system."

The writers felt a lack of credit for the key sequences they had devised with Murphy's character in mind, Krikes discussing some of the intended concepts that morphed once they were replaced: "One of the things we had in our earlier drafts that they took out was what happened when they first went through time . . . we had them using the slingshot effect around Jupiter and Mars. Also, when they first appeared in the 20th century, they were in a fog, and as they lowered, the monitors picked up all of the cheering and applause. As they come out of the fog, they find themselves over a Super Bowl game and everybody thinks it's a halftime show. Then, they cloak and disappear."

Meerson adds: "My favorite scene we wrote was between Bones and Scotty, where they talk about the fact that they're getting too old to be doing this. I personally think they [DeForest Kelley and James Doohan] would have loved to play it. It was two guys sitting on a park bench in Union Square, completely out of time and space, saying, 'We're really getting too old. If we ever do make it back, maybe we ought to give it all up and retire.' Then, they both decided that they'll never retire, because there's more to life than sitting on your duff."

Ultimately, as regards to Murphy, everyone involved got cold feet, including the actor himself: "The script was developed, but we eventually dropped the idea. *Golden Child* came along and I decided to do that film instead, because I thought it would be better for my career. In retrospect, I think I might have been better off doing *Star Trek* IV."

It is interesting to hear Murphy reflect on what might have been had he played the UFO-obsessed wacky professor so early in his career. Though *The Golden Child* was not warmly received by critics, and despite *Coming to America* soon on the horizon, Murphy's career arguably never hit the heights of the first few highly regarded pictures he made while a raw, electric talent in his 20s. Quite what would have happened to his career and *The Voyage Home* is a fascinating question. Murphy's absence nonetheless perhaps harmed his career more than that of *Star Trek*, as *The Voyage Home* romped to the biggest box-office success of the franchise to that point, with critical and fan adulation to boot, which continues decades on.

Though by no means the final big-screen adventure for *The Original Series* crew, with at least two more solo pictures to come as the 1980s gave way to the 1990s, the success of *The Voyage Home* led Paramount to finally see the potential, once again, of *Star Trek* on television. VHS copies of the film contained a snapshot of *The Next Generation*, set to launch in 1987, taking place almost 100 years into the future with a new *Enterprise*, new crew and new captain in Jean-Luc Picard who would, in time, become almost as iconic as Gene Roddenberry's first group to boldly go where no man had gone before.

Before we get there, however, there is one last 'what if' tale in the history of *The Original Series*, one which takes us back a decade, to before the production of *The Motion Picture*, to the mid-1970s and a moment where Roddenberry's long-gestating attempts to bring *Star Trek* to the big screen very nearly led to a TV series that passed into myth and legend.

This is the story of *Star Trek: Phase II* . . .

FIVE

THE LOST YEARS: PHASE II

OVER HALF A year after the cancellation of *The Animated Series*, following a truncated second season and an overall production of mixed quality, Gene Roddenberry decided to go for broke. He moved into his office on the Paramount lot in May of 1975 and started writing a *Star Trek* feature script with a distinct working title: 'The God Thing'.

The concept continued Roddenberry's ongoing fascination with the crew of the *Enterprise* tackling alien creatures who posed as deities or established themselves as false gods. 'The God Thing' follows a similar template that would be clear in the plot of *Star Trek: The Motion Picture*, ultimately released in 1979, as now Admiral Kirk and his reformed crew, having moved away to different Starfleet positions, take the *Enterprise* to confront a mysterious object approaching and threatening Earth, a creature considered to potentially be 'God'.

"The Object turns out to be more than just a vessel – it is a computer form so advanced it is a living entity itself. However we discover that this God they've worshipped is actually the Deceiver, the computer-programmed remains of a race who were 'cast out' from their dimension and into this one."

Roddenberry's plot for 'The God Thing' re-establishes the trickster entity from folklore, the Loki figure of mythology who will be evident in John de Lancie's Q from 'Encounter at Farpoint' onwards in 1987, while casting the idea in the frame of Judeo-Christian symbolism as fused through Roddenberry's preoccupation with technology. His script would have seen the Deceiver use parlour tricks to display its apparent god-like power (such as restoring Sulu's amputated legs that he lost in an accident) and almost everyone is convinced of the machine's deific status except Kirk, who goes mano-a-mano with the entity, ultimately revealing its true face, unlike the Christian imagery he had previously displayed.

Although shades of these conceptual ideas do end up in *The Motion Picture*, there is a very clear through-line to the fifth *Star Trek* feature in 1988, *The Final Frontier*, in the idea of a messianic alien creature who deceives 'lesser' beings into believing them a deity. Sackett adds: "Kirk inevitably goes one-on-one with the Entity, whose Christlike image dissolves into patterns resembling 'The Great Deceiver,' as Gene put it." This heavily recalls the climactic moment of *The Final Frontier* as Spock's zealot half-brother Sybok, on realising the deception, flings himself into a fatal tussle with the omnipotent being.

Perhaps the strangest aspect of this initial draft comes from the denouement, after the Deceiver's vanquishing: "At the end, Kirk wins out, the entity returns to its other dimension, and the *Enterprise* crew is left with a gift – they return to Earth and discover that the 'Deceiver-God' entity had made them a gift of time in which they are suddenly younger and are now returning from their first five-year mission."

Quite how this would have worked given the developing age of *The Original Series* cast is anyone's guess, but it suggests Roddenberry still had one eye on continuing the television series, so ignominiously by now cancelled, and saw an opportunity to reset the board and send them back on a similar new five-year mission that would later almost come to pass with *Phase II*. Regardless, Paramount's rejection was partly fuelled by a concern that Roddenberry's potent atheism, and downright suspicion of organised Christian religion, was too heavy a theme in his concept for the movie. Sackett claimed Roddenberry's script was "iconoclastically asking what if the God of the Old Testament, full of tirades and demands to be worshipped, actually turned out to be Lucifer. If so, was the serpent's offer of the Fruit of Knowledge actually a gift from the real God?"

As with Herb Solow's concerns that 'The Cattlemen' might have been too heavy a subject matter for audiences venturing out on a Friday night, Paramount seemed wary at Roddenberry's determination that 'Star Trek II' be a religious parable wrapped up in a big science-fiction project.

Nonetheless, intentions to make a movie remained, as we previously discussed.

'The God Thing' itself never truly came into being, despite the core narrative inspiring *The Motion Picture* and, indeed, influencing early development on *Phase II*. At the end of the 1970s, Roddenberry attempted through Bantam Books to develop his treatment into a novel, separate from *The Motion Picture* novelisation he did indeed pen, and Walter Koenig aided him in expanding the novel. It failed to come to pass, though Sackett herself around the point of Roddenberry's death in the early 1990s attempted to revive it, working firstly with Fred Bronson and Pocket Books, and later Michael Jan Friedman. Cover artwork for the book was even developed but, again, the project foundered.

The legacy of this foundational text, however, contained deep roots.

And in 1977, such roots would take hold.

*

On 10 June of that year, Paramount executives Barry Diller, Michael Eisner and Jeffrey Katzenberg announced plans for a fourth television 'network' under the umbrella of the studio, allowing them to eradicate the established model of licensing series out to other networks for a lesser profit. It would be named 'PTS' (Paramount Television Network).

One of their most profitable series across the 1970s in syndication, traditionally reached after a show clocks one hundred episodes, was *Star Trek*, discovering a new life in reruns across various television stations around the country. It had led to the birth of the popular culture 'convention' circuit, the existence of *The Animated Series*, continued plans for a movie, and now what fans desired most of all: *Star Trek*'s triumphant return to television.

Phase II would finally, after almost ten years, make that a reality.

Gary Nardino, the Paramount executive and friend of Roddenberry tasked to shepherd the series back to the screen, stated years after the fact: "I don't think *Star Trek* had the respect that it eventually earned, though at the time it was recognised as an asset they felt had probably [been] neglected."

Paramount intended PTS to consider *Phase II* a flagship project, aware even in the days before intellectual property on television and in cinema truly became a going concern, that *Star Trek* had a built-in fanbase eager for more content. Nardino adds: "It was worked on. It wasn't ignored.

There was suspicion that there was something of great value there. And that suspicion came awake because the figures would come out about syndicated properties, and even in those days *Star Trek* was an enormous leader in attracting male viewers in the syndication drama marketplace. That's what keyed the studio's decision to make a new series, and later a movie. They saw the power of the *Star Trek* pull out there, in the syndication of the old episodes."

A production crew was assembled as Roddenberry intended for *Phase II* to begin with a version of 'The God Thing' as a pilot episode, bringing on seasoned Desilu writer Harold Livingston to help him develop the script. Matt Jeffries, the iconic designer of the original USS *Enterprise* (who would later have a well-used tube named after him in-series), to update the look of the legendary vessel. His intention was for a second five-year mission for the original *Enterprise* crew, led by William Shatner's Kirk. All the main cast had enthusiasm for getting the band back together, bar one very noticeable example . . . Leonard Nimoy.

Roddenberry recalls the reasoning: "At about the time the *Star Trek* movie was canceled by Paramount, I had a meeting with Leonard Nimoy in which we discussed *Star Trek* and television. At that time, he told me that he might consider long-form television specials, but 'under no circumstances' would he return to play Mr Spock again on a weekly hour television series basis. He explained that the pressures of weekly television would interfere with his career goal of stage, film, and other things. I still hoped he would change his mind, but could not ignore reports that he continued to reject any *Star Trek* television possibilities in newspaper columns and in television interviews. Then when Nimoy finally became part of a successful play on Broadway, I had to accept that his rejection of *Star Trek* television was final. Convinced that no terms I could arrange would bring a willing and enthusiastic Leonard Nimoy into the role of Mr Spock on television again, I had no choice but to get on with the difficult job of inventing a new science officer."

Nimoy had grown considerably weary of Roddenberry since the end of *The Original Series*. Nimoy had sued Paramount over merchandising rights concerning his likeness and Roddenberry had not supported him during that fight. Nimoy had written his first autobiography, pointedly titled *I Am Not Spock*, in which he distanced himself from the franchise. He also used that forum to give his own take on why he refused to be part of *Phase II*: "I'll confess that when I first heard about the new show, I had major reservations. I was still very concerned about being perceived as a one-character actor, and still war-weary from the unpleasant struggles from Trek's third season. But I was at least willing to hear what Paramount and Gene Roddenberry had to offer. And here it was: a recurring role wherein Spock appeared in two of every eleven episodes. Quite honestly, the offer confused and startled me. Only two out of every eleven? I was being offered a part-time job. It made little sense for me to be technically tied up with a series and having to be unavailable for other challenging work, while at the same time making such a small contribution to the show. I passed."

There had been similar reservations from Shatner during his own *Phase II* negotiations concerning payment and the possibility of his character's presence being reduced as part of a cost-saving measure before he ultimately signed on. A back-door plan was developed to either have Kirk reduced to cameo appearances or even be killed off, paving the way for a replacement character in Commander Will Decker, the son of Commodore Matt Decker from 'The Doomsday Machine' in the 1960s, and a forerunner of the Will Riker 'Number One' character in *The Next Generation*. Decker himself would become a major part of *The Motion Picture*, as played by Stephen Collins.

The show bible says of him: "When not absorbed in his task of keeping the *Enterprise* at top fitness, Will Decker is a very humorous man. He particularly enjoys playing the 'too perfect' soulless marionette of an officer. The joke can be confusing to others because Will can become almost that kind of officer when Kirk's welfare or the safety of the ship is involved. We can see that Jim Kirk is very much in the process of training the young commander for the responsibilities of starship command someday. We will see that future captain begin to happen during this five-year mission."

Alan Dean Foster, who worked on *Phase II*, expands on this: "The original idea was to have more conflict between Kirk and Decker. He's supposed to be equal to a younger Kirk, but he comes across as kind of a postgraduate nerd when the character eventually showed up in the movie. It's like everybody is sitting around wondering how this guy could get command. You weren't supposed to think that when the character was conceived."

The idea of a *Star Trek* revival series without Kirk and Spock now feels unconscionable but it was, for a time during 1977, a genuine reality. Particularly for the latter and, as Roddenberry alluded to earlier, a replacement for Spock was swiftly designed to plug the gap of a character Roddenberry clearly believed *Star Trek* could survive without. Said character was to be Lt Xon, played by actor David Gautreaux, a full-blooded Vulcan who would have believed the only way to equal Spock's presence was to try and access suppressed emotion to engage with the crew, with a similar antipathy between he and Dr McCoy becoming evident as a result, with *Phase II* working to recreate the famous 'triumvirate' of Kirk, Spock, McCoy with Xon. He would, arguably, be an early inspiration for *The Next Generation*'s android Commander Data.

As the show bible states: "The new science officer accepted the *Enterprise* assignment with much trepidation. He has no doubt that he can competently handle the scientific aspects of his job, but he fears the crew might expect him to be a duplicate of Spock as well as a replacement. These fears have been realised and hanging over the early episodes. So also is the unsaid comment, 'Mr Spock never did it quite like that.' Nor is Captain Kirk overly fair to Xon in the beginning. Spock's friendship was a deep, important thing to Kirk and the Captain is now almost arbitrarily rejecting the possibility of a meaningful relationship with the young Vulcan. However, the more difficult Lieutenant Xon's situation, the more we'll like him and the more we'll want him to succeed in this difficult assignment."

Foster described his belief in the new Spock replacement: "I loved the character of Lt. Xon. I loved the idea that there would be a full Vulcan on board. It was a change. It gives you different personal and interpersonal conflicts and relationships. I'm not saying they're better than a half Vulcan gives you, but they would have been different. Particularly Xon on board with Kirk, because Kirk would have been thinking – and this is in the original treatment – that Xon is fully aware that he is taking the place of the legendary Commander Spock, and even though he doesn't feel emotions, from a logical standpoint it presented all sorts of interesting dramatic possibilities. Kirk thinking, 'This kid's good, but he isn't Spock.' So a whole different relationship and all kinds of interesting and new interpersonal dynamics to explore there."

The series 'bible', developed in 1977, was designed to flesh out many of these characters and aspects. It added planned returns for Grace Lee Whitney's recurring Yeoman, Janice Rand, and Majel Barrett's nurse Christine Chapel, now promoted to doctor. It also included plans to develop an entirely new character, a beautiful Deltan navigator called Lt

Ilia – who much like Decker would play a significant role in *The Motion Picture*, played by Persis Khambatta, and indeed would serve as a major inspiration for Counselor Deanna Troi.

Jon Povill discusses this: "We were helped out tremendously by the new characters. We wanted characters that could go in new directions, as well as the old crew. I particularly liked Xon. I thought there was something very fresh in having a nice young Vulcan to deal with, somebody who was trying to live up to a previous image. To me, that was a very nice gimmick for a TV show that was missing Spock. But we never wanted Xon to be a Spock retread. We wanted him to be somebody who definitely had his own direction to go in, and he had different failings than Spock. Xon's youth was also very important and he would have brought a freshness that people would have appreciated."

Livingston describes the intention: "The idea was to bring in a new generation. I think those characters would have developed well. Obviously you couldn't have a geriatric crew there; you have to have new people, and these were them. Gradually, Kirk would become an admiral and Decker would become captain. I thought on that basis we could develop some new directions with these people."

In outlining what *Phase II* would be, the bible is clear on the philosophy present: "We will still use science-fiction to make comments on today but <u>today</u> is now a dozen years later than the first Star Trek. Humanity faces many new questions and puzzles which were not obvious back in the 1960s, all of them suggesting new stories and themes. Also, television censorship has relaxed enormously during those same years, opening up still more new story areas . . . or certainly more honesty in some old areas."

This rationale is fascinating, not simply in how it suggests *Star Trek* might reflect an age after the failure of the Vietnam War, the scandal of Watergate and the realities of a global financial crisis that by the 1980s would beckon an entirely new fiscal, conservative order of globalisation and neoliberalism under which *The Next Generation* would appear. But also in how it recognises the evolving role of television during a decade where restrictions had loosened in film and television, with the former giving way to an age of the daring cinematic auteur. This would soon be subsumed by *Star Wars* and the oncoming age of the blockbuster and corporate box office mentality, but it places *Phase II* in a sweet spot – free of the 1960s allegorical restrictions but ahead of Reagan's America. The result would have been enormously interesting to witness.

Phase II, of course, never happened. Many of these characters and some concepts were parlayed into *The Motion Picture*. Even David Gautreaux would be given a cameo role as, ultimately, a very ill-fated Xon at the beginning of the movie. We do, however, know many of the stories *Phase II* would have told in the first year of the second, planned, five-year mission.

The first goes back not just to 'The God Thing', but even further into the recesses of Gene Roddenberry's failed, non-*Star Trek* ventures.

*

"My name is Dylan Hunt. My story begins the day on which I died."

The opening line of a made for TV movie, aired by CBS in 1973, written by Roddenberry and directed by John Llewellyn Moxey, called *Genesis II* – the intended feature-length pilot of a TV series.

It starred Alex Cord, best known a decade later for his role in hit 1980s action series *Airwolf*, as Dylan Hunt, a NASA scientist in 1979 working on 'Project Ganymede', a system that would allow astronauts on long spaceflights to be placed in suspended animation. He tests the project deep in the caverns of New Mexico, but an earthquake befalls him, causing the technology to keep him frozen until the year 2133, where he emerges into a post-apocalyptic future following 'The Great Conflict' – a third world war that wiped out most of civilisation and now sees numerous groups, including the villainous mutant Tyranians, seeking to control through totalitarian means. Hunt is drafted into a group called PAX (Latin for 'peace'), with the series concept revolving around Hunt seeking to help them establish a society while presumably battling the Tyranian menace.

Genesis II was one of three, post-*Star Trek* projects Roddenberry developed and made into TV movies, the others being *The Questor Tapes* and *Spectre*, which failed to make it past their TV movie pilot episodes. As we will see in the next chapter, Questor – much like Xon – informs the development of Data, while the name 'Dylan Hunt' will be revived in Gene Roddenberry's *Andromeda* in the 1990s, starring Kevin Sorbo and developed by Majel Barrett-Roddenberry following his death, based on notes he had for a high-concept science-fiction series. Very little in the Roddenberry imagination failed to inform projects that did end up happening.

The same can be said for one of the episodic concepts in *Genesis II* called 'Robot's Return', in which following a 1992 NASA expedition to

Neptune, advanced computers and machinery are discovered on one of its moons and by 2133 it has evolved into a sentient form of robotic life that visits Earth and seeks the 'God' called NASA. It finds Hunt, as a former NASA scientist, to be the 'messiah'. As an idea, it recalls Nomad from *The Original Series*' episode 'The Changeling' and would ultimately inspire the Voyager probe behind V'Ger in *The Motion Picture*, but in relation to *Phase II*, it served as a key part of the intended two-hour pilot episode which Roddenberry tasked Alan Dean Foster to write, based on ideas from 'Robot's Return', called 'In Thy Image'.

Foster recalls it: "When they were thinking of reviving the TV series, a number of writers were called in to submit treatments for hour-long episodes. Roddenberry had gotten in touch with me, because of the *Star Trek Log* book series. He felt that I was comfortable with the *Star Trek* universe, and comfortable and familiar with the characters. So I submitted three story ideas. Then Roddenberry gave me a page-and-a-half outline, or notes, for 'Robot's Return', a proposed episode of *Genesis II*. He thought that could be developed and wanted to see what I could do with it."

Foster developed a plot in which the refitted *Enterprise*, with new crew members Xon, Ilia and Decker in tow under Kirk and alongside the older hands, is sent out to face an energy cloud that is headed for Earth and has been destroying vessels in its path. During the story, they learn that the cloud is an ancient human space probe returning home to seek its creator. In other words, 'In Thy Image' was the chief basis for the feature story that would become *The Motion Picture*, and it very quickly became wrapped up in ongoing, swiftly changing realities within Paramount. In short, PTS collapsed. There would be no fourth network with *Phase II* as the flagship. As Shatner claimed: "I remember at one point giving a party at my home for the cast and production staff to celebrate the impending start of a new *Star Trek* TV series. Plans for it were canceled the day after my party."

Nevertheless, development for a *Star Trek* revival series continued, with Paramount executives intending to shop the series to other networks, albeit wary they might refuse based on Paramount's attempt to subvert them in attempting to unsuccessfully develop their own infrastructure. Foster's draft, commissioned by Roddenberry without consulting Livingston, who in a producing capacity was responsible for writing assignments on *Phase II*, was the subject of ongoing tension between Roddenberry and Livingston on who should develop the proof of concept that was 'In Thy

Image', a script that now existed in a strange 'halfway house' position between feature-length pilot and *feature* script.

Foster ended up walking away after an initial draft – largely turning his back on screenwriting to become a successful novelist across multiple decades – which left Livingston the task to pen the script. Paramount received it well at the end of October 1977, barring certain character dynamics between the new players. "I delivered it and Gene said, 'Great, you've done your job. Now just relax and I'll write the second draft.' He wrote it in two days. Seriously, it was that fast. Then he brought it in, gave it to us in a bright orange cover, and there it is: In Thy Image, Screenplay by Gene Roddenberry and Harold Livingston. He took first position. We all read it and I was appalled, and so was everyone else. There was Povill, Bob Goodwin, myself, and Bob Collins, who was the director. We sat around looking at each other and somebody said, 'Who's going to tell him it's a piece of shit?'"

Roddenberry's take on 'In Thy Image', submitted in November 1977, retained the same plot but saw scenes of light nudity between Kirk and his latest girlfriend, Alexandria, who ends up the victim of the kind of haunting transporter accident we see depicted in *The Motion Picture*; seductive female Yeomans questioning Xon about *pon farr* (the Vulcan mating ritual); Kirk even asks the admittedly sexual Ilia about whether she has had sex with a human. Chekov nicknames what became the V'Ger probe in the movie 'Tasha', when it takes control of Ilia, and she shows a deliberately sexual interest in Kirk. It also, unlike *The Motion Picture*, kept Ilia and Decker alive after Kirk scans a print from NASA to fulfil the V'Ger (here named N'Sa in a more on the nose reference) requirement of the 'Creator' – a less romantic ending than the movie.

The intended director of the pilot, Robert L. Collins, was not a fan of Roddenberry's script as much as Livingston, who confronted a crestfallen Roddenberry on the reality of it before a meeting in the office of Michael Eisner: "We sat around this huge table. Michael had the two scripts. My version was in a brown folder and Gene's version was in an orange cover. Michael had one script in one hand and one in the other, balancing them in his palms. And he said, 'Listen, this is the problem. This,' Gene's orange script, 'is television. This,' the brown script, 'is a movie. Frankly, it's a lot better.' Well, holy shit! Everybody was clearing their throats. The great man had had his feathers ruffled. Anyway, after some heated discussion, it was decided to let Collins write a third version using the best elements of both."

Collins discusses his draft and the *2001: A Space Odyssey*-style aspirations he imagined for it: "I had what I thought was a wonderful, spectacular idea for the end. Decker sacrificed himself at the end of the picture and unleashed a history of mankind. It would be a ten-minute sequence where we would flash images of mankind since the dawn of the apes up till the present. These flashes of images would be all over the ship and then, of course, all over the theater. All of this would be accompanied by a musical montage of Beethoven and Bach. It was a grand idea and very ambitious, and I think it would have set off the end of it in a very spectacular manner. I remember that I wrote something to that effect. Not particularly well, I imagine, but that was my thought on how the picture should end. I was trying to deal with what this animal known as man really is, and essentially I was saying that man was pretty good."

Though Decker sacrificing himself to V'Ger would remain in the draft that became *The Motion Picture*, Collins' own draft was disliked by Livingston, whose own draft became the primary script placed into pre-production when Paramount made the decision to make 'In Thy Image' into a *Star Trek* feature film. Collins was replaced by Robert Wise, a seasoned director from an older Hollywood era behind classic pictures such as *The Day the Earth Stood Still* and *The Sound of Music*, and the rest is history.

The Motion Picture was born.

As 1977 ended, however, numerous writers Livingston had brought in to develop outlines and scripts for *Phase II* still worked on the episodes they were writing for a *Star Trek* series of the 1970s that would never come to pass. We now turn to those fascinating stories, many of which influence *Star Trek* tales on television eventually to come, and some of which remain glorious curiosities of what many rightfully call the 'Lost Years' of *Star Trek*.

*

Paramount had ordered not just the *Phase II* feature-length pilot episode but thirteen episodes, roughly half a season of television in the now ageing network television model which would often yield a 'back nine' if the first run of episodes gained an audience, bringing the total up to a minimum traditionally of twenty-two for a full season. This might have been the fate of *Phase II* had it successfully launched the second five-year mission, running from 1978 through to 1983.

Jon Povill, as story editor, was the man tasked by Livingston to get treatments and scripts being written and pitched by a succession of hired writers to the stage they might be ready to enter production. "As I was under contract as story editor, I continued working with writers and bringing in commissioned scripts until my contract ran out, even though we were told that they were going to feature sometime in the middle of my story-editor tenure."

'Tomorrow and the Stars', written by TV veteran Larry Alexander – who had penned episodes of everything from *The Six Million Dollar Man* to *CHIPs* across the 1970s and 1980s – heavily evoked Harlan Ellison's classic 'City on the Edge of Forever' by placing Kirk in yet another historical, time-travelling, tragic love story. Alexander had previously pitched a tale called 'Ghost Story', in which Kirk is projected back in time on a planet in ruins and unwittingly contributes to its destruction, but Roddenberry preferred 'Tomorrow and the Stars'.

Following a Klingon attack that leaves Chekov badly suffering from radiation exposure, Kirk prepares to join a party to take him to Earth for treatment. A transporter glitch sees Kirk materialise in December 1941, the date of the attack on Hawaii's Pearl Harbor by the Japanese that draws the United States into the Second World War – though with an unusual physical effect – he cannot make physical contact with his surroundings and has materialised in ghostly, transparent form. He meets a young woman called Elsa Kelly, married to a man called Richard who Kirk fears might consider him a spy as Elsa takes pity on and helps the lost Kirk. While in the future, the *Enterprise* crew work to understand the transporter glitch and Sulu decodes Second World War-era Japanese transmissions, Kirk realises the significance of the date he has arrived at as he grows closer to Elsa.

Having figured out what happened to Kirk and where he is, Scotty attempts to transport him and fails, but it does reconnect Kirk with his physical form, allowing him to romance Elsa, the two beginning to fall in love. Richard, meanwhile, has begun to detect Kirk's presence and naval intelligence discover his communicator, suspect him of espionage and arrest him. As the Japanese approach for their surprise attack, Elsa helps Kirk escape as the *Enterprise* crew beam down, recover the communicator and try to find him. Kirk tells Elsa who he is, where he's from, and about Pearl Harbor to save her life, but she insists they warn Richard. Kirk, knowing he cannot change history, tries to stop her but Elsa flees, and

Decker and McCoy restrain him and beam him back to the *Enterprise*. Ilia and Bones help a heartbroken Kirk come to terms with Elsa presumably dying in Pearl Harbor and assuming her place in history.

As 'In Thy Image' was inspired by an unproduced *Genesis II* concept, so too was Alexander's story. Roddenberry had envisaged an episode called 'The Apartment', in which Dylan Hunt, trapped inside 20th-century ruins by a strange force field, is transported back to 1975 where he exists as a 'transparent ghost' by a girl living in an apartment nearby, who he falls in love with. Alexander morphed the concept into 'Tomorrow and the Stars', adding the historical element, and the similar moral dilemma Kirk found with Edith Keeler in the 1930s. A final draft was produced in January 1978, with Alexander frustrated that he never had the opportunity to write for the absent Spock, noting: "I had a moment in the script where something has happened to Kirk, and the captain says, 'Xon, what have you done to me?' So there was a little bit of resentment there that he wasn't Spock, which was fun to play with. It seemed like the 'logical' thing to do."

'Tomorrow and the Stars' likely would have been an expensive time-travel tale to mount, depicting the period Pearl Harbor setting, but it would have made an intriguing 'sequel' of sorts to Ellison's iconic love story, yet one perhaps shot through with a late 1970s sense of American trauma, depicting not a victory but the most tragic loss of American lives during the entire Second World War period and the one instance of American shores being attacked during that conflict. It feels a pointed choice after the misadventure of Vietnam. Perhaps the one lingering plot aspect that does filter through to a future *Star Trek* story lies in Kirk's unusual transparency, a plot *The Next Generation* utilises for Geordi and Ro Laren in the fifth season episode 'The Next Phase', where they are 'phased' from existence during a transporter accident.

Theodore Sturgeon, who had penned *Original Series* outings such as 'Shore Leave' and 'Amok Time', returned to develop 'Cassandra', a comedy romp in the style of episodes such as 'The Trouble with Tribbles'.

The *Enterprise* returns the foreign minister of the planet Manlikt, Hibchiba, from a peace conference, a world made up of the human-looking Manlikt and the snout-nosed, tail wagging Breet, who have signed a non-aggression treaty after years of war. Uhura discovers, however, that the Manlikt have threatened to use a doomsday weapon against the Breet unless they return the 'Sacred Monitor', a precious treasure, to their people, which Hibchiba claims they have stolen. Xon claims the treasure is a device that foretells the Manlikt people's future.

At the same time, a clumsy yeoman aboard ship, Myra Kart, discovers a strange egg on the shuttle used to take the transporter-phobic Hibchiba back to the planet, which in sickbay hatches to reveal a small creature bearing a deep, bassy voice called Cassandra who greets Chapel with a "Oh my, if you aren't just the cutest little bug!" Cassandra begins to cause havoc aboard ship, seemingly reading the minds of the crew and depicting what they are thinking or are about to say, as Kirk tries to stabilise the powder keg political situation on Manlikt and discovers – surprise surprise – that the 'Sacred Monitor' is in fact Cassandra (so named after the Trojan prophetess in Greek mythology). Xon figures out the treasure was swapped out with the express intention of placing Cassandra on the *Enterprise* as the crew work to find her.

Yeoman Kart continues to play a part in efforts to track her and capture three Breet spies who beam aboard claiming to be dignitaries looking to trap Cassandra, risking war to gain control of the creature themselves. Through largely comic misadventure, Kart manages to capture the spies and Hibchiba arrives, managing to gain control of Cassandra, which prevents the Breet attack as the plot is exposed. Kirk tells Kart: "For the good you have done, you are hereby raised two ranks in grade. For the trouble you have caused, you are hereby reduced two ranks." Xon comes to her defence and the episode ends with him musing on learning compassion amidst a final gag, in a very *Original Series*-style.

Indeed, 'Cassandra' feels very much akin to the lightness of the 1960s that *Phase II*, with a deliberately darker and more futuristic aesthetic, might have struggled to square in the late 1970s.

One of the major writing forces from the 1960s, John Meredyth Lucas, was to return for an ambitious two-part episode titled 'Kitumba', which would have focused expressly on the inner workings of the Klingon Empire. It was a story that, arguably, influences Klingon and Romulan politics as depicted in *The Next Generation* and beyond.

In the first part, *Enterprise* intercepts an old friend of Kirk's, Admiral Li, who warns him that the Klingons are building a vast fleet around the orbit of multiple planets and Starfleet are bracing themselves for a Klingon attack on the Federation. Li beams aboard Ksia, tutor of the titular Kitumba, the 'Sacred Ruler' of the Klingons, who has contacted Starfleet to try and avert war. Through him, they learn more about the race's culture – that 'Klingon' is a name for just the ruling class and the rest of their species are named Technos – the scientists and technicians – and Subjects, who are the commoners. Above them all are the Warlord, who rules in the name of the Kitumba, a god-king confined to the 'Sacred Planet' at the heart of the Klingon system. Ksia explains that the Kitumba is currently a seventeen-year-old boy made virtual prisoner by the dangerous current Warlord, Malkthon. Ksia represents the Baros, a rebel group of Klingon noblemen who oppose Malkthon's rush to war. Li gives Kirk his mission – penetrate Klingon space with Ksia, reach the Sacred Planet and find the Kitumba as a means of averting war.

The *Enterprise*, ordered to destroy itself rather than get captured by Klingon hands, heads off on its dangerous mission, with Ksia integrating with the crew as the *Enterprise* dodges patrols and encounters a Klingon craft that dies in battle trying to engage them, thereby accentuating their differing philosophies. Kirk avoids a Klingon small fleet near the Sacred Planet with the ship requesting sanctuary from Baro Tara, the deputy Warlord. He seeks an audience with the Kitumba, who Ksia claims was elevated to the post after the sudden death of his father several years earlier. Ksia cannot step foot on the planet but gives Kirk a ceremonial dagger to greet the Kitumba if Baro Kali, leader of the group that opposes Malkthon, is present. Kirk meets the Kitumba and makes his case for peace, with the dagger being a sign to Kali for a second, secret meeting with the leader alone.

Kirk beams down, disguised as a Klingon Subject, and meets Kali who tells him they believe Malkthon assassinated Kitumba's father to become Warlord, a role Kali held under him. Kirk meets the Kitumba in the streets and beams him to the *Enterprise*, educating him on ancient human cultures of history with similar beliefs as the Klingons, and for a reunion with Ksia. Having achieved his purpose, he commits ritual suicide with the permission of the Kitumba, who is returned to the Sacred Planet as Kirk goes with him to help him learn more about the Federation. The *Enterprise* crew mount a rescue mission, fearing Kirk is held captive, but Kirk begins proving his physical and intellectual mettle to convince the Kitumba that life is more precious than death. The cliffhanger sees Malkthon, on his neighbouring planet of Ultar, learning the Kitumba is falling under Kirk's influence and orders Taru's forces to kill him.

The second part sees Xon forcing Kali to help him on the Sacred Planet find Kirk's whereabouts, using Vulcan mind powers to implant a 'suggestion' in Kali that reveals Kirk's location in the palace. Kali reveals that spies on Ultar have learned the code word 'Kitumbala' has been used, meaning 'the spread of power', as a sign that the Klingons intend on conquering the galaxy after the Federation. Malkthon is also planning a non-aggression treaty with their old foes, the Romulans, but Kali believes Malkthon will ultimately turn on them too. Xon learns that they need the Kitumba to stand against Malkthon if they hope to avoid galactic war.

Malkthon soon arrives at the Sacred Planet and finds the Kitumba wavering against signing his decree for war, as Kali tells Xon – now spying on events having reached the planet – that he would need to kill himself in dishonour if the Kitumba ruled against his war. As Xon reaches Kirk, deploying the Vulcan neck pinch in his efforts, they learn that Malkthon has already ordered the attack and the Kitumba discovers he has sent his impressionable six-year-old brother, Klum, to Ultar with a plan to install him as the Kitumba once he kills the boy under Kirk's influence. As Malkthon arrives with a duplicate of a ceremonial sword Kirk gained at Starfleet Academy to slay the Kitumba, Xon poses as the leader in an illusion while Kirk and Kali try to get the Kitumba to the *Enterprise* and safety. Malkthon attempts to claim Kirk has killed their leader, thereby justifying his war, and heads to proclaim Klum as the new Kitumba on Ultar.

Taru is shown proof of Malkthon's deception and is stopped by Kirk in committing suicide, as he gets the badly wounded Xon to McCoy on the *Enterprise*. They make their escape with Taru as an ally to the *Enterprise* and Kirk hatches a plan to have the *Enterprise* warp into the middle of the Klingon battle fleet, beam the rightful Kitumba to the flagship and have him end the attack. Scotty naturally believes it's impossible. The plan works but they find Malkthon still commands a huge battle fleet only operating under his false orders. With half the Klingon fleet on their side, the *Enterprise* returns to Ultar and Xon prepares to make the Romulans aware of Malkthon's treachery as they sneak past his defences, beam into his control centre and unmask his plan. Malkthon tries to flee but Kirk chases him, defeating him in single combat. The Kitumba is restored and grants Malkthon's request to kill himself in honour, making Taru his new Warlord, and not quite granting Kirk the peace he wishes but promising there will be no war.

"People and habits take a long while to change. But to you, personally, I shall always be grateful," the Kitumba tells Kirk, who have earned each other's respect.

If there was ever a *Phase II* tale that should have been produced, it was surely 'Kitumba'. A rich, mythological episode, one indeed that might well have worked as a feature film, Lucas grounds it in a deep exploration of Klingon lore beyond the Russian allegorical stand-ins they presented during the 1960s at the height of Cold War tensions. Perhaps foreshadowing the deeper contact and perestroika between America and the Soviet Union in the 1980s, 'Kitumba' suggests a Federation-Klingon Empire who might live side by side in mutual respect.

It most conjures *The Undiscovered Country*, over a decade later, which as we shall see uses the ending of the Cold War and the Chernobyl disaster as catalysts to tell a similar story of Klingon dynasty and conspiracy. We can see the god-icon of Kahless in the Kitumba. We can see General Chang in Malkthon, as we can the villainous Duras in *The Next Generation*, the aggressive challenger to the Klingon Chancellorship, in episodes such as 'Redemption', which establish the power dynamics in Klingon society as the Romulans plot to destabilise them and the Federation – through Picard – work as a unifying force. Kitumba's ending especially evokes Azetbur's exchange with Kirk at the end of *The Undiscovered Country*, following the assassination of her Chancellor father: "You've restored my father's faith," to which Kirk replies, "And you've restored my son's."

Had *Phase II* existed, David Marcus' murder in *The Search for Spock* might never have fuelled Kirk's hatred of the Klingons that feeds into such an exchange, but 'Kitumba' nevertheless inspires the future direction of Klingon politics and society in *Star Trek* for decades to come, even if the specifics of this story are never precisely repeated.

It remains one of the great, never produced tales in *Star Trek* history.

Next on the list of unmade *Phase II* episodes is 'Practice in Waking', from Richard Bach, a novelist who had written a 1970 bestseller called *Jonathan Livingston Seagull*, and something of a coup for *Phase II* in enlisting to develop what would be a forerunner of *The Next Generation*'s beloved holodeck episodes.

'Practice in Waking' sees the *Enterprise* discover a long-lost spacecraft, Project Long Chance, launched in October 2004, the last craft launched before the discovery of warp drive (which differs from later, established 'future history' *Star Trek* canon). Of a crew of forty, only one now apparently survives in suspended animation. Decker, Scotty and Sulu board the craft and discover the pod of Commander Deborah MacClintock, who appears to be in some kind of waking sleep mode that has remained for the last 280 years. Scotty touches a panel and he, Decker and Sulu collapse, asleep, awakening in a 16th-century Scottish forest with no memory of their time or of the *Enterprise*. They witness the capture of a witch by an earl who Scotty saves. The witch is MacClintock.

On the *Enterprise*, Kirk learns the trio are in a coma and lifesigns are weakening, while Scotty discovers that MacClintock can see the future as the trio fight off soldiers with swords. The *Enterprise* crew discover they are in some kind of heightened dream state as Scotty, Decker and Sulu witness MacClintock's apparent witch powers of levitation in a tavern, drawn into a battle with guards as they see flashes of who they really are and their own time. As McCoy struggles to find a way to rouse the trio, Uhura learns they were sent into the dreaming by a protocol that allowed other Long Chance crew to go in and check on the dreamers before being 'shocked' to return. Kirk and McCoy work on a plan to replicate this as a means of shocking them out of the dream state.

Inside the dream, the trio and MacClintock are captured and locked away in the earl's castle, where they use both her 'magical' powers – in fact flashes of her technical acumen – and their own latent knowledge to try and escape, while MacClintock begins fighting against waking in her pod, flickering in and out of the dream existence. Their escape is thwarted, and the earl sentences them to death for sorcery, intending to burn MacClintock at the stake. Xon mind melds with Decker to try and break through with a message and MacClintock begins to remember the Long Chance, encouraging Scotty and the others to 'dream' their way out of the world. It leads to what appears to be more sorcery and magic to the 16th-century folk. MacClintock wakes up and is beamed to the *Enterprise*, where Xon is being drained as Decker, Scotty and Sulu begin dying in the simulation. She claims the only way to escape is by picturing what they love the most.

As Kirk tells Xon he is doing his best, strengthening their bond, Decker pictures the *Enterprise* and escapes before he's burned alive. Sulu imagines his sword fencing and escapes. Scotty, with the help of Decker, manages to escape and later, uniting with a fading MacClintock in sickbay, finds that she believes the *Enterprise* too is just a dream, given how long she has been 'sleeping'. She dies and Scotty is left saddened at the loss of his friend, remarking to Kirk, "But the *Enterprise*, if she is a dream I meet one time only, I'll not be wanting to wake early." The *Enterprise* sails off, leaving the Long Chance to its seemingly eternal sleep.

Arguably among the strangest of *Phase II*'s proposed episodes, 'Practice in Waking' evokes a historical setting that *The Next Generation* and *Voyager* would explore in holodeck stories – not to mention being something of a precursor to the 2010s hit series, *Outlander*, based on Diana Gabbaldon's books – but Bach rather than relying on futuristic technology to develop interactive illusions instead relies on the strange, haunting power of the mind. It would also have served as the kind of strong, character story for Scotty that he was never given the opportunity to enjoy in *The Original Series*.

Had it been produced, 'Practice in Waking' would likely have been one of *Star Trek*'s most intriguing hours.

David Ambrose, a British television and film writer who would soon go on to pen high-concept Kirk Douglas adventure *The Final Countdown*, contributed 'Deadlock' (later used as a *Voyager* episode title, although Ambrose's working title was 'All Done with Mirrors'), a tale about the alternation of reality and the perception of it, dated January 1978.

Answering a distress call from an uncharted region of space, the *Enterprise* discovers it is coming from another Starfleet ship, the USS *Intrepid*, though soon the distress call vanishes. Summoned by Commodore Hunter (a nod perhaps to the original Captain Pike, Jeffrey Hunter?) to Starbase 7, Kirk is told there was no *Intrepid* distress call, and the *Enterprise* is already part of a Starfleet training exercise – the call was faked and Hunter orders the ship to shut down all power systems and await further instructions.

Hunter's chief science officer, Lang Caradon, tells the *Enterprise* crew they will be relieved of their duties as part of the test but must remain on the *Enterprise* to take part in a series of 'games' where they will be studied. McCoy claims that Caradon is a controversial proponent of behaviour control and believes that is what is going on. The first 'game' is a series of flashing lights, psychedelic patterns and strange electronic sounds, with the crew tasked to predict what the patterns will be when they stop. McCoy believes it is hypnosis and Xon learns that a coded message was sent within the 'game' – a warning from a woman telling them to escape, that Caradon is part of a 'plot'.

Kirk confronts Caradon with the message when Hunter refuses to accept his communications, but he claims it is part of the experiment. Xon discovers that Caradon was fired several months ago and his research stopped and, believing the message real, they work to find the woman inside a Starfleet base. Kirk suddenly changes his mind once he's beamed down and tells the crew he believes this a training exercise. Decker and McCoy are suspicious, concerned Kirk might be controlled in some way, as Kirk finds himself in the base held in a force field by a team led by a Lt Commander Anderson, who claims something unusual happened to Kirk and his crew in the unexplored region where they intercepted the distress call that has altered their behaviour. Kirk wonders if this is another Caradon 'game', but Anderson claims that he's never heard of Caradon or any Hunter training exercise.

He tells Kirk: "Five days ago, we received an emergency signal from the *Enterprise*. You informed us that you had just entered unexplored territory zero-one-nine and had encountered a mysterious radiation that had affected your entire crew. You requested permission to return here for assistance."

Kirk is shown a message that seems to confirm this, showing Kirk in peril, and then one an hour later where he is calm and collected. On the *Enterprise*, Xon finds evidence of reprogrammed footage which shows Kirk firing a phaser at him and Decker on the bridge, suggesting some kind of deception, or part of the training exercise. Scotty programmes decoys to suggest Starbase 7 is being overrun by *Enterprise* officers to disguise Xon and Decker beaming down, who find Kirk captive as Anderson prepares to treat the *Enterprise* as hostile. As the trio escape, they are confronted by Caradon and Hunter, who at first attempt to gaslight them into believing it's part of the training exercise, but ultimately are revealed as aliens from the unexplored sector nineteen.

The aliens are a chameleonic race who can assume other forms and are studying Starfleet as they believe their presence a threat, though they remain vulnerable to physical and mental influence by those near them. They decide to let Starfleet destroy each other as proof of their violent ways and beam away. As Anderson attempts to enter the sealed base area with troops, Kirk tries to reason with the aliens over their fear, but their attempts to contact the *Enterprise* are jammed by Anderson who now believes Kirk and his crew are trying to seize control of the base. Anderson breaks through, refusing to believe Kirk's claim about alien scheming behind all of this, and following some back and forth with Scotty in command of the *Enterprise*, and some telepathy from Ilia, they manage to convince Anderson that the communications were faked, and tensions are calmed.

Kirk records the following in his log: "I recommend that no further passage be attempted in region zero-one-nine until we have received a formal invitation from the inhabitants there. I can only hope that whatever influence they continue to feel from us will be felt in a more positive light as a result of our demonstrated, if somewhat tenuous, self-control."

'Deadlock' very much feels like an episode born of the 1970s penchant for conspiracy thrillers, evidenced in Hollywood pictures such as *The Parallax View*, which intentionally distorted the lens through which America viewed itself, especially in the wake of Watergate. Ambrose engages a very traditional science-fiction trope, of aliens using illusions to trick humanity – indeed it was one *The Original Series* employed many times – but in the 1970s this has a greater level of paranoid potency. Ambrose's original treatment had a revised denouement, one in which the aliens were substituted for actual human fanatics seeking to overthrow the Federation, which would have leaned even more expressly into the conspiratorial aspects of the plot.

It would too foreshadow episodes such as 'Conspiracy', in *The Next Generation*'s first season, where alien parasites take control of Starfleet Command and threaten to destroy them from within, not to mention the Changeling threat behind the Dominion across *Deep Space Nine* and their ability to disguise themselves as anyone, best evidenced in conspiratorial terms in fourth season two-part episode 'Homefront' and 'Paradise Lost', in which a Changeling infiltrator attempts to stage a Starfleet military coup. Though future *Star Trek* series would exist in less depressed times for America, the anxiety of order being replaced by chaos would never leave the franchise.

'Savage Syndrome' was the next intended episode, developed by Margaret Armen – who had written *The Original Series* episodes 'The Gamesters of Triskelion' and 'The Paradise Syndrome', alongside a story co-credit on 'The Cloud Minders' – and Alfred Harris, presented in December 1977.

The *Enterprise* is charting a lifeless planet and discovers a derelict, battle-scarred craft in orbit. Decker, Bones and Ilia find aboard ship a skeleton in uniform who was impaled with a crude spear, suggesting conflict. A strange, ancient sphere then approaches the *Enterprise* and hits the bridge crew with a light that transforms their personalities into feral, snarling creatures. On the derelict, the trio find evidence that the same thing happened to this ship, learning it to be a space mine that emitted radiation that wiped from the crew their civilised instincts. They fear the planet below suffered the same fate and are concerned when they cannot contact the *Enterprise*.

On the ship, Kirk and the rest of the crew are now savages battling for control, as Kirk assumes command once again, Uhura and Rand as the submissive females at his side. Decker, Ilia and McCoy dock and discover the crew affected, the *Enterprise* turned into a battle zone, with McCoy tasked to try and find a way to synthesise an antidote. They battle their way to sickbay, only to be attacked by a feral Chapel, who stabs Decker before she is stunned. While Kirk and his tribe go hunting for food, McCoy runs tests on the subdued Chapel as Ilia suggests they attempt to free the crew of this collectively before they kill each other by reaching the bridge and flooding the decks with tranquilliser gas. Decker is too wounded, so Ilia sets off on the mission alone.

As Kirk and Scotty, with dual tribes, fight over food stores, Ilia reaches the bridge and finds she can't unleash the gas, meaning Bones' antidote is their only hope. Kirk and Scotty's battle reaches engineering where they inadvertently trigger a warp core breach countdown in one hour, forcing Ilia to try and shut down the generators. Kirk and his tribe reach the bridge again, he insisting Ilia become his submissive, but she escapes in the turbolift and with McCoy's help they subdue the aggressive Kirk. In sickbay, the trio find there is no antidote available, but Decker suggests they use the shuttle to get to one of the alien mines, reverse the radiation frequency and detonate it. "The savage syndrome was caused by pulsed light and electromagnetic radiations on a specific frequency. The effect can be reversed by altering that frequency and generating it from a similar power source," Decker reasons.

Decker volunteers for the dangerous shuttle mission, with McCoy and Ilia helping him reach the launch bay. Kirk revives and heads back to the bridge, where Xon has installed himself in charge, and they battle for control, which Kirk wins. Decker launches the shuttle while McCoy and Ilia head for engineering to try and stop the breach. They work on a 'tranquilliser bomb' to take down crew who try to get them as Kirk comes for them, while Decker works on the mine, but in his weakened state he begins blacking out and collapses before he can finish it. Deducing only a lucid Scotty can help them stop the breach in time, Ilia uses seductive Deltan mind powers to trigger Scotty's latent engineering skills but fails. McCoy tells Decker with all his final strength to complete the rewiring, with minutes until the breach, and he manages to do so. The light hits the *Enterprise*, and the savagery is reversed, with Scotty immediately stopping the breach with seconds to go.

With the crew saved and the *Enterprise* having narrowly avoided destruction, only Decker, Ilia and McCoy clearly remember what happened. Ilia nevertheless quips to Kirk that he made a "magnificent savage".

Another outing very much in the vein of *The Original Series*, 'Savage Syndrome' had all the elements of an action-packed romp, largely on the contained *Enterprise* sets, with the cast given the chance to ham up very accentuated, feral performances. Roddenberry liked the story for how different it was from other *Phase II* pitches and while it leaned toward the pulp, it nonetheless would have been a memorable, if throwaway, old-fashioned style of *Star Trek* tale.

'Are Unheard Memories Sweet?', also known as 'Home' and 'Id's Delight' had the potential to court quite some controversy, with a script that included nudity among other contentious aspects.

Penned by Worley Thorne, who would go on to script *The Next Generation* episode 'Justice' (alongside John D. F. Black, under the pseudonym 'Ralph Wills'), his tale sees the *Enterprise* looking for a lost starship, the USS *St Louis*, on a planet in the unexplored Hyades star cluster. Finding traces of human life, an away team led by Decker discover instead dilithium deposits – a substance that helps fuel the *Enterprise* – before becoming entranced by what appear to be visions and memories. Two crewmen find a lagoon of scantily clad women they frolic with. Decker finds himself back at Starfleet Academy in a clinch with a beautiful young cadet, Linda.

Transporting Decker back on ship, where he remains regressed and convinced he is still at the Academy, Kirk and the crew hunt for the other crewmen on the planet, as the captain's judgement is considered impaired given he was good friends as a youth with the *St Louis* commander, Michael Schwerner, as evidence suggests they might have suffered the fate of the hypnotic visions. 'Linda', an alien female in fact called 'Ronel', beams aboard the *Enterprise* and begins to place different crew members, such as Rand, under her spell as Decker – convinced Kirk is plotting against him – rushes to support 'Linda'. They end up destroying the stored dilithium on the ship before beaming away, causing the *Enterprise* to end up adrift.

Realising they need to get more undiluted dilithium to prevent the *Enterprise* grounding, as likely happened with the *St Louis*, Kirk is joined by Bones and Ilia in travelling to the planet surface. Kirk eventually finds himself placed into a seductive illusion by Ronel, who reveals the planet is called Grokh and her people, the Grokhoor, are suffering a profound cultural decay, partly down to the fact there are no rules on Grokh and nobody works, meaning their society has broken down as nobody can remember how to effectively maintain it. They discover Decker and the away team are attached to 'feeding tubes' overstimulating them with the illusions they're trapped inside, creating extensive hormones.

Kirk and the crew figure out this is the Grokhoor's plan – they trapped the *St Louis* crew to gain their hormones, as they are hermaphrodites, and need both sexes to survive. Though they ultimately manage to escape, managing to get the dilithium needed to power the ship, they are left to wonder if the Grokhoor's fate might be to ultimately destroy themselves.

Thorne's tale would have combined numerous ideas visible in *The Original Series* while also playing with the mythical idea of the Siren stranding sailors on the beachhead.

Perhaps the most eccentric concept pitched for *Phase II* was 'Lord Bobby's Obsession', written by Shimon Wincelberg, who had penned *Original Series* outings 'Dagger of the Mind' and 'The Galileo Seven' (with Oliver Crawford), popularising the growing concept of UFOlogy and alien abduction long before the heyday of such ideas in science fiction during the 1990s.

Heading for a Federation colony under supposed Romulan attack, the *Enterprise* comes across the Niobe, an abandoned Klingon destroyer which broadcasts, unusually, a 19th-century English folk song, decoded by an exolinguist aboard called Jennifer York. An away team led by Decker and York beam aboard and discover a strange passenger – Robert Standish, the Third Earl of Lancashire, otherwise known as 'Lord Bobby'. He claims Klingons abducted him around the year 1900, keeping him cryogenically frozen for long periods that prevented ageing. York and Bobby begin to bond as he is beamed aboard the *Enterprise*.

Lord Bobby turns out to be not what he seems. A shimmering bracelet he wears indicates he is some kind of alien and gives him powers over the Niobe, which he tethers to the *Enterprise* and plans to blow up apocalyptically unless the *Enterprise* returns him to England. A game of cat and mouse ensues as the childlike but powerful Bobby makes his demands, eventually after Kirk proves the England he seeks is long gone, ordering the *Enterprise* breach Warp 10 and go back in time to Victorian England.

As the crew plan to reach the Niobe and disable it, Lord Bobby explains to York – now falling in love with him – that his planet was colonised as a child by the 'Britannic Commonwealth', where he learned his obsession with England. A plan to disable the doomsday device on the Niobe fails but they find the key to disarming it just as Bobby, learning that they never intended to take him home, decides to blow them all up. Kirk shows mercy, allowing Bobby to remain adrift in the Niobe searching for home, and York declines to go with him, and Bobby returns to his obsessions, alone.

There are lots of intriguing aspects to Wincelberg's story, not least the idea that the British Empire would have been revived at some point in *Star Trek*'s 'future history' and colonised planets. Quite why Klingons might have wanted to randomly abduct humans is an open question, as this episode would have tied them to the post-Second World War 'Foo Fighter' craze, an idea better explored in *Deep Space Nine*'s 'Little Green Men' with the more appropriate Ferengi. Nevertheless, this episode recalls *The Original Series*' penchant for slightly whimsical, powerful beings with a childlike nature, such as 'The Squire of Gothos' and so on. In that sense, it might have been a throwback.

'To Attain the All' came from Norman Spinrad, who wrote 'The Doomsday Machine' for *The Original Series* and would have potentially introduced a sizeable new conceptual species to the *Star Trek* universe.

The *Enterprise* is flung while exploring into a different part of the universe with an altered set of physical laws, outside of normal space. A bald, blue being called the 'Prince' of a race billions of years old, the 'First Ones', and their transportation is connected to a machine designed to preserve the knowledge of their lost species and share it with younger galactic races. They must prove their worth 'to attain the All' or be stranded where they are for eternity.

As the *Enterprise* faces the physical threat of a black hole about to swallow them, as well as strange psychological effects on the crew, Decker and Xon on a nearby planetoid face the 'Prince's challenges, including puzzles and passing through fire. Though they succeed, Kirk realises the Prince has found a way to telepathically connect the minds of the entire crew and allow himself to speak through all of them. The First Ones gave up their corporeal bodies and became a collective existence, the 'All', but were trapped on the planetoid. Now free, they intend to spread through all races in the galaxy and provide them immortality and knowledge the All have.

The Prince, a projection only, tells Kirk and Decker (also unaffected) "Attain the All or meet your death."

They manage to fight off the 'possessed' *Enterprise* crew, taken over by the All, and beam the globe containing their shared consciousness to the *Enterprise*, where they lose control of their power, and the ship returns to normal space. Kirk instead of destroying the All sends them on a journey of billions of years to the Andromeda galaxy, where he hopes they will learn penance for what they have done.

In many respects, Spinrad's story evokes the Borg, who would be introduced in *The Next Generation* as a collectivised menace who threaten to consume the galaxy, although the All are presented in older-fashioned, grandiose science-fiction terms, with even a hint of the Lovecraftian, rather than the technological allegory for viral possession that the monstrous, zombie-like Borg suggest. Though unlikely to have struck such a chord within *Star Trek* as the Borg did, this might have been a *Phase II* highlight, given the blend of strange, otherworldly power, planetary adventure and creeping horror that Spinrad presents.

What could have been one of the biggest stories in *Phase II* came from Arthur Bernard Lewis, best known subsequently as one of the chief writers of US soap opera *Dallas*, who developed a tale with a grandiose title – 'The War to End All Wars', which came from a discarded concept developed by Richard Bach, the man behind 'Practice in Waking'.

The *Enterprise* arrives at a planet called Shadir, a planet of great culture despite living under an imperial yolk, which the Federation last visited two centuries earlier. However, the crew discover no signs of planetary life and debris from what looks to have been a major battle. One ship seems to have survived containing a beautiful woman, Yra, a Shadirian and survivor from a major domestic planetary war. As the *Enterprise* is targeted by surviving Shadirian ships from the other side, McCoy learns Yra is in truth an android and wishes to go back to the surface of Shadir.

Kirk, Xon and McCoy find a civilisation that looks like late 20th-century Earth if it had suffered the bombings and devastation of the Second World War. They soon find those on the planet are also androids led by the imperial leader, Plateous III, and that Yra was a spy looking to help them capture the *Enterprise*. They find a civilisation not built around culture but rather the meaning of war as a way of preserving life, a way that Plateous III has corrupted for his own ends. Yra ends up turning on the leader and helping Kirk and the *Enterprise* escape, with Shadir still ravaged by war and not the civilisation the Federation thought.

Arguably, the budget needed to realise 'The War to End All Wars' might have put paid to the story being produced, but Lewis certainly finds a large-scale science-fiction lens – evoking 1950s tales about wars in space – to tell a story in *Phase II*, one that would have brought together action, big ideas about peace and war, and very clear villains into a story that could well have, like 'Kitumba', sustained two parts.

We finish our look at the *Phase II* episodes that never came to be by discussing two *Star Trek* stories that did, eventually, materialise – only on *The Next Generation*.

'Devil's Due', developed by William Douglas Lansford, a writer on various TV series of the 1960s and 1970s and several movies, was considered akin to the Stephen Vincent Benét story of 1936, 'The Devil and Daniel Webster'.

Lansford's tale sees the *Enterprise*, exploring uncharted space, discover the planet Naterra, a world very similar to Earth in terms of life and ecosystem. Brought by friendly natives to meet their leader, Zxolar the Blessed, he anxiously considers Kirk and his crew portents of doom at first. They learn Naterra is destined to be destroyed in flame within twenty days and Zxolar appeals to the Starfleet crew to help them. As he collapses, a strange energy being envelops and abducts McCoy, a being seemingly materialising between different dimensions at will.

As Zxolar is treated on the *Enterprise*, and the energy being causes issues across the ship, Kirk and Xon return to the planet to try and figure out the truth behind it and learn Zxolar is one of six philosophers who saved their dying world, strangled by pollution, a thousand years before, after making some kind of bargain with the energy being, Komether. He delivered them a 'Thousand Years of Joy', eradicating Naterra climate issues as they banished technology, but then he would return and destroy the planet, leaving the ruined world as his. They learn that Komether wants Zxolar dead before this can happen and work to surreptitiously revive him using AI tech, given McCoy is gone and Chapel is badly wounded in an earlier attack.

Though bound by a long-held contract, Kirk figures out that Komether was created through the philosopher's collective energy, and he cannot take over while Zxolar is still alive. Letting the *Enterprise* computer be the judge, Kirk offers Komether a trial – if he wins, he takes the planet, the

Enterprise and her crew and if he loses he leaves this dimension forever. Kirk uses the will of Xzolar to defeat Komether and banish him, saving Naterra, restoring Chapel and bringing back McCoy. Zxolar is revived and stronger than ever as the *Enterprise* leaves the planet and her crew to a future where they will hopefully learn from their self-destructive mistakes.

Clearly a *Star Trek* allegory for the Biblical story of Lucifer and subsequent myths about a devil's bargain, it ended up forming the basis of the thirteenth episode of *The Next Generation*'s fourth season, given the same title. In that story, Jean-Luc Picard's *Enterprise-D* finds a similar issue on the planet Ventax II, of a being called Ardra who returns to claim the fruits of her bargain, but in perhaps a sign of *The Next Generation*'s deeper penchant for scientific rigour as opposed to *The Original Series*, this new version a decade later presents Ardra as a notorious con-artist – a feminine Harry Mudd, if you will – who uses advanced technology to trick the Ventaxians into believing she is their devil figure. It makes for something of a lighter piece.

Initially, producer Michael Piller asked writer Melinda Snodgrass during the third season to simply port the *Next Generation* characters into the *Phase II* script, but it quickly became apparent that the two were not a great fit. Multiple writers attempted to wrestle it into shape – including Lansford himself – but it was Phillip LaZebnik who struck gold, as Piller attests: "He turned it inside out and made it a delightful show. It was too funny, though, and the people felt it was playing it all for laughs. I loved that draft of the script, but not everybody did. It was put into rewrite by approximately 15 people between Phil's script and the final draft, which I took, changing the male devil into a female devil for fun. [I] put back as much of Phil's original script as I could."

Though not recognised as a great episode of *The Next Generation*, it was a successful example of *Phase II* cascading down into the future of the franchise.

Less successful a translation, however, was 'The Child', penned by Jaron Summers and Jon Povill, which transformed from an Ilia story into a Deanna Troi tale over time, and was likely based in part on one of Roddenberry's initial 'Star Trek Is . . .' ideas called 'Infection'. Povill expands on this: "In one of the [series' story] meetings, a writer named Jaron Summers pitched a story about space eggs that we were going to reject, but I suggested it could be reworked. Jaron agreed to have me work on it with him; and from that came our draft of 'The Child'."

Summers' story sees the *Enterprise* pass through an unusual nebula after which a bright light energy being passes into Ilia, after which she wakes up pregnant and very swiftly bears a seemingly perfectly healthy baby, who she names Irska, meaning 'pure light' in Deltan. McCoy is naturally uncertain, and Kirk is downright suspicious, especially as a strange alien cylinder soon intercepts the *Enterprise* made of the same composition as the nebula. McCoy can't tell Ilia what he's discovered – that her rapidly developing baby is likely to die within the week as she is developing leukaemia.

The *Enterprise* soon faces challenges as the cylinder spreads a lethal poison aboard ship that Irska helps devise a cure for, and later an energy field causes a major system breach that Kirk, as Ilia desperately tries to protect her child, knows only Irska can go in and help them prevent. As Xon mind melds with her to try and understand her development, with Irska remaining childlike as she tries to understand human nature, Kirk and the crew ultimately realise that Ilia and then the *Enterprise* were part of her birthing process, operating as 'wombs' for her development, as she beams onto the cylinder and it disappears as energy, thereby saving the ship and crew.

Livingston believed the resulting script by Povill was more his than Summers, and Povill himself was convinced that his version was far superior to that of *The Next Generation*, revised by Maurice Hurley as the second season premiere of the series, retrofitted to work around the Writers' Strike of 1988 in which no new scripts were able to be written while industrial action was taking place.

In that story, a similar energy source passes into Deanna and she bears a boy, Ian, named after her late father, who ends up dying in her arms for greater pathos as the same 'womb' effect is realised, though Hurley spends an equal amount of time introducing Diana Muldaur's ill-fated Dr Katherine Pulaski (who would only last a season) and a Wesley Crusher sub-plot; as a result, to an even lesser degree than 'Devil's Due', 'The Child''s ultimate similarity to the original *Phase II* version ends up being extremely slim.

Although these were the only *Phase II* stories to be directly revived for *The Next Generation*, the impact on that sequel series of all the tales never made for *Phase II* cannot be underestimated. It truly is the lost bridge between the 1960s and 1980s/1990s era of *Star Trek*.

*

Numerous writers continued pitching stories for *Phase II*, even as it became apparent that the series was not going to happen – Alan Dean Foster, Arthur Heinemann, Steve Kelly, to name a few. James Menzies pitched a story called 'The Prisoner', in which Albert Einstein no less would appear on the *Enterprise* viewscreen and claim numerous Earth scientists had been abducted and were being held as 'batteries', though this would be ultimately a plot by a sinister being called Logos, using illusions as a means of destroying humanity. The pitch was never accepted, though Einstein would one day appear on *Star Trek*, in holographic form on *The Next Generation*.

In March 1978, the decision was nonetheless made. *Phase II* would not happen in favour of *The Motion Picture*, which would bring Decker and Ilia to life, just once as opposed to many adventures, and see Spock return to a series that had been written to accommodate for his absence. *Phase II*'s shadow was nonetheless long, stretching even to fan fiction. The fan-made, professionally developed series *Star Trek: New Voyages*, launched in 2004 by Jack Marshall and James Cawley, sought to tell new stories with *The Original Series* crew, played by *Star Trek* fans and crowdfunded. Actors such as Walter Koenig, George Takei and Nichelle Nichols revived their characters. Writers such as D. C. Fontana and David Gerrold contributed scripts, including the latter's potentially controversial 'Blood and Ice' (more on that in the next chapter). They even filmed a version of 'Kitumba' as they rebranded in 2008 to, you guessed it, *Star Trek: Phase II*.

In 1995, *Star Trek: Voyager* would indeed serve as the flagship for a Paramount network – UPN – that did survive and in doing so honoured the legacy of *Star Trek*'s greatest, unmade, five-year mission. Had *Phase II* happened, we may never have seen *The Next Generation*, *Deep Space Nine* or anything that came in their wake. The human adventure would have looked very different.

We now turn to the series that cemented *Star Trek*'s longevity after the 1960s and 1970s. If the question was whether *Star Trek* could become a franchise on television that lasted, *The Next Generation* would make it so . . .

SIX

WHERE NO ONE HAD GONE BEFORE: THE NEXT GENERATION

"LET'S SEE WHAT'S out there..."

A statement of intent at the very end of 'Encounter at Farpoint', the pilot episode of *Star Trek: The Next Generation*, as uttered by Patrick Stewart's Captain Jean-Luc Picard as he takes the helm of the USS *Enterprise-D* and sails off into what would be seven years of highly successful adventures that spearheaded what remains, to this day, the Golden Age of *Star Trek* on television.

Decades on, it is hard to imagine a time that Picard and his 24th-century era crew, be it his charming 'Number One', Will Riker; curious android science-officer Data; or noble and proud Klingon security officer Worf, were both the new kids on the block and the strange, unwanted stepchildren of Captain Kirk and his iconic crew. As these words are written, in sequel series *Picard*, the entirety of *The Next Generation* crew is returning together for the first time in over twenty years for one final, extended voyage and a curtain down akin to *The Undiscovered Country*.

Yet back in 1986, as the success of *The Voyage Home* and the franchise's impending 20th anniversary celebrations led Paramount to finally go ahead and invest in a *Star Trek* sequel series set many years after *The Original Series* and with an entirely new crew, few involved or in the fanbase could imagine accepting new actors and new characters on the *Enterprise*. It was a whole new frontier and one that Gene Roddenberry, initially, turned down the chance to make.

Paramount pressed on with the father/son producing team of Sam and Greg Strangis, recruiting them to devise a show tentatively named 'Star Trek: A New Beginning'. "My premise was relatively simple: It was a time when, in the future in the existing *Star Trek*, the Klingons weren't enemies anymore and were allies. I wanted to create Starfleet Academy on a ship. You'd have a lot of younger players and older, senior leaders, and it was going to be the naval academy on a starship."

As we will see, ideas for a Starfleet Academy story were very much in the ether during the 1980s, and though Roddenberry's eventual change of heart – motivated by the reality of someone else making *Star Trek* other than him, despite his intentions to retire – saw the Strangis team out the door, a future setting and a thawed relationship with the Klingons, epitomised by Worf, certainly remained a core tenet of the series to come. Indeed, initially plans were to set the series even further ahead, in the 25th century (now the arena of *Picard*) on the *Enterprise-G*, until Roddenberry grew anxious about too great a number of ships bearing that name between this show and the original, and reduced the timeframe to just under eighty years.

Key personnel began to come aboard, such as Rick Berman, a Paramount executive who had no grounding in *Star Trek* but later, following Roddenberry's death in 1991, became the guiding light of the franchise for well over the next decade. Roddenberry returned to the well of 1960s writing staff on *The Original Series* and talked to faces such as Robert Justman, D. C. Fontana and David Gerrold, all of whom began pitching ideas for what the new series could be, as Gerrold describes: "Gene and I went out to lunch. We sat, talked, and he said, 'What would you do with *Star Trek*?' He did not say, 'I want to hire you.' I nonetheless outlined my ideas for *Star Trek*, which were to shift the show to a first officer and let the captain stay on the ship. This allows you to simultaneously run shipboard stories and planetside stories. Before, the focus of the stories always stayed where Kirk was. If you break it up and have a captain who's always on the ship, then you can stay with him if there are reasons to cut back to the ship, and yet you don't have him putting himself in danger on the planet. If your first officer is strong, then you have a focus there. So you have two heroes instead of one hero and a sidekick."

Although this concept didn't come to pass, with Riker certainly playing second fiddle to Picard, this was eventually tried out on *Discovery*, also a series that launched a new era of *Star Trek*, where Sonequa Martin Green's Michael Burnham took centre stage as a disgraced second-in-command.

Across the run of *The Next Generation*, a veritable phalanx of writers, some of whom eventually wrote for the series and others who did not, came in and pitched ideas first to Roddenberry and from the third season onwards, subsequent show runner Michael Piller. Enormous amounts of these were rejected, many of which were archived by Ronald D. Moore, whose spec script for 'The Bonding' under Piller's aegis saw the birth of a successful writing career for television: "I have binders of all the abandoned stories, and all the ones we bought, the ones we started to develop. But they filled, like, a three-ring binder; each season was filled with stories that we didn't get to. Some were pitches, some were internally developed, some never made it past just the one-page memo. But there are dozens, if not hundreds, of stories that we didn't do."

Maurice Hurley, who briefly under Berman gained creative stewardship of the series during the second season, pitched perhaps the most radical concept, which was rejected out of hand: "I'll build the second season on the absolute tragedy that the *Enterprise* exploded by unknown cause and lost everybody, and now we must find the new *Enterprise* crew." Even by the standards of future television eras wedded less to a conventional network model, killing and replacing the entire crew after one season was quite extreme, even given *The Next Generation* arguably takes two full seasons to find its feet on multiple levels. Other writers had more conventional approaches.

"We'd sit down and talk about the movie we'd just seen and spark ideas. Like after *Aliens*, Gene would say about Jenette Goldstein, 'That woman created a whole new style of feminine beauty. We should have something like that in *Star Trek*.' So we started off with a character named Macha Hernandez, who eventually became Tasha Yar. That sparked an idea for Gene."

The focus at the outset was, naturally, on the opening two-part episode (less a pilot given the series had been fully commissioned already), and Fontana delivered an initial draft in December of 1986 called 'Meeting at Farpoint', with key differences from the final product. Here, Jean-Luc is 'Julien' Picard, with a first officer named Kyle Summers, and Macha Hernandez as security chief. Riker had a different surname derivation in 'Ryker', while Dr Beverly Crusher had a daughter, Leslie, rather than a son, Wesley (although the imaginative name change as the sex of her child changed is clear). The plot contained a complete absence of John de Lancie's iconic trickster Q, focusing rather on a science vessel called the USS *Starseeker* which comes into conflict with a species called the Annoi, apes with advanced technology who have enslaved the Farpoint population, leading to the discovery of an alien lifeform the crew need to protect.

Many of these ideas would evolve into the final product which eventually arrived on screen in the fall of 1987, kickstarting a whole new *Star Trek* adventure.

*

The first two seasons of *The Next Generation* began, as will many a *Star Trek* sequel series, with significant growing pains as writers worked to try and figure out how to both write a series that honoured what came before while establishing a new tonal approach that would befit a whole new era of television, as Rick Berman commented: "There was nothing like that show on TV. That's the number one thing, so right away you're doing something different. Second, since you're doing something in the 24th century, you have this unique opportunity to explore all the stories that impact on what's going on today from the advantage and 'safety' of the future, which is remarkable. Third, because of the incredible success of the former Star Trek and the movies, Paramount really bellied up like no studio I've ever seen before to make this the best-looking, the best-produced series ever. There were no more cardboard walls or rubber monsters. They were spending the time and money to do it right."

Established episodes would develop from initial shapes, often into completely different products that might end up on screen. Roddenberry, whose health was faltering, steered a ship buoyed heavily by writers from the previous *Star Trek* era who he knew and trusted, but ended up growing extremely erratic as he took scripts away from freelance writers, threw out concepts that would allow for dramatic tension (known later infamously as 'Roddenberry's Box'), voiced opinions about women and ethnic minorities some of the staff found beyond the pale (sentiments that creep into early episodes such as 'Code of Honor'), and fostered a working environment that saw the entirety of *The Original Series* writers depart by the end of the debut season.

During this period, however, numerous episodic concepts were developed that provide fascinating roadmaps into stories that never made it to air. Perhaps the most controversial, indeed one of the most controversial proposed *Star Trek* episodes in history, was titled 'Blood and Fire', a story delivered in May 1987 by David Gerrold.

The plot sees the *Enterprise* answer a distress call from a medical research vessel, only to find upon beaming over that the crew are infected with 'Regulan blood worms', a deadly and supposedly incurable pathogen that Picard is ordered, as with any such ship encountered, by Starfleet Command to destroy. Gerrold's script intentionally features gay characters and strong allusions to the AIDS crisis, which reached during the late 1980s an apogee of press reportage and public hysteria. He explained the process behind initially developing the idea, based on a convention in Boston he and Roddenberry attended:

"One fan asked, 'Well, are you going to have gay crewmembers, because in the 60s you had Black and Asian and Latino, etc.?' Gene said, 'You know, you're right. It's time. We should.' I was sitting on the side, taking notes, of course. So there it was: Gene had said it in front of an audience of 3,000 people in November of 1986. I was a little bit surprised and delighted that Gene was willing to go there. We got back to L.A. and Gene said it again in a meeting, and somebody in that meeting – I won't say who – said, 'What, we're going to have Lt Tutti-Frutti?' Gene balled him out and said, 'No, it's time. And I promised the fans we're going to have gay characters.'"

Via Berman, the network signed off on the conception of a story revolving around AIDS, or at least providing an allegorical framework to explore it, and Gerrold picked up Roddenberry's baton and ran with it: "I wanted 'Blood and Fire' to be about the fear of AIDS – not the disease but the fear – and one of the plot points involved having the crew donate blood to save the lives of the away team. I thought, 'If we do this episode right, where blood donorship is part of solving the problem, we can put a card at the end telling viewers that they could donate blood to save lives, too.' I thought it was something Trek should be doing, raising social awareness on an issue, and if we did it right, we could probably generate a million new blood donors at a time when there was a critical shortage."

Gerrold developed the draft, not shying away from the homosexual subtext amongst several of the guest characters he wrote, called Hodel and Eakins: "There were two characters who were not very important to the story, but they were the kind of background characters you need. At one point Riker says to one of them, 'How long have you two been together?' That was it. The guy replies, 'Since the Academy.' That's it. That's all you need to know about their relationship. If you were a kid, you'd think they were just good buddies. If you were an adult, you'd get it. But I turned in the script and that's when the excrement hit the rotating blades of the electric air circulation device. There was a flurry of memos, pro and con."

'Blood and Fire' was subsequently canned by a network who became jittery about the perceived response amongst female and conservative groups regarding the alluded gay content, with ostensibly a greater problem regarding these aspects than any commentary on the AIDS phenomenon. Gerrold's relationship with *Star Trek* and Roddenberry subsequently broke down and he allowed his contract to expire, channelling many of his story ideas into a litany of subsequent novels and, indeed, eventually adapting his version of 'Blood and Fire' many years later into a two-part story for the fan-made series, *Star Trek: Phase II*. "I said, 'Gene made a promise to the fans. If not here, where? If not now, when?' But the episode got shelved anyway and that's when I knew I wasn't going to be allowed to write the very best stories we should be writing. The original show was about taking chances. If we weren't going to take chances, we weren't doing *Star Trek*."

Gerrold's rejection was not the end of the story for this concept, however, as Roddenberry handed staff writer Herb Wright the opportunity to rewrite Gerrold's draft, turning in a script that was re-titled 'Blood and Ice'. The essential tenets of the tale remained present and correct – except for the gay characters and allusions to AIDS. Wright substituted them for zombie crewmen, attempting to develop a story that leaned toward *Night of the Living Dead* in a science-fiction context. This too never made it to air, though Wright never quite gave up on the idea: "When I came back during fifth season, I read the script again because they were hardup for stories and I brought it in. I mentioned it to [Co-Executive Producer] Michael Piller and he said, 'What was it?' because he thought he had read everything when he came in. I said, 'You probably never saw this draft. If anything, you probably read "Blood and Fire", and this one was called 'Blood and Ice'. I printed it out and brought it in. The staff loved it, Rick loved it, but Piller said, 'Nice script, but it's really a first season type of show.'"

This story remains an indictment of *Star Trek*'s unwillingness to venture into territory that would have pushed the liberal aspects of the series' mandate into bold new areas, and despite stories pitched that would have tackled gender – such as Fred Bronson's 'The Mnemonic Enemy', in which the male and female contingents on the *Enterprise* were separated; a story that ultimately became the much less progressive 'Angel One' – the reality of *The Next Generation*'s limitations was already clear.

Much later, toward the sixth or seventh season of the show, a 'gay-themed' episode centred around Wesley Crusher was suggested by writer René Echevarria, which would have followed up from the fifth season episode 'The First Duty', in which Wesley was put on trial by Starfleet Academy after a shuttle accident and explored his relationship with gender-fluid friend Los, who stood by him during that ordeal. The genre-twist would have been that Los can only change gender for a few hours at a time and would have delved into gender-based ideas as Wesley fell for them. It again was rejected.

The Next Generation might be going where no one had gone before, but not in many of the ways that mattered.

Another early first season show concept was 'The Dream Pool', developed by Tracy Torme, one of the writers who didn't depart at the end of the season and remained as a writer and consultant on the second. After being invited to read the show bible for the intended *Next Generation* series, Torme pitched a story about addiction inherent in the Federation, unaware that producer Bob Lewin was going through similar issues at the time: "That might be why Bob liked my addiction script. My addiction show was kind of like the cocaine allegory show that sweeps through the Federation."

Though 'The Dream Pool' was never made, it was enough to get Torme on staff, and he later pitched another concept for the opening season that was never produced called 'Genius Is Pain': "I was on another one of my quests to create a new character for the show, so I had an idea: who would be a really interesting alien on *Star Trek*? And I got the idea of John Cleese. So I created an episode called 'Genius Is Pain' and it was about a race of aliens who are mathematical geniuses – they spend the first twenty or thirty years of their lives devoted to mathematics, and they're off-the-chart geniuses, they can do things that engineers can't do, the whole race. But once they turn thirty, they have a philosophy of life that all life should be devoted to bohemian pursuits, so if you invite them to your house and they feel like spray-painting a four-letter word on the wall of your nursery, they're going to do it, because to suppress it would be against their nature."

There is some genesis here, in terms of the mathematical genius aspect, of the Bynar species of advanced cybernetic humanoids who in the first season episode '11001001' update the *Enterprise* systems and cause a crisis in the process, but Torme's concept was only embraced by Roddenberry in terms of how he viewed his own process in terms of life being made up of 'pleasure' and 'pain', breaking into a long and rambling speech that took Torme off guard, to say the least: "And then he started to list things that he found painful: the pain of dealing with network executives, the pain of going through divorce, the pain of seeing your children's faces when you have to tell them you don't love their mother anymore, the pain of spending eighteen straight hours writing a perfect scene and someone saying it has to be changed for some fucking stupid reason – so he's going on and on. It was really one for the ages."

It was, at the time, yet another signal that Roddenberry was beginning to lose perspective as the illness that would eventually lead to his death began to take hold.

During these early days of production, there remained a determination to connect back to the elements of *Star Trek* from the 1960s that fans still adored. DeForest Kelley had reprised the role of (now 137-year-old Admiral) Leonard McCoy in 'Encounter at Farpoint', episodes such as 'The Naked Now' and 'Where No One Has Gone Before' had served as veritable sequels to *Original Series* episodes, and though the Klingons would return in 'Heart of Glory', an earlier concept known as 'Once a Klingon' from D. C. Fontana and Herb Wright was proposed, and indeed both writers also pitched an episode that would have seen a return for Leonard Nimoy's legendary Spock and his father, Mark Lenard's Sarek. "We're taking on a mysterious Vulcan visitor who, of course, turns out to be Spock, and his mission is to rescue his father, who has been captured by the Romulans while on an exploratory peace mission. Now he's being held hostage, and they want Spock."

Though the story was rejected due to the perceived difficulty of getting Nimoy (who was also directing *Three Men and a Baby* around the same period) or Lenard to reprise roles they were now playing on film for television, a similar concept would end up forming the basis of the fifth season two-parter 'Unification', in which Spock did return, as did

Sarek after his third season showcase 'Sarek', where he boarded Picard's *Enterprise*.

Speaking also of Romulans, a story revolving around the enigmatic species introduced in *The Original Series* arrived in the form of first season finale 'The Neutral Zone', although earlier in the season's production, a script by Greg Strangis with the same name and a completely unrelated narrative also almost ended up becoming a reality. Strangis' concept would see Picard leading a mission to bring trade delegates to a negotiation with the Romulan Empire alongside Billings, a Starfleet security expert who led the mission to liberate Tasha Yar from her homeworld, now confined to a wheelchair. As the crew face a battle of wills against Gar, a Romulan commander, over a transporter malfunction, the sidelined, Romulan-hating Worf, alongside Wesley Crusher, would end up assisting Dr Beverly Crusher's attempts to cure Billings from fluid removed from Data's android spine. These two narratives would come together by the end of the episode.

The concept was rejected, with some ideas making their way into the first season episode 'Too Short a Season', instead the writing staff choosing with 'The Neutral Zone' to introduce a Romulan Empire emerging from a long period of isolationism, potentially as a dangerous, recurring threat.

Maurice Hurley, however, as he began a tenure heading the writing staff under Roddenberry – who retained the power of green light and veto – had broader plans. 'The Neutral Zone' seeded the idea of a terrifying new enemy destroying colonies on the edge of the titular border between Federation and Romulan space, eventually revealed as deadly cybernetic colonising force the Borg, but Hurley intended to open the second season with a much bigger story that would reveal the Borg and force Starfleet and the Romulans to join forces in stopping them. The 1988 Writers' Strike put paid to these ambitions and the Borg, ultimately, were introduced in second season episode 'Q Who?', before stamping an eternal mark on *Star Trek* lore in third season finale, 'The Best of Both Worlds'.

Hurley's intention to immediately inject a greater sense of action and dramatic tension into *The Next Generation* for the second season certainly rubbed up against Roddenberry's well-known aversion to anything that might contradict his Utopian mindset about the 24th century, but Hurley was determined to retain the purity of Roddenberry's vision for the show, even if it ran contrary to his own instincts at points: "*Star Trek* has absolute rules that cannot be broken and nobody knows that until they get into it. It's a problem that all writers have had for the most part. My ability comes from character and action, so what I thought they wanted from me was character and action. They didn't want that. They wanted writers who could take the *Star Trek* parameters – Gene's vision – and put a shine on it, button it, and not change anything. That's a hard lesson for writers to learn, especially those writers coming in with bona fide credentials and a lot of ego."

Hurley's bullish determination caused more internal political issues within the writing staff, as Roddenberry's erratic decision making had in the first season, causing numerous writers to eventually depart – including Torme – but interesting possible storylines were still being devised amidst a difficult atmosphere.

'Ferengi Gold', written by Roddenberry, was intended as a two-part story for the second season and would have revived the Ferengi, introduced in the first season's 'The Last Outpost' as intended major new villains for the franchise, before their impish nature and silly make up design very quickly reduced them from tenable threat into comedic relief, which later series *Deep Space Nine* would heartily embrace. 'Ferengi Gold' would have featured several concepts Roddenberry often mined on *The Original Series* – dual alien civilisations developing similarly to Earth, attractive women, the strong morality of the Federation and the Ferengi using technology to pose as god figures. Though the story would not be made, a similar concept years later would be utilised in the *Voyager* episode 'False Profits', bringing back Ferengi crooks who first appeared in *The Next Generation*, who appear across the galaxy to gaslight an alien population into believing them as deities for their own ends.

'Past Lives', later rejected by Hurley and subsequently by Michael Piller, was devised by Fred Bronson and Susan Sackett, who teamed up to pitch after realising both had, independently, been rejected multiple times with their own pitches. Their latest unsuccessful attempt featured time travel, in a story which has echoes of the later *Deep Space Nine* episode 'Visionary', centred around Chief Miles O'Brien: "[It] at the time was unexplored territory, but now would sound old hat. It involved a woman from the Future coming back, and accidentally causing the death of Captain Picard, and them having to fix that damage in Time. And it involved Romulans and Klingons."

Perhaps the most tantalising unmade story for the second season is 'Return to Forever', a planned two-part story from Torme, which he describes: "One thing that happened was very exciting. They came to me and said, 'We think we can get Leonard [Nimoy] to do the opening episode of the second season, and we want you to write it. Would you come up with something that you think would be really cool for him?' So I cooked up a sequel to 'The City on the Edge of Forever' and I called it 'Return to Forever'. They were going to go back to what was now the most forbidden place in the galaxy, which was that time portal, and they were going to have to actually violate the rules about non-interference, and it was going to create a Pandora's box with a whole terrible, unforeseen thing which only the Spocks from the two different time periods coming together could actually fix."

Torme believed that bridging the older series with the newer would be an ideal way to kickstart a new season: "What I had going was that a small research team was allowed to work with this thing [the Guardian] and were all found dead and Spock ended up coming through from the past. There was a circular story where I had two Spocks on the ship at the same time, one was in a coma and the one from the present was still alive. The reason the Spock from the past came through was all tied into the one in the present, yet the one in the present didn't have any memory of this. Then at the end, the present Spock puts his hands against the past Spock and tells him to forget, so he goes back in time not remembering that he will meet himself."

Quite how *The Next Generation* characters might have featured in such a Spock-heavy story remains unclear, but a return for the Guardian – despite reappearing in *The Animated Series* as earlier discussed – would have been a thrilling prospect. Torme explained that the idea never made it to script as negotiations with Nimoy fell away, though there was an attempt to revive the Guardian during the subsequent Piller tenure of the show, roughly around the end of the fifth season, when 'City on the Edge of Forever' writer Harlan Ellison was asked to write an episode of the series, after writer and producer Jeri Taylor had concocted a story, which Ellison described: "The idea was this: *Back to the Future II* uses *Back to the Future*, except you see it from a different angle. Using the original 'The City on the Edge of Forever', you have the people from *Next Generation* going back to the same time, the 1930s, because what was changed [on TOS] was okay for their time when they did it, but two hundred years later during *The Next Generation*, or whenever it was, the changes have been disastrous, and they have to set things back the way they were. Edith

Keeler's got to be left alive. Everybody who was alive in that show is still alive, but you didn't have to have any of the original characters. All you had to use was pre-existing footage. Put it in the background and put your characters from the new show acting and doing what they have to do, so what looks like her being killed, for instance, isn't."

Ellison later claimed it was rejected both as Piller couldn't imagine tampering with the original story, and that Nimoy had just appeared in 'Unification' and Piller was wary at having Spock return so soon. Again, it could have been a fascinating mechanism to revisit one of *The Original Series*' foundational classic episodes, and while it was not meant to be, the Guardian did decades later make a reappearance in *Discovery*'s third season episode 'Terra Firma Pt 2'. It is likely that return, in the 21st-century era of *Star Trek*, will not be the last.

As the second season came to an end, a darker year of *The Next Generation* – perhaps the darkest of all – Hurley, who despite not being the most beloved of leaders left a legacy in the form of the Borg, decided to move on to pastures new: "Two years was enough time in space for me. I did some good, some bad, some mediocre, but it's not a show that I could continue to do. It's not where I come from. The second season became a hassle where you were hassling for mediocrity. You weren't hassling for excellence, and that's always a debilitating kind of feeling. That's not a lot of fun. I told Gene at the beginning of the second season that I was only doing one more year."

Though he would be replaced by Michael Wagner, an experienced science-fiction show runner and producer, his tenure would be even shorter as he struggled to adapt to Roddenberry's Box. The man who would replace him, the man who would transform *The Next Generation* into an iconic *Star Trek* series even beyond Roddenberry's death, would shepherd some of the series' most powerful stories, and equally turn down some of its potentially most intriguing.

*

Michael Piller, at the beginning of the third season of *The Next Generation*, walked into a mess: "It was complete turmoil there at the time. *Star Trek: The Next Generation* was considered the worst place to work in Hollywood, and the reason for that was that Roddenberry had very strict rules. His vision was sacrosanct, and he didn't care about excuses or explanations.

He didn't want to argue about it. He just wanted you to do it his way, and a lot of writers couldn't see his future his way. Gene really didn't want any conflict between human characters, so the problem that Mike Wagner was having was the problem that every writer on staff was having. They felt that they were suffocating."

Piller immediately set about ensuring *The Next Generation* would escape the curse that befell *The Original Series*, survive to a fourth season, and become profitable for the network in syndication. He also worked to bring in a new team, flanked as he was by experienced hands such as Hans Beimler and Melinda Snodgrass, and ultimately buoyed by fresh talent thanks to an open-door spec script process that saw scribes such as Ronald D. Moore, René Echevarria, Naren Shankar and Brannon Braga brought into the fold, many of whom would become staples of the Berman era before graduating on to other projects. Ira Steven Behr, who would join the staff later in the season, would steer his own ship some years later as *Deep Space Nine*'s chief show runner.

"When Maurice Hurley left, there was basically a weeding-out process by trial and error, trying to bring new people on board. *Star Trek* is not an easy show to write. There are some people who could be Emmy Award–winning writers on a lawyer show or a police drama who just can't grasp what it is to write for a somewhat-stylized twenty-fourth-century world where the conflict between characters is very, very subtle. Because of the way our people treat each other, there are a lot of writers who just don't get it or who have a lot of difficulty at it. It's nothing to do with how smart they are, but how they fit into writing Star Trek. So you end up getting turnover."

Some departed, such as Snodgrass and Beimler, while others flourished under Piller's aegis as the quality of the storytelling improved, as subsequently did viewing figures as the third season saw the main cast truly begin to find the essence of their characters and *The Next Generation*'s distinctive tone and style fell into place. Moore was one such writer who got his break on the third season, as Piller – in dire need of scripts – picked out 'The Bonding' from the so-called 'slush pile' and put it into production – coincidentally an earlier proposed episode for the first season from 1987, by Lee Maddux, shared the same title, but beyond that there was no connection.

Moore pitched a story during the third season, dated December 1989, called 'Only the Lonely', a title likely used coincidentally by

Chris Columbus for his John Candy-starring comedy of the same name in 1991. The plot sees the *Enterprise* experiencing intense feelings of loneliness and hallucinations after they pass through a sector of space: "People from their pasts appear and disappear without warning: old friends, family members, people they haven't seen since childhood. All of these apparitions share one common trait: they seem to be attempting to reach out for the people who see them."

Picard and Deanna Troi figure out where these feelings came from so the *Enterprise* returns to that specific sector and the experiences begin again, stronger this time, with the hallucinations promising to stay with the crew if the ship never leaves. Troi ultimately learns there is an alien presence behind this, a being part of the fabric of space itself: "This being exists primarily in an inter-dimensional 'bubble' that cannot be detected in normal space. The alien was 'born' at almost the same instant as our own universe (the Big Bang) and there were many such beings that thrived in the early years of the universe. As the universe expanded, these beings (that exist as a section of space itself) expanded with it. The result was that they gradually lost contact with each other. The alien is basically lonely."

After the *Enterprise* learn the alien has been alone for billions of years and just wanted to make contact with other life, Picard promises to have a science station placed there to maintain contact and study the alien, with Moore concluding his pitch with this rationale for the idea: "This show would give us an opportunity to dig into some of our characters by getting a glimpse at the people and places they miss the most. We should come to see that each person is unique in certain ways and that on some level each individual has no one to really share everything with: there is only one Klingon aboard, no other empaths, only one boy-genius, one Captain, etc. We will also come to see how much our people mean to each other and how the ship has become 'home' for those who might have no other place to call home."

While the episode would never make it to air, *The Next Generation* would frequently produce stories about space-bound entities, as far back as the pilot episode indeed, which were often ultimately benevolent. Equally, episodes as early as 'Where No One Has Gone Before' would present alien-influenced hallucinations of people from our main character's past, such as Picard seeing his mother Yvette on the *Enterprise* corridors – a character eventually central to Picard's story arc across the second season of *Picard*.

Late in production of the third season, David Livingston, who began work on *The Next Generation* as a unit production manager, discussed with Rick Berman a pitched story in April 1990 – by an unknown writer in this case – called 'The Changing Seasons', which aside from utilising time travel and focusing on a father/son relationship, would have seen the death of Will Riker. Livingston commented in a memo: "I didn't buy this one for an instant. Implies that time travel will be simple in a few years. NO WAY! Also, do we really want to establish Riker's death. (This whole idea of dealing with one's mortality was done a lot better in 'Yesterday's *Enterprise*'). If we're going to do a father/son piece, I like my idea of a renegade son of Picard."

Firstly, although *The Next Generation* had previously killed off a main character in Tasha Yar during the first season episode 'Skin of Evil', killing the established Riker and Jonathan Frakes would have been a much bolder and riskier move. Livingston referencing 'Yesterday's *Enterprise*', which added an unexpected wrinkle to Yar's past and is considered one of the series' finest episodes, makes sense as a touchstone, in how it used time travel to explore character. Moreover, his desire for Picard to have a renegade son would surface several times – in the seventh season episode 'Bloodlines' through the character of Jason Vigo, via the unerring 'clone Picard' reality of Shinzon in *Nemesis*, and finally the swaggering form of Jack Crusher in the final season of *Picard*.

Another pitched script to feature time travel was 'Somewhen', by Vanna Bonta, which saw the *Enterprise* respond to a distress call from the *Pleides*, a transport ship caught in the Docleic Triangle (a variant on the famous Bermuda Triangle in the Atlantic Ocean). On entering this area of space, the *Enterprise* ends up creating several different time continuums which see Picard gain a beard, the original Jack Crusher (his best friend and Beverly's husband) returned to life and now serving as first officer, and a Geordi who could see, had a wife and children, and never joined Starfleet. As Data figures out the differences due to be unaffected by the time changes, and convinces Picard on a way to escape them, Beverly stays behind in a timeline which presumably contains a living Jack, and Wesley as a result is never born. Picard convinces her to give that life up, return with them, and the *Enterprise* escapes to their original timeline.

The story here is, in many respects, very reminiscent of 'Yesterday's *Enterprise*', whereby the *Enterprise* passed into an alternate reality where only Guinan (played by Whoopi Goldberg) remembered the differences and had to convince Picard of the changes, a timeline where Tasha lived and stays behind with a man she falls in love with. Whether this is coincidence or 'Somewhen' helped form the basis of that famous *Next Generation* episode is unclear, but Bonta's story would have perhaps been a slightly lighter touch on similar themes.

While on the subject of the late Jack Crusher, Mike Sussman tried three times to pitch spec scripts for *Next Generation*, one of which involved Crusher, although Sussman had no idea he was one of many to try and include the barely seen character in the show: "What was funny, though, was that I later submitted that Jack Crusher story, separately, to apply to the *Voyager* internship program and got in! However, they were not interested at all at Next Gen to [put it into production]. You know, again, they were just looking at the idea. I'm sure as soon as somebody said, 'Jack Crusher,' they said, 'Not interested. What's next?'"

Regarding time travel, during the seventh season, Joe Menosky pitched 'Out of Time', focused on Worf's son Alexander Rozhenko, who during a trip with his father to a Klingon hunting planet suddenly vanishes into a time portal, surfacing seconds later as an embittered old man. Jeri Taylor described it: "Worf looks around and calls out for him. A second later Alexander's voice answers 'Here I am.' Worf looks up and there is Alexander, now a scarred, battle-hardened [man] . . . Through various sci-fi reasons he was winked to another kind of dimension and was deposited there as a nine-year-old in a very harsh cruel environment, sort of a *Mad Max* kind of place where he had to fight and survive without anybody or anything. To him, he lived . . . years more in this really rotten environment, abandoned in a sense by those who loved him, and turned into this battle-hardened kind of warrior."

Worf and the older Alexander would return to the *Enterprise* where Worf must deal with losing his son's childhood, while Alexander is angry and resentful towards Worf for what happened. Menosky wrote it as a way of dispensing with Alexander, who he disliked, but Piller repeatedly rejected the concept, Echevarria claiming: "We never did that show because Alexander was Michael Piller's mother's favorite character." Whether this is true or not, Taylor regrets the fact it never happened: "I thought it was a dynamite story and always wanted to do it and Michael just wasn't comfortable with it for a lot of reasons. It's the one story I regret we didn't do [on TNG]."

Alexander would be given a time-travel story in the seventh season's 'Firstborn', and Echevarria liked the idea enough that he pushed for it to be developed in the sixth season of *Deep Space Nine* as the Molly O'Brien-focused 'Time's Orphan'. Sometimes good ideas never truly fade away.

Returning to the third season, one of the lighter episodes produced was 'Captain's Holiday', where Picard takes a vacation to the pleasure planet Risa and finds romance while facing time-travelling villains, but Behr originally envisaged an entirely different adventure for the Captain on Risa, where Picard finds a holodeck: "It said, 'Face Your Greatest Fear!' and it was like a carnival place. It wasn't what it became, this sensual, open-sexuality place – Gene turned it into that! It was like this carnival atmosphere place; a true vacation resort. And he thought, 'Oh, cool, this is going to put me in a good mood. What I need is to fight some Klingons without thinking about the repercussions of it, or go after some Romulans or whatever it is.' And he goes into this holodeck, and it was all about the captain being promoted to admiral, and losing the *Enterprise*, and Riker being bumped up to captain of the *Enterprise*. Basically, though we never really hit it on the head, it's about growing old. Not to grow old, but your time of life changing and suddenly you're not going to be the guy going off on adventures, you're going to be sitting at a desk somewhere, SENDING people on adventures. That's his greatest fear."

Roddenberry, still consulting as Piller made day-to-day decisions, was not happy with the notion of Picard having any element of fear, although he did like the pleasure planet aspect which ended up retained as the story morphed into a blend of *Indiana Jones* and *Casablanca* in space. Behr's concept nonetheless prefigures ideas that would one day be explored in *Picard*, with an aged Admiral Picard grappling with his own listlessness.

Moore provided a second rejected episode concept in January 1990 with an episode named 'Errors of Judgement', the premise of which he described as: "The experiences that have had the most impact on us and on our lives are not our successes, but our failures. By an examination of these defeats, we can learn more about who we are and from where we come."

In a one-page treatment, the plot saw the *Enterprise* contact a new species, highly curious about the Federation. They are telepathic and seek mental contact with the crew, not satisfied by mere historical documents, their abilities triggering memories in the crew which leads the characters to relive the biggest mistakes of their lives. Moore added: "The point of doing this show is not to say that our people are running around with these big problems over their heads. The point is to see what made them the people they are today. Picard and co have dealt with their regrets and can live with them . . . indeed their pain only made them stronger in the end. But I think we could make a really interesting show out of learning what drives these people and what private demons they've learned to deal with."

To some degree, this feels familiar to the recently released, at the time, *The Final Frontier*, in which villain Sybok uses a mind-meld to unlock Spock and McCoy's latent feelings of sadness and pain, but it also serves as a key example of how Piller's insistence on maintaining 'Roddenberry's Box', convinced it made for greater challenges in how to create drama, meant Moore was devising a tale that didn't see the *Enterprise* crew grappling with regret but showing how that regret makes them the well-adjusted people they are.

One tale that would have pushed the edges of that box was 'Leap of Faith', one of several stories that perennially unlucky duo Fred Bronson and Susan Sackett pitched to Piller during season three. "[It] involved Deanna Troi getting stuck in Time on a planet, and living a whole second life where she had children. But Michael said 'No I don't [think] that works!'"

Interestingly, a similar story was ultimately produced for the fifth season called 'The Inner Light', in which Picard experiences an entire lifetime as an alien man called Kanin, an episode which subsequently went on to win both Hugo and Emmy awards, considered one of the finest episodes of the series. That too, very nearly, had a sequel, called 'The Outer Lights', pitched by the same writer, Morgan Gendel, in which the *Enterprise* would have encountered the scientist who formed the basis of Picard's wife, Eline, during his experience with the probe from the planet Kataan. "Picard was married to this woman, made love to her, and grew old with her, so it's not like a dream. It's real to him, and now his dead wife has come back to life, which is a really powerful thing and made more so by the fact she doesn't know who the hell he is. And she's married to one of the scientists also on board the probe. I have a personal attachment to this episode, and I thought my passion for that would get it through. The idea is so powerful. His whole family has been destroyed in a natural holocaust, a nova explosion, and now he finds out his wife is alive. I pitched my heart out, but they thought it was best not to tamper with the memory of "Inner Light."

Regardless, both Bronson and Sackett were convinced 'Leap of Faith' would have been as powerful and successful as 'The Inner Light'. We shall sadly never know.

*

The fourth and fifth seasons of *The Next Generation* saw Piller consolidate the writing staff as the series equally consolidated its position as *Star Trek*'s future, given *The Original Series* crew would sail off on their final voyage in 1991 – more on which we will discuss in the next chapter.

Though Behr departed before he began his stint on *Deep Space Nine*, a major new hire was Jeri Taylor, a strong female voice who would ultimately succeed Piller as show runner and help create with him and Berman the third sequel series, in 1995, *Voyager*. Taylor would provide a calming influence on a staff who, following a chaotic third season, could see the ship righting itself, to which Moore attests: "The third season was the toughest. It was by far the worst just in terms of organization and pace and workload. It was never that bad again. You're trying to do twenty-six episodes, which now looking back on it, is unbelievable. But, you can only write so much, and freelancers are out writing episodes and those are coming in, but they all need to be rewritten because none of them were good."

With less immediate stress in breaking stories, buoyed by more of a harmonious staff environment, Piller had more space to think about what stories *The Next Generation* should tell, and what stories they shouldn't.

One considered story for the fifth season would have brought together all the 'family' accrued by Data across the run of the series to date, including his villainous brother Lore (also played by Brent Spiner) and his 'daughter' Lal, seen in the third season episode 'The Offspring'. Lore would have stolen the emotion ship developed by their 'father', Dr Soong, in the fourth season episode 'Brothers', attempting to revive Lal with it for presumably dastardly ends. The idea was never fully developed but the emotion chip was utilised again as a key factor in Data's character arc in *Generations* and movies beyond.

Jose Molina, who subsequently staffed on shows such as *Agent Carter* and *Firefly*, also pitched a post-'Brothers' Lore episode called 'Endangered Species', roughly around the end of the sixth season: "It features the return of Lore, who seeks out Data with a dual purpose. First, he wants to return the emotions chip he stole in the season-four episode 'Brothers', and second, he wants Data to deactivate him. Yes, the 'issue of the week' was assisted suicide. In returning the emotions chip to Data, Lore cautions him about the human feelings he so desperately wants. He explains that it was the overwhelming torrent of emotion from his own chip that once made Lore so dangerously unbalanced, and that now makes him want to end his life. Because just like the twin androids can process millions of calculations in a second, they can also feel millions of emotions in that time. The androids can experience lifetimes of human anguish in minutes. Data has an opportunity to reflect on his brother's crisis as he mounts a holodeck presentation of 'Frankenstein'. The Monster's Promethean rant against his maker, and the sheer agony of his solitary existence, help Data arrive at a better understanding of his long-suffering brother. In the end, Data helps Lore find a new lease on life; he tasks his big brother with acting as caretaker to a species as unique and misunderstood – and endangered – as himself. Alone in his quarters after dropping Lore off at his new home, Data faces his own dilemma: Does he install his long-lost emotions chip? Heeding his brother's warning, he crushes it under his boot instead."

This would have been a fascinating and perhaps more rewarding final *Next Generation* appearance for Lore than we were given in 'Descent', where he rises to lead a group of Borg drones as a sinister villain, exploring deeper themes of euthanasia and utilising Mary Shelley's Gothic tome in line with the series other dabbling in 19th-century literature. Lore would later return in the third season of *Picard*, receiving a rather bittersweet final goodbye in 'Surrender', but 'Endangered Species' could have been a more rewarding version of *Deep Space Nine*'s 'Sons of Mogh', where Worf honourably gives his brother Kurn a whole new life after he seeks to die.

Speaking of recurring characters, one significant omission from the fifth season was Q. Two intended Q stories for that season were developed and both, unusually, were rejected.

'Q Makes Two' would have seen Q duplicate the *Enterprise* and her crew, as Brannon Braga explains: "Q comes on board and Picard's saying people are inherently good and we have managed to get rid of our darker elements in the 24th century and we're better people. Q says, 'So you don't think you have dark components and you think you're better without them, well I'm going to show you a thing or two,' and so he extracts the darker components and puts them into doubles. The clean, good components suffer and so do the darker components and neither functions without the other. We see that dramatically . . . The image in my mind that we never really got to was the two *Enterprises* shooting at each other, that's what you want to see."

Aspects of this story recall *The Original Series* episode 'The Enemy Within', whereby a transporter accident duplicates Captain Kirk into a Jekyll and Hyde duplicate pairing, and Braga's later *Voyager* second season episode 'Deadlock', in which he splits the ship and crew into two duplicates thanks to a schism.

Braga nonetheless struggled with breaking 'Q Makes Two' on a practical level, penning at least three drafts, with René Echevarria contributing two. He expands on the difficulties, claiming Taylor told him: "'These are the four or five ideas we have rolling around; which one appeals to you?' and foolishly I said that one. I wrote a first draft that Michael [Piller] said wasn't workable, and we ran it by him three times before he finally approved the teleplay. From a production standpoint, we had to ask ourselves, 'How produceable is this?' Almost every scene would have to be done as an optical, and it wasn't practical, and Michael said the story wasn't working practically dramatically. That story was killed."

A second Q episode proposed for the fifth season was called 'I. Q. Test", credited to Herb Wright in January 1992, and would have depicted Q wagering against another member of the Continuum, his omnipotent species, leading to a contest between the *Enterprise* crew and a dangerous race called the Zaa-Naar. Picard and his crew would have been thrown into an Olympic scenario, with Q having selected the *Enterprise* crew as his combatants against his rival Q's Zaa-Naar aliens. Rumours circulated that Arnold Schwarzenegger, at the height his fame at this point thanks to *Terminator 2: Judgment Day* amongst other films, would appear, likely perhaps as one of the fearsome Zaa-Naar, but Moore claims this was never the case, adding that Piller junked the idea: "In defense of Michael, the Q-Olympics story was ludicrous and needed to be deep-sixed."

Moore himself, separately, had his own concept toward the end of the series for a Q story during the series run that never made it to air, one in which a fracture within the universe led to the being experiencing a period of insanity. "It was a totally nutso beginning – Picard is suddenly walking down [a] New York street dressed in his uniform but carrying a brief-case and wearing a fedora. He passes Riker who is pounding on the side of a building with a loaf of bread – that's Riker's job, to pound the side of a building with a loaf of bread. And a Klingon driving a taxi cab drives by and a knight in shining armor is the cop, all this insane stuff."

It was a story the writing staff loved but the producers of the show vetoed, perhaps out of a sense of it being too unusual to make work. Moore continued about the plot: "All our characters are there and they are doing things that make zero sense, and then the camera pans by an alley and there lying by a trash can is Q who is dressed like a homeless guy and he is mumbling to himself 'I used to be a super-being' . . . It's all about us trying to figure out that none of this is the way things are supposed to be and that nutty guy who is saying he used to be a super-being is actually right."

Braga added: "They come to realize that something's not right, and it turns out that Q has gone insane, and somehow he folded the laws of physics and the universe into his insanity. In this bizarre reality, where different time periods converge, Q is this homeless person going on and on about how he used to be a super-being. It was kind of our homage to *The Prisoner* and it didn't get approved. That could have been a classic."

Piller wasn't sold on this tale but did then start to consider the idea that a Q story should bookend the conclusion of *The Next Generation*, thereby directly influencing development of legendary series finale 'All Good Things', and moreover the conceptual idea of a crazed homeless figure out of time would ultimately appear in *Voyager*'s 'Future's End' two-part story in the form of 29th-century Starfleet officer Captain Braxton.

Q and meddling with time also featured in a story pitched by Robert Hewitt Wolfe, who ended up a major creative force in the success of *Deep Space Nine*. He wanted to port a *Quantum Leap*-style narrative into *The Next Generation*. *Quantum Leap* ran concurrently with the series, starring future (or more specifically past) *Enterprise* captain Scott Bakula as Dr Sam Beckett, a scientist unstuck in time who 'leaps' into different bodies through 20th-century American history, learning lessons and helping people overcome moments of adversity. Wolfe's plot saw Q transform Picard, Data and Troi into Romulan officers aboard one of their ships: "There was no Romulan makeup involved; they weren't possessing the bodies. The visual gag was the same as Quantum Leap, where we would look at them and see them as themselves and maybe in a reverse shot we might see them as other people completely."

Troi did, of course, end up transformed into a Romulan officer in sixth season episode 'Face of the Enemy', as was Major Kira Nerys a Cardassian in the similar *Deep Space Nine* outing 'Second Skin', in the third season of that show. Both tales, however, had nary a Q in sight.

Also without Q, during the sixth season, was the planned sequel to the episode that saw his return following his fifth season absence, the much admired 'Tapestry', in which Q takes a seemingly dead Picard back to his raucous youth at Starfleet Academy to relive an incident where he was almost killed in a bar fight. Ron Wilkerson and Jean Louise Matthias suggested a plot in which Picard attended an Academy reunion, meeting old friends Maria Batanides and Cortan Zweller, the latter of whom – a failed Starfleet captain – is embittered by Picard's success, as Matthias describes: "So here they were coming back to face each other and there is a great amount of pressure to perform for your friends." Wilkerson adds: "Corey wanted to involve Picard in a new scheme and Picard realized he could help his friend, but only by taking a risk, putting himself on the line for friendship."

While this story was well received, including by producer Taylor, Piller rejected taking it forward, perhaps aware of how cherished 'Tapestry' was. Numerous 'sequel' episodes failed to materialise across the run of *The Next Generation*, both during, before and after Piller's tenure, in part thanks to the anxiety of not despoiling what came before. Early on, a sequel to *The Original Series* episode 'Charlie X', featuring the gifted prodigy Charles Evans, as played in the first season by Robert Walker, was pitched by Nick Sagan, during the period when episodes such as 'The Naked Now' suggested the series was less against drinking from the well of the 1960s.

Much later, during production of the final season, Moore sought to have the *Enterprise-D* visit Sigma Iotia II, where in *The Original Series* episode 'A Piece of the Action', Kirk and crew discovered the Iotians had parallel development of Earth's history as 1920s Prohibition gangsters. Moore's suggestion was for the Iotians, almost a century on, to be now imitating the crew of Kirk's *Enterprise*, and was considered as a possible story later for *Deep Space Nine*'s 30th anniversary episode in 1996, which turned into 'Trials and Tribble-actions'. Marvel Comics also eventually turned the idea into a one-shot issue of their series *Star Trek: Unlimited* in 1998, named 'A Piece of Reaction', written by Michael A. Martin and Andy Mangels. It won't be the last we'll hear of attempts to revive this classic episode either.

A sequel to sixth season episode 'Ship in a Bottle' was for a time intended, whereby sentient hologram Professor Moriarty would be trapped in a virtual world with his nemesis Sherlock Holmes, and requests Data via a distress signal enter to save him. Moriarty would eventually return, albeit briefly, as a holographic guard of Daystrom station in *Picard*'s third season episode 'The Bounty', decades later. Much earlier, Nick Sagan would pitch a return of the villainous Armus, the oily skin creature who killed Tasha Yar, but he would eventually return years later on a comedic level in *Lower Decks*' second season episode 'The Spy Humongous'.

There was also a belated attempt, toward the end of the series, to give Michelle Forbes' Ensign Ro Laren a focused story about the murder of a Cardassian for which she is blamed, thanks to her Bajoran heritage. Ro would eventually return, decades later, albeit briefly, in 'Imposters' during *Picard*'s third season, but there remains a fascinating alternate story for Ro's character that we shall save for a future chapter.

One sequel that never happened on *The Next Generation*, and not for the want of trying, was an episode following on from *The Original Series* tale 'Mirror, Mirror', set in a parallel universe filled with evil doppelgängers of our heroes. "We've been pitched 'Mirror, Mirror' sequels since *The Next Generation* began, and I wasn't interested," Piller admitted. Few of these stories became public knowledge, or perhaps were developed far enough to be made available, but David Gerrold did jokingly claim in February 1987 that a story existed where "'he *Enterprise* returns to the 'Mirror, Mirror' universe and Edith Keeler is eaten by carnivorous tribbles." Jerome Bixby, who wrote the original story, pitched a sequel which would have involved *Original Series* characters, but Paramount rejected the notion of using them, even while they indulged Roddenberry calling back to other 1960s stories and tropes.

This suggests the idea of returning to 'Mirror, Mirror's' pulp sensibility never sat well with *The Next Generation*'s cooler, scientific approach to *Star Trek*, particularly in the Piller era. *Voyager*, designed and presented in a similar manner to *The Next Generation*, also never ventured to the Mirror universe, whereas the darker and in some respects pulpier *Deep Space Nine* and *Enterprise* both did, as did *Discovery* for a much broader arc. Only in comic form did *The Next Generation* finally dabble in the Mirror universe with several series from IDW Publishing during the 2010s, but seeing Picard and his crew in their sinister alter-ego's remains one of the more fascinating 'what if' notions in *Star Trek* history.

Also linked to *The Original Series* were multiple attempts, toward the end of *The Next Generation*, to bring back Walter Koenig's Pavel Chekov as they had done McCoy, Spock and Sarek, and indeed James Doohan's Scotty in sixth season romp 'Relics'. Koenig claims he had meetings early on, but a good Chekov idea never stuck, with the writers anxious to involve time travel, or descendants of the original crew. Koenig came up with an idea about a Worf-focused story about Chekov whereby he would be a hallucination, possibly thanks to Worf's Russian connections in the Rozhenko family, but his reasons why this never proceeded are intriguing: "We were in a room, and they had pads and pens ready to take notes. But just when we finished the introductions, the phone rang and it was [a producer] telling them they had to leave, that they were needed somewhere else. Because I am who I am, and have a level of neuroticism that includes paranoia, I concluded that this may have been done purposefully, that the writers had contacted me without consulting [the producers] and they ordered them out of the room. I may be wrong; I never got the full story."

Naren Shankar came the closest to realising a Chekov story in the seventh season, devising a plot idea that again focused on Worf: "It never went anywhere. I was working on a Chekov story where he returns as a prisoner-of-war from a planet where he was imprisoned for many years and finally released. Now he has come back as an ambassador to help the Federation open up diplomatic relations, like Vietnam, essentially. The story was going to be about Worf and Chekov, because they're both Russian and Worf has heard about him and they kind of strike up a relationship together. Throughout the course of the negotiations with these people, it appears as though Chekov is sabotaging them. It turns out he is plotting to use the *Enterprise* to lay waste to their capital for revenge and to screw things up for the Federation because he feels they abandoned him and let these people torture him."

One wonders how *Star Trek* purists might have reacted to Chekov returning as an embittered, villainous, tragic hero, but it could have been a genuinely fascinating approach to one of the less-developed original Starfleet heroes.

It speaks to how *The Next Generation* writers remained cautious about how to approach the past, how to return to storylines and characters, and just how carefully they sought to leave a mark in established *Star Trek* canon.

*

By the end of the fifth season, *The Next Generation* had achieved what *The Original Series* failed to do – complete a five-year mission, even though Roddenberry's sequel never stated they were on such a time-specific journey. The crew of the *Enterprise-D* experienced a cultural and viewership stability that *The Original Series* was never fortunate enough to weather, and this bled into the production too according to Moore: "Ironically, the final seasons of *Next Gen* were characterized by stability among the writing staff, which bred a consistent level of quality among the episodes. I think the shows were better. There was more of a family feeling to the crew, which is reflected because there was more of a family feeling on the staff."

In the final seasons, before cast contracts came to an end and *The Next Generation* was geared to transition into cinematic outings, the show grew bolder in allegorical storytelling. 'The Outcast' for example, albeit clumsily at points, tackled LGBTQ issues as Riker fell in love with a genderless alien, and there was talk of an episode that focused on the thorny issue of abortion, before the idea was canned, as Echevarria describes: "Michael didn't feel that it worked. He was very concerned with it being too pro-life, and though it was ultimately pro-choice, the basic idea we came up with was that we have an alien on the *Enterprise* that has been on there for years, and some super alien species comes aboard and says, 'This is our fetus and it is time to make it either be born into one of us or abort.' The alien never had to feed and never understood why. It took in nutrients through its parents, these energy beings, so there was this dependence, and they had the right to terminate the dependence of the fetus, but Michael was concerned that our sympathies would be with the fetus and it would come off as being too pro-life."

Given how the repeal of Roe vs Wade in the United States in 2022 opened the debate wider than in fifty years, this could have ended up in one of the most powerful and resonant episodes of *The Next Generation*, had they been brave enough to tackle it.

One of the more intriguing concepts fostered in these later seasons involved a radical change to Geordi La Forge, as described by Taylor: "We wanted to make Geordi an alien. He was going to discover that his father was not who he thought he was, and his mother had an almost *Rosemary's Baby* – kind of thing and had been impregnated by an alien. As a result, Geordi was actually half alien and now, at his present age, his people were coming back to get him. I thought that would have given

Geordi's character a lot of elaboration." This feels in step with attempts to add a sense of threat and danger to Geordi's character, as seen in episodes such as 'The Mind's Eye', where he is brainwashed to be an assassin by the Romulans but would have been a permanent character conceit difficult to write around if necessary.

Numerous concepts were pitched and failed to materialise that would have made for striking episodes. Marc Bernardin, later to write for shows including *Alphas* and *Castle Rock*, came in with a story called 'Past Present': "The basic thrust of it was that, during one of what had to be many stretches where the *Enterprise* was just flying between worlds – *Star Trek* always pretended that space was a crowded place, when in reality, even with warp capabilities, the distance between populated systems is impossibly vast – Picard was concerned about the crew's level of preparation. Even though the *Enterprise* wasn't a warship, a knife still needs to be kept sharp. Picard vented his frustration to Data, who can't share his concern, as circuits don't get dull from lack of use. Later, there's an attack on the *Enterprise*, from seemingly out of nowhere. It cripples the ship. The culprit: Khan Noonien Singh. Somehow, delivered from the clutches of the Genesis device (which does, after all, create life out of lifelessness) and pitted against a new generation of Starfleet captain. I don't remember the ins-and-outs of the plot, but the upshot was that Data took Picard's musings as an order and created a simulation that would challenge the entire crew – with a little holodeck trickery and inertial dampener manipulation, Data turned the *Enterprise* into a big-ass motion simulator ride."

This sounds a little far-fetched for *The Next Generation* and bringing back presumably Ricardo Montalban as Khan would likely have been the ultimate in stunt casting, not to mention invalidating the climax of *The Wrath of Khan*. Bernardin's narrative oddly could work better in the more action-driven, nostalgia heavy 21st-century *Star Trek* series.

Lisa Klink pitched a Geordi-focused story in 1993 as a spec script called 'The Empath', which she describes: "The crew needed to get information from an alien race about how to get through a dangerous part of space. But the aliens only communicated telepathically, so the universal translator was no help. Troi couldn't understand them either. However, the neural interface of Geordi's visor allowed him to perceive their thoughts. The problem was that these aliens were highly emotional, and Geordi found it overwhelming. So he turned to Troi for advice about how to handle and interpret the emotional overload. My idea was to take the chief engineer completely out of his element and force him to solve a different kind of problem, leading to some reflection about why he chose to work with machines instead of people, and why his best friend was an android. It was a perfectly good episode, if nothing spectacular."

Andre Bormanis, a science advisor on the final season of the show, and later a writer on *Voyager* and *Enterprise*, discussed with me an idea revolving around Data that he pitched for the seventh season: "It was a story where Data got separated on an away mission. His shuttle crashed and he found himself compromised mentally somehow. And he took the risk of introducing himself to this sort of relatively primitive village of humanoids. And he was trying in some way to figure out where he is, how to get in touch with the ship. And he met a couple of people. He tried to keep a low profile. And the next day he came back to this village and it was occupied by entirely different people. And he came back again a few days later and again, different people and what the hell is going on? And the reveal was that this was a species of sort of mayflies. They lived an entire life cycle over the course of 24 hours. And so they had never progressed beyond a very primitive level of technology, despite the fact that they were intelligent at language and presumably were born with a certain vocabulary and racial memories or species memories. And when I pitched that Jeri Taylor, she said, 'Oh, I got to stop you right there. We're developing this new series, *Star Trek Voyager*, and one of our principal characters has a very shortened lifespan.'"

Said character turned out to be Kes, although the conceptual idea behind her differed from Bormanis' Data story here, though he admitted the emotional core of the tale and what it would say about Data as a character had not been broken.

Naren Shankar, a working staffer on the series, pitched a story called 'Blackout', akin to the fifth season episode 'Disaster', about a massive power outage across the *Enterprise*: "What happened was Data got zapped some way and he started to dream. And the idea was: Can an artificial life-form and android actually experience dreams, and if so what do they mean? I'd read this really interesting article in the Atlantic about a neurobiologist who was talking about dreams in the context of kinda refuting Freudian dream theory. It just talked about the random firings of memories in your brain. And so it suggested an interesting angle into something that hadn't been explored at that time with that character,

Data. I suspect a lot of people wrote specs about Data, 'cause he was one of the most interesting characters on the show. And you're always able to use him as a way of commenting on human behavior or aspirations. I seem to remember I didn't want it to be like the holodeck, so it wasn't like a literal dream – it was more impressionistic than that."

If Shankar often sought a scientific approach to his stories, Echevarria intended in one pitch on an environmental focus, based on a script idea that Piller gave him following production on the third season episode 'Transfigurations': "It involved every environmental story that people had done and seemed fairly obvious. They in fact commissioned a teleplay that was literally smokestacks, and it would have been very obvious to the audience that it was the cause of the blindness and mutations in a tribe that was kept on a little island called the Island of Tears. They were kept there, hidden from view, in order for the rest of the society to be able to maintain its mode of production, which was highly exploitative and environmentally unsound. The audience would have guessed at the end of the first act what was going on. What I came up with was a Federation colony that mined dilithium and they're natives to the planet. The twist was that what was causing the problems were these organisms that had evolved in the presence of electromagnetic fields of dilithium. Its removal was creating mutations."

Writers on staff were often encouraged to chase or explore story ideas that spoke to their sensibilities. Ron Moore, for example, long wanted to produce a musical episode, in the vein of *Buffy the Vampire Slayer*'s sixth season episode 'Once More with Feeling' that years later would pull the concept off well, but even despite the holodeck serving as the perfect vehicle to realise this, his was the only enthusiasm for the idea. Moore told me more about the intended plan for it: "It was late in the run of TNG — probably the sixth or seventh season — and this idea came up in the room about doing a musical episode where something happens to the ship and they end up having to sing their way through the story. We tossed around a few notions of maybe it's a virus or an alien mind game and so on, but we never really advanced the idea past the concept because Michael Piller and Rick Berman were dead set against it. I loved the idea, however, and I kept trying to get them to at least consider it, but to no avail."

Strange New Worlds would eventually realise this dream in the penultimate episode of its second season, 'Subspace Rhapsody', three decades later.

What he considered his 'white whale', however, in *Moby Dick* parlance that would entertain any fan of *First Contact*, was his desire to tell a story entirely in reverse, where time flowed backward for the characters and the audience. Moore discussed the idea with me: "We actually took several days trying to make this concept work in the writers' room, but kept floundering on what to do with the characters' memories of events that had already occurred and still maintain jeopardy about where the story was going and also how to keep the audience from getting confused. We went round and round trying to break the tale (which had some kind of sub-space phenomenon as its catalyst) but ultimately decided to shelve it. I never quite got over wanting it to work. Years later, I saw the Seinfeld episode 'The Betrayal' and realized they'd done the best version we'd never thought of."

Though his attempts would be frustrated, Kenneth Biller did eventually realise this concept on *Voyager* in the third season episode 'Before and After', while in 2000, Christopher Nolan's *Memento* would popularise the idea and spawn a litany of television shows that would attempt their own version. Moore on this was ahead of the curve.

For Jeri Taylor, it was a two-part story involving the mysterious Breen, who would play a big part in the conclusion to *Deep Space Nine*, that she envisaged as a potential two-part story to end the sixth season and open the seventh. In her untitled story, dated January 1992, the *Enterprise* would be told that they no longer will be exploring deep space and have been reassigned to patrol near Earth, organising diplomatic conventions, peace treaties etc . . . with the flagship, given its prestige, seen as the perfect ship to function as this emblem. Her pitch document continues: "Picard and the others, of course, receive this news somewhat differently, and with varying amounts of surprise, anxiety, and dismay. Picard tells his senior staff that they have a choice – to remain on board and serve in prestigious but ceremonial positions, or to make other decisions about their lives and careers."

As the crew grapple with their decisions, the *Enterprise* is sent to escort a Breen delegation to Earth, who Taylor describes as a "bellicose, brutal species who inhabit a distant but expanding empire. We have long been aware of the Breen and have been happy they were so far away; we've always felt that they would be trouble." There are echoes in this description of the unseen Tzenkethi from *Deep Space Nine*'s third season episode, 'The Adversary'.

The Breen having made the first entreaty toward relationships, the Federation decide to talk, but subsequently Starfleet officers are sent on a mission with Breen scientists to investigate a newly discovered phenomenon. The ship vanishes after a distress call and, as the Breen rage, Picard takes the *Enterprise* on what could be its last mission to find out what happened. "Near a never-before charted star system is a horrendous gash in space which, even for our intrepid explorers, is an awesome sight. They have no idea what it is or what might have caused it; nothing like it has been seen or reported. The readings are perplexing, mystifying."

The Breen ship is found in the anomaly but as tensions rise with the Breen, and despite Geordi's efforts, the ship slips deeper into the phenomenon which threatens to swallow the *Enterprise* itself. "On the bridge, the situation is dire. Shearing stress threatens to rip apart the saucer and battle sections. Riker takes a small crew to the Battle Bridge; they must separate or risk a violent wrenching apart." Geordi eventually figures out the *Enterprise*'s warp drive is what is causing the rupture, so the saucer separates and as the rupture causes damage, it plunges toward a nearby planet, out of control "and already glowing red from the friction of the planet's atmosphere, screaming down to an inevitable, cataclysmic explosion".

Taylor ends the first part there, giving context: "This is a story which gives us a lot; deeply personal dilemmas as the crew struggles to make decisions about what to do with their lives; the opportunity to introduce a new adversary, the Breen – a move which I think will infuse new energy into the 7th season; a way to deal with the sizeable issue of the warp drive destroying space without diminishing it (in that we learn what it is in Part One, and have Part Two to wrestle with the way to deal with the problem); and a highly dramatic cliff-hanger ending which will have the fans wondering who will survive (i.e., return to the series) and who will not."

There is a great deal to unpack here. Firstly, Taylor's story has echoes of the third/fourth season tale 'The Best of Both Worlds', as Riker faced a huge career decision while the *Enterprise* faced off against a deadly new enemy, leaving the audience wondering if a key cast member would survive. It is also markedly different from 'Descent', which ultimately did end the sixth season and kicked off the seventh, though that too featured a major villain in the Borg and did separate the saucer section, an effect used back in the pilot episode but sparingly across the run of the show for budgetary reasons. The saucer crashing on a planet, moreover, would eventually serve as the major action set piece in the first *Next Generation* feature, *Generations*, in 1994.

Taylor's creation of the Breen as a way of revitalising the seventh season with a recurring antagonist is a tantalising prospect, had this been taken forward, with the suggestion being that *Next Generation* had grown somewhat stale as it approached the finish line. There is more than a sense of that in Taylor writing a 'final voyage' for the crew in the penultimate season. It feels like a story that could have worked as a series finale, in some respects.

In a revised concept for the sixth season finale, dated February 1992, Taylor posited a new story, retaining elements of the earlier draft, which, again, tethered back to 'The Best of Both Worlds', focusing as it did on Riker: "Profoundly affected by his experiences in 'Second Chances', Riker decides to seek the captaincy of another ship, and is quickly given command of the Indiana, a Nebula-class starship. He goes to Picard, who of course wishes him well, and states that he'd like to offer senior staff positions to some of the *Enterprise* crew. Picard acquiesces, and Riker proceeds to put some of his friends in a difficult dilemma."

As the *Indiana* is scheduled for a five to seven year tour of the Gamma Quadrant, Riker's offer sees Deanna wanting to go but worrying about her mother; Worf equally interested but concerned about whether he would leave his son Alexander; Geordi open to it, if Lieutenant Aquiel (from the sixth season episode 'Aquiel') will go too, Geordi as ever being led by his chaste, romantic heart. Beverly won't leave Wesley so stays, as does Data – promoted to first officer – but the others leave.

Heading for the DS9 wormhole, the *Indiana* is hailed by a Breen delegation, and Riker is assigned as the *Enterprise* was to escort them to Earth, before they encounter the new space phenomenon, and the joint Starfleet/Breen mission vanishes. Riker is deemed to have failed and is irritated when Starfleet sends the more experienced Picard and the *Enterprise* to investigate and clean up the mess. They encounter the gash in space, trying to rescue the ship, end up caught in it, just as in Taylor's first story, but here Riker decides – against the Breen's wishes – to take the *Indiana* to help the *Enterprise*. "Picard comes aboard the Indiana to confer with Riker and encounters the volatile Breen. The decision is made to use the tractor beam of both ships and engage full warp drives in a mighty effort to pull the science vessel from its trap." Disaster then strikes for both ships and, as Picard moves to transport back over, the bulkhead ruptures "and Jean-Luc Picard is blown out of the rupture in the hull – and into the deadly, hard vacuum of space".

While the idea of presumably killing Picard at the end of the sixth season did not last very long, Taylor's focus on Riker continued a persistent anxiety over what to do with the character. Ever since 'The Best of Both Worlds', where he was established as a captain in the making holding himself back due to his love of the *Enterprise* (and probably Deanna), through to when he finally does graduate at the end of *Nemesis*, Riker had been a character multiple writers considered killing off, as earlier discussed. Following 'Second Chances', which saw Frakes play a morally dubious transporter accident-created double called Tom Riker (shades again of *The Original Series* episode 'The Enemy Within'), Taylor again believed killing Commander Riker was a way to energise the final season, but not lose Frakes by replacing him with Tom and "let Lieutenant Riker come onto the ship as a rejuvenated, energetic, driven, ambitious character. He wouldn't be Number One, he would be at ops and have to prove himself and build his career and get into conflict with the others, because he had these rough edges from having lived that arduous experience. It gave it a wonderful life that would energize the seventh season with everyone in a different place and a new character, and yet our same character there, and I was very, very taken with that. It was just too bold."

Ron Moore expanded on this for me: "I thought it was a great way to refresh the show and let Jonathan Frakes stretch into a different character toward the end. The writers were all in favor, but again Michael and Rick shot it down — although I think Michael was a little bit more on the fence. Rick couldn't get over the idea that viewers would be confused if they missed the episode where we made the transition and that it would change the fundamental DNA of the characters from that point. I thought it was a bold and risky chance that we should have taken and I still do."

In hindsight, for the rather safe network television model of the 1990s, this was indeed too radical. Frakes would play Tom Riker again in *Deep Space Nine*'s third season episode 'Defiant' but otherwise the promise of the character was never truly explored, nor were Taylor's ambitions to infuse new energy into a show that had become quite content to tell steady, often well-written but stand-alone, unintrusive stories week on week that never threatened the status quo.

This brings us to 'All Good Things', though not the seventh season finale and curtain down on *The Next Generation* that we might imagine. As Taylor developed her Breen/Riker finale for the sixth season, Moore and Braga worked on their own two-part story for the season bearing the famous title, which also – like Taylor's story – featured the *Enterprise* saucer separating and crashing on a planet, as seen in *Generations*, which Moore and Braga eventually wrote and which Moore describes: "The genesis of the saucer crash was in a story called 'All Good Things', which was not the series finale, but a story that was going to be a cliffhanger for the sixth season of *Next Gen*. Brannon and I had come up with a story where Starfleet recalls the *Enterprise* home and is going to split the crew up. The *Enterprise* is going to become the Queen Mary, basically, and on the way home, the characters all decide what they're going to do with their lives. But in the course of returning home, there's a big battle and the saucer separates from the battle section, which explodes, and the saucer crashes on the planet's surface. The producers hated that story for the cliffhanger and we tossed it aside, but when we were doing the movie, the crash of the saucer was one of the first things Brannon and I came to Rick with."

It is very intriguing that all three writers came up with a similar concept, about the *Enterprise* and her crew being put out to pasture, but by this point the adventures of Picard and his loyal officers were looking to a bigger stage – a series of cinematic adventures that would have their own intriguing, alternative possible directions, and suggest by no means that Picard, Riker, Data etc . . . were ready to sail off into the sunset. Their human adventure was in some respects just beginning.

We shall return to the *Enterprise-D* – and indeed *E* – crew later, but first there is one last story to tell with *The Original Series* crew, as they head at the end of the 1980s into their final adventures . . .

SEVEN

THE FIRST AND FINAL ADVENTURES: *THE FINAL FRONTIER* AND *THE UNDISCOVERED COUNTRY*

THE ENDING OF *The Voyage Home* in 1986 reset the board for the crew of the USS *Enterprise*. Cleared of their crimes in rescuing Spock, the only 'punishment' being Kirk's demotion to captain, they were reunited and given a brand-new, upgraded *Enterprise* to boot, warping off for more adventures together.

Leonard Nimoy, having directed the previous two pictures, stepped away for the fifth movie that would be immortalised as *The Final Frontier* in favour of William Shatner, who despite having never directed a movie previously triggered a clause in his contract to allow him to produce and direct the film, as well as star.

While Paramount sought a film with the kind of box-office successful lightness of touch *The Voyage Home* espoused, Shatner also had lofty and mythical themes in mind for his *Star Trek* showcase. He originally sought out fantasy and thriller author Eric Van Lustbader to write the screenplay, having been interested in his work: " . . .[he] had written some wonderful novels about an American in Japan and how out of place he felt. I thought, 'God, that'd be perfect for a Spock movie.' I went to see him and we walked the streets of New York pondering the plot of Star Trek. He was a fan. I thought, 'God, I've got a bestselling author ready to do a Star Trek.' And then they couldn't agree on the novel rights. So I lost him and my movie was going downhill before it even started."

Shatner's intentions to focus somewhat on Spock carried through into *The Final Frontier*, which sees the USS *Enterprise* respond to a distress call from Nimbus III, the 'Planet of Galactic Peace', only to find a mysterious Vulcan named Sybok (Laurence Luckinbill), also Spock's half-brother, has brainwashed an entire group of people into helping him steal a starship in order to travel through the Great Barrier at the centre of the galaxy, convinced that he will find God. Stealing the *Enterprise* and bewitching most of the crew, Kirk sets off on a quest that sends them truly where no man has gone before, only to find Sybok has been tricked by a false god, a dark entity, who needs the *Enterprise* to escape, leading to Kirk's immortal one-liner "what does God need with a starship?".

The biggest inspiration for the Sybok character came from Shatner's fascination with the televangelists of the 1980s, characters such as Tammy Faye Bakker, Robert Tilton, Jimmy Swaggart – Christian evangelist zealots who became incredibly rich and fruitful on cable television espousing the gospel with a powerful zeal, people Shatner considered to be transparent salesmen at best. He began crafting a combination of many of these figures into a character he first called Zar, and while he quickly started to develop scenes and ideas that became immortalised in *The Final Frontier*, Shatner readily admits his first treatment – which he called 'An Act of Love' – was markedly different from the finished product:

"In my rudimentary version, as in the film, Starfleet orders Kirk and company to rescue the hostages and apprehend Zar, but that's where the train leaves the tracks, because almost immediately, Spock surprises his shipmates by staying that he knew this renegade holy man back in Vulcan seminary. Surprise turns to shock when Spock makes it clear he feels this man is indeed so brilliant, and so advanced, that he could genuinely be the messiah."

It is indeed a startling change from the Spock who is more entranced by the reality of his half-brother in the film, the idea that he would be possessed by the belief in a heretofore largely unacknowledged Vulcan sense of religion. Zar, too, stood to be an intriguing creation, as Shatner's daughter Lisbeth recounts as "a relatively dark and violent character, who rode a unicorn throughout his planetary adventures. This unicorn was an extension of Zar's violent nature, to the point where my father had envisioned a battle scene where the unicorn had speared an unfortunate soldier, who lay writhing and screaming in agony upon the unicorn's horn while Zar rode on in triumph."

Shatner further details how Starfleet forces battle Zar on Nimbus III in Paradise City, but Spock – enraptured by Zar's magnetism – sells Kirk and his people out, leading to their capture. In a similar vein to the film, Zar uses mind-powers to show McCoy the death of his father and Spock's birth, but Kirk – despite being shown his son David and dredging up anger and guilt that will become more visible in the next movie – feigns acceptance the others have found for Zar's ideology.

Reaching the planet of 'God', Shatner describes that it "could have come from Dante's Inferno – a fiery, uninhabitable, completely barren wasteland. An awesome God-like image appears, surrounded by angels, and demands that the *Enterprise* transport him back toward more populated sections of the universe. As it escalates, 'God' begins showing his true colours, and his image begins to transform, ultimately becoming unmistakably satanic. The angels simultaneously change into hordes of gargoyles, the Furies of Hell."

The climax of *The Final Frontier* is perhaps where the greatest changes in Shatner's vision for the film lie. Though God, in the form of actor George Murdock, is presented initially in the form of the benevolent, Christian male God of the Old Testament, the finished article loses the deliberate Hell iconography and specific reference points to angelic or demonic beings that might have tied *The Final Frontier* more specifically into Judeo-Christian mythology.

In this treatment, Kirk, Spock and McCoy run from the God figure, the latter falling and breaking his leg as he and Spock are surrounded by the 'Furies', McCoy being carried away by the demonic creatures into 'Hell'. "Descending together into the river Styx, Spock and Kirk fight off their hideous attackers and save their injured friend, with Kirk carrying McCoy on his shoulders as they flee."

David Loughery, who would contribute to the script, said: "Paramount liked Bill's outline, but they thought it was a little too dark. After the success of Star Trek IV, they wanted to make sure that we retained as much humor and fun as possible, because they felt that was one of the reasons for the big success of that film. They wanted us to inject a spirit of fun and adventure into the story."

Loughery and Harve Bennett developed their own draft, which just in the manner Gene Roddenberry disliked his overt references to human religious constructs, Shatner had issues with their approach: "The script had almost nothing to do with anything that preceded it. Now, instead of searching for God, the crew of the *Enterprise* was being led by Sybok to a land of great peace and enlightenment, a land where no one ever grows old. In short, Harve and David had revisited Lost Horizon, with Shangri-La now hiding beneath the cheesy pseudonym of Sha-Ka-Ree."

Shatner famously named the planet after Sean Connery, who he desired for the role of Sybok, and which sadly never came to pass, but the concept by Bennett and Loughery removed the deliberate iconographic religious aspects of Shatner's idea and moved the 'final frontier' more in line with an Edenic lost land, in line with 19th century literature and myth that preceded it. There are parallels with *Insurrection*, a decade later, that would see a different *Enterprise* crew battle for their own version of regenerative 'paradise', albeit in a variable context.

The original idea of seeking God was reinstated, with Roddenberry suggesting he was a trickster alien (very much a throwback to numerous *Original Series* episodes), but Shatner as pre-production began became acutely aware that the budget for *The Final Frontier* was spiralling. "With erasers and red pencils flying at warp factor eight, I lost my band of angels, lost the resultant horde of gargoyles, and in their place we concocted a mere handful of monsters, made of solid stone, which would become animate upon God's 'command', rising up out of the planet's surface."

Shatner ended up having to make do with one 'rockman', which itself did not end up making the final cut, as producer Ralph Winter describes: "We never ran out of money. We ran out of good ideas and good execution. What we thought with the rock creature was just completely silly and we bagged it. It became obvious that it was just silly, and it would have been more expensive."

One additional concept that failed to materialise was a greater sense of dramatic impetus behind Captain Klaa, the ambitious young Klingon commander who follows the *Enterprise* into the Great Barrier to earn his spurs, as Loughery explains: "One of the things that was cut out of the movie is that the reason Captain Klaa was so passionate about chasing down Kirk was that he not only wanted that feather in his cap, but because there was still a bounty on Kirk's head. That was a thematic thing that would have joined into the next movie. Then they had this ridiculous reshoot that was done without me in which Kirk comes aboard the *Enterprise*. In the original script he walks in on the Bird of Prey, the chair turns, and here's Spock. They have this embrace – 'Please, Captain, not in front of the Klingons' – and there's a big laugh. But they went back and shot this bit where Klaa is forced to step out and say, 'I apologize.' Their thinking there, I guess, is that he had gone off on his own after Kirk. That was something that bugged me."

The Final Frontier ultimately went down in history as something of a crusade for Shatner, an excess of ego where the second-biggest star of *Star Trek* believed he could copy the success of his colleague without realising he lacked the acumen in a multitude of ways. The film opened to poor notices but was by no means a flop within a crowded summer blockbuster marketplace including *Indiana Jones and the Last Crusade* (the film Connery chose to make instead), Tim Burton's *Batman* and *Ghostbusters II* among others. It managed to keep the flame alive, even if it has never truly been critically reappraised.

The question is whether Shatner's original intentions, his combination of religious iconography with mythological scope, might have delivered a stronger and more powerful picture, as he has long attested. He certainly believed in this approach for *Star Trek*: "Having done a quick course with Joseph Campbell, I've realized the magic of *Star Trek* is to provide a mythology that this culture doesn't have. As he pointed out, mythology relates man to his environment and tries to explain some inexplicable dilemmas and the dichotomies that face us. Because of the construction of our culture, we don't have time for that because all of us are busy solving these problems with science. I think mythology is best served by an individual, along with his hearty band of brothers, as was done so many times, so well by the Greeks."

Perhaps in Paramount's own quest for a romp in line with *The Voyage Home*, the breezy *Star Trek* they believed would be a winner with audiences, they misjudged the possible impact of Shatner's vision. Maybe he was forced to compromise too heavily, and the heavier but more intriguing version of *The Final Frontier* remains unproduced.

Whatever the truth, his film was born out of an intention to retain the sense of adventure and combine it with a youthful exuberance, as *The Final Frontier* in the manner we know it was very nearly never made at all. A year or two earlier, plans were set in motion for an idea that would have revitalised the entire destination of *Star Trek* on cinema screens, an idea that has its foundations much further back than anyone might have anticipated.

*

Shortly before the premiere of the third season of *The Original Series* in 1968, Gene Roddenberry attended the 26th World Science Fiction Convention aka World Con and, outside of discussing the TV show, he talked about the possibility of a *Star Trek* movie: "Gene spoke to an adoring crowd, and he said that he was talking to Paramount about making a feature film version of *Star Trek* that would tell the story of how Kirk, Spock and McCoy met at the Academy."

This was the genesis of a foundational story in the history and lexicon of *Star Trek* that would not be told until long after Roddenberry's death, long after the end of the original crew's adventures on television or in cinema, and by writer/director J. J. Abrams in his big-budget 2009 re-conception of *Star Trek* as a blockbuster entity. In that film's first act, we would see the swaggering young Kirk, anxious younger Bones, and officious youthful Spock as they came together on Captain Christopher Pike's *Enterprise*, albeit in a different, alternate timeline and reality.

Despite how *The Motion Picture* came together, in the wake of *Phase II*, telling this origin story always appears to have been Roddenberry's instinctual concept for *Star Trek*'s evolution to the big screen. In November 1976, *Starlog* reported on the status of the intended film, which had missed a July start date: "When Paramount Pictures announced they would be producing a Star Trek movie for theatrical release – nearly a year and a half ago – Gene Roddenberry immediately began work on possible screenplay ideas. His first was one concerning the formative years of the characters – their days at the Space Academy, their first assignments, their coming together to man the starship *Enterprise*, and the construction and launching of the UFP Starfleet. This idea never made it to the submittal stage."

The concept never left Roddenberry, even as the big screen success of *Star Trek* was built on the ongoing adventures of the middle-aged crew. As we have seen, initial ideas around a sequel series to *Star Trek* in the mid-1980s concerned, according to Rick Berman, "making it a prequel to the original *Star Trek* and thoughts of it being set on a starship that was run by cadets in Starfleet Academy". Whether this would have involved Kirk, Spock and company is unknown, but Roddenberry and those around him saw strong potential in returning to the beginning, the origin story, of these beloved characters.

One such person was Harve Bennett, who as we have seen had great success in developing the cinematic franchise from *The Wrath of Khan* onwards, and was following the fourth movie, *The Voyage Home*, looking ahead to the fifth picture as *The Next Generation* was being developed by Roddenberry. His fellow producer Ralph Winter sparked the idea in him: "I had pitched Harve an idea, The Academy Years, at his daughter's bat mitzvah. I remember saying to him we shouldn't make *Star Trek* V. We should make *Star Trek* V, VI, and VII. We've just demonstrated with *Star Trek* III that we can do a young Spock. We should see how these guys meet for the first time. And build something that would be a reboot of this with younger characters to pick up with when these older characters don't want to do this as much. He loved the idea."

Paramount were also keen on this approach, aware that each negotiation for the *Star Trek* pictures had been a time-consuming balance of financial demands and egos, and Loughery was tapped to pen a draft. Winter continues: "It was set in Huntsville, Alabama. It was the training ground for Starfleet Academy. It was young Kirk and Bones and Spock, who was the first off-worlder to attend. The three of them become friends and they're all the extremes that were presented in the TV series. Spock is überlogical, Kirk is the ladies man and always out there, and Bones is trying to be a medical student." McCoy would also have been recovering from the euthanasia he conducted on his terminal father as a young man, seen in *The Final Frontier*, and seeking Starfleet as a path to give him meaning.

Loughery continues: "When I heard about the idea, I thought it was terrific. Not from the point of view of recasting, but from the point of view of storytelling, because I worked so closely with these characters on Star Trek V, that the idea of doing an origin story – where you show them as young cadets and kids – was tremendously exciting. What it was, was a real coming of age story."

Bennett added: "It's a great story finding out about this young cocky character on a farm who goes to flight school and meets up with the first alien that comes from Vulcan and how they meet the other characters. It would have been a gift for the fans on the twenty-fifth anniversary."

Initial ideas for the story would have been set across one year at Starfleet Academy, Loughery claimed: "Kirk and Spock are sort of put to the test and they begin as rivals and end up as friends and comrades who learn that they have to combine their talents for the first time to defeat a deadly enemy. In the final scene, where they say good-bye at graduation and go their separate ways, we're able to see the legends that these two boys are going to grow up to become." He described it as "*Top Gun*-style

Star Trek", suggesting a more youthful, high-octane approach at the end of the 1980s for a series that had coasted into middle age.

Plans for what became known as 'The Academy Years' began entering fruition in the wake of *The Final Frontier* as Bennett approached Paramount studio head Ned Tanen with the view of tackling the prequel as opposed to another potentially expensive adventure with the original, ageing cast. "Our model, or mock-up, was Santa Fe Trail, a Warner Bros. movie made in 1940 about John Brown's raid on Harpers Ferry. We gave Kirk a genuine love affair with an eighteen-year-old, her first. The girl dies heroically. Kirk, insane with grief, performs his first heroic act against all odds. And Spock saves the day in a struggle with racist overtones, getting the medal of honor. The prequel story ends over the grave of his lost love, giving some insight into why Kirk never falls in love again for the rest of the Star Trek series."

Almost certainly unintentionally, but the idea of a youthful Kirk's first love dying feels reminiscent of Peter Parker's Spider-Man losing Gwen Stacy, which took place in Marvel comics in 1973. The concept of a tragic origin story for the protagonist would have placed Kirk akin to many such superhero characters, and indeed provided something of a thematic through line later to the figure we see in *Generations*, in the Nexus, seeking to return to a former love. There was also a means considered to include both William Shatner and Leonard Nimoy in the finished product: "At the end of the film, while the older Kirk is contemplating her passing, Spock beams down and asks him if he's going into teaching or back to the ship. They have a sentimental exchange and Bill says, 'Beam me up.'"

In March 2006, *Ain't It Cool News* reviewed a proposed outline of the film titled 'Star Trek: The Academy Years', which would have opened in the wake of *The Voyage Home* with DeForest Kelley's Dr McCoy addressing Starfleet cadets who ask him about Starfleet legends Kirk and Spock. "What were they like?" "Were they friends?" are all questions asked. Bones laughs: "I never met two less likely candidates for friendship in my entire life," claiming they were as different as night and day, or "Vulcan and Iowa".

This leads to the story flashing back to Iowa, where a young Kirk is scolded by his brother George Samuel 'Sam' Kirk (as seen both in *The Original Series* episode 'Operation: Annihilate' and across the first season of *Strange New Worlds* in multiple episodes) for flying a 'futuristic crop duster' recklessly, in strong shades of the opening to Abrams' 2009 film where young Kirk steals his step-father's vintage car to the strains of the Beastie

Boys. Ralph Winter even has suggested that Abrams' film took a cue from the script that Paramount had been sitting on for almost two decades with these similarities: "In the opening scene of the screenplay we developed were cornfields and a mailbox that is flapping back and forth in the wind and it says, 'Kirk' on the mailbox. It sits on that for a moment, and then you hear something in the distance, and coming right at camera is a crop duster. A futuristic crop duster. And this young kid is at the wheel of it trying to fly it like a fighter jet. And he crashes it into the farm and burns it down. That's the opening of the *Star Trek* screenplay."

As Kirk is accepted into Starfleet Academy, we find a young Spock on Vulcan being dissuaded from joining by Shardik, a fellow Vulcan, who claims he would be singled out thanks to his Vulcan lineage. Kirk gets to San Francisco, the home of Starfleet and the academy, and meets Cassandra Hightower, who becomes his love interest during the film; meets Kalibar, a fellow cadet he gets into a fight with (reminiscent of the bar fight Kirk gets into in Abrams' film with 'Cupcake' while trying to charm Uhura); and meets his new roommate, McCoy, who he christens 'Bones' immediately. He also meets Montgomery 'Scotty' Scott, an engineer who worked with Kirk's father, a pilot also named George, presumed dead after the *Bonaventure*, his test ship, vanished during an experimental warp drive test.

The outline suggests that Kalibar is not just a cadet but next in line to the throne on his homeworld, his species still practising slavery, with racism still rife across the Federation world. When Spock does join the academy, Kalibar and his crew beat him, a situation Kirk rescues him from (inverted in Abrams' film as Spock beats the Vulcan bullies who try to beat him for being half human). Kalibar is expelled from the Academy as he learns his father has been killed in a coup related to a proclamation by Kodaris, an ambassador on his world, seeking to ban slavery from their world.

At the Academy, Kirk and Spock get in trouble as the latter helps the former cheat an exam through a mind meld, while Bones and Cassandra are assigned to an old starship which the outline describes as "a war horse, battered and patched. Its design may not be familiar, but its name is: U.S.S. *Enterprise*". This suggests the *Enterprise* here would not have been Christopher Pike's command, as seen in 'The Cage' or Abrams' alternate continuity, but rather an older model, perhaps even Robert April's original ship, or a variation on it.

The mission is to return Kodaris, ambassador to the Federation, to his world, but Kalibar attacks the *Enterprise*, threatening to destroy it unless Kodaris is handed over. Kirk, Spock and McCoy steal the *Bonaventure II*, a prototype warp ship similar to the one Kirk's father piloted, from a Starfleet Museum and race to save the *Enterprise* once they hear of the attack, but they find the crew in dire straits. They take command, with the help of Bones, Cassandra and an assigned Christine Chapel, rigging the *Enterprise*, and taking on Kalibar and his ship, defeating him. They all return to the Academy, and some go their separate ways, for now.

In an epilogue scene, back in the present day, McCoy finishes his tale and his communicator beeps, Scotty asking if he's ready to beam aboard the *Enterprise*. McCoy takes a last look around as he excuses the cadets, says "beam me up, Scotty" and beams away as the film ends. This wraparound storyline echoes the idea of bringing elder Kirk and Spock into the tale, though it lacks something of the poignancy with McCoy narrating rather than the two key players of the film.

Bennett decades later commented on the intended film, which by this point had changed McCoy to Kirk and Spock: "It was the best script of all and it never got produced. It was at the end of my run. Ned Tanen, who was Paramount's head of production, had green lighted it before he left. We even had location scouts and sent feelers out for the cast. I had an eye on John Cusack for Spock, which would have been great. Ethan Hawke could have been Kirk. There were so many possibilities. But basically it was a love story and it was a story of cadets, teenagers. And, in order to get Shatner and Nimoy in, we had a wraparound in which Kirk comes back to address the academy and the story spins off of his memory. At the end, Kirk and Spock are reunited and they beam back up to *Enterprise*, which would have left a new series potential, the academy, and a potential other story with the original Trek cast. All the possibilities were open, the script was beautiful, and the love story was haunting, but it didn't happen."

Part of the reason the idea faltered was, arguably, Roddenberry himself, who was non-plussed with the idea, despite spending years talking up the possibility of a prequel origin tale: "I didn't like it. Who was going to cast the new Kirk and Spock? I could have done so if I thought it was a good idea, but it didn't fit in with the rest of Trek. It wasn't good. Some of it was like *Police Academy*. You could hardly do this without the magic of a group of characters tailored for *Star Trek*, which this was not."

The idea of a prequel story equally caused friction with the original cast members who felt akin to being put out to pasture, with Walter Koenig suggesting had it been successful, the entire original crew would likely have never appeared again. Fans began to get wind, perhaps through the negativity espoused by people close to the project who were dubious about its viability, that it would have been a spoof of the show and films they held so dear, which had never been the intention.

"The Academy Years may have looked like a mistake but look at the franchise as a whole. We had a successful series of feature films, then a new television series, and with the [original] film series ending, it made sense to start a new series of films. You could have opened a whole new frontier. When *Star Trek: The Next Generation* came out, the people said, 'This will never work, how can we have a new captain? It will never equal Kirk and Spock.' But they achieved their own success. It could have been the same with a prequel cast."

Bennett adds: "The Academy Years, like *Star Trek IV*, would have reached beyond the cult. It would have interested people who had never seen a *Star Trek* film which did not exclude the regulars, but it simply said, "If you don't understand what it's all about, come see how it all began."

There is an argument to suggest Bennett might be right, given how Abrams' film, which though not exclusively about the Academy experience certainly features that period heavily at the beginning and is without doubt the Kirk and Spock origin story (albeit one in a different timeline) that Bennett, Loughery and Winter sought to produce, was the second-highest grossing *Star Trek* movie of all time (second only to sequel *Into Darkness*) and revitalised the franchise, kickstarting the third age of the series on television following a new successful run of movies, at a point people genuinely believed *Star Trek* might be dead and buried.

Ultimately, Paramount CEO Frank Mancuso turned the project down upon realising that most of the beloved elder cast and crew would not be involved in the film, and after Bennett turned down an offer to make an academy movie after producing a sixth picture with the *Original Series* cast, though Bennett remained keen to make the film even years after *Star Trek VI: The Undiscovered Country* had been released and *The Next Generation* crew had graduated up to feature films. In 2004, Bennett approached Paramount chairman Sherry Lansing, convinced following *Nemesis* – the last *Next Generation* movie – that the time was right to make 'The Academy Years', claiming: "We would have made it, but then she said the television department had asked her not to do it, because *Enterprise* was being produced and they thought that should be the prequel. Therefore, we did not do that."

Five years later, Abrams' film went where no academy film pitch had gone before, successfully bringing the concept to the screen, and in the early 1990s the *Star Trek* franchise pivoted back to the original crew. Rather than depicting their first adventure, however, *The Undiscovered Country* would end up being their final voyage.

*

The 20th anniversary of *Star Trek* had passed with a movie, *The Voyage Home*, and the promise of a new television series to debut a year later, but as *Star Trek* approached a quarter of a century old in 1991, everybody involved knew – aside from the success of the established *Next Generation* – that it needed to be celebrated in style.

There was, however, no specific idea. No script. No producer, given Harve Bennett walked away after *The Final Frontier* and failing to mount 'The Academy Years'. And no director. Only one element seemed, among everyone involved and Paramount, to be set in stone: this would be the swansong of the ageing *Original Series* crew.

Embers of previous approaches to a sixth film concerning a passing of the torch to youth nonetheless lingered. Walter Koenig devised his own treatment for a movie subtitled 'In Flanders Fields', based on the famous First World War poem by John McCrae, which sees the Romulans unexpectedly join the Federation thanks to losing too many of their young officers in combat, triggering war with the Klingon Empire. As part of wartime, all Starfleet officers are given fitness tests, but of the *Enterprise* crew, only Spock passes. The rest are put out to sunder and the *Enterprise* is handed to a younger crew; however, when she goes missing, Kirk hauls the rest of his crew out of mothballs to find her, and a kidnapped Spock who was commanding the young crew, abducted by an alien race who drain youthful members of races for their own survival, and who had been killing the young Romulan officers that dragged them into the situation to begin with.

Koenig describes the attempt to outwit creatures he described as "not stunt guys in suits, not blue-skinned furries with horns, but truly repulsive sewer-dwelling worms of slime and putrefaction . . . things that the monsters in Aliens evolved from".

Depicting such creatures would have seen a sixth *Star Trek* film operating in line with CGI breakthroughs of the 1990s such as *Terminator 2: Judgment Day* and *Jurassic Park*, no doubt fuelling the kind of unlikely budget that also thwarted Shatner's rock monsters in *The Final Frontier*. The crew race against time to save the *Enterprise* and Spock, but at great personal cost. Koenig admits he devised the story with a sense of finality: "I ended up submitting it on paper. I had three of the characters dying in the story. I thought we were all done. Certainly after *Star Trek I*, I thought we were done."

Indeed, only Spock and McCoy survive the rather bleak ending to 'In Flanders Fields', the rest falling on the battlefield trying to save the youthful, captured crew against the alien creatures, with Kirk dying as he deals the final blow to the last surviving alien villain. Bones and Spock would have walked among the dead, as Koenig's tale evokes the bodies of no-man's-land in the Great War, flashing back as he does to moments shared with his fallen comrades (likely taken from the *Original Series*). Spock reaches Kirk and falls to his knees in grief. The treatment describes: "In this loneliest, most desolate of moments, Spock [permits] himself the one expression of friendship that he has never before admitted to: his need for Leonard McCoy. Spock leans against the doctor for support, and the two men – adversaries in a thousand arguments over the years – walk off together."

Perhaps due to how sombre a conclusion to the story of these legendary characters Koenig's idea would have been, his concept was never developed further. Mancuso and Paramount instead, concerned about the approach Shatner had taken on *The Final Frontier*, decided the time had come to start passing the torch to the next generation. Eventual co-writer of an early draft, Mark Rosenthal, claims this was the principal concept as the film was developed: "Our initial response was that we should do something where *The Next Generation* has to come back in time and work with the classic cast. The poster would be Patrick Stewart, William Shatner, Leonard Nimoy, and Brent Spiner. That would have easily been a hundred-million-dollar film. Feelers were put out on that and there were some very strong negative responses. The TV department was totally against it. The TV series was doing extremely well, and everyone was afraid that the old guys' egos would get involved and they would say that it was a sign of a lack of confidence that they could carry the film. So that was the end of that."

The man deemed necessary to save the project was the other main star of the series who had previously shepherded two successful predecessors in the run: Leonard Nimoy. He sought out Nicholas Meyer, who had contributed to the script for *The Voyage Home*, asking him to write and direct, approaching him with the core concept that underpinned the film.

The Undiscovered Country begins with the explosion of Praxis, a Klingon moon; a Chernobyl-esque moment for their species who, aware they are a dying race economically and structurally, reach out to the Federation to make peace, which Spock helps engineer alongside forward thinking Chancellor Gorkon. Kirk is full of hate toward them for the death of his son and when Gorkon is assassinated on the *Enterprise* as it transports him to the peace accords, Kirk and Bones are arrested and sentenced to hard labour on a prison planet, Rura Penthe. As Spock and the *Enterprise* crew work to expose a conspiracy to sabotage peace that goes deep into Starfleet, Kirk tries to survive, escape and lead his crew to prevent the collapse of peace and beginning of a galactic war.

"At one point we had a discussion about using Chernobyl, and that really opened the floodgates. Then we began to look at specific events. Everyone was paranoid that someone is going to try and sabotage the peace between the Soviet Union and the United States. Why not have the same thing occur between the Klingons and the Federation? It all kind of led to the idea of assassination. What if Gorbachev was assassinated and the blame fell on Kirk? That was really the key."

Rosenthal and his co-writer Lawrence Konner worked with Nimoy on the concept, who took it to Meyer, and he subsequently decided to revise the screenplay and work on the idea himself. Rosenthal claims there was various ideas and concepts he intended for the movie that fell by the wayside once his draft was revised: "I very much wanted to have Kirk fall in love with Saavik, a Vulcan, so that they would produce a people who would be like Spock, who himself had a human mother and a Vulcan father. I thought it would be a wonderful way to bring the characters and their relationships to a close. Obviously they changed that to Spock falling in love. Frankly, I don't feel it's as satisfying."

Rosenthal refers to Spock's relationship with Valeris, his Vulcan protege played by Kim Cattrall, who is ultimately revealed to be part of the conspiracy to sabotage the peace process. The intention was for the role of Spock's protege to be filled by Saavik, first portrayed by Kirstie Alley in *The Wrath of Khan* and later Robin Curtis in *The Search for Spock* and *The Voyage Home*. It would have been curious to see if the age gap between Shatner and Curtis could have been surmounted to convince audiences of a Kirk/Saavik romance, which might have been easier to swallow during *The Wrath of Khan*, although it seems Curtis wouldn't have been the target here.

As Denny Martin Flinn claimed: "There was a desire to get Kirstie Alley to play Saavik. When that looked like it was going to be impractical, we couldn't stand around waiting for a decision – maybe the money was too much – for whatever reason. We reached a point where Kirstie Alley could not be counted on to do the film and we said, let's forget it. Let's create another character, which led to some nice changes."

The writer discussed more aspects of his and Konner's original draft that fell by the wayside: "Instead of Kirk just going to the Klingons, he was arrested by Sulu and turned over to them, which was a very dramatic moment for Sulu. We also wanted to do this thing where while he was in prison, some of the characters they had met over the twenty-five years would be there, which we felt really would have tied up the entire series."

The last point certainly intrigues. Quite who Kirk and Bones might have encountered on Rura Penthe is tantalising. An older, recast Harry Mudd, perhaps? There are numerous possibilities. Rosenthal continues: "We also discussed the fact that the Klingons are this aggressive race. Originally, they supposedly had this reptilian background. In regards to this whole thing about Kirk and his search to uncover the conspiracy behind the assassination, we come upon more primitive Klingon tribes who had an almost religious representation for the Klingons. They would be much more primitive and violent. We were going to do a whole thing on the anthropology of the Klingons, but all of that was dropped because it would have been too expensive."

Such an idea would also have added an additional layer of complication as to the portrayal of Klingons between *The Original Series* and *The Next Generation* that *Star Trek* would eventually even devote narrative screen-time to try and explain in-universe. The writer adds: "What we did was we had a literary reference from a wonderful poem called 'The Idle King', and it was about Ulysses and the end of his life, where he and his crew are very old and they decide to go off on one last voyage, and it was very clearly a voyage to death. You know, old men rowing the boat again. So we had this bit where Kirk mentions it to Spock. Then Kirk is turned over to Sulu who turns him over to the Klingons, only it turns out that the president of the Federation arranged it all secretly so Kirk let himself get arrested. Ours had a little more twists and turns."

Though Meyer retains the Federation president as a character, the Rosenthal/Konner draft suggests more devious machinations from the highest brass in the Federation than Meyer chooses to depict on screen. "We had this thing where Kirk at the beginning is talking to Spock about the Trojan horse, and the way they get him out is they let the Klingons capture the *Enterprise*, which they seem to have abandoned. But they've stowed away, like Ulysses and the Trojan horse, and that's how they free Kirk. So we had different literary references. I think that ours was a lot more textured."

Meyer penned a draft with his friend Denny Martin Flinn that included various dropped ideas and plot points. We would have seen the entire *Original Series* crew drafted, one by one, from their personal lives of choice, for a final mission on the *Enterprise*. We would see Spock playing the role of Polonius in a production of *Hamlet* – further exemplifying the strong Shakespearian themes and references core to the final film. Bones would be seen drunk at a medical dinner for the elite. Scotty would be teaching engineering at Starfleet Academy as we see the Klingon *Bird of Prey* from *The Voyage Home* pulled out of San Francisco Bay – we can assume something like this happened given we spy the vessel during the third season of *Picard* in a Starfleet fleet museum. Chekov plays chess at a club, Uhura hosts a call-in radio show and Kirk is now married and settled with, yes, Carol Marcus, the mother of his late son, who would once again have been portrayed by Bibi Besch. "This sailor is in port for good," he promises her, before being dragged away as Carol shouts "but he's retired . . . you're retired!" Kirk would then travel to collect the rest of his compatriots before they all headed for Starfleet Command and the briefing sequence.

It was, by all accounts, one of the sequences Meyer was desperate not to lose. Flinn explains: "What I had done originally was to give every one of the seven principal actors an entrance. The scenes demonstrated who those people were and what they did when they weren't on the *Enterprise*. They were either retired or rotated to R and R, and it added some humanity and humor to the characters. I called it the roundup. It would have been a very effective sequence and we held on to it until the very last minute, but Paramount was saying, 'We're going to discontinue preproduction unless you cut another million dollars out of the budget.' We just had to drop fifteen pages. Maybe what I'm thinking of would have been rambling and slow and dropped in editing anyway, but there was a kind of The Over-the-Hill Gang Rides Again attitude."

In quite a break from his promotion to captain of the USS *Excelsior*, we would see Sulu driving a cab in an overcrowded futuristic metropolis, although another draft names him as the character – the captain – who pulls the characters back together into service. This serves as a good point to briefly discuss the long-held lobbying of George Takei for Paramount to consider a 'Captain Sulu' television series in the wake of *The Undiscovered Country*, where he impresses as commander of the slick *Excelsior*.

Takei has talked about how the International Federation of Trekkers supported the notion: "Back in the 1990s, Russ Haslage contacted me about a campaign to launch a new *Star Trek* series called *Excelsior*, which would have been based on the adventures of the U.S.S. *Excelsior* and Captain Sulu. And of course I have a deep and profound love and interest in Captain Sulu. And I must say, Russ and IFT mounted a very impressive campaign. It was a substantial idea. There was a huge following for it. And after all, *Star Trek VI* seemed to have opened the door for an *Excelsior* television series. But for whatever reason, Paramount didn't pick up the idea. So despite that massive and heroic effort that was launched by all of the people, and I was absolutely convinced that the audience was there based on the reception of *Star Trek VI*, the idea didn't go through. I was absolutely baffled."

Haslage, of the IFT, truly began lobbying for the idea at the beginning of the 2000s as *Voyager* was ending, and merchandising sales alongside general interest in the franchise was beginning to slip away. The '*Excelsior* Campaign' boasted, at the time, over a thousand fans, with more becoming interested. "There are 80 missing years in the stories of *Star Trek*. We've gone from the original crew into the next century to see its recent incarnations. There are a lot of missions and a lot of adventures in those 80 years."

Some of this was covered non-canonically in tie-in books such as *The Lost Years: The Sundered*, and *Star Trek Excelsior: Forged in Fire*, not to mention a series of audiobooks voiced by Takei in the mid-1990s called the 'Captain Sulu Adventures'. He reprised the role in *Voyager* episode 'Flashback' (more on which later) and finally in 1997 in the *Starfleet Academy* video game, both as Captain Sulu, but beyond these efforts a TV adventure for the iconic character has never materialised.

Takei perhaps had the last laugh here in 2012 when he announced on social media a startling press release: "Friends, I'm thrilled to share this news with you today. As announced at Emerald City Comicon, where I'm appearing this weekend, Paramount Pictures has greenlit a new *Star Trek* Movie entitled *Excelsior* in which I will play the captain. This announcement is part of Paramount Studio's 100th-year anniversary campaign. The studio has acknowledged the fan enthusiasm for this concept ever since I appeared in command of the vessel in *The Undiscovered Country*." J.J. Abrams will direct, with Robert Orci again writing the screenplay. My co-star in Allegiance, Paulo Montalban, has been cast opposite me to play the mercurial 'Agha,' the grandson of Khan (played by Ricardo Montalban in the Second *Star Trek* Movie). Also featured are Gilbert Gottfried (playing a wily Ferengi First Officer) and Lisa Lampanelli (as a Bajoran security officer). More to come on this breaking story soon. Thanks again for the years of support, and I'll see you on the Bridge of *Excelsior*."

There was just one problem with this: the date was 1 April. As Takei himself might quip, oh my!

*

Though he maintained a role as 'Executive Consultant' on the *Star Trek* movies and had stepped back to let Michael Piller run *The Next Generation*, Gene Roddenberry by the early 1990s was in far from rude health.

Having suffered a stroke in 1989 that facilitated the use of a wheelchair, Roddenberry's health went into rapid decline, especially following a second stroke in October of 1991. As a result, his contributions to *The Undiscovered Country* as it was being written in 1990 and filmed in 1991, for release at the end of the year, were limited, though Nimoy attests that he regularly visited and updated him, seeking his counsel through production. Roddenberry was, however, deeply unhappy with aspects of Meyer's script, as Nimoy explains: "He [Roddenberry] said, 'I don't feel good about *Enterprise* crew talking that way.' We pointed out these are bad people who are racists and who turn out to be assassins. 'I'm just uncomfortable with a couple of guys walking around in Federation uniforms talking that way about another race.' And I understood it. It's a danger. By and large, he was quite taken with the idea of a Klingon détente. It was his idea to put a Klingon in the Federation on *The Next Generation* and this was the beginning of that link."

Producer Ralph Winter explains: "I screened the movie *Star Trek* VI for Gene Roddenberry about a week or two before he died. He's a character. He had a great idea and he executed the great idea, but he couldn't follow through and he was not a people person. He was cantankerous and he had some kind of weird deal that if he found a problem with any of the scripts, they had to pay him to fix it. So he always had problems. He had to accept it. If he didn't, they had to pay him to fix it and change it. And so he was always employed. His wife was down in the cutting room taking short ends of film prints and cutting them up and selling them for a dollar apiece. It was an odd group. But he loved the last movie. He watched it in a wheelchair covered with a blanket. He was cold and he was clearly on his way out. He had a great idea and he sponsored a great franchise."

The Undiscovered Country was screened for Roddenberry just two days before his death, featuring a climactic moment as the *Enterprise* heads off into the second star to the right, as the signatures of the cast appear on screen from lowest billed to Shatner at the top. The intention was originally slightly different, as Flinn explains: "My original script read that the signatures were James T. Kirk, Mr Spock, etc. What we were doing was offering them a chance to sign the final log. I thought that would be rather touching, especially since it was the last film [with the original cast]."

The Undiscovered Country was released in December 1991 to critical acclaim and a decent commercial box office. It arrived just weeks before the dissolution of the Soviet Union and the end of the Cold War the film had very distinctly chosen to parallel, in a moment of narrative symmetry. Roddenberry, sadly, did not live long enough to witness the success of the film. He passed away on 24 October 1991, following the second stroke and having seen a cut of the film in his ailing state, to which he reputedly gave his approval, even if numerous issues he had remained in the film.

The film was dedicated to his memory.

Star Trek was now indeed sailing into less a final but certainly a new frontier. *The Original Series* cast would never grace the screen together again and, for the very first time, the franchise was about to enter a world without the shadow of a man known as 'the Great Bird of the Galaxy', his vision, his beliefs and, in many cases, his rules for what he believed *Star Trek* would be.

The fringes of that vision would be tested by what came next, not just the first spin-off series from *The Next Generation*, but the first *Star Trek* show to break, in so many ways, from twenty-five years of tradition . . .

EIGHT

THE RIFLEMAN IN SPACE: *DEEP SPACE NINE*

FOLLOWING THE SUCCESS of *The Next Generation*, a possibility was raised that would see *Star Trek* truly going where the franchise had never gone before – producing a second sequel series that would air simultaneously with the adventures of the *Enterprise*.

Rick Berman and Michael Piller, now the experienced hands running the universe for Paramount after the passing of Gene Roddenberry, were given the challenge in developing what would launch in January 1993 as *Star Trek: Deep Space Nine*. Roddenberry did not live long enough to see the project come to fruition, though he was aware of the possibility, as Berman states: "I went to Gene and mentioned we were thinking about a spin-off, and he said, 'Great,' and that we should talk about it some time. Unfortunately we never did, because he was not well then and he got worse and worse."

Some, such as Deanna Troi actor Marina Sirtis, suggest Roddenberry would have rejected the very concept of *Deep Space Nine* as not holding to the principles of *Star Trek* that he considered sacrosanct, and led to the infamous 'box' discussed in earlier chapters that writers found themselves bound to. Others such as Susan Sackett and Gene's son Rod Roddenberry back up this assertion, while Berman and Piller long rejected it. Whatever the case may be, it was the new Paramount Pictures president Brandon Tartikoff who approached Berman about seeking to evolve *Star Trek* beyond just a singular 24th-century setting, as Berman explains: "I went up to his office and he said to me, 'I want to do a new series, I want you to do it, and I want it to start next year.' What I learned later is this was a traditional fashion of Tartikoff's, and he said, 'My idea is *The Rifleman* in space . . . a father and son out in space.' He didn't know anything about *Star Trek*. So, I got together with Michael Piller and we started thinking about a father and a son in space. That was the beginning of *Deep Space Nine*."

The Rifleman aired on ABC between 1958 and 1963 and starred Chuck Connors and Johnny Crawford as Lucas McCain and his son Mark in the fictional town of North Fork in New Mexico, circa the 1880s. One of the first primetime American television series to depict a single parent raising a child, the show focused on the residents of North Fork with the McCains a core centre, around which Western storylines would flow.

David Weddle, a writer on later seasons of the show, saw the connective tissue between both shows: "This genre does have a lot in common with westerns. I didn't realize it when we first started on *Deep Space Nine*, but I came to realize it because I brought up westerns all the time in the writing room as analogies for whatever we were working on. And the fact is that they are both allegorical forms of storytelling. The American westerns, they exist in a sort of imagined world. It's not exactly what the West is like. They're mythic storytelling, and it's very much like outer space, because you have people going across an uncharted wasteland where there is no rule of law, no civilization, and they have to face existential choices about what choice am I going to make here for myself? What am I going to decide is right or wrong? And there's no authority to tell me or guide the way. They're stripped-down morality tales."

Piller acknowledges how, based on Tartikoff's edict, this factored into his and Berman's conceptualisation of the show: "We pretty much knew that there were only three kinds of series that you could do in space. One was going to be on a ship, one was on a space station, and one was on a planet's surface. We talked about the planet's surface for a while, doing a Wild West town, but we realized that we were going to wind up having to shoot on location up in the mountains above Hollywood and thought that was untenable. We basically turned our attention to the space station idea. So then it became, where do you put the space station?"

Berman and Piller assembled a team of writers, including a returning Ira Steven Behr after his stint on *The Next Generation*'s third season and experienced hands such as Peter Allan Fields, who set about brainstorming concepts across the summer of 1992 after Berman and Piller had devised the show Bible and the 'premise pilot' that forged itself into the two-hour opener, 'Emissary', in the same format of 'Encounter at Farpoint' six years earlier.

Their concept built naturally out of the world *The Next Generation* had constructed, with the very first moments connecting to the iconic 'The Best of Both Worlds' and the character of Commander Benjamin Sisko (Avery Brooks), a father and widower, his wife Jennifer killed in the Battle of Wolf 359 against the Borg, who following the Cardassian withdrawal from occupation of the planet Bajor, is sent to run a new Federation peacekeeping outpost in the area, a sundered Cardassian space station called Terok Nor re-designated as 'Deep Space Nine'. As he finds opprobrium from established figures such as Bajoran officer Major Kira Nerys (Nana Visitor) and security chief Odo (René Auberjonois), and reverence from a Bajoran religious group, his new Starfleet science team end up discovering a 'wormhole' to the distant Gamma Quadrant part of the galaxy, instantly making the station one of the key outposts for the entire Federation.

"Mike and I knew that if we were ever going to do another *Star Trek* show, it would have to take place somewhere where adventure could come to us as opposed to us going to adventure. It was very important to us that *Deep Space Nine* had to be different, because it was going to be on the air for three years along with *Next Generation*, so we really couldn't plunk seven people on another spaceship and have it plopping around the galaxy. It just didn't seem right."

It was a far richer and complex set-up than the adventures of the *Enterprise*, with a whole tapestry of characters, backstories and conflicts that immediately became apparent during 'Emissary', as Starfleet officers clashed with Bajoran and Cardassian officials amidst a deeply political and emotional set of circumstances, which made writing for the show to come difficult as aspects of the pilot continued to morph and evolve as Berman and Piller constructed the scenario, which Fields explains: "At that stage in the season, the writers are the ones who do shape it. The executive producers are the ones who have an idea about what the characters should be like, and the idea can change from episode to episode. In the beginning, though, I was the only one there. Michael and Rick were somewhere over in the other building writing the pilot, and I was sitting there, wondering what I was supposed to do. I remember saying, 'Geez, we now boldly sit where no one has sat before.'"

An early treatment, dated April 1992, was titled 'The Ninth Orb', and had many of the constituent elements that would be seen in 'Emissary'. The plot concerned a black-market presence aboard DS9 controlled by Rulod, an alien of an unspecified race, which Sisko vows to Bajoran religious leader Kai Opaka he will stamp out. Ferengi barkeep and part-time crook Quark points him toward Rulod and Sisko threatens to arrest him, kicking his chair out and lifting him by the collar when he is obstinate. Scenes also concern an asteroid base of Rulod's in the Denorios Belt, and Rulod makes the sinister Cardassian ex-commander of Terok Nor, Gul Dukat, aware of the wormhole when it is discovered. One or two characters had different names – Dr Julian Bashir was here Dr Julian Amoros, of Hispanic heritage. Principally, the draft contained one major regular character who was removed before the series aired – Ro Laren, mentioned in the last chapter as a recurring *Next Generation* character, and the first Bajoran seen on *Star Trek*, who was designed for the role later immortalised by Kira – Sisko's first officer. She meets Sisko before he has a fateful confrontation with a visiting Jean-Luc Picard, who he finds difficult to meet given his Borg alter-ego Locutus was responsible for the death of his wife.

The aforementioned *Deep Space Nine* Bible describes the intention behind Ro's character on the show: "Established on ST:TNG. She is properly addressed as Lieutenant Ro since Bajorans put their family names first. (Note: She will receive a promotion from Ensign to Lieutenant on an episode of ST:TNG before this series begins.) As a Bajoran, Ro cares passionately about her people's independence. That's why she volunteered for duty on the space station. Sisko originally refused to accept her transfer . . . He didn't want anything to do with someone with her undistinguished service record and reputation. But during the first episode, she proves her value to him and becomes his first officer."

As Piller describes, Ro's presence simply wasn't meant to be: "Michelle Forbes is a wonderful actress, and her character of Ensign Ro created the entire canvas for this new series. It had always been assumed that she would be one of the people spun off and moved over to DS9, but she wanted to be a feature actress."

Other Bible entries concerning different regulars suggest how Ro might have related to other established characters, such as Jadzia Dax: "Ro, who forms a very close relationship with Dax, often tells her to loosen up. Dax admires Ro for her youthful energy, her purpose and her drive and becomes something of a mentor to her." Ro would have been an adversary of Quark, and in regard to Odo, she "finds Odo's negative attitude to authority delightful and they have a Bajoran fellowship". These are all traits largely ported over into Kira once she is created, although who knows whether Ro and Odo might have enjoyed a friendship that blossomed into romance, as we saw happen between he and Kira.

Perhaps in another life . . .

"I found there was a great deal more conflict in having the Bajoran not be Starfleet. Immediately you have different priorities and agendas, and the two people immediately have a conflict with each other the moment they step onto the station. The one between Sisko and Ro would have been a much different one, because ultimately she's Starfleet and has to do what the boss says. Kira Nerys could do things that are not appropriate Starfleet behavior."

Though neither Ro, nor indeed Rulod, would survive future drafts of 'Emissary', nor would an overly Western-inspired tone to a script that suggested the core of Sisko's endeavours would be as a sheriff rooting out organised crime. A second draft from Piller focused more heavily on allegory linked to a very recent 1992 event that had shocked American society, as Berman explains: "It was a rewrite that brought into it the ideas that we had discussed all along that had to do with the 1992 Los Angeles riots; the idea of people rebuilding and of people living in an area that had been damaged and had been violated. And the spirit that goes into the rebuilding of it. It was a good change, but not a major change."

The eventual pilot would, rather, highlight Sisko's difference to Picard as a competent, honourable but gruff reluctant hero, a man who slowly begins to learn over the course of the story that he might have a connection to Bajor, to its people, and the newly discovered wormhole that he never could have imagined. The building blocks to a series that would not only be wildly different to *The Next Generation* in the long run, but also every other *Star Trek* series before or since, had been sown.

Now came the challenge of writing *Deep Space Nine*, sailing into territory the franchise has never previously ventured.

*

"I would like to take everyone out who has tried to write a story, written a story, got hired to write a story and got cut off on a story and buy them dinner. It's like, into the valley of death rode the six hundred. These people took a wing and a prayer, some of them went off before we cast the show, while the sets were being built, and all they had to read was this pilot with all these new characters and a new environment that none of them knew. It's tough to hit a home run under those circumstances as a writer. I would not like to have tried it."

Ira Steven Behr certainly understood this plight, especially for those pitching stories for *Deep Space Nine*, many of which would be turned away as the series shifted into the shape it became known for. Often writers would pitch ideas concerning Klingon or Cardassian conflicts, many of which were being woven by the core writing staff – Behr, Fields (in the earlier seasons), Robert Hewitt Wolfe, René Echevarria and Ronald D. Moore, to name a few. Some were writers who would go on to pen episodes at later dates, or had written for *The Next Generation* – Lisa Klink, David Weddle and Bradley Thompson, for example.

Some would combine forces – such as 'Yesterday's *Enterprise*' writer Eric Stillwell, novelist David R. George III, and Quark actor Armin Shimerman, as the latter discussed: "David George, partnered with Eric Stilwell, asked if I would join them to pitch episode ideas for *Deep Space Nine*. We worked for several months honing our plot points and eventually had our shot with writer/producer René Echevarria. Unfortunately, No sale." They did come close, however, with a story that would have tackled a powerful topic: "The episode would have focused around inherent racial prejudice, not just for Ferengis but for other entities [and/or species] as well . . . I just wanted to explore that theme."

Though Shimerman would never get to head down such a road for the Ferengi, and perhaps his character Quark, he did team up with George to develop a *Deep Space Nine* non-canonical tie-in novel based on these ideas, called 'The 34th Rule', released in January 1999. The story saw Quark amid an interstellar incident between the Ferengi Alliance and the Bajoran government, after the financial leader of the former, the Grand Nagus, refuses to sell a lost Orb of the Prophets to the Bajorans, which leads the Ferengi to be banned from the sector, Quark to lose his bar on the station, and his freedom. Though Ferengi stories became increasingly comic in nature, Shimerman aspired for the tale to have connections to a dark period of the Second World War, a conflict *Deep Space Nine* was broadly obsessed by: "Of course I wanted to tell a Ferengi story. I believe it was Eric [Stillwell] who first ventured the idea of an episode based on

The crew of *Star Trek: The Original Series*. Alamy

The animated version of Captain Robert April, the original *Star Trek* captain, from *The Animated Series*.

Robert Lansing as Gary Seven, the intended star of Gene Roddenberry's spin-off, *Assignment: Earth*.

Concept painting by Ralph McQuarrie of a prospective design for the USS *Enterprise* for the unproduced *Star Trek: Planet of the Titans* feature film. *The Art of Ralph McQuarrie*

First draft image of the script for *Phase II*'s intended premiere, 'In Thy Image', by Harold Livingston, when it was still known as *Star Trek II*.

Xon intended for *Phase II*.

Sketch art for a young James T. Kirk and Spock from the abandoned *Star Trek: The First Adventure*, in the late 1980s.

The *U.S.S. Enterprise-D* from *Star Trek: The Next Generation*. Alamy

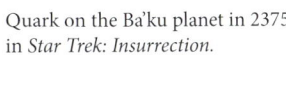

Deep Space Nine aka *Terok Nor*, the former Cardassian space station setting of *Star Trek: Deep Space Nine*. Alamy

Quark on the Ba'ku planet in 2375 in *Star Trek: Insurrection.*

Genevieve Bujold as Captain Nicole Janeway filming 'Caretaker', the pilot of *Star Trek: Voyager*.

The main cast of *Star Trek: Voyager* from the first season. *Alamy*

The main cast of *Star Trek: Enterprise* from the first season. *Alamy*

James T. Kirk and Spock as their 'Abramsverse' versions in 2009's *Star Trek* reboot. *Alamy*

A poster for the animated series, *Star Trek: Lower Decks*.

The reunited crew of the USS *Enterprise-D* in the final season of *Star Trek: Picard*.

the plight of the Nisei in America who were isolated from the rest of the population and interned in camps during World War II."

As writers joined the staff, and others pitched episodes, the first season began getting underway with a great deal less internal strife and conflict than evidenced at the birth of *The Next Generation*, and while both seasons have in common a debut year where the actors take time to find their characters, and certain stories work – typically those which didn't resemble recycled *Next Generation* plots – and others don't – see 'Q-Less' as evidence of the *Next Generation*-style that never worked on *Deep Space Nine* – the first season has, in many places, an assuredness of tone, situation and place that allows it a greater robustness.

"Robert Wolfe, our story editor in the first season, explained it best: DS9 was unlike TNG and the original series, where you go out into the great void and explore and map and meet people and have adventures and then you leave. We knew every move that Sisko made, every thought he had, every action he took, had repercussions that we could go back to and work on and play with. That's why we had the best supporting characters on television. From Dukat to Garak and Rom and Winn and all these wonderful people that we can continue to explore, because they didn't go away. We could leave as much as we wanted to, but we always came back and the station was still there."

A greater focus on character led to story possibilities, early on, which would have altered the complexion of narrative arcs that eventually developed. Michael McGreevey, a producer, and writer on the TV series *Fame* who would go on to write first season episode 'Babel', early in development pitched a romantic story that saw Dax and Bashir fall in love: "It was a love story, a simple concept. I don't know why they didn't want to do it. The symbiont inside Dax becomes ill, making her ill, and Dr Bashir must separate them in order to treat the symbiont. We would come to see the personality of Jadzia, which of course is different from Dax. Bashir falls in love with her, and she feels for him, too. But the most important thing in life is to be joined with the symbiont. Bashir realizes that the only way to save the symbiont is to put it back into Jadzia, and thereby lose the girl he loves."

With hindsight, it is clear why this story was rejected, given the complexity of the Trill and how Dax and Jadzia are both the same entity, with shared experiences and memories – had Bashir fallen in love with Jadzia alone, we would have been robbed come the end and the characters would have needed to wrestle with the consequences. Bashir certainly was in love with Dax anyway, unrequitedly, for most of the series, which Behr and his writers would confront after Jadzia's death in Season 6 finale 'Tears of the Prophets'. In the following final season, Jadzia's new host Ezri would, in a discarded story called 'Dysfunctional', arrange to have the Dax symbiont removed, struggling as she was to cope with her new joined lifestyle. Though this episode never came to pass, Ezri finding her transition as a Trill joined quickly and unexpectedly would ripple through the seventh season.

The climax of the first season, which ended examining Bajoran politics on the station with 'In the Hands of the Prophets' – a singular concluding episode à la *The Next Generation* with 'The Neutral Zone' – originally had a much bigger scope. 'Emissary' had featured Patrick Stewart as Picard, the earlier discussed brittle scene with Sisko, and loosely crossed over with the *Next Generation* sixth season two-part story 'Birthright', centred on Worf but saw the *Enterprise* docked at DS9 and featured Dr Bashir. There was, in short, a pre-existing direct crossover between the two, but the plan was to have the two series, and their characters, come together once more to face an intergalactic invasion force for *Deep Space Nine*'s season finale, likely involving a cliffhanger ending.

This was vetoed by Berman, as Behr explains: "[It] had to do with the Cardassians deciding they wanted DS9 back, and we looked at it and what it would cost to do it right. It would have required a lot of money."

It was a few years too early for such a move, which did end up taking place in fifth season finale 'Call to Arms', by which point a mythology had bloomed on the series to the point that both the stakes were emotionally far higher for the cast, and there was no need to include Picard and his crew at all. The intention of introducing a powerful new enemy certainly bled into 'The Jem'Hadar' a season later, albeit in a very different context. Nonetheless, seeing all the *Next Generation* regulars interact with the *Deep Space Nine* crew battling the Cardassians, and likely Dukat, would have been an enticing proposition.

The second season opened with a three-part Bajoran-focused tale, advancing elements from 'In the Hands of the Prophets', which saw the station ultimately held under siege by a rogue extremist faction of the Bajoran government, but 'The Homecoming' – the story that began *Star Trek*'s only, to date, three-part story – had roots in *The Next Generation* under Jeri Taylor, who pitched the same core idea during the sixth season of that show.

In the developed 'The Homecoming' story, a legendary Bajoran resistance fighter from the Occupation called Li Nalas (Richard Beymer) is discovered to be alive and a prisoner of war, which leads Kira to stage a rescue mission. Kira subsequently learns that Li was not the hero, the talisman, he was mythologised to be. Taylor's original story would have seen the *Enterprise* firstly find a Bajoran woman desperate to find the leader of the Bajoran resistance being held by Cardassians long after the end of the conflict, and later the woman in Taylor's story became Ro Laren (before she was intended as a *Deep Space Nine* regular). Both plots had the same outcome – the icon is rescued, discovered to be a weary soul, but becomes a hero once more and sacrifices his life for the cause.

Piller wanted to adapt the story for the first season of *Deep Space Nine* but Taylor at first refused, convinced it would work for *The Next Generation*, and when later it repeatedly wasn't being developed either for *Deep Space Nine*, Taylor grew more frustrated: "I went to him and said, 'Michael, if you're not going to use that story, give it back.' And he said, 'No, no, no. It'll surface, I promise you.'"

He was, in the end, true to his word, and while 'The Homecoming' would no doubt have made for a great showcase for Ro on *The Next Generation* as a one-off story, it arguably works a great deal better as part of Kira's continued development and the ongoing story of Bajoran religion and politics in *Deep Space Nine*.

Though the second year of *Deep Space Nine* would mostly adhere to the stand-alone storytelling style of *Star Trek* established by *The Next Generation*, steadily components of broader narrative concepts were introduced across the year, hinting at larger threats such as the Dominion, or seeding character stories and personal arcs that would play out across the run of the show. Robert Hewitt Wolfe explains the thought process regarding this in the writer's room: "The premise of the show is one of serialization. The whole point, and we realized this very quickly, is that the show was about consequences. How the things we do ripple and echo and sustain, and we did not warp away every week at the end of the episode. The premise of 'come to a planet, have an adventure, warp away' is inherently an episode-by-episode stand-alone premise. The premise of 'come to this place and take control of it and build it into something better' is not that. It is a serialized premise; it inherently lends itself to that kind of storytelling. That is a part of what we were figuring out, but it didn't take very long to figure that one out, to be honest. It was a quick realization."

Writers continued to pitch story ideas, nonetheless, geared around specific ideas that didn't factor into any broader sense of serialisation. Christopher Teague pitched an idea inspired by the magician Jeff McBride, a veteran stage performer who had opened for acts as sizeable as Tom Jones, Tina Turner and Diana Ross, often during seasons in Las Vegas, after Piller saw McBride's show and invited Teague – a mutual friend – in to pitch material that could feature him. Ron Moore claimed that the episode concerned a circus that came to *Deep Space Nine*, and McBride would be a character within it. Echevarria expanded: "It was an Odo show, about Odo's dreams, or a figure that he was chasing." The figure would have been McBride, inspired by masks that the magician wore in his show, repeatedly taking them off to reveal another mask underneath, with the character revealed as a murderer.

Ultimately, the idea of a circus didn't enthuse the writing staff and Teague's idea was shot down, though it did end up inspiring elements of the third season Dax story 'Equilibrium' enough, written in the end by Echevarria, and which featured McBride as the sinister, hidden Dax host Joran, a serial killer hidden in the symbiont's past. Teague gained a story credit and would later in the 2000s work on a Piller script, posthumously, with Piller's son Shawn for a show called *Wildfire*, a show about a New Mexico family that co-starred Nana Visitor and ran for four seasons.

Regarding Dax and her symbiont, one writer whose rejected spec script for *The Next Generation*, 'The Empath', discussed in a previous chapter, was invited on the strength of her work to pitch for *Deep Space Nine*. Lisa Klink, early in production on the second season, developed another spec revolving around the theft of the Dax symbiont, but in a stroke of bad luck ended up submitting her idea on the very day the fourth episode of *Deep Space Nine*'s second season, 'Invasive Procedures', aired, an episode about, you guessed it . . . the theft of the Dax symbiont. "I just tore my hair out. I couldn't believe it, because you can only submit two spec scripts without an agent, and those were my two! I figured I had just used up all my chances."

It certainly didn't end up being Klink's last opportunity to write for *Star Trek*, indeed she would conceive another *Deep Space Nine* story that never made it, which we will discuss later, but it did show how multiple writers, completely coincidentally, often touched on similar material and concepts for stories. Even titles would often end up coming up more than once, as was the case for 'Persistence of Vision', which ended up being the name of a second season *Voyager* episode, but also served as the title for a story by Wolfe during production of the second season following a discussion with Behr about the possibilities of virtual reality, with the latter wondering: "How scary is it going to be in the future when you won't be able to tell what's real and what isn't?"

The holodeck had, of course, already posited a future where people could enjoy virtual environments where often events could go fatally wrong thanks to technology, and episodes such as 'Profit and Loss' in the second season would suggest Quark operates a murky trade in virtual prostitution based on the images of real people (in that case, Kira), but Wolfe was interested in exploring VR as it related to the real world. His story saw Miles O'Brien (Colm Meaney) and Jadzia Dax entering a virtual reality prison, only to believe they've escaped before realising they remain trapped. "Then they escape again, and I wanted the tag to be where Keiko was telling O'Brien how good it was for him to be back, and O'Brien saying, 'I don't know whether I'm back or not. I'm never gonna know.' Fade out."

Several of these concepts ended up forming aspects of episodes to come, including the bombastic third season opening two-part story 'The Search', and principally the second season story 'Shadowplay', written by Piller after he rejected Wolfe's story, retaining the character of Rurigan from Wolfe's story and lightening the tone for what became a story driven through Dax and Odo.

Wolfe nevertheless continued to seek a good vehicle for Meaney's O'Brien during the second into the third season, returning to a story he originally developed with *The Next Generation* in mind, given O'Brien had for the run of that series served as a background character, first a helm officer and later transporter chief, before *Deep Space Nine* promoted him to full regular status. Wolfe sought to return to 'The Wounded', arguably O'Brien's greatest showcase in the fourth season of *The Next Generation*, where the *Enterprise* worked to stop the Captain of the USS *Phoenix*, Benjamin Maxwell, from going rogue and starting an interstellar war between the Federation and the Cardassians, a Captain who O'Brien served under years before on the USS *Rutledge*.

A wellspring episode for the creation of *Deep Space Nine*, 'The Wounded' not only featured Marc Alaimo as a Cardassian character, later immortalised as the villainous Dukat on *Deep Space Nine*, but also debuted the Cardassians as a race *The Next Generation* would return to several times before they became a major part of *Deep Space Nine*'s mythology and tapestry. Wolfe's inspiration was the Q episode he envisaged that would have seen Troi becoming a Romulan, later under different circumstances adapted into 'Face of the Enemy', but here he believed the tale could be converted into a story for O'Brien, who would have been revealed to be a Cardassian in disguise who had been replaced years before while serving on the *Rutledge*, meaning the man we grew to know all along was a spy.

"The replacement [in O'Brien's case] was a deep-cover agent who'd been given O'Brien's memories [and didn't know he was Cardassian]." It was a concept utilised for the character of Raymond Boone in another second season O'Brien story concerning the Cardassians, 'Tribunal', but Wolfe abandoned it after realising the Cardassian version of O'Brien could never have fathered the very human Molly. Refusing to give up on the idea, Wolfe instead transformed the story into one for Kira, which became the produced third season episode 'Second Skin'.

In Wolfe's story, Kira is abducted by Tekeny Ghemor, a member of the Cardassian Obsidian Order (their equivalent of the CIA or KGB) and wakes up to find herself a Cardassian. She is told her name is Iliana Ghemor, a Cardassian spy who was surgically altered to look like Kira Nerys and assume her role in the Bajoran Resistance, and now they plan to reverse the memory loss she suffered so she can return to Cardassian life. Kira eventually discovers it was a Cardassian plot and she is ultimately Bajoran, but she grows to care about Ghemor, who just wanted the daughter he loves back. He would later return as an ailing figure in fifth season episode 'Ties of Blood and Water' and be an example of Cardassian figures humanised in Kira's eyes which begin to soften her approach toward the race who enslaved her people.

'Second Skin' originally, however, would have revealed Kira wasn't Bajoran at all, as Echevarria claims: "Robert wanted to say that Kira was Cardassian, that the arc of the show was that the real [Bajoran] Kira died, but she [Kira's Cardassian counterpart] is essentially Kira now and it doesn't really matter." Both Berman and Piller were unhappy with the idea. "I think Rick and Mike . . . thought that it was too weird, too alien a notion for the audience to really hold on to a character they had invested themselves in . . . They were probably right in that decision." The idea also has strong similarities with Jeri Taylor's desire to kill Will Riker and replace him with Tom Riker, his transporter double from 'Second Chances', an idea also aborted early on.

In a twist of fate, Tom Riker would reappear on *Deep Space Nine* just a couple of episodes later in 'Defiant', posing as Will Riker to steal the USS *Defiant*, having joined the Maquis resistance fighter organisation, kidnapping Kira – who he was charming beforehand – as part of a mission into Cardassian space. As an aside the seeds of this story were originally designed for Ro Laren, who after not graduating to *Deep Space Nine* had in the *Next Generation* seventh season episode 'Preemptive Strike' been revealed as an agent of the Maquis, who would make a significant return in the second season of *Deep Space Nine*. The writers couldn't make a Ro in the Maquis story work for *Deep Space Nine*, which saw them port the concept into Tom Riker. This would be the first and last time Jonathan Frakes would appear on *Deep Space Nine*, but he certainly lobbied the writing staff in the wake of the episode to make a reappearance: "I keep thinking Tom is coming back . . . Don't you think it makes sense for them to send Kira over there to free Thomas? It's a no-brainer."

Despite Frakes being a major guest star on the show, playing a darker variation on the Riker archetype, and reprising a character who fans enjoyed, the *Deep Space Nine* writing staff actively discouraged writers who might pitch for the show during the subsequent fourth season about sending ideas concerning a Tom Riker reprisal, although possibly thanks to the writers already considering a return for the character. Ron Moore suggested a loose plan for having Tom rescued from his Cardassian prison at the end of 'Defiant' was discussed: "We'll probably see a return-of-Tom Riker episode. What's nice is he's not really a part of *Next Generation*, so he's ours, and we can do what we want with him and not worry about what the movies do with Will Riker."

Though, during the seventh season, Frakes suggested to Moore that Tom could reappear as part of the Cardassian rebellion movement against the Dominion colonists of their world led by resistance leader Damar, nothing came of it. Tom Riker, to date, has never escaped his Cardassian cell. Given, however, 21st-century *Star Trek*'s propensity for bringing back old favourites, and Frakes still heavily involved with the series, nothing remains impossible.

*

These stories took place during a third season of *Deep Space Nine*, which saw the show graduate, for a year at least, into the solo *Star Trek* series on television. *The Next Generation* had ended in the summer of 1994 with 'All Good Things' and later that year would release *Generations*, the first of four cinematic outings over the next decade. *Deep Space Nine*, until the arrival of *Voyager* in 1995, would be flying the flag.

It came nonetheless with a caveat, as related by Behr: "At the start of season three, Michael came into my office and said, 'Look, Ira. I want you to know I love DS9 and I think you're doing a great job, but you just have to prepare yourself that Voyager is going to be the flagship show of the franchise. DS9, no matter what you do, will never be that show. It will always be overshadowed by Voyager, because it's going to have the ship, it's going to be on a journey to get back home. It's just going to be way too in the pocket of the franchise for DS9 to compete.' Well, you can imagine my reaction. My reaction was 'Fine. Okay.' There was no conflict between Mike and myself, but talk about waving a fucking red flag at a bull. It was, like, 'Okay, the Eye of Sauron has moved away; it's looking in another direction. We are going to go for it. Take that as an advantage. Yes, the actors will be disappointed if that's true. Everyone's egos will take a hit.' But it was already becoming clear to us that we were our own separate little isolated thing. The bastard child, as the actors still talk about it. But if we were going to be the bastards, we were going to be inglorious bastards!"

This edict led to a third season, led by Behr and a team including Hewitt Wolfe and newly imported gains from *The Next Generation*, René Echevarria and Ronald D. Moore, plus Hans Beimler who would arrive for the fourth season, all of whom became the key assortment of writers who would steer *Deep Space Nine* further away from the established *Next Generation* template, further toward challenging storylines, serialised narratives and character conflict and drama that often strayed further from 'Roddenberry's Box' than the 1987-era of the series had ever strayed before. Beginning with 'The Search', which introduced the *Defiant*, the Changeling/Dominion threat, and revealed Odo's mysterious heritage, *Deep Space Nine* became, in the main, a bolder, richer and more thrilling series than it had been during the first two seasons.

The pitched ideas that failed to resonate reflected such a change. Wolfe imagined a story called 'Cold and Distant Stars', which would have seen Sisko awaken on a Santa Monica beach, circa 1995, claiming to be a Starfleet officer but considered crazed and dishevelled by 20th-century humans around him. "I wanted Sisko to be saying, 'I'm the captain of a starbase in the year twenty-three-whatever, and I don't belong here.'

And everybody's telling him, 'You're a homeless schizophrenic, take your Thorazine.'" Though the idea was deemed too similar to Brannon Braga's fourth season *The Next Generation* episode 'Frame of Mind', which put Riker through a similar psychological breakdown, the seeds that would blossom in the sixth season *Deep Space Nine* episode 'Far Beyond the Stars' and later 'Shadows and Symbols', with Sisko's 1950s science-fiction author alter ego Benny Russell, are very clear.

Behr wasn't convinced by the idea, though Wolfe was persistent. "I sold him the idea that Sisko would wake up on Santa Monica beach. He would say, 'I am a starship captain,' and the locals would say, 'Yeah, right.'" The concept served as the building blocks for third season two-part story 'Past Tense', in which a transporter accident throws Sisko, Dax and Bashir into the 2020s and Sisko is forced into a historical role during a key part of American history called the 'Bell Riots'. It would go on to be one of *Deep Space Nine*'s most successful and profound episodes, with ideas that resonate strongly with fascistic aspects of American governance in the actual 2020s.

As part of the genesis of 'Past Tense', Wolfe also envisaged a mechanism designed to utilise time travel without actually travelling into the past: "I had an idea where Sisko's consciousness gets disconnected from his body, and hooked into the mind of an ancestor with a similar genetic makeup, like two radios tuned to the same frequency. The idea came from the fact that my wife has been a counselor for the mentally ill homeless for a long time, and I've learned that just because they say they are something they couldn't be, doesn't mean it's not true for them." Echevarria expanded on this: "Part of Robert's idea was that Sisko would see a cop and it would be René Auberjonois without his makeup. The homeless counselor would be Dax without the spots. Sisko would be seeing these blurry things and realize he was seeing through some weird filter. Robert wrote different drafts of the story with different tech."

Once again, though 'Past Tense' would emerge quite differently, DNA is clear between this story and 'Far Beyond the Stars', which featured actors such as Auberjonois and Terry Farrell sans make-up in human guises, which may or may not be simply Sisko's imagination. Indeed, the same title – 'The Cold and Distant Stars' – would be reprised when developing that Season 6 story, with Marc Scott Zicree's original concept focusing around Jake Sisko, who would have travelled through time rather than experiencing a vision, into the 1950s, and encounter a similar group of struggling science-fiction writers, only to come the conclusion that the time travel was fake and that he had been tricked by an alien being seeking to learn about humanity. Behr rejected the idea of the alien – considering it a gimmick – but liked the rest enough to build it around Sisko as he faced racism and, well, the rest is future history.

Though Jake didn't end up taking centre stage in this story, the actor who played him – Cirroc Lofton – had designs earlier on crafting his own Sisko story, around the point of the fourth season. Sisko and Jake's long-held love of baseball, which was fully explored in seventh season episode 'Take Me Out to the Holosuite', is a key facet of their bond, and Lofton's pitch would have seen an argument regarding it leading to Jake taking up an interest in basketball, designed to get NBA star Michael Jordan – then at his peak and even now arguably still the most famous basketball player in history – to guest star as a holographic version of himself. With Lofton claiming that the A-plot of the episode would have revolved around Quark poisoning his customer's drinks with an additive, the B-plot would have seen Sisko-based comedy.

Lofton claimed the sentiment amongst writers was that "Michael Jordan's not going to come here and do that!" and the idea was never pursued. There was always across *Deep Space Nine*, however, no aversion to a comedy or romp, evidenced chiefly through the Ferengi-centred episodes around Quark, his brother Rom and a growing retinue over time of characters including Rom's son Nog, Grand Nagus Zek, officious investigator Brunt and Quark/Rom's 'moogie' Ishka. Ron Moore at one stage pitched an episode that would have entirely revolved around Quark's bar over the course of a day. Indeed, one of the most enjoyable Ferengi stories, the fourth season's 'Little Green Men', originally came to life as a possible *Next Generation* episode, from writers Jack Trevino and Toni Marberry.

Trevino explains: "'Little Green Men' came to me one night as I was working on a college assignment in my den. With the TV playing in the background, I heard the familiar *Unsolved Mysteries* theme music. On the show, there was a segment about the crash at Roswell, New Mexico, 1947. I listened as an older woman told a story of how her husband had flown dead aliens to an airbase, and how he later described the bodies to her. According to the wife, her husband told her the aliens were short, with big heads and sunken eyes. My mind immediately conjured up a Ferengi. We pitched this premise on our first pitch, taken by René Echevarria . . . We presented a story of Captain Picard and his crew pursuing four Ferengi back to Earth in the mid-1900s. Unfortunately, the Ferengi ship crashes and the military recovers the wreckage and bodies. The task of removing all traces of this extraterrestrial existence falls upon *Enterprise-D*."

Had this been a *Next Generation* episode, 'Little Green Men' might have resembled *Original Series* outing 'Tomorrow Is Yesterday', where the original *Enterprise* is mistaken for a UFO, but Echevarria rejected the idea due to a limit of one time-travel episode per season. Ultimately, pitching the story again as a *Deep Space Nine* Ferengi episode where Quark, Rom and Nog end up *becoming* the Roswell aliens of UFO myth, made for a lighter episode which still connected to the mid-1990s fervour over alien abductions and conspiracy lore, as evidenced by *The X-Files* capturing the zeitgeist of the time.

Trevino and Marberry also contributed an earlier story in the fourth season, 'Indiscretion', which saw Kira forced to help her sometime nemesis Dukat search for Ziyal, his long-lost half-Bajoran daughter, who was originally designed to be Kira's sister: "After reading our script, an agent turned us down, citing it violated the Trek guidelines. I couldn't bring myself to give up on the story because I knew it had dramatic potential. So, I re-tooled it, omitting the part about Ziyal being Kira's sister. Instead, I focused on placing Dukat and Kira in a most difficult situation: Dukat having to ask Kira for help and Kira being forced to help him locate his daughter. A friend at work told me that when Dukat finally finds his daughter, he should kill her. I said, I couldn't do that. But after thinking about it, I told my co-worker there wasn't any reason why the audience couldn't be led into believing he's going to kill her."

Returning to the Ferengi, a pitch from Steven S. DeKnight, who would later create Marvel's Netflix adaptation of *Daredevil* as well as working on Joss Whedon's *Angel*, sought to take a unique approach to the now comic aliens, as he describes: "The spec was called 'Giant'. It starts out in Quark's bar and Worf is there with Jadzia Dax. He goes up to the bar to get a drink and he comes back to the table to discover there's a Ferengi hitting on his girlfriend. He tells the Ferengi to get lost and the Ferengi gets feisty. Worf says, I remember this line, 'There's no honor in fighting a single Ferengi.' And he hears a voice behind him saying, 'I'd say the same thing about Klingons.' And he turns around and there's a giant Ferengi behind him that's bigger than he is. So that's the start of it and when we come back it's your classic bar fight with Worf and this giant Ferengi, who goes toe-to-toe with Worf. And from there, everybody gets thrown into the brig."

The concept of a gigantic Ferengi able to hold their own against a Klingon such as Worf would likely have raised eyebrows, as DeKnight continues: "You find out as the story unfolds that these two Ferengis are brothers, the regular Ferengi and the giant Ferengi. The big one is a scientist and he discovered there's a secret the Ferengi have been hiding for like a thousand years: The Ferengi used to be big, they used to be like Klingons. And slowly they evolved, they got smaller, and basically sneakier, as an evolutionary survival tactic. Because, as you find out in the story, people underestimate you when you're small. They don't consider you a threat. And that's how you can screw them over. So the scientist discovered that there's a genetic modification he can make to restore Ferengi to their rightful place. And he has this dream of Ferengis becoming large again and being respected."

This idea resonates with the Klingons on a different level, serving as an alternative idea to the one later evinced by *Star Trek* to explain why Worf and subsequent Klingons had cranial ridges, when in *The Original Series* they do not, as suggested in 'Trials and Tribble-ations' and later expanded on in *Star Trek: Enterprise* episode 'Affliction'. DeKnight concludes: "The story from there basically goes that Worf and Dax have to transport these two guys, because they're wanted fugitives from the Ferengi empire, and hand them over. And on their way transporting them, they get attacked by a Jem'Hadar ship. From there it becomes this adventure, as they crash land on this planet, of Worf and Dax having to work together with these two Ferengi to get off the planet and escape the Jem'Hadar. And at the end of the episode, Worf has gained a lot of respect for this giant Ferengi. And he lets him go. He helps him escape."

Though we don't have exact details on why the idea was rejected, it perhaps moved too far away from the established idea of the Ferengi for comfort, although 'The Jem'Hadar' at the end of the second season had certainly displayed how you could bring together comedy plots and deadly alien races without them being a jarring concoction.

The Jem'Hadar indeed would feature significantly in fourth season episode 'Hippocratic Oath', where Bashir is forced to help a group of the Dominion soldiers with their addiction to a drug called 'ketracel-white', a story that came from an original idea by writer Nicholas Corea that ended up combined with an unused concept by the aforementioned Lisa Klink, who had devised a story about Bashir being thrown into an alien prison, as Echevarria expands upon: "It was a planet where we end up in this camp; we think these are the people who live here, but it turns out that they are not native to this planet and that they are fighting the natives off. We realize we are on the wrong side and that we have been helping fight off some kind of aliens living in the forest, when in fact they are the natives who are fighting a war of rebellion."

Bashir's imprisonment was the only idea retained as part of what became 'Hippocratic Oath', as the fourth season balanced stories of light and darkness. Ron Moore still retained his desire to produce a musical episode, as he had wished for on *The Next Generation*: "On record, I wanted to do a musical version of Trek well before *Buffy* or *Chicago Hope*. I wanted to do a musical episode, and nobody would f***in' do it . . . There's just some tech virus that infects the crew and they can only communicate in song, you know? And just do it! And have a ball."

In truth, such a concept would not have been a million light years away from several of the romantic love stories that *Deep Space Nine* would engage in during the third and fourth seasons, with 'Fascination' and 'The Muse', both of which brought Lwaxana Troi (Majel Barrett-Roddenberry) over to *Deep Space Nine* after numerous memorable appearances across *The Next Generation* as the flamboyant Betazoid mother of Deanna Troi. Indeed, before his death, Gene Roddenberry had suggested a cable TV sitcom project featuring Lwaxana as a main character in 1991, but his passing put paid to the fascinating concept, despite Barrett-Roddenberry's reputed strong interest. On *Deep Space Nine*, however, Lwaxana continued to wreak amore, as Barrett-Roddenberry suggested Lwaxana return pregnant claiming Odo, the focus of her adoration, was the father.

The story never happened but it triggered Behr and the staff to begin considering love stories they could produce: "We decided to do a very soft show about different romances: Rom and Leeta, Sisko and Kasidy, O'Brien and Keiko. And the fourth romance would be Odo and Mrs Troi."

Echevarria added on the subject that plans were suggested for "Bashir and O'Brien and Keiko and Leeta, some kind of weird double date, Bashir having an infatuation with Leeta . . . or something like that." He also later suggested Kira and Shakaar, the dashing Bajoran resistance hero come politician who she had an off-on dalliance with, would be one of these romance-focused storylines. Ultimately, drafts were developed for some of these plots but Echevarria claims they went nowhere: "It just didn't gel. Nobody was very excited. We decided that the plan was a little too soft."

Ultimately, Lwaxana returned one final time to *Star Trek* – discounting a fleeting cameo in *Nemesis* at the wedding of Deanna and Will Riker – in 'The Muse', which condensed these aspirations into the episode's B-plot. Though about weddings, it should be noted that toward the end of *The Next Generation*, Moore suggested that Deanna should marry Worf, and they did indeed have a fleeting romance in seventh season episode 'Eye of the Beholder'. Riker was always meant to be with his imzadi, ultimately, but Moore did get his wedding wish, seeing Worf and Jadzia Dax married in Season 6 episode 'You Are Cordially Invited'.

Though, it's perhaps best not to ask if they lived happily ever after.

*

Deep Space Nine, perhaps more substantially than any *Star Trek* series before or since, became known for a true character ensemble of main and returning players who, especially as the series moved toward its fifth, sixth and final seventh seasons, gained an increased amount of traction in the show's storytelling.

Garak, as played by Andrew Robinson all the way back to the second episode of the series, 'Past Prologue', emerged as a key example of *Deep Space Nine*'s scope in this regard. A florid, conversational but enigmatic Cardassian tailor, the only one to remain on the station after the Occupation ended, Garak builds a close friendship with Bashir and repeatedly plays with theories he might be a spy, until the second season episode 'The Wire', which revealed he was an agent of the Obsidian Order living in exile when he discovered his former mentor, Enabran Tain, was attempting to kill him.

Judy Klass, a freelance writer, proposed a follow up focused on both characters which would have revealed Garak to be Tain's son. Wolfe stated, "We were never able to do the full-blown show about that," Nevertheless, the concept of Tain being Garak's father was retained and incorporated into the two-part fifth season Dominion arc story, 'In Purgatory's Shadow' and 'By Inferno's Light', which added greater depth to Garak's history.

Before this climactic story in the middle of the fifth season, there had been plans among the writing staff to create their own version of *The Great Escape*, the iconic 1963 Second World War film by John Sturges starring Steve McQueen, on the station. The team looked to create variations on classic films where possible – take how 'The Nagus' stylistically borrows from *The Godfather*, the strong James Bond and Matt Helm influences on 'Our Man Bashir', or the sixth season episode named 'The Magnificent Ferengi' – but here they wanted to develop the central McQueen character as recurring Maquis separatist and Starfleet traitor, Michael Eddington.

Behr explained that it would have started ". . . with him in the brig and showing how he breaks out, forcing the audience to kind of root for the guy. It never worked out, because we weren't confident that the fans were really behind the character." The concept of a prison break was eventually utilised in 'By Inferno's Light', but the aspirations in making *The Great Escape* and providing more of a rousing return for Eddington faltered, and he eventually met his maker in more dramatic fashion, evoking Victor Hugo's *Les Miserables*, in the fifth season episode 'Blaze of Glory'.

Speaking of cinematic adaptations, Michael Taylor was drafted during the sixth season to pen an episode inspired by *The Guns of Navarone*, another Second World War adventure based on the 1957 book by Alistair MacLean, released in 1961 and starring amongst others Gregory Peck, David Niven and Richard Harris, which saw an Allied commando unit working to destroy a seemingly impregnable German fortress that threatens Allied naval ships in the Aegean Sea. Taylor later claimed that after moving to California to write what he described as a "military adventure", the writing staff lost interest and he ended up instead writing the Mirror Universe love story for the sixth season, 'Resurrection'.

During the fourth season, continuing the Second World War-influenced theme, Behr remarked regarding the episode 'Starship Down' that: "We were trying to do a submarine movie and if we want to, we can try again sometime." 'Starship Down' saw the *Defiant* outwitting a Jem'Hadar ship inside a nebula in a tactical game of cat and mouse, but originally the intention was to feature the *Defiant* filling with water, sinking in ocean, as opposed to filling with gas, but it was considered too prohibitive. It certainly wasn't the exact adaptation of *Das Boot* that writers David Mack and John J. Ordover hoped for, and created a running joke in the writer's room that they could eventually nail the 'submarine' episode. The Second World War influences across the series remained powerful.

Numerous characters aside from the Ro Laren were considered for a reprisal during these later seasons. Sisko's wife Jennifer, who died in the opening prelude to the series in 'Emissary', and later returned in the form of a Mirror Universe variant several times, would have been revealed as an assimilated Borg in a pitched story by writers Robert Simpson and

Marco Palmieri. Outside of the brief Wolf 359 battle, however, the Borg were entirely avoided during the run of *Deep Space Nine* and left as the province of *Voyager*.

A less memorable character, this time from *The Next Generation*, was posited for a return in Sito Jaxa, a Bajoran-born Starfleet crewman who appeared in the seventh season episode 'Lower Decks', which focused on a group of minor-ranked crew officers as opposed to the series regulars, and decades later influenced Mike McMahan in the creation of animated spin-off comedy series, *Lower Decks*. Sito was presumed dead at the end of that episode, having volunteered for a mission to transport a Cardassian defector, but an episode by Wolfe would have revealed Sito had been captured by the Cardassians and kept under inhumane conditions, with her now suffering from post-traumatic stress disorder.

Ron Moore explained why the idea never happened, despite Sito as a Bajoran presumably making sense on *Deep Space Nine*. "We talked about this for quite a while, but then decided that bringing Sito back would rob 'Lower Decks' of a great ending." Wolfe's plot would have revealed Sito had killed the cellmate she had grown close to, triggering her PTSD, and later worked a similar concept into the O'Brien story for the fourth season, 'Hard Time': "I took the end of the Sito story and threw away the rest." Sito Jaxa never would return from the dead.

As discussed in the previous chapter on *The Next Generation*, Ron Moore attempted to revive the Iotians from *The Original Series* episode 'A Piece of the Action' for that series, without success, but he attempted again to mount a sequel for the 30th anniversary celebrations of *Star Trek* during *Deep Space Nine*'s fifth season. In a tweak to his original idea of the Iotians now worshipping the adventures of the original *Enterprise*, Sisko and his *Deep Space Nine* officers would arrive on Sigma Iotia II and discover the race had an entire religion based on the Federation. Moore would have used it in a meta context relating to the *Star Trek* audience: "To me, it was to send the [DS9] characters to a *Star Trek* convention, which I thought would be fun, and a kind of comment on fandom, and people's involvement with the show from afar."

Several of the writing team, including producer Hans Beimler, had concerns about the message such an episode might send as part of a celebration of the fandom: "We really weren't comfortable with it, although we were having a lot of fun. There was something that was bothering all of us, but especially Ira [Steven Behr], which was that in a way we were making fun of the people who watch and are our fans. That didn't feel right to Ira, to sort of poke too much fun at them. After all, they are the fans, they are what makes the show work. We owe our livelihood to them. So it wasn't quite sitting well."

The more fan-friendly nostalgic re-tread of 'The Trouble with Tribbles', 'Trials and Tribble-ations', ended up being produced instead, but *Deep Space Nine* daring to dabble in pre-social media commentary on the nature of *Star Trek* fandom through the Iotians is perhaps one of the great, lost possibilities of the series and the anniversary celebrations.

As *Deep Space Nine* raced toward a conclusion, a continued focus on character arcs, amidst the broader storylines all coming together that had been constructed across the seven years of the show, saw some very intriguing alternate storylines be considered and ultimately rejected. During the sixth season, following the end of the Dominion occupation of the station, Odo would have become a recluse, motivated by his guilt for actions he took during the first six episodes of the season. Rene Auberjonois interceded, concerned at how radically different Odo's portrayal would have been from such a long-term storyline, and how it would have sidelined him from the rest of the characters in the show. Though a bold move in theory for the character to show ongoing development and repercussions from him almost being seduced by his fellow Changelings, the writing staff abandoned the idea after his misgivings.

Around the same time, similar consequences were being considered following 'Waltz', the sixth season tour de force for Gul Dukat, and actor Marc Alaimo, in which Sisko – transporting the war criminal to trial – crashes on a hostile alien planet and is forced to confront home truths about his relationship to the man, as Dukat is haunted by visions of those closest to him, sliding further and further into madness. Dukat come the end, making his escape, rants about his intentions to destroy all of Bajor, but instead was originally planning to more specifically threaten Jake, telling Sisko he would "learn what it's like to lose a child". Moore decided this would be "an awkward thing to have to work into every episode" and the threat was changed from Sisko needing to protect Bajor from Dukat's vengeance as opposed to simply Jake.

Many of these storylines filtered into the concluding, serialised, eight-part finale to *Deep Space Nine*, from 'Penumbra' through to series conclusion 'What You Leave Behind'; a feat of storytelling not repeated in *Star Trek* history until two decades later. Few could argue that *Deep Space Nine*'s ending was anything short of definitive for the concept and characters, despite doors being left open for future adventures and storylines for the ensemble. Nana Visitor at the time believed those were doors that could be walked through: "I think, maybe foolishly, but I think we could have gone on. I think there were more stories to tell . . . I think it could go on from the way the last episode is. I think you could start again the next year, with what's happening now, but it's got to end sometime."

*

That next step, a hypothetical eighth season of a franchise that to date has never progressed beyond seven seasons, finally came to be realised in *What We Left Behind: Looking Back at Deep Space Nine*, a retrospective documentary released in 2019 directed by Behr. In March of 2015, the original writer's room was assembled, including Behr, Wolfe, Echevarria, Beimler and Moore, to break a Season 8 premiere episode set twenty years after 'What You Leave Behind', in the year 2395 – placing it just four years behind *Picard* when it finally returned to the 24th-century *Star Trek* era beginning in 2399.

Moore discussed the experience: "[The reunion] was really fun. I knew going in, when Ira and I first talked about it, when he pitched it to me, I was like, 'That's a really cool idea. I wonder what that'll be like.' And then going in, it took a little while to kind of sink into just talking about it as a show again. Because at first, you're just kind of catching up and you're kind of trying to remember the names of characters and what we'd established and, 'Oh wait, where did we leave the Dominion and what was this?' And after an hour or so, it just became another writer's room."

The untitled episode begins with Nog, the wily Ferengi nephew of Quark's brother Rom who across the series becomes the first member of his race to join Starfleet, as captain of the *Defiant*, escaping attack from a mysterious ship by fleeing through the wormhole and arriving at the station. DS9 is now a religious shrine to Benjamin Sisko, the Emissary, Kira still in charge as a religious Vedek, Quark remains running his bar, and Bajor still not a member of the Federation. O'Brien runs the department of mechanical engineering at Starfleet Academy, his daughter Molly now in Starfleet. Ezri is now captain of the USS *Emmett Till* (named after the young black boy lynched in the 1950s, in another nod to *Deep Space Nine*'s commitment to tackling racism and human rights); married to Julian Bashir, who joins her in their mission of exploration through the Gamma Quadrant. Worf is being lined up to succeed Chancellor Martok as leader of the Klingon Empire, while Jake Sisko is a successful but isolated author living in New Orleans, with a younger brother – Joseph Yates-Sisko – serving on the station in Starfleet.

Moore continues: "By the end of that day, our biggest disappointment was that we had just broken a story that wasn't going to get made. It was like, 'Wow, this was cool and this was fun.' The next step should be somebody writing the story outline, somebody who's going to get to write the script. It was like, 'Oh, but no, we just did this for fun.' The fun stopped once we realized that it wasn't going to get made, but it was great. You just lost yourself in it. You just really, at a certain point, you'd forgotten it was an exercise and you really were debating story and tossing ideas and pitching things, wrestling around structure . . . It was really fun to be back in that for a day."

As many of these characters are summoned back to *Deep Space Nine* to bid farewell to the 'dying' sentient hologram Vic Fontaine, the *Defiant* explodes, killing Nog as he was about to deliver a mysterious message. The Starfleet contingent clash with the Bajoran military as they begin to investigate, while Worf learns from Garak – now on Bajor – that Kira can't be trusted as she was converting Jem'Hadar soldiers into a new Bajoran army, which Nog discovered. This connects to a plot by Section 31 – the sinister Federation black ops intelligence group, introduced in *Deep Space Nine* – to eradicate any trace of religion from Earth, planning to destroy the wormhole and the Prophets within, which will make Bajor finally join the Federation. Bashir is revealed to now be secretly running Section 31.

Behr discussed this development: "Section 31 came very late in the game. As we show in *What We Left Behind*, if there was an eighth season, Section 31 is the direction the show was going in. After the Dominion how can you come up with another villain? The villain would have to be on the inside, and it seemed like an absolute normal progression for *Deep Space Nine* to see how the Federation would stand up if the villain was us. We showed restraint with Section 31 because we ran out of time."

Major Palik, a Bajoran military official, believes the Bajoran government might be implicated in the crime Nog discovered, with Kira under pressure to expel the Federation. Joseph and Jake, now investigating the death of his friend as Grand Nagus Rom returns to give him a 'state funeral', realise Section-31 killed him after he learned of their plan.

Tensions grow high as Starfleet prepare to be expelled, with Klingon and Bajoran ships around the station. Kira ultimately chooses to stand with her friends just as a white light appears simultaneously before multiple characters in multiple places at once and from it appears . . . Benjamin Sisko, returned from the Prophets, facing Jake in the DS9 station office where he holds his father's old baseball as Sisko says: "I'm sorry, Jake. I lost track of time." On that, the episode ends on a cliffhanger.

Behr talked about the big reveal of Sisko's return: "Well, obviously we're never going to know, because there's never going to be an actual *Deep Space Nine* show starring Benjamin Sisko. Certainly not one with Avery Brooks in that role. It's all theoretical. But I will say, what I would think was next for Sisko was that he would have to re-find his humanity. Because once you've basically lived with the gods, or become a wormhole alien which is almost the equivalent of being a god, it's finding your way back to your simple humanity that matters. People sometimes get too above the fray. I think that's happening in this country, in a weird way. In the last couple of years we thought we were above all this, and people now are realizing that they have to come down and fight for the right to have the freedoms that they were thought were theirs by birthright. And this country and its freedom and democracy could all be taken away very fast. There will always be people who want to take it away, so you have to be willing to fight for it. How much would Sisko's sons mean to him in order to reach back into his humanity?"

Where such a hypothetical Season 8 would have gone from here remains an open question. One suggestion in the writer's room was for Kira to bring Odo back from the Founders homeworld where he joined the Great Link at the end of 'What You Leave Behind', but Behr suggested it would be a stronger story later in the season. Just a few years later, *Picard* would canonically place Worf less on the path of a future chancellor and closer to a Klingon samurai contractor, while the Changelings would return as villainous secessionist terrorists, but plenty of scope remains in the world of *Deep Space Nine* for these story ideas to one day become reality, should the modern era of *Star Trek* choose to return to that world in the late 24th or early 25th centuries.

Though Behr understands that, in truth, you can never go home again: "It was never meant to be canon, that is what season eight of *Deep Space Nine* was. We had one day to talk about it. We never came back to talk about it more. It was just a chance for the audience to see how the process went down, and that's all that was meant. So the idea that this is exactly what we would have done is false. No comic book, no novel would make it any less false. It was just a wonderful day to be with everyone back in the room."

Deep Space Nine remains unlike any *Star Trek* series before or since, retaining a distinct sense of its own identity. It was, for some, perhaps *too* different. Those who came in the slipstream of Gene Roddenberry, once *Deep Space Nine* was firmly consolidated on air, felt that with *The Next Generation* over, *Star Trek* needed to boldly go where no one had gone before once again.

It was time for *Star Trek* to set a course . . . for home . . .

NINE

DAMN FINE CUPS OF COFFEE: *VOYAGER*

THE ARRIVAL OF *Star Trek: Voyager*, the third spin-off show from the original *Star Trek*, coincided with the arrival of the United Paramount Network in January 1995, a fourth cable network the corporation had, as we have previously seen, tried to launch almost twenty years earlier around the ultimately aborted *Phase II*.

Now, in a climate where *Star Trek* was more profitable and popular than ever thanks to *The Next Generation*, and with *Deep Space Nine* still on the air (albeit with much lower ratings than its predecessor), UPN was deemed to be the home of the next adventure for, in this case, another Starfleet crew, as Rick Berman describes: "They felt that the great tentpole of this new network would be the *Star Trek* show. So one piece of good news was that we were in a position to go back onto a spaceship, because *Next Generation* was going off the air. And Jeri Taylor, who had been one of our co-executive producers and eventually an executive producer on *Next Generation*, I adored; she's a wonderful writer and she ended up being the show runner on *Next Generation* near the end. I invited her to join Michael and myself in creating this show. Again, we knew we were going back on a spaceship, but we had to do something different."

Berman, Piller and Taylor developed the core idea of a Starfleet vessel, the USS *Voyager*, newly launched under Captain Kathryn Janeway (Kate Mulgrew), on a mission into a region of space called the Badlands – a hostile collection of nebulae known as a 'Bermuda Triangle' where ships disappear – to hunt down the rebel Maquis 'terrorists'; resistance fighters introduced in *The Next Generation* and *Deep Space Nine* who were trying to prevent the Federation ceding planets in a demilitarised zone of space to their former enemies, the Cardassians. During the mission, hunting Maquis rebel leader Chakotay, both ships are swept 70,000 light years (aka around 70 years distance in travel) away into the uncharted Delta Quadrant of the galaxy by an alien called the Caretaker. Both Starfleet and Maquis crew are forced to integrate on *Voyager* as they begin their journey home, which by default is a mission of exploration along the way.

"We remembered the episodes, many episodes, where Q would show up and throw one of our ships or one of our people off to a strange part of the universe. And we'd have to figure out why we were there, how we were going to get back, and ultimately – by the end of an episode – we'd get back home. But . . . we started to talk about what would happen if we didn't get home. That appealed to us a great deal . . . You have to understand that Rick, Jeri and I had no interest in simply putting a bunch of people on another ship and sending them out to explore the universe. We wanted to bring something new to the Gene Roddenberry universe."

Voyager in that sense both was and was *not* much different from *The Next Generation*. She was a ship led by a strong captain, in this case matriarch, with a crew who grew to become a family unit over seven years of adventures, encountering many a strange anomaly or unusual alien, not to mention the Bor, along the way. The only sizeable difference was that, unlike *Deep Space Nine* – which had the luxury to integrate characters and storylines from *The Next Generation* if it wished, and at points it certainly did – *Voyager* for most of the series run was completely untethered from the established *Star Trek* universe, as Taylor describes: "We are forced into creating a new universe. We have to come up with new aliens, we have to come up with new situations. We knew we were taking some risks. We decided, in a very calculated way, to cut our ties with everything that was familiar. This is a dangerous thing to do. There is no more Starfleet, there are no more admirals to tell us what we can and cannot do, there are no Romulans, there are no Klingons, there are no Ferengi, no Cardassians. All those wonderful array of villains that the audience has come to love and hate at the same time will no longer be there. This is a tricky thing to do."

One of the biggest innovations was, for the first time, the presence of a female captain. Not that *Star Trek* hadn't presented women in charge of starships before. The captain of the third USS *Enterprise*, indeed, decades before the beginning of *The Next Generation*, had been Rachel Garrett, seen once in the episode 'Yesterday's *Enterprise*'. She remained arguably the most prominent example to this point, despite the presence of commanding and strong female Starfleet officers across both series, or indeed a character such as Kira in *Deep Space Nine* – first officer on the station and often commanding operations or at points the USS *Defiant*. Regardless, none of these actors were the main character, the first name on the call sheet, the iconic captain to follow in the footsteps of Kirk, Picard and eventually Sisko. Mulgrew and Janeway broke that mould.

Berman claimed: "It's something we felt it was time to do and it gave us a new direction. Gene Roddenberry was never averse to the idea of having female captains in guest roles, but this was something that we never did get a chance to discuss with him. Jeri Taylor, Michael Piller, and I all agreed that when we took this on, that it was the next logical step for us. I'm sure Gene would agree."

Though Mulgrew remains synonymous with Janeway's combination of logical, compassionate leadership and dry sense of humour, she was not the original choice to play the role. Genevieve Bujold, a French-Canadian actor nominated for an Academy Award for the 1969 historical drama *Anne of a Thousand Days*, the Anne Boleyn to Richard Burton's brooding Henry VIII, plus films such as Brian de Palma's *Obsession* and David Cronenberg's *Dead Ringers*, came aboard in the role, attracting the producers in a similar manner to how Patrick Stewart had as Picard almost a decade earlier.

Kenneth Biller expands on this: "I think they thought it was kind of cool that she was not American per se in the way that Jean-Luc Picard had not been American, and that that kind of spoke to the international quality of it all. It wasn't just interplanetary, but that the human characters were of the international variety. That it wasn't just about Americans. She was considered a very serious, really interesting actress."

She was originally Elizabeth Janeway, altered to avoid legal complications with someone living (though the person in question was reportedly flattered), and later at Bujold's request she became Nicole Janeway, so named after the actor's original given name. Bujold began filming scenes on the bridge of *Voyager*, footage of which still exists as a fascinating document of an alternate reality for the series, at which point concerns immediately started being raised by Berman, Winrich Kolbe – directing the *Voyager* pilot episode 'Caretaker' – and others.

Berman goes on to explain: "I spent a lot of time with this woman and I could just see that there was a fragility to her and the way that she talked about making movies, the way that she talked about the kind of relationship that she had with her directors and with her writers. It was a whole sensibility that told me there was no way this woman was going to be able to do an episodic television show; working ten months a year, fifteen hours a day. So, I took her to lunch and I sat her down and I kind of painted the darkest picture I could of what it would be like. That she would be getting pages five hours before she would go on set. Which, in fact, does happen sometimes. That she would be working with directors that she never met before. That she would be doing seven pages a day as opposed to one and a half, which is what her life had been. I remember she said, 'I will go talk to my children and I will let you know on Monday.' And she called me the next day and said, 'I've spoken with my children and the answer is oui, oui, I will do it.' I just went, 'Oy, I know I'm right about this. I know this isn't going to work.' Anyway, to make a long story a little shorter, she quit on the second day. And as chaotic as it was, it was a wonderful sense of vindication for me that I had been right on this."

Bujold arguably was never given the time or space to grow into Captain Nicole Janeway, but it is hard to argue she looks and sounds out of place amidst actors such as Robert Duncan McNeill (Tom Paris), Garrett Wang (Harry Kim) and Tim Russ (Tuvok), who already feel quite at ease with characters they would play for seven years. She retains a certain Gallic sense of remote distance that Stewart brought, with an English flavour, to Picard at the beginning of *The Next Generation*, but she struggles to bring 'technobabble' dialogue to life (a challenge for any actor) or inject Janeway with a sense of command vital to the role.

Mulgrew came in, as the newly minted Kathryn Janeway, and immediately finds that rhythm, one can argue faster indeed than either Stewart or Avery Brooks themselves did. It perhaps helped that 'Caretaker', the two-part opening story, in the same style as both 'Encounter at Farpoint' and 'Emissary', was designed to be a rip-roaring adventure around establishing the central concept of the show, introducing the main characters, and providing a central point of conflict in the Starfleet and Maquis crew members.

The introductory tale, and the series premise, was devised across the summer of 1993, as notes by Taylor from August 1993 show: "Starfleet sends a ship and crew on a dangerous covert mission . . . To accomplish the mission, we must take along someone who has fallen from grace – a former Starfleet officer who may even be in prison. Given a chance to redeem himself, he agrees to help us. During the course of the mission we must find two other nefarious characters; our former officer may have information about them, or know them, or know the area in which they are working. The mission unfolds, and during the course of it – perhaps near the end? – we are somehow zapped to the far reaches of the galaxy, somewhere so far that, by conventional means, it will take ten years or so to get back. The Captain steels herself for this journey, and offers uniforms to the three misfits. Two of them accept and take positions on the bridge; the other won't take the uniform, but agrees to serve in Engineering. The Captain makes clear that the journey home will fulfil their Starfleet job descriptions: they will map and investigate and explore this unknown space. They will get back, and when they do they will have a wealth of information and research to bring to the Federation."

There are naturally differences here from 'Caretaker' and the series more generally. *Voyager* is 'zapped' into the Delta Quadrant at the very beginning, and the length of time is extended from 10 to 70 years to increase the stakes and anguish for a crew who might never live to see Earth again. Characters refusing to adopt the uniform was championed by Piller, as a means of suggesting the conflict between the Starfleet and Maquis crew, but Berman shot the idea down, convinced audiences did not want to see weekly conflict between the main cast, despite the very nature of the premise.

Ron Moore, who joined the series as a writer in its final years after *Deep Space Nine* ended, and who has documented in detail his disappointment in the show and the working environment, believed this to be a key factor in why *Voyager* did not ultimately work as a series: "By the end of the pilot, you have the Maquis in those Starfleet uniforms, and – boom – we've begun the grand homogenization. Now they are any other ship. I don't know what the difference is between *Voyager* and the *Defiant* or the *Saratoga* or the *Enterprise* or any other ship sitting around the Alpha Quadrant doing its Starfleet gig. That to me is appalling, because if anything, *Voyager* –

coming home, over this journey, with that crew – by the time they got back to Earth, they should be their own subculture. They should be so different from the people who left, that Starfleet won't even recognize them any more. What are the things that would truly come up on a ship lost like that? Wouldn't they have to start not only bending Starfleet protocols, but throwing some of them right out the window?"

We will return to Moore's thought process, and his belief in what *Voyager* should have been, later. 'Caretaker' continued to be formed as Taylor mentions a short-lived alien called a 'Mayfly', which never made it to the final episode, a creature from a world that had been the victim of squatters known in the document as 'Crips and Bloods' (eventually the Kazon). It is clear the Mayfly aliens evolved into the childlike Ocampa, as Taylor suggests "we may lose an older Mayfly and take the young one with us", referring to how Kes (Jennifer Lien) joins the *Voyager* crew.

The document also refers to 'misfit' characters including a tactical officer (ultimately Tuvok, the Vulcan friend of Janeway undercover in the Maquis for Starfleet), an assistant engineer (who became feisty half-human/half-Klingon ex-Maquis, B'Elanna Torres), and a conn officer who ultimately became charming rebel Tom Paris, though initially McNeill was in the frame to reprise the character of Nicholas Locarno, a Starfleet cadet from *The Next Generation*'s fifth season episode 'The First Duty', responsible for the death of a fellow cadet which he covers up, embroiling Wesley Crusher in the conspiracy. Locarno was expelled from the Academy.

Taylor expands on why Locarno was never ultimately reprised, and Paris was born: "We had liked the idea of a character like Tom Paris ever since we had done 'First Duty' and had Lecarno [sic.]. We didn't make Lecarno the con officer, because he was somewhat darker and more damaged. We felt Lecarno couldn't be redeemed and we wanted to be on a journey of redemption."

A later document from August 1993 from Taylor lays this out in more concrete detail, following *Voyager* being flung into the far reaches of the galaxy: "Our first instinct is to try to find out how we got flung out here, and if we can get flung back again. But there's no information, no clues – except the bad guy ship, strangely deserted. We investigate it, and decide we'd better find those two guys. They might, through their experience in coming through, have some idea what's happened and how to get back. We're able to track them to the planet of the Mayflies, and find they've been taken prisoner by the Crips – a gang which, in conflict with two other gangs, competes for territory in this region of space. During this time we encounter our Mayfly and another of her species – an older one, near the end of a brief life span. Our adventure allows us to rescue the bad guys from the Crips, and we end up with them, and the Mayfly, on board. But the rescue has incurred the wrath of the Crips and we must extricate ourselves from them. One possibility: we forge a truce, or understanding with them – only to learn that in doing so we have ensured the enmity of the Bloods, who swear to eliminate us."

Subsequent story drafts began to expand on these ideas, refining the plot, as more characters and concepts were added. Names evolved – Janeway was initially just 'Kate', Tuvok was named 'Vicon', Harry Kim known as 'Jay Osaka', a medic named 'Dah' (who became Kes), a guide named 'Felux' (later impish Talaxian cook Neelix), and a doctor named 'Zimmerman'. The holographic Emergency Medical Hologram would just be known as the Doctor, but *Deep Space Nine* introduced the scientist who created him, Dr Lewis Zimmerman (also portrayed by Robert Picardo, in a similar nod to Brent Spiner playing Data's creator Noonien Soong in *The Next Generation*), in the fifth season episode 'Dr Bashir, I Presume'.

Another character set to be named 'Dumas', a female, was developed but later dropped as the story moved closer to the finished article, and while Mayfly was now named as the Ocampa, a plan existed to more overtly sexualise the scenario by having who would become the Kes character from the J'Naii race, an androgynous species featured in fifth season *Next Generation* episode 'The Outcast', where Riker falls in love with a non-binary character in an early example of LGBTQ representation in *Star Trek*. This was later dropped and the 'Dah' character, originally removed, reappeared.

'Caretaker', when it finally arrived at the beginning of 1995, launched a series which had the potential to become a new fan favourite. *Deep Space Nine* had a passionate core of fans, and indeed writers working on it, but it never had the broad popularity of *The Next Generation* or, after the fact, *The Original Series*. It was dark, complex and uncompromising, especially the longer it was on television. *Voyager* was brighter, lighter and back to the core series premise – a ship, a crew and the final frontier.

"One of the biggest challenges that faced the show was that expectations were inevitably high when it comes to *Star Trek*. What gets forgotten is that the franchise may be around for so long, but this was a whole new show with a whole new set of characters and a premise that had its own set of complications and difficulties. In the first year we did some really great episodes and others that weren't quite as great, and I think that's true of any show. When you look back at *Next Generation*, which when taken in its totality is a wonderful show with some of the best stuff done on television in a long time, it's because we only remember the best episodes. When people look back at the first two seasons of *Voyager*, there are a few episodes that you can look back upon as being really good *Star Trek* and really good television."

The journey was underway. *Voyager* could have been the most exciting and successful *Star Trek* series in history. What we ended up with was a great deal of unrealised potential.

*

"We had a lot of shows about planets with people that look just like humans, whereas I felt that one of the promises of this premise was to be *The X-Files* of *Star Trek*: expect the weirdest, blackest, most dangerous shit you can imagine."

This was Brannon Braga describing a very different series from the one eventually produced or indeed devised. The premise of *Voyager*, lost in an unknown region of space, very quickly worked to establish itself as a purveyor of storylines that echoed the explorations of *The Next Generation*. Across the run of the show, and especially in the earlier and indeed later seasons, *Voyager* even attempted to figure out ways to insert well-known *Next Generation* characters and races into the series, despite the concept. 'Eye of the Needle', early on, brings back the Romulans thanks to the Doctor being transported to an experimental Starfleet ship in the Alpha Quadrant.

'Projections', early in the second season, an episode in which the EMH ends up on a station near Jupiter and learns about his creator, Zimmerman, saw Braga bring back Lieutenant Reg Barclay (memorably played in recurring fashion during *The Next Generation*'s run by Dwight Schultz), though he originally intended on a much bigger character: "We came up with the idea of putting Geordi La Forge in there, but then I thought it would be much more fun to have Barclay [a recurring character from TNG] and the doctor." Geordi would appear years later as a captain in the hundredth episode 'Timeless', set in an alternate future. Just two episodes beyond 'Projections', in 'Non Sequitur', when Harry awakens in an alternate timeline, when back on Earth, Braga planned another significant *Next Generation* character appearance – Deanna Troi: "I had actually written Counselor Troi into a big scene where Kim is being interrogated. It's the admiral now, but it was Troi working for Starfleet, where she really grills Kim. But we couldn't work it out with Marina [Sirtis], so I rewrote it." All of these key *Next Generation* characters would go on to play interesting, and indeed significant, roles in *Voyager*'s future much later.

Across the first and second seasons, there were also established episodes that contained intriguing aborted or lost directions for the stories told that would have made for different and perhaps quite unique outings for the show. 'Phage', which saw *Voyager* raided by the Vidiians, a race who steal organs, was originally titled 'Heart and Soul' and would have focused on Paris, pitched by writer Timothy DeHass: "Tim had a wonderful idea, which was that Paris is injured and gets a holographic heart, and we were very captivated by that." It was moved away from when Braga grew concerned it would restrict the story to sickbay, given Paris would have been forced to stay where the Doctor's holographic emitters were established.

Also in the first season, 'Prime Factors', in which Janeway attempts to bargain with a planet who have technology that could transport the ship halfway home, was originally pitched by Eric Stillwell and David R. George III to have a connection to classic *Original Series* episode 'Assignment: Earth', as Stillwell explains: "David and I speculated what might happen if the *Voyager* crew happened upon that civilization. What if they had the ability to transport our crew back to Earth, but because of some terrible failure caused by their intervention on another world in the past, they'd adopted their own kind of Prime Directive to avoid any such disasters in the future? This was the essence of our pitch."

George continues: "As we pitched the story to the producers, though, we realized that they did not want such a strong tie to the original series, and so we spontaneously dropped that aspect of the plot. Fortunately, the producers liked enough of the rest of the tale to send us off with a few notes and an invitation to pitch a second draft. Eric and I did so, and that version of the episode sold."

The second season episode 'Cold Fire' directly connected back to 'Caretaker' as it introduced the twin being of the original entity who sent *Voyager* hurtling into the Delta Quadrant, a concept devised during the making of the pilot following anxieties by Paramount executives that audiences would not warm to the idea of the ship being lost so far from home. The being called Suspiria – a darker entity in a nod to Dario Argento's celebrated 1970s horror film of the same name – was a 'get out clause' for the very premise of the series, as Berman explains: "The studio was very concerned when they first heard the pitch [. . .] We convinced them that it didn't have to be bleak [. . .] And frankly we made a concession to finally finish the sales job . . . we put the one-armed man out there – which is the other entity that we met in the pilot. It's out there somewhere. We will try to find that entity more than once during the next several years because we know that the entity has the ability to send us back home." Though Suspiria appearing and being dealt with put paid to such anxieties, it suggests Paramount were less confident in *Voyager*'s pitch than might otherwise have been considered.

Elsewhere in the second season, 'Investigations' began to conclude an ongoing story arc involving Paris and a traitor aboard *Voyager*, a storyline that writers such as Taylor were bored of, in a marked example of how little the series embraced serialisation – which the second season certainly experimented with – unlike *Deep Space Nine*. The episode opened with an on-ship news item called 'A Briefing with Neelix', which proves crucial to the plot, and Piller wanted to do much more with that quirky idea, as Taylor explained: "Michael wanted to use the electronic newspaper as a stylistic device in order to tell the story in a different way. That meant that we would only experience the story from Neelix's point of view." The idea was rejected by Paramount executives as it would have precluded audiences seeing Paris' heroic moment against the recurring Kazon villains, which the writing staff agreed with.

The penultimate episode of the season, 'Resolutions', in which the diagnosis of a terminal illness strands Janeway and Chakotay on a planet as the *Voyager* crew seek a cure, leading them to almost develop a romantic connection, was intended by Kenneth Biller as a more expansive look at a life they could have had together: "I had a hand in 'Resolutions' in the sense that I wanted to do a story about Janeway and Chakotay stranded on a planet, but I wanted to do a more sci-fi twist on it where they get stranded and *Voyager* literally left through a time eddy to get home. When they come back Chakotay and Janeway have aged 40 years and have a whole family. Jeri [Taylor] felt it was too reminiscent of [*Star Trek:*

The Next Generation episode] 'Inner Light'. That was kind of the twist I wanted to do on it."

Many episodes of *Star Trek*, and television in general, go through development and a range of changes, from episode titles to entire concepts, but most *Voyager* episodes in the early seasons came relatively fully formed, with the above as the most potent examples of stories that might have ventured in different directions. As the third season approached, and Michael Piller moved on from *Star Trek* completely to develop a show called *Legend* for TNT – his final contribution being the second season finale 'Basics' – we begin to see an increased amount of rejected concepts for where the series might have gone, as it fights any and all attempts to break free of the established *Star Trek* style and form of *The Next Generation*.

Piller, to his credit, had observed how television as the 1990s progressed was beginning to morph and embrace the kind of serialisation that would become more apparent in the decade to come, earlier in the second season: "I took a look in a cold, analytical way at the television scene, and frankly, it had changed remarkably in the seven years I was with *Star Trek*. *ER*, *Law and Order*, *NYPD Blue*, and other hour shows told stories in very different ways than we did. I realized that some of these television shows were writing twenty-second scenes, and it was less a combination of traditional three- or four-page character scenes and more like a scrapbook, telling stories with a mosaic of images. So I came back and I looked at those four shows of ours, and I read the three other scripts that were completed, and I said, 'This is just nineties television.'" I came in and sat down with the group and I said, 'Guys, I don't think we can get away with this anymore. The pace of these shows is languid. Yes, we have a loyal audience, but I think we have to look at ways of telling stories in a much more vigorous, energetic fashion.' Well, people started looking at each other, like, 'Wow, he's just going to change *Star Trek*. He's going to come in here and he's going to change it completely.'"

Biller had voiced his concerns about how *Voyager* was attempting to retrofit this approach, as it devised a narrative about undercover Cardassian spy Seska working with the Kazon to sabotage *Voyager* over multiple stories: "The idea of a season arc was done wrong. The mistake that was made was a clear one. Michael Piller had this notion that we should tell a continuing story, sort of à la *Hill Street Blues*, *L.A. Law*, or *NYPD Blue*. But if you watched those shows, the continuing story elements are the character threads, the relationships. Somebody's having an extramarital affair and that keeps playing out through the whole season. The A-story, whatever the big case was, gets solved. They arrest the bad guy, and these personal stories continue along. We did it backward. I wrote this episode called 'Lifesigns', but that episode will never be a little gem, because right smack in the middle of it are these two bizarre scenes with this guy sending messages off to Seska."

Viewing figures went down, with audiences less attracted to *Deep Space Nine*'s level of mythology and recurring characters tuning into *Voyager* for a less complicated and more escapist approach being disappointed, and once Piller moved on – though not entirely from the franchise, as we shall see in the next chapter – Jeri Taylor began to recalibrate the series for the third season as one built on a greater sense of adventure: "I wanted to try to recapture some of the spirit of the original *Star Trek*, which I think everyone would agree was the most fun. We wanted to inject more humor into the show. We did not want to do stories in which the crew complains about not being at home, or stories about almost getting home and not making it so that everyone is depressed. Exploration and adventure is the reason why all these people joined Starfleet. And so it seemed to me that they have the joyous kind of time in their exploration that Starfleet people always have."

One of the first ways in which *Voyager* would embrace looking back to the 1960s would be with a certain, fast approaching, *Star Trek* anniversary.

*

As we have seen, *Deep Space Nine* celebrated the 30th anniversary celebrations of *Star Trek* in 1996 with 'Trials and Tribble-ations', taking the series back to the original *Enterprise*, so *Voyager* – once Paramount decreed that they also wanted the show to celebrate the milestone – had to approach the idea with a different tack for the episode that would ultimately become 'Flashback'.

Braga recalls the intention: "We already had on hand the story premise of a memory problem for Tuvok that Janeway saves him from, and when the request came down from the studio for a 30th anniversary show, that seemed like a natural to get us back into that era without yet another time travel plot."

Time travel was considered initially, however, for the story as Braga describes: "And back [in] time, that was what we were going to do [originally]. We were going to see Janeway's first commission. It was going to be more about Janeway and that relationship. We just used that story as a departure and it worked very nicely. But the gag was always the same, to do a time travel story without doing time travel, by doing a meld."

The key tether to *The Original Series* in 'Flashback' is, of course, what would be the final on-screen appearance of George Takei's Hikaru Sulu, as the episode reshoots, replays and re-contextualises scenes from *The Undiscovered Country*, tweaking continuity to reveal the character Tim Russ played on the bridge of the U.S.S. *Excelsior* during that movie was, in fact, a younger Tuvok. Braga initially planned to also bring back the only *Original Series* character never to make an appearance beyond that final movie in 1991 – Nichelle Nichols' Nyota Uhura, which Takei described: "She would have communicated with me, as Uhura to Tuvok, over the viewscreen. I pleaded with her on the phone to do it because it would have been wonderful to have her back as well. She felt the part did not do her justice, so she passed on doing it."

Braga confirmed that Nichols said no, forcing a deletion of the scene which led to the episode briefly running short, and while Sulu's appearance certainly gave 'Flashback' an appropriate link to the past, the missed opportunity of seeing Sulu and Uhura again together is part of the reason 'Flashback' lacks anywhere near the same punch as *Deep Space Nine*'s frothier, pulpier alternative.

One such pulpy concept that would have fitted Taylor's intention to drive the third season with a greater sense of adventure came from the duo of Jack Trevino and Toni Mayberry, last seen pitching a version of what would become *Deep Space Nine*'s memorable 'Little Green Men'. Trevino explains their idea: "We pitched one story to *Voyager* staffers called 'Visit to a Small Planet.' In this story, the crew arrives at a world where the entire population has been observing their life on *Voyager* (through ship log entries) for the previous three years. When the away team beams down, they discover everyone, and I mean everyone, is dressed like members of the crew. Of course, there are a limited number of people dressed as Neelix, as he was the least popular *Voyager* crew person. For Toni and I, this story represented a perfect way for the crew to truly see themselves in a different light – as they were perceived by others (alien populations, which really represented *Star Trek* fans)."

This concept sounds remarkably similar to Ron Moore's pitch for how to bring back the Iotians from *The Original Series*, suggested on both *The Next*

Generation and *Deep Space Nine*, and the same misgivings that led to that idea being turned down came into play here for Trevino and Mayberry: "In this pitch, we told the producer the story represented a wonderful opportunity to make a few observations about Us, the fans. The producer responded, '*Star Trek* fans would never accept the show having fun at their expense.' For that, I countered, saying, 'Fans would love it, as long as the fun poked at them was light-hearted and not cruel.' In fact, I suggested the studio could have an open casting call for fans (dressed up as *Voyager*'s crew for a scene depicting members of the planet's population) to be in the episode. Still, the powers that be passed on it. Two years later, a movie called 'Galaxy Quest' came out and it was a huge success."

Galaxy Quest, directed by Dean Parisot and starring Tim Allen, Alan Rickman, and Sigourney Weaver, remains a cult favourite comedy in how it sees the actors from a *Star Trek*-esque TV show recruited by aliens to play the very characters they portray, with more than a few nods and winks to actors such as William Shatner and Patrick Stewart. It is enormously charming, and *Star Trek* during the 90s, anxious as it was to burst the bubble of its own success and analyse itself, lost more than a few interesting opportunities to play with ideas around fandom and stardom as they related to the franchise.

The third season instead evoked past glories. John de Lancie's Q returned for the second time, after second season episode 'Death Wish' (which also saw Jonathan Frakes cameo as Will Riker); two-part time-travel romp 'Future's End' very much called back to the spirit of *The Voyage Home*; and 'Unity' quietly introduces the Borg as a threat in the Delta Quadrant, their queen having been seemingly destroyed during the events of *First Contact* when the Borg attempt to change history. *Voyager* edges further away from the mission statement of charting new waters in the third season and closer toward serving as a semi-sequel to aspects of *The Next Generation*.

Taylor stepped away as show runner as the fourth season began, making way for Braga to take a lead on the series under Berman, both of them having conceived the major two-part episode 'Scorpion' to bridge the season, which fully introduced the Borg, a new major threat in Species 8472, and crucially Jeri Ryan's Seven of Nine, a detached ex-Borg drone (physically and psychologically), who joins the *Voyager* crew and becomes a major focal point of the series going forward. To say her arrival caused tensions is an understatement, with cast and crew during the fourth season at loggerheads (Mulgrew and Ryan particularly), but there is little doubt these changes – inspired partly by flagging ratings – helped to galvanise the series into what is probably the best season of television it produced.

"I thought *Voyager* could be a big, expansive, cinematic show. I wanted to up the ante from the production point of view. I would eventually get that chance. I remember Joe Menosky and I went to Jeri Taylor and said we wanted to start doing a series of two-part episodes that would let *Voyager* make its own stamp. Every single two-parter we did was fucking great and a barn burner. Real scope, and from a really high concept. I always thought *Voyager* could be high concept."

The initial idea of how to end the third season came from a phrase used in the Biller-written episode 'Before and After', the phrase "year of Hell", which described an alternate timeline where *Voyager* is almost repeatedly destroyed and becomes a shell of its former self. A two-part episode in the fourth season, 'Year of Hell', was eventually produced, as *Voyager* is consistently attacked by Annorax, a member of the Krenim Empire, who has technology which can change time through the power of a weapon. It sees *Voyager* battered, the crew bruised, some even killed, and the whole *Voyager* family almost brought to their knees. The normal, cleaner timeline is eventually restored, with none of those events having technically happened to *Voyager*, but the story remained powerful. And it was meant to be much bigger, as Braga describes: "One of the criticisms the show got was the fact that there was little carryover from episode to episode. There was a two-part episode called 'Year of Hell', which was arguably the best two-parter we did. My original pitch for that was 'Let's do a season called "The Year From Hell" where *Voyager* gets its ass kicked and the entire season is *Voyager* barely surviving,' and we would play a real continuity between episodes. I don't remember the specifics, but I know it was rejected and it did not become a serialized show. So I said, 'Okay, I'll do a two-parter that takes place over the course of a year,' and that's the closest I ever got."

Bryan Fuller, later briefly one of the creators of *Discovery* who joined the *Voyager* staff this season, added: "In season four, the entire season was going to be *Voyager* getting its ass kicked and the show was really going to go to a gritty and rich place of 'we are out of our element and we are in danger and all we have is ourselves,' Janeway being this situational, ethical leader who was willing to do whatever it took for her people to survive in these circumstances. And it was so much bolder than what you saw.

That's not to say that there weren't some great episodes in that season. You had the 'Year of Hell', but Brannon had so many bold visions that were brushed aside by Rick just not seeing it and not wanting *Voyager* to be as gritty and bold as *DS9*."

Berman was greatly concerned that Ira Steven Behr was 'out of control' running *Deep Space Nine*, which had blossomed into a genuinely unique approach to the franchise, and he did not want *Voyager* to be anywhere near as serialised or experimental, despite Michael Piller's earlier belief that *Star Trek* was being left behind as a result. Fuller continues: "One of the things that Brannon really wanted to do is to say we don't have a Federation starbase nearby that we're going to get backup supplies from, so he wanted to start cobbling together an aesthetic for this ship that was a mixture of new technologies that we found in the Delta Quadrant. It was that desire to really change the aesthetic of the show and do something different with *Star Trek*. And what he was told was that the *Voyager* had to look like a starship."

Braga very much wanted to adhere to Piller's suggestion about *Voyager*'s direction but was stymied: "Non-serialization was more or less a mandate. It wasn't the way we did things. Honestly, that's why I did these two-parters. I wanted to do three-parters and that was rejected. I was yearning to tell stories on a larger canvas and stories that required more than forty-five minutes. I have vivid memories of writing those two-parters with Joe Menosky, and it became part of what I was hoping *Voyager* could be. My influence on the show began in season four with the high-concept stories. Like I said, to me the Delta Quadrant should be the weirdest fucking place in the world and weird shit should happen. It's where the Borg live."

A different concept for how to end the third season lay in the use of 'biomimetic lifeforms' that would serve as exact duplicates of *Voyager* and the crew, who would return to the Alpha Quadrant and be celebrated as heroes, as later depicted in the alternate future of series finale 'Endgame'. Taylor described the idea: "Everybody thinks that *Voyager* is home and there are celebrations, and they see their loved ones, etcetera, etcetera. And it turns out to be an invasion or a dark plot of some kind."

Joe Menosky, one of the writers on *Voyager*, added more detail: "Brannon [Braga] had some great images. One was opening with *Voyager* above Earth, this great homecoming sequence. There are fireworks in the sky, and everybody is going down to their homecomings. Janeway has a wonderful tearful reunion with Mark. She kisses Mark and she then snaps his neck, end of teaser. Then he had this image of like a thousand *Voyagers* converging on Earth. Somehow, these duplicate *Voyagers* were being created that didn't even know who they were."

Again, some of the imagery here would be eventually utilised in 'Endgame', but the concept of mimetic lifeforms – essentially another *Star Trek* variation on *Invasion of the Body Snatchers* – struggled to work for the third or even fourth season finale, where it was considered, not to mention as repeatedly a two-part episode during the fourth season, consistently replaced by stories such as 'Year of Hell' or 'The Killing Game'. "The mimetic aliens got to have this really weird reputation as being a negative muse. It was this weird thing that no one wanted in the room." Taylor continues: "The more we discussed it, the more we thought that once they go home, even if it isn't really our characters, well, it undercuts whatever will happen when the real crew actually does get home. Which we do intend to have happen."

Prophetic words that would be lived by, in the long run, but the mimetic lifeform concept was ultimately dealt with across two different episodes, the fourth season's 'Demon' and fifth season's 'Course: Oblivion', even if the concept never took flight in the dramatic manner the writing staff intended.

One of the two-part stories Braga mentioned above was 'The Killing Game', in which the Hirogen – a hunter species of aliens akin to the Predator from the successful franchise of the same name – take control of *Voyager* and trap the crew in a simulation of occupied France in the Second World War, playing the role of Nazis as the crew form part of the Vichy resistance in combating them. The Hirogen had appeared memorably in 'Hunters' and 'Prey' earlier in the season, and writer Joe Menosky originally had an alternate idea of how to use them: "In my original story, I had the Hunters have a kind of hunting scenario planet. It was like a planetary Holodeck, and we found ourselves down in a simulation because they drove us there. But in working out the story, when we were all together as a staff team, Ken Biller came up with the idea that it was on our own Holodeck."

'The Killing Game' stands as one of the strongest holodeck stories not just in *Voyager* but in *Star Trek* as a whole, thanks to the changes made here. It typifies the 'high concept' storytelling Braga wanted to bring to his tenure on the show, missing from earlier seasons. The fifth season would continue this trend, increasing the amount of Borg-focused stories around Seven, especially the two-hour showcase that was 'Dark Frontier', not to mention in certain abandoned story ideas.

Though Q would eventually reappear in the final season's 'Q2', an earlier reappearance was suggested by John de Lancie himself, as Menosky describes: "Brannon [Braga] and I went to Rick Berman's house for Thanksgiving dinner, and Brent Spiner and John de Lancie were there... John had an idea for a Q episode. He had a couple of interesting images, of Q on an ocean somewhere on a beach, either having lost his complete identity as Q, or lost his will to live. Somehow he gets involved with an everyday kind of person, and that person's fate and life somehow affects Q. That was his pitch, and it had some nice images."

While the idea of fate playing a role would inform development of 20th-century set Janeway-ancestor story '11:59' later in the season, the notion of a listless Q, largely powerless, intervening in the lives of others, would arguably factor into his return during the second season of *Picard* decades later.

Three of *Voyager*'s main cast around this time, Paris, Seven and Kim, all were the subject of rejected storyline pitches for shows that would have echoed memorable parts of popular culture. The eventual writer of 'Drone', Harry 'Doc' Kloor, pitched numerous ideas, including Paris being pursued in his bespoke shuttle, the Delta Flyer, and crashing on an unknown planet. He finds his arm has almost been ripped off, but a friendly indigenous alien of an advanced race reattaches it using Borg technology. It was a concept deemed too gory.

Along similar lines from Kloor was an idea known as 'The Terminator Drone', in which Seven's Borg nanoprobes infect the ship's holo-emitter, creating a deadly and unstoppable killer drone, in the vein of the Terminator. Working with Bryan Fuller, the idea eventually adapted into Seven and the Doctor becoming 'parents' to a rapidly matured Borg, with the killer aspect being softened into that of a child. 'Drone' emerged through the *Voyager* machine into the kind of character story as opposed to action pieces that characterised later seasons.

Garrett Wang, who played Kim, claimed there existed an idea for his character based on the popular series *Quantum Leap*, as had almost happened during *The Next Generation*. "There was an idea that I heard about, which they affectionately called around the office the Quantum Kim episode, similar to the show *Quantum Leap*. They were talking about that at the beginning of this season, for the end of the season, but I think after 'Timeless' they wanted to save a show of that magnitude for the next season . . . it's a *Fugitive* kind of thing, the Harrison Ford thing, the wrongly accused fugitive who ends up having to become the action hero."

'Timeless' had been the celebrated hundredth episode of the series focused heavily on an older Kim who changes history to prevent *Voyager* crashing on an ice planet, killing most of the crew in the process, and displayed not just what Kim – often underserved as a character – could do, but also the kind of epic scope that *Voyager* often did not feel brave enough to try.

As the final seasons approached, one writer who joined the staff following the end of *Deep Space Nine* had the kind of aspirations for *Voyager* that would frustrate both him and other staff on the show. Ron Moore's tenure on *Voyager* coincided with some of the most fascinating, and disappointing, rejected concepts for the future and indeed the conclusion of the series.

*

"Ron came aboard as a writer and – God, I have a lot of regrets – he came aboard wanting the show to do all sorts of things. He wanted the show to have continuity. When the ship got fucked up, he wanted it to stay fucked up. For characters to have lasting consequences. He was really into that. He wanted to eradicate the so-called reset button, and that's not something the studio was interested in, because this thing was a big seller in syndication. It wasn't until season three of *Enterprise* that we were allowed to do serialization, and that was only because the show needed some kind of boost to it, because it was flat. I made a big mistake by not supporting Ron in that decision or in supporting Ron in general when he came aboard the show. That was a dark chapter for me and Ron and Rick. It was a bad scene."

Braga's description of Moore's intentions underscored the creative tension happening as *Voyager* sailed toward the end of its run. After the 'Year of Hell' season-long plan floundered, Braga had made do with two-part blockbuster stories, though even they had disappeared largely during the fifth season. Now, entering the sixth season, as the 1990s were about to end and cable television was beginning to beat the drum for serialised fare, *Voyager* was beginning to run in place as the only *Star Trek* series on television.

Moore was frustrated from the get-go, witnessing how the story that bridged seasons 5 and 6, 'Equinox', cemented no lasting stakes among the characters, even though Janeway and her crew had come up against another Starfleet ship lost in the Delta Quadrant and a darker, mirrored reflection of herself in the captain of the *Equinox*. He recounts how he began thinking in terms of stories that would challenge the stand alone, board resetting thinking of *Voyager*'s storytelling: "When we were talking story before the season began, I thought, 'One of the shows you should do is the trial of Captain Janeway. You should have the crew, one day, put her on trial.' That would be a real major thing in the life of the ship, if the crew can do that, if they really have the power to take command away from her at any moment. If they are really willing to put her under that kind of microscope, it calls into question the entire structure of the show, the entire social fabric, the command structure. Why are we behaving in this way? Why do we hew to these rules anymore? Do the rules still apply to us? What do we find within the rules that work? What do we find that doesn't work? What does it say about Janeway? I thought that there is ground to play there. Nobody wants to go there. On the one hand, you hear them say, 'We don't want the Captain to look weak.' They don't want to make Janeway look foolish. But then the things that you do make her look weak and foolish anyway. It's this strange, schizophrenic attitude about their lead character."

Moore ultimately didn't see many of the more radical ideas he wanted to bring into *Voyager* late in the series run incorporated and admits a great deal of them ended up being worked into the fabric of his successful 2005 remake of Glen A. Larson's *Battlestar Galactica*: "I kept saying that I want the internal culture on *Voyager* to change over time. Why don't they put the leadership of the starship to a vote at some point? Is Janeway literally going to captain this ship until she's eighty? Is Chakotay always going to be the number two? If these guys really don't think they're getting back to the Alpha Quadrant for seventy or eighty years, shouldn't they start thinking long-term? Shouldn't they sort of let their hair down a little bit? What if they don't want to wear their uniforms on a Friday? What if they want to decorate the halls? What if they start customizing this ship because it's probably a generational ship? And they were not open to those concepts."

Instead, the sixth season continued with business as usual, focusing significantly on Seven and the Doctor, including the Borg, and initiating the beginnings of what would be a slow, steady thematic and dramatic return to the Alpha Quadrant, as planned from the beginning. Space still existed for potentially quite fun and format breaking exercises, however, such as Bryan Fuller's pitch for an episode called 'Who's Killing the Great *Voyager*'s of the Delta Quadrant?'. It was designed as a play on the now little remembered 1978 film *Who Is Killing the Great Chefs of Europe?* (otherwise known as 'Too Many Chefs'), which featured George Segal and Jacqueline Bisset amongst others in a romp about, surprisingly, murdered chefs across Europe.

Fuller describes his idea: "We'd follow the crews of several alternate *Voyagers*. There was a Klingon crew with a 'Mistress Jan'toch' – Captain Janeway in Klingon make-up – that was native to a universe where the Klingon Empire conquered the Federation two hundred years ago, a holographic crew that was essentially The Doctor to the infinite power, and several others. In each of these instances, some unseen force would destroy the alternate *Voyager* and its crew. Ultimately, the real Captain Janeway and her posse would discover that another alternate *Voyager* with a twisted Chakotay in command was responsible. He was from a universe where the Maquis overthrew the Starfleet crew. He had a personal vendetta against Janeway and *Voyager*, and wouldn't stop until he had snuffed each and every one of them out of existence. It was a fun, broad concept and for a brief time there seemed like a possibility that we might do it, but ultimately it never came to pass."

It sounds the closest *Voyager* would ever come to a pulpy Mirror Universe concept, and would likely have been fun, but pitches were heading in perhaps more character-specific directions by this point. Reg Barclay, who appeared in 'Projections', had been in the mind of Berman, Piller and Taylor right at the conception of *Voyager* during production of the final season of *The Next Generation*. In an episode they considered for the seventh season of *The Next Generation*, Barclay would have been seen to be the creator of the Doctor, debuting Picardo's character before the arrival of *Voyager*, as Taylor describes from a 1993 set of notes: "Barclay would have been working on this program and finally takes a leave to put on the polishing touches (on a TNG episode). He creates the character in his own image."

While the revelation of Zimmerman makes more sense in a literal context of creating a hologram in one's own image, Barclay being creator of the EMH certainly would have worked as a reflection of Barclay's own neuroses, often explored in *The Next Generation* in episodes such as 'Hollow Pursuits' and 'Realm of Fear', both of which concern Reg's anxieties over technology. It would perhaps also have added a deeper level of attachment and context, beyond 'Projections', as to how Barclay later becomes obsessed with finding *Voyager* and bringing her home, especially in the sixth and seventh seasons, starting with 'Pathfinder', where he almost relapses into holographic addiction as he recreates the *Voyager* crew.

This is a further example of how *Voyager* works to tether back directly to *The Next Generation* to a degree *Deep Space Nine* avoided, given how Deanna Troi is finally incorporated into the show as the person who supports Reg through his issues. Marina Sirtis relates her involvement: "Troi wasn't originally as heavily featured in the episode as she ended up being. But after I had told them I'd do it, they kept writing more and more scenes for me. I think Barclay originally had a wife, and they wrote her out and possibly gave me some of her stuff."

Barclay being married could well have inspired, in the alternate 'Endgame' future, the authorial Doctor, now named 'Joe', himself having a flesh and blood wife. Arguably, the two characters remain tethered through episodes such as 'Life Line', 'Inside Man' and 'Author, Author' as the series wraps up, further developing the connection between both men. Barclay perhaps plays an even more significant part in *Voyager*'s history than he does that of *The Next Generation*.

As the season developed, amidst a fractured writer's room, pitches were still being received in the hope of finding stories that would shake up the *Voyager* template. Jamahl Epsicokhan, a regular reviewer of the series at the time, came in during early 2000 to pitch four stories Bryan Fuller's way. All were rejected but each one offers an unusually detailed glimpse into stories that came from the mind of a devoted *Star Trek* fan, someone with just as much investment and knowledge of the series as the writers.

'Momentum' was the first story pitched, running as follows: "*Voyager* receives an urgent communication from an uninhabited solar system they're passing through. A small alien medical research colony (limited resources) is mining a rare substance from an asteroid belt here. It is essential for them to mine as much of it as possible to stop a deadly epidemic threatening their homeworld. They tell *Voyager* they need someone to investigate a potential threat that they can just barely make out on their long-range sensors. Whatever it is, it's BIG, and it's headed their way. They don't have the resources to investigate right now. *Voyager* sets course, warp 9 for this object. It's huge. What IS it? A new type of Borg ship? No; it's millions of times more massive than even the largest Borg ship would be. Guess what? It's a PLANET, moving at warp 1. It's an entire society moving their planet from one solar system to another because their star is on the verge of supernova and their rich culture needs to be preserved. It's a massive undertaking that's taken decades of planning and three years of moving. They are days away from entering the solar system."

Epsicokhan describes the 'problem' to surmount: "The planet movers are going to have to wipe out the asteroid belt in order to attain the proper orbit, and thus possibly destroy the cure to the plague in the process. It's a delicate procedure that requires exact timing and execution. The plan is practically unchangeable without threatening the planet and its population. The planet-movers are sympathetic toward the other aliens' plight, but make no mistake – they've got nowhere else to go and they are COMING THROUGH. Period. Destruction of the asteroid belt must begin no later than several hours before the planet arrives. Race against the clock. *Voyager* agrees to try to help both sides hammer out a solution that will hopefully solve the problem for everyone. Tuvok, Seven, and B'Elanna venture to the planet to look for logical tech solutions. Janeway and Doc beam down to the research station to investigate ways of replicating the substance. We watch as both sides of the problem are worked. On several occasions it looks like a possible solution is being reached. But these possible solutions result in failure. For a long time it looks like a breakthrough in replication is imminent, but it continues to fail, resulting in the production of worthless matter. It looks impossible. Destruction of the asteroids begins. With time running out, Tuvok and B'Elanna realize with flash insight that the solution is to use the planet's speed and gravity in their favor, adapting the planet's technology in a way that distorts the gravitational forces and sweeps the asteroids out of the way into a farther orbit in the solar system. It's a calculated risk, but the planet-movers see the merit in the procedure and reluctantly agree. *Voyager* must put itself at risk to help destroy rogue asteroids that do not get swept out of the way. The other aliens are evacuated and their research station is destroyed in the process, but the planet-movers, once establishing final orbit, pledge to use their resources to help the aliens mine the materials and cure their epidemic."

Epsicohkan handily also recounts Fuller's thoughts following each of these pitch ideas, describing the feedback for 'Momentum': "Bryan was intrigued by the image of the rogue planet, but he thought my application of the planet was too much of a Trek formula, involving two 'warring alien races' (although my point was that both were well-intended but at the mercy of larger problems) and the starship *Voyager* as a mediator to fly in and solve the problem. He thought this was a story that would work better on *The Next Generation* rather than *Voyager*'s action/adventure style. He suggested that I rework the rogue planet into something more action oriented and pitch it again."

The second idea pitched was 'Human Option', a Seven-focused episode at a time Jeri Ryan's character was being heavily developed on the show: "Away mission. An accident zaps Seven with some sort of powerful electromagnetic shock. She's rushed into emergency surgery and nearly dies. She wakes up in sickbay where Doc tells her that 75 percent of her Borg nanoprobes have been eradicated. Her human immune system reasserts itself and attacks the nanoprobes like a cancer. This gives Seven a sense of extreme illness and discomfort. With her human systems overpowering her Borg systems, she can't regenerate. The alcove doesn't do anything for her. She must SLEEP, which she finds strange and chaotic. Symptoms are severe: headaches, insomnia, nausea, oversleeping, nightmares, falling asleep while on duty, physical weakness. Seven does NOT like functioning like this. Doc tells her the symptoms will subside as her body destroys the rest of her nanoprobes. This will cause her remaining Borg systems to 'die' and her human physiological systems to reassert themselves. Physiologically, she will become almost completely human. The Borg in her will be gone."

Epsicokhan continues: "Seven is reluctant. She fears becoming human. She feels more vulnerable already. Janeway convinces her that she has a huge opportunity here, to take another step toward regaining her humanity. But Seven is in too much pain to think in those terms. She lashes out, she screams, she cries. It's unbearable. Doc gives her a treatment that relieves the symptoms. Seven feels better, and begins considering the possibilities of sleeping rather than regenerating. There's something about it that's appealing. Perhaps being human wouldn't be so bad. She finds that activities like eating are more fulfilling now. Things look to be improving. Then Seven has an especially bad attack of painful side effects. Doc didn't predict them, and Seven is wondering what else he didn't predict. She decides the disorder isn't worth it. She wants her nanoprobe production restarted. Doc tells her it's a risky, complicated procedure that really isn't necessary. Janeway urges Seven not to do it, and then ORDERS Doc not to perform the surgery, saying the risks are too high. Seven is angry. Doc is on the fence. Seven, still in much pain, wears down Doc until he agrees to disobey Janeway and perform the surgery."

The interesting factor here lies in how Seven actively chooses to reconnect with her Borg self, for reasons Epsicokhan describes: "Meanwhile, Tuvok comes to Janeway and asks her: 'Do you remember a person named Tuvix?' Janeway is caught off-guard. Tuvok explains that Janeway made a decision in that situation, and it wasn't necessarily hers to make. This gives Janeway a dilemma: Is she really looking out for Seven's best interests, or is she simply enforcing her own idea of humanity upon her? Is it really Janeway's choice to make? Janeway decides to let Seven have the surgery if she so wishes. By then, however, Doc has already performed the surgery. Seven's partial Borgness is returning, restoring her to her pre-accident self. Janeway isn't happy with Doc for going against her orders, but she understands. Janeway and Seven both come to realize that being partially Borg is part of who Seven is as a person. Humanity and individuality don't necessarily go hand-in-hand. Being part Borg is what makes Seven unique."

This sounds like a strong, *Star Trek*-flavoured means of exploring Seven, and Fuller had already beaten Epsicokhan to the punch, as he described: "As I got about a quarter of the way into this pitch, Bryan stopped me and said that just this week they broke a story for season seven where Seven's inner technology fails and a choice has to be made. In this version, one of the Borg children offers to donate a piece of technology to save Seven. The problem is that the donor will die if she gives up the implant to save Seven. After Bryan's warning, I continued with my pitch just to give an idea to him where I was headed. Ultimately, he said the stories were too similar – but at least I was in the game creatively."

Epsicokhan hoped for more luck with his third pitch, 'The Warning', which he described in full: "An alien, a sole pilot in his ship, wakes up groggy and dizzy with massive gaps in his memory. Slowly he's coming to his senses. He's repeating to himself, 'I must stop *Voyager*.' Meanwhile, *Voyager* receives a distress call from a nearby planet that had been experimenting with a new type of artificial-wormhole-creation technology in a station orbiting their planet. They have no idea why, but there was a massive explosion that left a tear in space-time, which is causing major disruptions (tremors, etc.) on their planet. The explosion killed all 50 people on the research station. Now they fear the tear will grow and threaten lives on the planet if not sealed as quickly as possible. They need assistance from a ship with high-warp speeds to transfer enough dilithium (or other tech) from a distant mining colony to combat the problem. *Voyager* is nearby and agrees to help. They make a warp 9 run out to the mining asteroid to get the dilithium. En route back to the planet, the mysterious 'must stop *Voyager*' alien (we'll call him Bob) intercepts *Voyager* and tells Janeway they must turn around. He is CERTAIN that *Voyager*'s involvement will cause a catastrophe. But he isn't certain how or what that catastrophe is, just that *Voyager* is directly involved. His memory is hazy about everything else. He just knows that *Voyager* MUST stop."

Epsicokhan continues: "Janeway doesn't have time for this; a catastrophe is precisely what will likely happen if she doesn't take action to help seal the rupture. She does not yield to Bob, but passes his concerns on to the alien officials. They say they aren't sure who Bob even is, although we know he's one of their race. One thing is certain: The aliens want *Voyager*'s help more than they want to put stock in Bob's cryptic prediction. They've assessed the situation; this is the action to take. But Bob is CONVINCED that *Voyager*'s presence is a disaster waiting to happen. He continues to contact *Voyager*, sounding more and more desperate. Janeway reluctantly agrees to beam him aboard to talk. While the crew, in conjunction with the aliens, work on refining the dilithium to deploy to seal the rupture, Tuvok agrees to mind meld with Bob to see if he can resolve the vagueness in Bob's uncertain prediction. He can't, although Tuvok does become more convinced of Bob's urgency. But Bob's mind is a muddle; he can't find anything there except the overrunning thought of 'I must stop *Voyager*.' This leaves Janeway a little troubled, but there's no time to waste pondering the situation."

Thus far, the episode does not seem to focus as specifically on one *Voyager* player, perhaps opening up scope for 'Bob' to be played by a significant guest star: "Bob is panicked. He says he must get as far away from this disaster as possible. He beams himself back to his ship. Everyone else wonders why; there's no indication of any problem. The rupture is closing as hoped. But when Bob returns to his ship, he crazily opens fire on *Voyager*, disrupting the energy transfer that's sealing the rupture. The rupture expands suddenly, and Bob's ship is pulled inside. *Voyager* tries to tractor him out, but to no avail. With no more chances to take, *Voyager* seals the rupture. The planet is safe. Bob is gone. Later, Torres finds a sensor log that took a reading of the rupture after Bob had entered it. The crew realizes that the wormhole rupture led back through time just a few hours, to exactly when the explosion happened. She believes Bob somehow ended up in that time frame unharmed, possibly having CAUSED the explosion in the first place because of passing through the rupture. Sensor logs indicate that not far away another rupture opened and sealed itself at exactly the moment of the explosion. This is apparently where Bob had been sent. When we met him at the beginning of the story, it was right after he had emerged from this other rupture's exit. The trauma of moving through time must've had some strange effect on his memory. All that remained was his certainty that *Voyager* was the cause. The paradoxes are troubling, and the crew ponders them. Where did Bob come from? Was he ever a real person, or did he exist only inside this loop? How did he get there? Was *Voyager* responsible for the explosion and the 50 deaths? Or was Bob? Or was anyone? Was the situation avoidable, or was it destined to happen no matter what? Is there a cause or an effect?"

A fascinating time-travel devised dilemma that Fuller found perhaps a touch too dense, as Epsicokhan relates: "He thought the story was too complex, and that the paradox issue at the end would confuse viewers. He said the writers go out of their way to avoid and ignore time paradoxes because they're so baffling. He also thought the 'must stop *Voyager*' alien was too similar to Captain Braxton and his motives in third season's 'Future's End.'"

Epsicokhan had one more roll of the dice with his fourth and final pitch, entitled 'Do No Harm', a Doctor story with a much shorter description: "While on a medical mission of mercy on a violent, war-torn world, the Doctor is forced to fire a phaser and kill someone to protect a fellow crew member when a violent situation suddenly breaks out. The killing leaves Doc disturbed, as it directly contradicts his Hippocratic Oath programming. It's the first time he has taken a life, and he isn't sure how to deal with it. He has a number of discussions with crew members on their own personal experiences with violence, which hits a number of nerves with those who have experienced violence in their lives, particularly Torres and Chakotay in the Maquis days. Doc finds himself working through a number of violent/war holodeck programs to attempt to understand/relive the visceral impacts of violence."

The writer admits he didn't have as strong a grasp on the idea going in, as Fuller responded: "He thought the central dilemma was too similar to 'Latent Image'. He also didn't think Doc would be as naive concerning death and violence as this story would require him to be."

Though Epsicokhan's trip to Los Angeles – which included a set tour – yielded no story credit for him, sadly, it nonetheless continued to display how open the *Star Trek* engine room was toward new talent around this point, as well as returning writers and established professionals pitching work. It would continue into a seventh and final season where, despite *Voyager* ramping up to an ending, the unrealised possibilities of *Voyager* tales arrived thick and fast.

*

Burned out by years of working on multiple shows and movies at the end of the sixth season, Braga stepped away and yielded control for *Voyager*'s final season to Kenneth Biller, a stalwart of the staff since the show's early days.

"Rick Berman and the studio basically said to me, 'Okay, this is the last season and whoever's watching the show in the seventh season are people who are already invested in the show and characters.' They allowed me to take a more serialized approach in the final season. So we did storylines that had to do with whether or not Tom Paris and B'Elanna were going to get married, and we got to play that out over a number of episodes. And the quest to get home got played out in a more serialized way than it had been in previous seasons. The lack of serialization before wasn't really driven by the creative desires of the writers or the cast, but driven by the economic realities or at least the perceived economic realities of the long-term health of the show and the ability to show it in repeats and to foreign viewers."

This became apparent in how Biller wanted to develop the idea of *Voyager* making regular live communication with the Alpha Quadrant early in the season, positing a possible Tuvok story as a result that never came to pass: "Tuvok may get a call from his daughter, from whom he is somewhat estranged. She's a little rebellious for a Vulcan, and she needs his help solving a mystery." While this plot line failed to materialise, 'Author, Author', late in the season, saw Biller institute the communication idea that drove the ship closer and closer to home.

'Fury', early in the seventh season, had seen an aged Kes return, filled with vengeance toward *Voyager*, and while eventually she made her peace with the crew and headed home, Biller claimed the writers discussed the character reappearing at points during the season, as another example of growing serialisation and continuity. This never ultimately happened but the change of mindset toward storytelling on *Voyager* was very apparent.

This is not to say the entirety of the seventh season was one long continuing story, à la the conclusion of *Deep Space Nine* or the third season of *Enterprise* to come. Plenty of space remained for stand-alone stories within *Voyager*'s fabric, such as an intended piece teaming Tuvok and Chakotay together from Biller: "Exploring a kind of archaeological puzzle that turns out to be a lot more than either of them thinks it is. It's kind of a game." The plot would have concerned a holo-program based around an alien mythological construct of tunnel mazes that created a huge logic problem, "the two of them [working] on the puzzle together, and it turns out [to be] much more than they realized". The story is, in some ways, reminiscent of the strange 'Masks' on the seventh season of *The Next Generation*.

Speaking of Chatokay, he was a character who actor Robert Beltran often felt was under-serviced by the *Voyager* writing staff, with pitch meetings alongside writers often not returning decent storylines. He would have been well-serviced by an idea pitched late on by Marc Guggenheim, later heavily involved in the DC comics television universe, and shows such as *Arrow* and *Legends of Tomorrow*, in a story called 'Home': "Captain Chakotay and the crew of the *Voyager* encounter a space-time anomaly with what appears to be a Federation starship from the future. On it, they find their lost Captain Janeway (in stasis) and Admiral Janeway, Kathryn Janeway from 20 years in the future. Admiral Janeway offers the crew what they want most – a way home with the help of future technology, explaining the time paradox by the revelation that her future self was always meant to come help them. Chakotay and Tuvok begin to suspect that Admiral Janeway and her crew are not what they seem, and find they're actually Shapeshifters impersonating a Federation starship. By taking the form of the *Voyager*'s crew, the Shapeshifters are able to take the entire crew hostage. The *Voyager* crew must work together to stop the Shapeshifters and save the real Captain Janeway."

The utilisation of shapeshifters would have connected *Voyager* to *Deep Space Nine* in a rare way, and we would one day see Captain Chakotay

– albeit in animated form, voiced by Beltran – in the youth-orientated *Prodigy*. Beyond that, Guggenheim's pitch has remarkable similarities with 'Endgame', the finale of *Voyager*, partly set in a distant future with an aged Admiral Janeway plotting to return to the present and change *Voyager*'s history, using futuristic technology against the Borg Queen and sending *Voyager* home decades before they originally succeeded, with Chakotay among those killed before they could return.

In bringing the series to a conclusion, many possible avenues were posited, as Berman states: "When ending the show, we considered everything. We considered having Janeway die, we considered having Seven of Nine give up her life, we considered so many things. We knew that the Borg Queen was going to be involved in the final episode. And that there was going to be a great showdown between her and Captain Janeway."

Fuller continues: "We had talked about so many different things to end the series. One of them we sort of used earlier in the season, the idea being Janeway, to get everyone home, allows the crew to be assimilated knowing that the Doctor can activate and disassimilate the way he did Seven of Nine and that *Voyager* was going to cross the finish line in the belly of a Borg cube and then, as it explodes, come bursting out of the debris with everyone safe in this bold gambit that only Janeway could have pulled off."

Reflecting on the finale, Braga added: "My only regret about the Seven of Nine character is that I would have killed the character in the *Voyager* finale. I remember sitting in a room with Rick and Ken Biller. Ken was running the show in the final season, so I had stepped away and couldn't really impose my will. I had written one episode in season seven called 'Human Error', where Seven of Nine realizes she can never develop feelings for anyone, because there's this Borg chip in her that will kill her, so she's a woman between worlds. She can't be human and she doesn't want to be Borg again. She's a tragic character, and I really felt she should sacrifice her life at the moment of truth to get her crew home. It would have added a real pathos and would have been a fitting end to a very tragic character. I just can't believe they didn't want to do it."

The future fabric of the *Star Trek* franchise would have looked different had Seven died in 'Endgame', given what a key role she would go on to play in *Picard*, as would Janeway's death given Kate Mulgrew openly wondered if the captain should go down with the ship at the end – which thanks to time travel, she kind of did. Nonetheless, returning the

Voyager crew to the Alpha Quadrant, getting them home, did create some discussion amongst the staff, as Braga related: "The biggest decision, of course, was whether or not we actually wanted them to get home. That was a decision that really came down to the wire."

Though *Voyager* did not show the fallout from the crew's return, leaving that to Christie Golden's future non-canonical tie-in novels, they do reach Earth, in a sudden and swift moment, gaining the prize they had sought for seven years. Yet while the characters on *Voyager* might have been shocked at returning home, the series itself had been laying the groundwork for audience expectations on this for over a season. People wanted to see Janeway and her crew get the ending they deserved, which Biller attests perhaps to why the series' shelf-life – at one point the franchise's most watched series on Netflix – continues to exist: "There's a generation of people for whom *Voyager* was their *Star Trek*. We did really cool character stuff, but it was also an adventure show and a slice of adventure in that universe that in some ways was closer to the original series than *DS9* and maybe even *Next Gen*. I think we created some cool stuff on that show. It may not be everyone's favorite *Star Trek*, but I've been surprised to find out that it's a lot of people's favorite version of *Star Trek*."

Crucially, 'Endgame' was not just the end of *Voyager*, but the final show for many years to serve as an ongoing sequel to the series that came before it. A journey further back than *Star Trek* had ever ventured was coming next on television.

First, however, before we return to the beginning, let us return to a stage *Star Trek*, while *Voyager* and *Deep Space Nine* before it were on air, was simultaneously stepping up to: the silver screen. *The Next Generation* were on their own voyage in *Star Trek*'s second age of motion picture adventures . . .

TEN

THE MOTION PICTURES: PART II

TWO CAPTAINS. ONE DESTINY.

So promised the tagline for *Star Trek Generations*, 1994's vaunted elevation of *The Next Generation* crew to the big screen after seven seasons of television adventures that had, arguably, taken *Star Trek* where no series had gone before and achieved widespread critical and ratings success. *The Original Series* crew might have passed into legend but Picard, Riker and co. had steered the franchise into a golden age, and now it was their moment in the cinematic sun.

Production on what would become *Generations* started at the beginning of 1993, while *The Next Generation* was in its sixth season, a film that would eventually see the iconic meetings between both beloved *Enterprise* Captains, Picard and James T. Kirk, pulling William Shatner back for one last appearance following *The Undiscovered Country*'s swansong.

It was Rick Berman who sought a story that bridged old and new *Star Trek*, as he relates: "When I was first asked to do this, I was not asked to do anything with the original series characters. Paramount wanted a *Next Generation* movie. I went to them and said, 'I would like to integrate the characters from the original series, do you have any problem with it?' Sherry Lansing and John Goldwyn, the people I was dealing with in the motion picture division, said, 'Great. Contact Bill and Leonard and see if they have a problem with it,' and they did not. The plan was,

I would write two stories with two separate writers, and that I would be involved with selecting which one was the best. One writer for the film was [former TNG co-executive producer] Maurice Hurley, who worked with us before, and the other was the team of [then current TNG writers] Brannon Braga and Ron Moore."

Ultimately, Braga and Moore won out as the writing team – with Michael Piller rejecting the chance to pen a script, although his adventure with *Star Trek* wasn't quite over yet, as we shall see later in this chapter. Hurley, who departed working on *The Next Generation* at the end of the 1980s, provided a draft in October 1993 for the as then untitled *Next Generation* movie, which saw Picard and the *Enterprise* faced with "a fold in space, through which an adversary is blown into our universe and who, in trying to get home to save his own species, must basically destroy ours".

In seeking to discover the alien race's purpose in attacking Starfleet, he goes to the holodeck and consults with Kirk, who would have been the only *Original Series* character to appear in Hurley's film. Based on Kirk's similar experience in the 1960s episode 'The Tholian Web', Picard sees him as the perfect avatar for advice, as Hurley explains: "It's the only other time on record that this has ever happened and the only person who witnessed it was Kirk. Picard attempts to get a point of view from the Kirk character that is different from what he's getting from pure facts. But that's not enough, so he starts manipulating the image, which produces a couple of bizarre scenes between Picard and Kirk – and they get pretty confrontational at certain moments."

Hurley believed Kirk to be an innately confrontational character and his script was designed to have his scenes with Picard be filled with tense back and forth, allowing the classically trained Shatner and Patrick Stewart plenty of dramatic fodder. "You want to bring back Kirk and not have it get confrontational? Kirk will get confrontational with anyone. In *Star Trek V*, Kirk got confrontational with God."

With Hurley reputedly never finishing the draft, Berman chose the safe hands of Moore and Braga, both of whom were now established, talented stewards of *The Next Generation* who understood how to write the characters involved. Aware that penning a big-screen adventure with not just *The Next Generation* but also *The Original Series* crew would be challenging, they began to work on devising how the two sets of characters, separated in time by almost a century, would integrate, as Moore explains: "The image that Brannon and I were most in love with was the idea of a movie poster for the film showing the *Enterprise-D* and the *Enterprise-A* locked in combat, shooting at each other. If you could have a situation where you had the two ships coming to blows, that would be really cool. It quickly became apparent that finding the motivation for the two to be at such odds and then keeping them both sympathetic and heroic was going to be a real tough sell. It was going to be too much trouble to get to this one cool scene at the end of the film. We knew that we didn't want to do a time travel story, and we didn't want the original crew to all be ancient like McCoy, who was in the 24th century in the *Next Generation* premiere, so Rick came up with the idea of a mystery that started in the 23rd century and picked up seventy-eight years later in the 24th century."

Generations begins several years after *The Undiscovered Country* as Kirk, Scotty and Chekov are present at the launch of the *Enterprise-B*, a brand-new ship with a new captain and crew, which goes tragically wrong as they save a transport ship from the Nexus, an energy ribbon which seemingly kills Kirk in the process. Almost a century later, as Picard reels from the devastating death of his brother and nephew in a fire, the *Enterprise-D* crew investigate the explosion of a star and face Dr Tolian Soren (Malcolm McDowell), a troubled scientist attempting to reach the Nexus, a space/time anomaly where people can return to and live in moments from their past. As the *Enterprise* is wrecked trying to prevent Soran destroying an entire planet for his aims, Picard is flung into the Nexus and must recruit Kirk, trapped there for decades and living comfortably, to travel back in time and help him save the galaxy once again.

Early drafts of the script intended the opening sequence revolving around the launch of the *Enterprise-B* was intended to feature the entirety of *The Original Series* crew but ultimately only James Doohan and Walter Koenig agreed to the small appearances the script warranted, the focus being understandably on Shatner. Leonard Nimoy and DeForest Kelley – as Spock and Bones – were the most sought after to appear alongside Kirk, but both felt *The Undiscovered Country* had been a sufficient adieu to their characters.

Bryan Fuller read the initial draft containing more of the original cast: "The opening had the entire crew of the original *Enterprise* saving the *Excelsior* and all the transplants from Guinan's race. So, you had Uhura there working the con and telling somebody that you have to treat it like you're going to treat a woman. So there's all the sort of fun, anachronistic charm of that crew. And then, of course, that got reduced to Shatner. But when you see Spock and Uhura and the entire crew sitting on the bridge of the soon-to-be *Next Gen* era, the connective tissue, it was pretty exciting to read."

Ron Moore told me about how he wished they could have spent more time with the original cast at the beginning of *Generations*: "We'd written a longer prologue that involved the entire original cast and we wanted to make it an even bigger part of the movie, but Paramount wanted that part to be greatly truncated. In the first official draft, each of them had something to do in the opening, but we'd had even bigger ambitions to really showcase them all before they arrived aboard the *Enterprise-B*, but the studio made us shrink it down drastically before we sent it out."

Moore expands on the intentions for the opening: "Originally, the opening was much more prolonged than it is in the final draft. There was all sorts of stuff about getting this new ship out of space dock, and when it came out of space dock we were gonna have the *Enterprise* do a barrel roll, which I'd always wanted to see. And initially, the original crew's role in this ceremony was to pilot this ship out of space dock on their own while the new crew stood by and watched. Y'know, the old guys were gonna be given one last spin around the block before the new crew took over. Kirk would have been in the captain's chair, Sulu at the helm, the whole bit, just for old time's sake."

Nimoy also rejected an overture to direct the movie after script changes he requested were rebuffed, which Braga expands on: "Nimoy read the script and hated it and felt the only aspect of the script that was interesting was Data's emotion chip story, but he hated everything else. By the way, he probably wasn't wrong. Rick and Leonard were very good friends, but he refused to direct the picture without a rewrite, and Rick said no, and they never spoke again. They were both pissed at each other."

Shatner discusses this in his memoirs: "Leonard, surprisingly, wasn't all that upset with this unusual turn of events. As you know, on Treks III, IV and VI, Leonard had been very involved very early on, nursing his projects through the story level and the scripting process, while simultaneously functioning as director and ultimately producer. However, this time around, that simply wouldn't have been his job. This story came from Rick Berman. It was written by his own handpicked writers, and essentially, Leonard was being asked to shoot their script as written, and he wasn't all that interested."

Nimoy, many years later, added context to his rejection of *Generations*: "There were five or six lines attributed to Spock [. . .] but it had nothing to do with Spock. They were not Spock-like in any way. I said to Rick Berman, 'You could distribute these lines to any one of the other characters and it wouldn't make any difference.' And that is exactly what he did. There was no Spock function in the script. I have always tried to make a contribution to these movies. There was no contribution to be made in that movie. It was just sort of 'let's get Nimoy in here too.' I said there is nothing here I can do so I said 'thanks, but I'll pass'."

While the opening sequence is relatively fleeting, it would have been a powerful moment in *Star Trek* history to witness Spock and McCoy's reactions to the apparent death of Kirk on screen. Emotions portrayed through Scotty and Chekov simply never feel quite as potent as they would have coming from Kirk's two greatest friends, his brothers in all but name. The *Enterprise-B* ends up developing another tether in Demora Sulu, daughter of Hikaru, at the helm (which George Takei confusingly claimed was written for him, despite Sulu becoming a captain in *The Undiscovered Country*), but *The Original Series* tethers ultimately end up thinly connected in *Generations* beyond Kirk.

Shatner, for his part, was concerned that the script lacked enough of Kirk to make him integral and devised with Moore and Braga a sequence in which Kirk would be shown skydiving as opposed to just discussing his love of it, an idea serving as an extension of the rock face free climbing we saw Kirk enjoying in *The Final Frontier*. The sequence was filmed, with a rough-cut existing that shows Kirk – having circled the globe – parachuting to Earth filled with excitement for his new hobby, already planning his next trip as he tells Scotty and Chekov, who greet him. Chekov breaks the news that they're due at the *Enterprise* christening ceremony, for which Kirk is less than excited. "When I retired from Starfleet, I swore I'd never set foot in another starship again. I'm not going, and that's final!" Kirk claims.

Interestingly, director David Carson intersperses the scene with the footage of the champagne bottle spiralling through space which opens *Generations*, finally striking the hull of the new *Enterprise* and exploding, seemingly intending on this exciting reintroduction to Kirk being artfully contrasted with the inevitability of his fate. It is a fun scene, and it remains disappointing that it never made the final cut.

Further changes from earlier drafts included Soran's character named

Moresh, altered as it sounded too similar to David Koresh, the Waco cult leader recently in the press; the Duras sisters, Lursa and B'Etor, well-established recurring Klingon villains across *The Next Generation* series, not simply dying in battle on their ship but battling the crew of the *Enterprise* in the jungles of Veridian III; plus the manner of Picard's brother's death, which Moore described initially had a calmer origin: "We wrote that Robert [Picard's brother] just died of a heart attack in his vineyard, and there was a nice line for Picard where he says he wears this uniform and there are risks that go along with being a starship captain, which he accepts, but Robert walked out to his vineyard one morning and died of a heart attack, and his only enemy was time."

Though the sentiment around time remained, Stewart pushed for a darker and more tragic manner to Robert and Rene's deaths, believing it would have the required shock value for Picard's emotional story in the film.

Bryan Fuller suggests that the original intention of Moore and Braga's script was for a greater sense of spectacle and excitement than *Generations* ultimately provided, thwarted by budget cuts and Paramount's intention to shoot a film that looked like an expensive version of the television show, perhaps evoked by hiring Carson – a competent small screen director behind well-made *Star Trek* episodes, such as the *Deep Space Nine* pilot, but someone who had never before helmed a movie.

"When they are sailing on the ship and they get the distress call that a science outlet has been attacked by Romulans, in the original draft they're in the middle of a battle. They come and they battle it out with Romulan war birds, and there's a huge battle. And then in the new one they come, the battle has already happened. It's all past and it's boring, comparatively. And then when they crashed on the planet, it was significantly different. Data had to open negotiations with Lursa and B'Etor, essentially by Deanna Troi sensing that they're in need, and so Data has to go in and power-fuck the both of them into opening negotiations. And then the Klingons and the crew of the *Enterprise* are working together to get people off the planet. It was just bigger, it had more ideas, and all of that came crashing down when they were, like, 'Okay, let's produce this like a television show.'"

Moore admits that budgetary concerns were a factor, following the crash of the *Enterprise* saucer on the Veridian planet, as he expands on some of these aspects: "We crash in the jungle and we know that Soran is going to extinguish that star pretty soon – and when he does, the shock wave is going to destroy the planet. So they are going to evacuate the children [in the one surviving shuttlecraft] and are leading kids out across the destroyed hull of the *Enterprise*, when all of a sudden these laser beams come out of the jungle and pin them down. It turns out Lursa and B'Etor have survived with a few of their men. There is a standoff and a mediation that takes place in Ten Forward, which has been completely trashed. It was fun stuff, but the script was 140 pages, and at some point it had to go. David Carson said, 'Cut it all,' and we said, 'But it's got our favorite stuff.' When we took a hard look at it, though, we realized he was right. The first draft came in and they budgeted it at some ridiculous figure."

Generations was not the smoothest of productions. Many of the *Next Generation* cast felt excised, to a degree, from their own big-screen debut, relegated to supporting roles in a similar manner that *The Original Series* crew often were in relation to Kirk, Spock and McCoy. Here the principal characters were Picard, Data, Kirk, Soran and Guinan, with Whoopi Goldberg reappearing for a slightly expanded role. And one of the key concepts from the very beginning of production, as if to underscore that *Generations* was never entirely about *The Next Generation*, was the intended death of Captain James T. Kirk.

"One of us just kinda threw out, 'What if we kill Kirk?' And we all kinda looked at each other and said, 'Wow. That would be amazing.' . . . From that point on, Kirk's death became part of the fabric of our story, and as a big surprise to us all, there was never a moment where it really came into question."

Picard would find Kirk trapped in the Nexus living out a fantasy part of his past living with an unseen love called Antonia on a farm in Iowa, cooking eggs, chopping logs and riding horses – returning to the all-American homestead as a grounded cowboy rather than a space-bound one, though critics wondered why *Generations* didn't instead revive one of Kirk's old flames from *The Original Series*, such as Edith Keeler – Joan Collins' iconic guest character from 'City on the Edge of Forever'. Moore explains the reasoning behind why this didn't happen: "We talked about having it be Edith Keeler, but, again, that got into the fact that the studio was so worried about continuity with the TV show. They didn't want it to be a 'fan movie', whatever that meant. Things have changed since then. At that point in time, on the television level there was still a great fear of any kind of continuity or serialization and a worry that the audience would be lost. They had the same fear about feature films. 'People would be lost. They won't know who Edith Keeler is or care. They barely know who Kirk and Spock are.'"

Test screenings suggested issues with the climax of the film where Picard, having convinced Kirk to join him in stopping Soran launching his weapon, heads back in time to before Veridian III and the *Enterprise* is destroyed. The original script has Kirk battling Soran while Picard works to stop the launcher, as we see in the finished film. Kirk quips, thinking they've succeeded, "The 24th century isn't so tough," at which point Soran looks up from a nearby rock face and shoots Kirk in the back. Soran stops Picard, but he has already reprogrammed the missile to veer off and explode harmlessly, at which point Picard kills the villain and stands over Kirk, who dies with his immortal words: "It was . . . fun . . .", again as depicted in the film.

Shatner discusses this: "Somehow everybody lost sight of the fact that I was being shot in the back and the whole ending kind of slipped away. They wanted more and they were going to change the shot in the back, but the dialogue remained the same."

Reshoots saw the ending altered whereby Kirk is trapped under a falling bridge and dies in a similar manner, with Picard present at the end, burying him on Veridian III – although three decades later Picard's own swansong series reveals his body was recovered by the Daystrom Institute and remains on ice in a secret lab . . .

Braga is not backwards in his reticence over Kirk's final end: "Kirk should have died on the bridge of a ship, not under a bridge. It was terrible."

Shatner nonetheless was sanguine about what would turn out, despite future possibilities, to be his final on-screen performance as Kirk: "I believe you die the way you live. Captain Kirk lived pretty much the way I wanted him to live. He was a distillation of all that I would like to be: heroic and romantic, forceful in battle and gentle in love, wise and profound. The ideal soldier/philosopher."

With the torch fully passed, and *Generations* having been successful enough – if not critically widely adored – to warrant a further *Next Generation* movie outing, the stage was set for the crew of what would now be the USS *Enterprise-E* to fully embrace, for the first time, their own solo big screen adventure.

Resistance to this was, ultimately, futile.

*

Shatner, as it turns out, was not quite done with Kirk yet.

He co-wrote a non-canonical *Star Trek* novel, *The Return*, in which Kirk's body is recovered and revived by the Romulans and the Borg and he is reunited with Spock and McCoy, who travel with him to the Borg homeworld where he sacrifices himself to end the Borg threat. Shatner wrote himself the heroic ending *Generations* failed to afford him, presenting the idea to Rick Berman and Paramount chief Sherry Lansing as a potential option: "Bill talked to me a lot about taking advantage of what happened in the last movie and reviving Captain Kirk, but we did kill him twice in *Generations*, if you think about it, so we had to leave him dead for a little while. The overall feeling was that, although it was an interesting idea, it was not really the direction we wanted to go at that point. We wanted to do a film that was pretty much isolated to the *Next Generation* characters."

What everyone agreed on quickly, from Berman to Moore and Braga – returning to pen the sequel – through to Stewart, was that the film that would become *First Contact* should be lighter in tone than *Generations*, a movie ultimately weighed down with heavy concepts built around loss, the passage of time and death. Everyone wanted a greater sense of adventure, with Berman himself keen on a time-travel narrative: "All of the *Star Trek* films and episodes I have been most impressed with – *Star Trek IV: The Voyage Home*, 'Yesterday's *Enterprise*', 'The City on the Edge of Forever', and I could give you half a dozen more – have all been stories that deal with time travel. In a way, *Star Trek Generations* dealt with time travel. Nick Meyer's wonderful movie *Time After Time*, dealt with time travel. The paradoxes that occur in writing, as well as in the reality of what the characters are doing and what the consequences are, have always been fascinating to me. I don't think I've ever had as much fun as being involved with 'Yesterday's *Enterprise*', and having to tackle all the logical, paradoxical problems that we would run into and figure out ways to solve them."

Braga, who often played with time travel in his television episodes, liked the idea of going into the past, but he and Moore very quickly had also fixated on the Borg – separate from Shatner's own ambitious pitch – as natural antagonists, given how crucial they were to both *The Next Generation* and Picard's character. "But I have to say, our initial ideas for the movie were pretty lame. We were talking about the Borg traveling back to medieval times, the 1500s. It was just insane. We talked about that for a few weeks, and Patrick got wind of it through Rick, and he refused to wear tights on the big screen. That was his quote. But it was a dumb idea to begin with."

In an early draft labelled 'Star Trek: Renaissance', Picard and the crew, in searching for a group of time-travelling Borg, would hear stories of creatures taking over neighbouring villages in the Renaissance period: "We begin to realize that these horrific monsters . . . were the Borg. We track them down to a castle near the village where a nobleman runs a feudal society. We suspect the Borg are working in there, but no one can get in. So Data becomes our spy, impersonating an artist's apprentice . . . Data became friends with Leonardo da Vinci, who at the time, was working for the nobleman as a military engineer . . . you would have sword fights and phaser fights mixed together, in fifteenth-century Europe . . . it risked becoming really campy and over-the-top."

Trace elements of these ideas, intentionally or unintentionally, fed into future *Star Trek* plots, such as the inclusion of a holographic *Da Vinci* on *Voyager* (introduced as Captain Janeway's crew face the Borg, no less), and in *Picard*'s 'Hide and Seek', Picard would defend his French chateau from a marauding army of Borg drones.

Moore added: "We went through a variety of time periods during the development process, from the Italian Renaissance to the present to the Civil War. Nothing really got that far, but we talked about a lot of different periods in terms of what would be interesting, where the Borg would go and why, and what we could do there. We realized fairly quickly that there's been a lot of time travel done. Almost any period you go to has been done in one way, shape, or form. Then we came up with the idea of doing the near future and to involve what is essentially the birth of *Star Trek*."

First Contact sees the newly christened *Enterprise-E*, as Picard is haunted by dreams of his time assimilated by the Borg, races to help defend Earth from a Borg invasion. In doing so, they fail to prevent one Borg ship travelling back in time and assimilating Earth in the past, thereby changing history so the Federation never exists. Following the trail back to the early 21st century, where the Borg are attempting to sabotage humanity's first contact with the Vulcans, the crew must help legendary warp drive inventor Zefram Cochrane (James Cromwell) complete the launch that leads to first contact, while Picard's dark obsession with the Borg as he prevents the *Enterprise* being assimilated leads him into the path of the seductive, sinister Borg Queen (Alice Krige): "The initial couple of drafts actually did not have the Borg Queen in it, and also did not have Picard on the ship. Picard was on Earth having a Frank Capraesque adventure with a photographer, which was bizarre, and Riker was fighting the Borg. That draft of the script got to Patrick, and I remember we flew to New York where he was doing a play. We sat in his apartment and he was very nice, but he was, like, 'This shit ain't gonna fly. I have to be on the bridge fighting the Borg.'"

In that draft, known as 'Star Trek: Resurrection', the Borg attack Cochrane's Montana compound, critically injuring him, and while Dr Crusher works to save his life, Picard – in a similar vein to Commander Sisko in *Deep Space Nine*'s two-part story 'Past Tense' – assumes Cochrane's place in history, preparing the warp drive test while becoming romantically involved with Ruby, a photographer and X-ray technician, who helps him assemble the ship. Meanwhile, on the *Enterprise*, Riker faces down a horde of faceless Borg drones.

Notes from Paramount resulted in concerns about the Borg being a dull, zombie antagonist, leading to the creation of the queen and the swap of Picard and Riker's roles in the narrative. Cochrane becoming injured and largely sitting the movie out, and a notion of a romantic interest for Picard in Ruby (who became Lily subsequently), were scrapped. Picard's one romantic storyline on the big screen would be saved for the next movie.

In switching around the roles of Picard and Riker, very quickly the tone of both segments of the film, those on Earth (lighter, evocative of *The Voyage Home* in places) and on the *Enterprise* (darker, more akin to *The Wrath of Khan*), fell into place. Picard would forge a dynamic with Lily Sloane (Alfre Woodard), Cochrane's assistant now rather than her original incarnation, not on the planet but on the ship, seeing her childlike wonder at the future world she was glimpsing, all the while serving as Picard's conscience as his Borg obsession grows.

"Interesting side note is that *MAD* magazine came out with a parody, a satire of *First Contact* when the movie came out, but the satire they did is based on the first draft of the script. It's completely different from the movie. Mort Drucker drew it, but he has got Alfre Woodard playing a photographer on Earth. The whole storyline is different – they obviously got a copy of the script to get a jump on it, but it's not the movie."

With Cochrane now back in the frame as a major character, designed here as a legend of future history to the *Enterprise* crew who in real life turns out to be a hapless drunk, attention turned to who might play the role. Excitingly, none other than Tom Hanks was rumoured to be interested, but at the time was busy working on his directorial debut, 1996's pop fable *That Thing You Do*. Moore suggests that it was only ever just that, rumour: "It never got that far," Moore says. "At that point in the process, there are lots of names on a wishlist for many, many reasons. I'm sure his name was floated in some capacity, but it was never really on the table."

Nonetheless, Hanks recently in a podcast appearance confirms, had he been asked, he would have said yes: "The guy who invented warp drive? Oh come on! I would have jumped on that. I would have come in and brought gift Tribbles to everyone on the first meeting. I would have done that!"

The role ultimately went to James Cromwell, celebrated and Oscar nominated around the time for family friendly hit *Babe* and a seasoned veteran, not just of TV and film but also numerous appearances on *Star Trek* shows. He would even go on to play an older Cochrane, once more, in 'Broken Bow', the pilot of *Enterprise*, in a brief cameo speech. Equally regarding casting, while Alice Krige memorably essayed the queen, overtures were made to Anjelica Huston, who expressed interest but was concerned it would be too similar to her role in *Captain EO*, a 1986 musical short film starring Michael Jackson, written by George Lucas and directed by Francis Ford Coppola, in which she played, you guessed it, an evil queen.

Shooting commenced on what was known, for all intents and purposes, as 'Star Trek: Resurrection', until 20th Century Fox announced production on the fourth film in their *Alien* series, entitled *Alien: Resurrection*. Subsequent working titles were 'Star Trek: Destinies', 'Star Trek: Future Generations', 'Star Trek: Regenerations' and 'Star Trek: Borg' (the latter eventually was given to a video game). *First Contact* was finally made official in May 1996 during shooting.

In no small measure, *First Contact* was a hit. Critics enjoyed it. Fans loved it. The box office was the strongest of any *Star Trek* film to date. All the uncertainties and misgivings of *Generations* melted away and with *Deep Space Nine* beginning to find its identity on television, and *Voyager* going strong, there is a strong argument that the end of 1996 going into 1997 was *Star Trek* at a creative and cultural peak.

Having bested his greatest enemy, and seemingly putting to rest a long-held demon, Captain Picard was free with his crew, and glistening new ship, to sail off on more big-screen adventures. *The Next Generation* had proved themselves and even begun to establish a formula. What came next was, again, designed to evoke the spirit of the original show and edge further away from what came before.

In doing so, we see the return of the man who made *The Next Generation* what it was, for what turned out to be a bittersweet final voyage in the *Star Trek* universe.

*

Since departing *The Next Generation* at the end of the sixth season, Michael Piller had, as noted earlier, turned down the opportunity to pen a script for *Generations* and focused his attentions on *Legend*, a short-lived but critically acclaimed series starring Richard Dean Anderson (later of *Stargate SG-1*), developed several TV pilots and written screenplays, one of which director Sydney Pollack had optioned. None of them, however, were being made.

The timing, it appeared, was right for Piller to consider a return to *Star Trek* as thoughts turned to the third *Next Generation* adventure.

"Rick Berman wasn't sure that I'd want the job. The first thing he said when he came into my office was 'Don't say "no" until I finish talking.' And when he finished talking about his hopes for the next *Star Trek* movie, he asked me if I would be interested in writing it. I surprised him by saying 'yes.' It may seem odd that anyone would even consider passing on a chance to write a feature film, but Rick knew I'd been moving away from the *Star Trek* franchise."

Though Braga and Moore had been approached to write the movie that would become *Star Trek: Insurrection*, the latter turned it down, convinced he wanted to go out on a high with *First Contact*, while the former agreed he was too busy show running *Voyager* on television. Berman turned to Piller and in early 1997, they began looking at concepts.

"Rick thought it would be interesting to find a classic story in public domain and adapt it to *Star Trek*. His first idea was *The Prisoner of Zenda* the novel by Anthony Hope that had been filmed several times, most memorably in the 1937 version starring Ronald Colman. It's a 19th century adventure story of two men who look alike, a common man and a king, both played in the movie by Ronald Coleman. When the king is kidnapped, the common man is recruited to take his place on the throne. Rick suggested that perhaps the Captain of the starship *Enterprise*, Jean-

Luc Picard, is kidnapped and another man, cosmetically altered to look like him, takes his place as Captain. He felt that it would offer actor Patrick Stewart a unique opportunity to do a dual role."

Piller's immediate realisation, in watching *The Prisoner of Zenda*, was that such a storyline would result in Stewart playing Picard for only a fraction of time in the film, with the bulk focused on the pretender. Audiences might baulk at the thought of their hero sitting out much of the picture in captivity, especially after seeing him in such a strident context in *First Contact*. Piller instead fixed on a different piece of classical literature, Joseph Conrad's 1899 novella *Heart of Darkness*, which told the story of sailor Charles Marlow sailing upriver for a Belgian company in the heart of Africa, widely seen as a critique of colonial African rule and memorably the principal inspiration for Coppola's dark Vietnam War treatise *Apocalypse Now* in 1979.

Piller describes returning to Berman with a story he called 'Heart of Lightness', based on Conrad's going 'up river' central idea: "'We open at Starfleet Academy in Picard's youth,' I told him, establishing Picard as a curly-haired, high-spirited cadet. We give him a best friend, another cadet who is as close to Picard as any man has ever been and ever will be. Flash forward to the present day and find adult Picard being given a mission by Starfleet Command. His old friend is now a wanted man – he's been attacking ships in an unexplored region of space and no one knows why. Picard has to track him down and if necessary, kill him. The *Enterprise* sets off through this mysterious region and the crew begins to act in unusual ways. We don't know why yet. After several curious incidents, they finally find the hiding place of Picard's old friend. Picard transports down to the planet and discovers that he looks exactly the same as he did at the Academy! We ultimately learn that this is a fountain of youth and somebody is trying to steal it from the people who live there. Picard's friend has been defending the natives on the planet."

Already in this concept, which Berman immediately took to, the seeds of *Insurrection* are strongly laid down, even if constituent elements will change. He did originally consider different and far better-known antagonists for the film: "The Romulans, an imperialistic, fascist race of aliens, had been long-standing enemies of the United Federation of Planets (the good guys) and had never been used in a movie before. Perhaps the story could be set against the threat of a new outbreak of war with the Romulans."

Directed by Jonathan Frakes, his second step in the chair following the success of *First Contact*, *Insurrection* sees the crew of the *Enterprise-E* called to a planet in the middle of the Briar Patch, an area of space with unusual radiation, after Data's programming goes awry and he exposes a secret Starfleet mission to study the Bak'u, natives on the planet, in league with a neighbouring, more aggressive race called the Son'a. Picard and Worf successfully manage to capture Data and subsequently learn he lost control upon discovering that the Bak'u planet contains a 'Fountain of Youth' which the Federation are working with the Son'a to gain control of, planning the forced relocation of the innocent, peaceful Bak'u people. Seeing this as a betrayal of the Prime Directive and all his principles, Picard leads a mission to save the Bak'u while Riker, on the *Enterprise*, is drawn into battle with the villainous Son'a and their sinister leader Ru'afo (played by F. Murray Abraham).

Berman had concerns that Stewart would not react well to the idea of the Bak'u planet rejuvenating Picard, as it does the rest of the ageing crew (Riker and Troi rekindling romance, Geordi's eyes repairing, etc), with the tacit suggestion that Picard was by this point an old man. Stewart liked the idea as following the tragedy of *Generations* and the intense obsession of *First Contact*, this allowed him to play a lighter version of Picard. Once seen, one can never forget him dancing the rumba . . .

Piller developed a draft initially titled 'Star Trek: Stardust', based on the initial 'Heart of Lightness' idea about Picard and his childhood friend. The title came after he heard the Nat King Cole song of the same name on the radio.

His treatment for 'Stardust', dated May 1997, goes into depth at what the first iteration of *Insurrection* looked like. His story begins with a twenty-one-year-old Picard at Starfleet Academy, many years before, and establishes his friendship with fellow cadet Hugh Duffy. "Duffy, more than Picard, would be more comfortable in the Starfleet of James Tiberius Kirk than in the new Starfleet coming with the 'next generation'. We begin to learn that Duffy is decidedly a non-conformist. He proudly claims to be a capitalist, believes that the elimination of currency in the Federation took power away from individuals and gave it to the government. And he embraces the ancient human custom of religious worship as a Buddhist. He's trying to talk Picard into joining him in a protest against the Academy dress code. We get the impression this is not the first time these young men have ruffled the feathers of authority at the Academy. Picard is wary of the latest scheme. But Duffy argues with youthful impudence that it is dissent that keeps a society vital and vigorous and alert. Conformity breeds apathy. Picard is more conservative than Duffy . . . yet, he too has a youthful arrogance and he goes along."

Given Piller was a strong advocate of 'Roddenberry's Box', discussed earlier in this book, his creation of Duffy as someone challenging the very precepts the late Roddenberry laid down in *Star Trek* – the abolition of money, the elimination of human religion – are fascinating additions. 'Stardust' would have tracked the impetuous, youthful Picard we glimpsed in 'Tapestry' during *The Next Generation*'s sixth season. Again, *Star Trek* remains desperate to tell an Academy story as it has done for nearly three decades.

Piller side-tracks to discuss a character he excised from Picard and Duffy's backstory and the remainder of the treatment: "You've never met Meredith, but as recently as Tuesday of this week, she was 'The Girl' in the picture and in all these scenes and many more to come. She eventually marries Duffy, goes on the trip with Picard to bring him back and as I continued to write her, a voice kept telling me she was in the way. That she was adding nothing and slowing things down. On the ship, there was arbitrary sexual tension between her and Picard while she sat around and served no other useful purpose, plus, by being there, she took Picard away from scenes with his crew (the family). On the planet, it seemed, she was just going to be a third wheel, again adding sexual tension perhaps, but if it's a love story about the two men getting back together again, I could see she was going to wind up a cheerleader. Perhaps the strongest influence on my decision came from the Kipling movies – where there really was no place in the men's lives for women, except as a brief recreational diversion. If it was only about these three (i.e. 'Butch and Sundance'), it might be worth exploring more about their triangular relationship, but we have so many other characters to service, I decided we had more important things to accomplish here so I took her out. It's the right thing to do, I think."

Moving forward to the present day, the *Enterprise-E* is battling Romulans who are attacking a colony on the edge of the Neutral Zone between the Star Empire and the Federation, and Piller introduces a key character: "During the battle, we establish one of the pilots in the Romulan fighters – a man who is half-Romulan and half-Klingon, the child of a Klingon woman who was taken at Khitomer and raped by her

Romulan captors (thus he is roughly Worf's age). His name is Joss and he is a fearless combatant in the skies, a Red Baron for the 24th century. Furthermore, from the glimpse of him we get here, he enjoys his work. Not sadistically. But as a confident competitor used to winning."

Protecting the colony, Picard learns from Norton, a liaison to the Federation Council, amidst the backdrop of a peace treaty between the Romulans and the Federation to bring down the Neutral Zone by a wizened Vulcan named Semark, that somebody is staging attacks on colonies to create instability, someone hiding in the so-called Briar Patch, where a mysterious xenophobic race fled the Romulans years ago. They believe that someone is now Lieutenant Commander Hugh Duffy.

"Picard reacts, knows Duffy was reportedly killed in a fight with the Romulans after he violated orders, crossing the border trying to prove that the Romulans were building a secret installation in the Neutral Zone. That assertion was never proved, and even the *Enterprise*'s efforts to investigate it proved futile. (Hard core fans will remember relevant episodes from the third season of TNG, others won't notice.) New evidence suggests Duffy and his ship may have survived."

The *Enterprise*'s mission is to enter the Briar Patch and find the ship, and perhaps Duffy, causing these attacks, lest the peace negotiations fall apart. There is some suggestion the friendship between Picard and Duffy didn't last as they haven't spoken for many years. Meanwhile, Piller devotes space to a sub-plot for Data, questioning the new feelings he has been given thanks to his emotion chip, and he visits the Daystrom Institute where he finds a lab full of less-developed androids, all of whom are in awe with how Data has evolved.

Piller considers this story as a sidebar: "Now, originally I wrote this as sort of a throw-away scene of self-exploration for Data . . . it seemed like an interesting counterpoint to Picard going back to the Academy. But as I wrote it, I became infatuated with the idea of Data as the object of hero-worship by other androids. I mean, all these years he's wanted to be like us. Now, the tables are reversed and their great wish is to be like him. I began to wonder if there wouldn't be fun in bringing one or more of the androids along to fuel a Data subplot. You know the old saying about the teacher learning from the pupils he's teaching [quoted in the verse to Rodger and Hammerstein's 'Getting to Know You', I believe]. Still not sure what it is Data should learn however. Have to be careful that we don't retell the Lal or the exocomp story again. And the risk is, of course, that it not turn into the new androids' story but that the new androids serve as a catalyst to tell a Data story. Data might get weary of being a hero to these guys. Perhaps, ironically, because they have a simulated self-awareness, he doesn't take them seriously and has to learn to. Although it steps on the exocomp ending, I can see an android sacrificing himself to save Data [rather like Gunga Din]. There is a lot of potential for humor in these androids following Data around. I'm not going to develop this much further until we talk but if we go this way, and I'd like to try, then Data has come to Daystrom to pick out a few androids because the mission requires it."

Though the android plotline was dropped for *Insurrection*, Piller remains interested in exploring Data's evolution as a synthetic being, and his interactions with the Bak'u child where he learns to play and have fun are arguably an outgrowth of Piller's musings on Data in 'Stardust'.

The treatment meanwhile brings back the character of Academy gardener and legend Boothby, played by Ray Walston in both *The Next Generation* and *Voyager*, to counsel Picard over reconciling his differences with Duffy if given the chance. The *Enterprise* gets underway but: "The first complication comes as the *Enterprise* enters the Neutral Zone . . . a Romulan Warbird decloaks, apparently poised for a fight. The Captain is Joss who insists that his ship will be accompanying the *Enterprise*. This was not part of the arrangement, but the Romulans do not intend to let Starfleet go in and cover up all the evidence of their own mis-deeds. As the political liaison on board, Commander Norton encourages Picard to accept the Romulan escort. Joss says he looks forward to closer relations between our peoples . . . and he seems to have his eye on Troi when he says it. Worf clearly doesn't like the fellow."

Back and forth with Joss in the treatment at dinner evokes *The Undiscovered Country* scene between Kirk and co. and General Chang, with Piller giving Worf additional character work given Joss' connections to Khitomer, a devastating milestone in Worf's childhood, and gives them a bat'leth battle on the holodeck as a test of honour.

The *Enterprise* enters the mysterious Briar Patch and they and the Romulan Warbird are attacked by small ships before discovering a Federation starship, Duffy's ship, hiding behind a moon. "Joss launches a full-out assault on Duffy's ship . . . and now Picard must fly the *Enterprise* between the Romulan ship and the smaller starship to protect it, all the while demanding the Romulan captain to cease fire. Finally, the smaller ship is damaged and is forced to land on an M-class planet that has a golden ring around it . . . Picard is convinced by the events that it must be Duffy in there and decides to go to the planet's surface to try and talk him into coming back. He takes Worf, Beverly and Geordi with him on the away team."

They find on the planet what Piller describes as a 'Garden of Eden' with natives who greet them in friendly fashion, and immediately they notice changes to their biology – Geordi's vision, Worf's injuries from the fight with Joss, etc, begin to heal. The leader of the natives presents himself and it's Duffy . . . looking no older than he did at the Academy, to Picard's astonishment. Duffy explains that the planet is made up of sarium krellide (aka 'stardust'), which provides regenerative effects that increases the lifespan of those involved by centuries.

"The relationship between Picard and Duffy is civil, even cordial but not intimate. When Picard asks him why he's been attacking the Romulans, Duffy says the Romulans have, in fact, established an illegal installation in the Neutral Zone driven by their need for sarium krellide. Their exploratory missions brought them close to this system . . . they'd sent probes into the Patch designed to detect the ore and were trying to follow the readings . . . any time they got too close, we took action to stop them. Picard: Without consideration for the consequences to the Federation. Duffy: The Federation can take care of itself – these people can't. Picard: So you chose to ignore the Prime Directive . . . Duffy gets angry with Picard: I knew what the Romulans would do to this planet if they found it. And what would happen to the people who lived on it. Check your history books under Bajor or American Indians for reference."

We are now seeing in 'Stardust' the core plot that *Insurrection* will deliver, except Duffy has been swapped out, come the filmed script, for Admiral Dougherty (played by Anthony Zerbe), with the personal connection to Picard excised. There are also trace elements of Ru'afo here too. Duffy believes the Federation are complicit in the Romulans being aware of this and it leads to conflict between them, with Picard refusing to countenance that the organisation he has devoted his life to would do such a thing.

Troi inveigles her way onto Joss' ship and learns some dark truths: "This is what she discovers: after the Romulan probes had found a significant source of sarium krellide, the treaty negotiations were accelerated with an understanding that the Romulans and the Federation would share the medical ore found in this sector. Then the attacks by Duffy and the aliens began, threatening the agreement. But the Romulans couldn't find Duffy and couldn't penetrate the Patch. So, the Federation agreed to send in their flagship. Picard is horrified to learn that he was in fact being used to lead the Romulans to the ore. And no one even seemed to give a second thought to the aliens who claimed that space as their own. The communications with the Romulans had been handled throughout by Commander Norton."

Picard confronts Norton who, much like the earlier scene with Duffy, resembles the eventual character of Dougherty in defending the Federation's plan to relocate the natives, which Picard considers tantamount to killing them: "Norton vaguely tries to assure Picard that it won't come to that, but his empty promises are interrupted when Picard does something I don't believe we've ever seen him do. He punches Norton in anger. Looming over him like Clay over Liston, he asks Norton if this was done with Semark's approval. Norton doesn't answer as he rubs his chin, only says: I'll have you up on charges, Picard. Picard answers simply, *You're damned right, you will.*"

This seems out of character for Picard until the factor of the regenerative properties he has been exposed to come into play, activating the impetuousness we have seen he displayed in his youth. He subsequently is joined by Data in leaving the *Enterprise* and heading down to the planet to support Duffy's efforts in resisting the joint Federation/Romulan relocation. Data quips, at Picard's initial resistance to him coming: "Very well, sir. I hereby consider myself taken hostage. Or: I believe that pesky emotion chip is malfunctioning again, sir. I'm not sure I can be held accountable for my actions." Piller takes this idea and runs with it for the opening of *Insurrection*, where this precise scenario serves as the inciting incident on the Bak'u planet.

As Picard and Duffy begin to bond once more, they stage Robin Hood-style raids against the enemy forces. Joss leads the charge in hunting them down, as Riker follows Norton's orders to find them, wanting to protect them from Joss' intentions to kill. "As the sequence continues, we begin to realize that Picard is getting younger, first psychologically and then gradually physically as well. We see that swashbuckling spirit of an earlier era revived in his heart. At the end of a particularly satisfying victory over the Romulans, he hugs Duffy with exhilaration. In a way, Picard is embracing his own youth, feeling again the bond of his lost friendship. It turns into a deeply emotional moment for him."

Picard ultimately asks Riker to take the *Enterprise* back to Earth and inform Semark about the conspiracy before the Romulan treaty is signed, believing the Federation will make the right choice. They realise they need to capture the Romulans hunting them to prevent them taking the planet once the *Enterprise* leaves, so they turn the tables. Picard battles Joss in a bat'leth fight and almost loses until Worf steps in for round two and kills him. Duffy, however, during the battle has been mortally wounded.

"They take him to the ship to try to save his life... and as they rush him to Sickbay, we see Picard begin to age rapidly . . . until he looks his real age again . . . In Sickbay, Duffy and Picard say a last, touching farewell between best friends. Picard promises that Duffy will not have died in vain. When he dies, Duffy also returns to his normal age."

The climax takes place at the Federation Council where Picard and his crew confront Semark as the treaty vote is about to commence, who refuses Picard's accusations and claims he and his crew have committed criminal acts, intending to arrest them and end their Starfleet careers. "He orders the guards to take him away and calls for the vote to begin . . . As the guards begin to escort Picard from the chamber, someone begins to clap in the gallery . . . and Picard pauses to look up and sees it is Boothby applauding, standing . . . and as the two men's eyes connect, a second person in the gallery joins Boothby, then a third, and another and another until the whole gallery is cheering Picard by name. As he's led out, the council members look at each other understanding the people have spoken. We can infer the treaty will be defeated and that Semark may have won the battle but has lost the war. As for Picard's future and the future of his crew, we will have to wait until the next movie to find out . . ."

Evoking *The Voyage Home*'s conclusion with Kirk and his crew facing the Federation Council, Piller ends 'Stardust' on something of a cliffhanger. Berman, however, was not won over. He believed the story and Duffy's motivations to be too political. It was he who suggested the Colonel Kurtz figure, to borrow from *Apocalypse Now*, should be Data rather than the new creation of Duffy.

A second draft, marked simply as 'Star Trek IX', dated late June 1997, retained the Romulans as villains and continued building elements constructed in 'Stardust'. Piller introduces 'Matt' Dougherty, a younger character than in *Insurrection* who serves as an envoy to the Romulans.

Picard and the *Enterprise* are informed that Data was recruited for a top-secret mission to contact a race inside the Briar Patch, detected by Romulan probes, but he went 'crazy' and started attacking Romulan forces. Picard is faced with the reality he might have to kill Data to stop tensions between the Federation and Romulans escalating out of control. "Picard: I've been his tutor in all things human, his drama coach, his art professor . . . now I'm asked to be his executioner . . ."

Joss is retained as the adjutant to a Romulan admiral, with a flirtatious interest in Troi remaining (a trait that oddly will carry over into the next film despite Piller's absence). And Piller keeps the colonial, 19th-century mariner flavour he instilled in 'Stardust', with the Kipling reference point of the Briar Patch (named after Br'er Rabbit) and the Conrad influences, framing the Patch as unexplored territory as earlier adventurers would have found 'darkest' Africa to be. "As a long time sailor, Picard knows the best information about a particular area of space can often come from Federation mariners – traders, ferry operators, and just plain adventurers – who traverse the quadrant. As a boy, he once even considered shipping out on the 24th century equivalent of a 'tramp steamer'. The *Enterprise* travels to an extraordinary location where the mariners dock and refit. They're quite a bunch — spirited ex-patriots, colorful rovers and indomitable free-spirits – hearty, well-fellows and lusty women who are not impressed by Picard's uniform. Imagine the captain of an aircraft carrier in the Caribbean arriving at Margaritaville to meet with an odd assortment of free souls who don't care much for authority figures and you get the idea. In an amusing sequence, Picard must earn their trust and cooperation."

This evokes Nicholas Meyer's sensibility with *The Wrath of Khan*, and his belief that *Star Trek* should mine the Hornblower inspirations Gene Roddenberry himself held for the original concept, for stylistic touches. The only way this is retained in *Insurrection* lies in Picard and Worf humorously singing Gilbert and Sullivan's 'HMS Pinafore' operetta to calm Data while hunting him.

Piller retains many of the plot choices from 'Stardust' from then on. Joss' fight with Worf over honour, Picard taking an away team down to the planet, but he also includes a battle with Data in the run-up. Piller alters the natives to add a deeper connection to Troi's telepathic powers: "They're stranger than any aliens we've ever encountered . . . small, with wide foreheads and piercing eyes . . . they're mute, apparently using telepathy (which we do not hear) to communicate with one another.

There is no way for us to communicate directly with these people. Our brains are simply not up to the task. Picard's efforts to make them understand us are extremely frustrating, setting in motion a theme that will continue throughout the story. In time, we will come to understand them as a gentle people with an extraordinary intellect who would harm no one." This frames them as different to the hero-worshipping settlers in the thrall of Duffy, or the relaxed, open, attractive humanoids the Bak'u would be presented as in the final film.

After being taken captive by Data, who Kurtz-like has gone fully native as his programming malfunctions, Picard is forced to kill him before he can destroy the *Enterprise* when they try and rescue him. Data's death is a definitive catalyst for an angry Picard to investigate – with the help of a native child who grew close to Picard, and Troi again inveigling herself with Joss – the conspiracy on the planet which exposes the ore, the joint Romulan/Federation plan and leads to Picard confronting Dougherty in a conflict closer to the one we will witness in Insurrection.

The remainder of the treatment plays out in similar terms to 'Stardust', with the natives resurrecting Data, Picard and his crew breaking orders to help the natives, Joss battling Worf and being killed, and following a battle the Romulans retreat. There is no grand confrontation with the Federation Council, no Semark, and Dougherty survives, with the whole Briar Patch incident ready to be covered up, though Picard is less keen to let it go. The treatment does not end on a cliffhanger this time, rather the *Enterprise* in time-honoured fashion warping off to another adventure.

It was Stewart this time who wasn't happy. He felt the story gloomy and dull. He didn't like that, again, Picard was placed in a dark position having to kill his friend. He disliked the use of the Romulans, believing they were played out. He thought it was not the best use of Data as a character. "In the first draft, Picard and Data are brutal, bitter enemies. In the film there's a wonderful moment where they battle in a dogfight while Picard sings Gilbert and Sullivan. That used to take seventy pages, and in that battle Picard was ultimately forced to kill Data. That was all very interesting, but by the time you had Picard go down to the next planet, you basically had a miniseries worth of plot. Neither side of it was good enough to support the elements. It was Patrick, frankly, who said, 'This is dark and dreary and it's not fun,' and he was the one who put us back on the fountain of youth course that ultimately really leads the story to its current state."

Piller's third treatment, later in July, added flesh to these bones as the story heaved closer to the 'Heart of Lightness' aspects of the 'Stardust' draft. Duffy is reintroduced but instead of Hugh he is Eleanor, who we see in an Academy prologue as friends and possible romantic interests. Data remains the Kurtz figure, but Eleanor is part of the Starfleet team on the mission to the Briar Patch, and she like Hugh is youthful when Picard meets her on the planet and starts to recapture his youth, and they become lovers, providing Stewart with a love interest character for the first and only time in cinematic terms. She would eventually evolve into the Anij character for *Insurrection*, portrayed by Donna Murphy, though Stewart and Murphy would be frustrated in how the romantic and sexual aspects of their dynamic would be cut and toned down in the final film.

"There was a whole sequence, a portion of which is still in the film, where I'm leading Picard through this altered reality, stepping inside a moment and kind of suspending time. It was more kind of a sensual exploration, a heightened sensory response to different ways of touching each other, and that led into this kiss. When I saw that that was cut, I thought that it may have been to give a greater payoff to a kiss that was at the end of the movie. And when I saw that *that* was cut, I was surprised. I initially had a negative response to that, because you shape performance thinking that there are certain pieces of the puzzle that are a given, and if you take those pieces out you might have chosen to shape the performance differently if you knew that those pieces were not going to be there. Patrick and I played that relationship as if there was an intimacy that had taken place at a certain point. I was told it was a studio decision that the kisses were not necessary."

Piller's third draft names the natives as the Bak'u, swaps out the Romulans for a new race called the Son'i (destined to become Son'a, perhaps to avoid confusion with a certain technology conglomerate), introduces Ru'afo as the villain and the revelation that the Bak'u and Son'a are the same biological race. The primary elements of the finished film were in place, although the film cycled through several other titles, including 'Star Trek: Prime Directive' and 'Star Trek: Nemesis' before settling on *Star Trek: Insurrection*.

Several *Deep Space Nine* connections were cut, unlike in *First Contact* where Worf is introduced by steering the *Defiant* into battle with the Borg. Berman vetoed an intended reference to the death of Worf's wife, Jadzia Dax, at the end of the sixth season of the show. And a scene was filmed featuring a cameo for Quark, who would have been present on the Bak'u planet, though only stills exist and the scene has never been released. Armin Shimerman gives more detail on this: "While I was doing *DS9*, Michael Piller was writing *Insurrection*. We would have dinner parties every now and then and he would say 'there's a scene for Quark'. At one dinner party, he would say I was in, and another he'd say I was out. Eventually he said that he had put [Quark] in the final version and I was in. Rick Berman called me at home and offered me the part a couple of days later. I pretended to not know anything because that's the Hollywood thing to do, and the next thing I knew I was shooting the movie."

While not as successful or critically beloved as *First Contact*, *Insurrection* did well at the box office, but it left everyone involved with a sense that something was missing from a final product that had been difficult to corral into a script and story that everyone – from Piller and Berman to Stewart to Brent Spiner and beyond – had been happy with. *Insurrection*, on that basis, remains the least memorable of the *Next Generation* movies, even if it perhaps, of them all, the film most attuned to the spirit of the series, thanks to Piller's storytelling decisions.

Piller ruminated once the film was complete about what he might have done differently second time around: "I'm not satisfied that, when all was said and done, we adequately established the odds against Picard. Yes, maybe one less cut in the ground action might have helped – the attack comes from only three Son'a shuttlecraft and the drones – but that's not really at the heart of the issue as I look back at it now. The true villain in the picture is the Federation leadership, but as written, their crimes are mostly philosophical. That leaves the Son'a, whom I described in dialogue as 'petty thugs', to provide the entire threat. I think the film might have had more scope if I'd pitted Starfleet forces as well as Son'a against Picard and crew."

He also believed a great deal of Picard's 'personal journey' was lost: "I wish I had started with a more substantial arc for Picard – one that could have withstood the loss of a scene or two. The clutter arc as written was just too subtle to survive. I have to reiterate that, based on the assembled film, I fully endorsed the cuts that Jonathan, Rick and the studio decided to make. But a trip to the fountain of youth deserves a profound re-birth of some kind for the hero and we didn't quite get there. That's a missed opportunity, one that bothers me a lot. I keep thinking back to how the script might have changed if we had faded in to find Picard weary from two years of war, first with the Borg and now with the Dominion, having lost many crew members fighting to protect the ideals of the Federation. Now, he discovers his own command is about to sacrifice those very ideals to steal the Ba'ku planet. In that scenario, the peaceful world would have provided an immediate contrast to Picard's dark days of war."

This was the final ever *Star Trek* script that Michael Piller would write, as he tragically passed away of head and neck cancer in 2005, following a long illness. *Insurrection* would be a passionate final voyage on the *Enterprise* for the man who made *The Next Generation* the success it was, and who remains a key figure in the development of *Star Trek* as a franchise.

He understood that for all his regrets, once a writer's work is out there, that in many ways is the end of the story: "My colleague, Alan Spencer, tells the story of the artist who is caught trying to steal his own work from the Louvre. 'I just want to finish a few things in my painting that aren't quite right yet,' he says. 'It's not yours anymore,' says the Louvre guard as they take him away. 'It's ours now.'"

*

The pedigree behind *Star Trek: Nemesis* should, on paper, have assured it the greatest critical and commercial success of any *Next Generation* picture to date. Stuart Baird, director of *The Fugitive* spin-off *U.S. Marshals* and renowned editor who had trained under various directing masters, stepped in to helm a script from John Logan, the Oscar-winning screenwriter of Ridley Scott's *Gladiator*, and later the iconic James Bond movie *Skyfall*.

The result, however, was both *Star Trek*'s most critically derided picture to date and the lowest-grossing film in the franchise of all time. It was not simply 'A Generation's Final Journey' as the tagline billed the film but a major contributor to what many believed was the second death of *Star Trek*.

Rick Berman admits the studio were not passionate about a fourth *Next Generation* film following the lukewarm *Insurrection* and a four-year gap, during which the franchise's two *Next Generation*-era series had drawn to a close. "The head of the studio had really tried to convince me to do a movie without the TNG cast. The feeling was, 'These guys have all gotten kind of older. It's time to introduce some new, fresh blood.' There was an attitude that I should go out and find a new Tom Cruise. I felt strongly against that for two reasons. One reason was that when we were developing this movie, the *Enterprise* series was coming out, so the *Star Trek* audience was about to get introduced to a whole new cast of young characters on television. For us to simultaneously introduce them to a whole new cast of young characters in a movie seemed to be insane to me."

This would be a conceptual wish of Paramount's that would become more apparent as *Star Trek* fully entered the 21st century, in various iterations both made and unmade, but ultimately everyone involved decided to make what they considered to be a final voyage for the ageing *Next Generation* cast. With Frakes not returning as director – busy as he was directing a teen adventure picture called *Clockstoppers* – nor the established writing hands of either Moore and Braga or Piller, *Nemesis* operated from two conflicting opposites as production began – a director in Baird with zero experience or seemingly interest in the franchise, and a celebrated writer in Logan who was, first and foremost, a devoted 'Trekkie': "My agents said, 'You want to do what?!?' The whole thing for me is that I'm a lifelong Trekkie, and utterly proud of it. My sort of obsession or fascination with *Star Trek* began with Captain Kirk on his original mission. Even as a kid, I was, like, "This is extraordinary." The chance to be a part of that story was just too exciting to even think about logically or in any other way."

Logan worked heavily on the story with Brent Spiner, who as the role of Data has increased across the *Next Generation* films had taken, after Stewart and Frakes as director, a more sizeable developmental role over production of the films. Spiner claims that Logan first produced a draft very different from the eventual movie, plus that they struggled to create something entirely fresh: "How do you come up with another story after you've done 180-odd hours? Actually, John Logan and I came up with a story that it turned out had already been done on *Deep Space Nine*, and neither of us had seen that. Rick, being there all the time, knew the story very well and said, 'We've already done it.' Then the three of us sat around together and thought about what would be interesting. We tossed around ideas and finally something stuck, and it evolved from there."

Nemesis begins, following the mysterious assassination of the ruling praetor and senate of the powerful Romulan Star Empire, with the *Enterprise-E* crew preparing for the wedding of Riker and Troi after they rekindled their romance during *Insurrection*. Very swiftly, Picard and his crew are ordered – unusually – to Romulus where a new praetor, Shinzon (played by Tom Hardy in a breakout role), has assumed power and seeks peace with the Federation. Picard eventually discovers that Shinzon is a cloned version of him from a secret Romulan plot to replace him, who grew up in the mines of Remus, has seized the empire and with his powerful ship, the *Scimitar*, plans to attack and destroy Earth and the Federation with a deadly new weapon.

Logan, a self-confessed fan of *The Wrath of Khan*, sought an approach to *Nemesis* that provided Picard with a powerful antagonist equivalent to the Borg Queen, or as Khan himself was to Kirk: "I thought that it would be really cool to have Patrick Stewart playing off an antagonist who is young and vibrant and very much like he is, and from that came the obvious connection between them. We played around with a lot of different avenues before we got there. We played with the idea, is this his long-lost son he never knew he had? Or is this a son he knew he had but no one ever knew about – but that just ran so contrary to the Trek canon that we sort of didn't want to go there."

Berman expands on this: "A script was written and it was too long and way too wordy. It was always a bit too Shakespearean. The idea of the story went from Picard's son to a Picard clone that was the same age as Picard, where Patrick would play both characters."

No such concerns for canon were in place twenty years later, in *Picard*, when the captain was indeed revealed to have a long-lost son, but that's a story for further down the road . . .

Akin to the fairly random inclusion of Quark in *Insurrection*, much as it did not make the final cut, Paramount lobbied for Berman to include Jeri Ryan as Seven of Nine somewhere in the film, keen as they were to include cameo appearances from previous *Next Generation* stars at the Riker and Troi wedding, which included Whoopi Goldberg as Guinan, and Wil Wheaton as Wesley Crusher, who much like Armin Shimerman failed to make the completed version of the film, bar the briefest of appearances in one shot at least confirming his presence.

Ryan, however, turned the overture down: "I was, like, I did four years in a catsuit on *Voyager* and I just got on a David Kelley show, which was my one chance to break out of *Star Trek*, which was still a fear that I had that I wasn't going to be able to escape that. Why would she be there? It was just odd. It wasn't the right thing to do. They understood, but then Rick was, like, 'Do you want to do a cameo at the wedding?' And I was, like, 'No! I don't know these people, I don't want to go to their wedding!'

The original wedding sequence as written contained an appearance by Dr Leah Brahms, played by Susan Gibney in *The Next Generation* third and fourth season episodes 'Booby Trap' and 'Galaxy's Child' and who had been established as a love interest for Geordi. Here, their relationship is confirmed, and the alternate future as depicted in 'All Good Things . . .' establishes they had three children, including two girls called Alandra and Sidney. The third season of *Picard*, in the canonical *Nemesis* future, introduces both children as adult Starfleet officers, but given Leah's appearance in *Nemesis* was cut, it is unclear and perhaps unlikely given casting that Alandra and Sidney are Leah's daughters.

It was just one of many unfilmed or deleted scenes from the final version of *Nemesis*, up to fifty minutes of which ended up on the cutting room floor. One confirms that Wesley, who left the *Enterprise* to voyage with the mysterious Traveler at the end of the seventh season, was returning to Starfleet and would serve under the newly minted Captain Riker on the USS *Titan*. Wesley would eventually reappear in 'Farewell', the second season finale of *Picard*, where he had remained very much a Traveler, his life a mystery.

In the coda of the film, following the death of Data and the transfer of Riker, Picard gets a new first officer in Commander Martin Madden, played by Steven Culp but, given he was deleted from the film, his presence in this role remains non-canonical. In an amusing scene, a departing Riker tells him Picard likes informality, pranking Madden who initially gets short shrift from Picard. Nonetheless, the film ends on a different, hopeful note to the scene between Picard and possible Data replacement B-4, with him preparing to depart to a new system for a mission of exploration. "It should be exciting. It's a place . . . where no one has gone before."

The *Enterprise* warps away, seemingly bringing the adventures of Captain Picard and his crew to an end. Though, had events played out slightly differently, it might not have entirely been the final chapter of *The Next Generation* story on the big screen.

In an interview almost a decade after *Nemesis* brought the curtain down on *The Next Generation*, Patrick Stewart suggested there were plans for a fifth film featuring the *Enterprise* crew being hatched between Logan and Spiner: "It was a very exciting idea for a screenplay. It would have been a real farewell to *Next Generation*, but it would have involved other historic aspects of *Star Trek* as well. I can't go into details because the project wasn't mine. When that didn't happen, the studio announced in its own inimitable way that we were suffering from franchise fatigue and that there was to be no more, and I am absolutely content with that."

Spiner expanded a little on the idea elsewhere: "One of the ideas that John Logan and I had about what the next film would have been was a Justice League of *Star Trek*. Something would bring all the great *Star Trek* villains together, from Khan to Shinzon, and Picard is the only person who could stop them and he actually has to go through time and pluck out the people he needs to help him. He goes back to the moment before Data blows up and takes him back to get Kirk and Spock, and go even further back and get Scott Bakula's character, Archer. The problem with that more than anything is cost – how do you pay for that?"

When the poor box office and critical reaction of *Nemesis* became apparent, and *Star Trek* focused entirely on *Enterprise* the television show, these ideas very quickly disappeared and were not revived for the reunion of ultimately the entire *Next Generation* cast on *Picard*, the final season of which was considered widely to be an unofficial fifth 'movie' and conclusion for the characters. Nonetheless, the ambition to bring together past heroes and villains in *Star Trek* history, in the style of comic-book storytelling, presaged the cinematic pop-culture behemoth that would dominate in the 2010s, even when *Star Trek* did return to the big screen: the Marvel Cinematic Universe.

Indeed, as early as the late 1990s, Brannon Braga was suggesting to Berman that a *Star Trek* film that brought together characters from across the requisite television series for a big-screen adventure would be a viable option. "We were gonna get Picard, Data, Odo, the holographic Doctor . . . all the Star Trek characters on one ship, like a think tank . . . It was like *Star Trek: The Avengers*." Though Berman didn't recall Braga suggesting this, or indeed when, he quipped that he liked the idea in retrospect: "You might as well throw Kirk in there as well."

Could this have worked? Could, in an age when comic-book cinema focused on solitary heroes in sequels, *Star Trek* have beaten Marvel to the punch and combined the cast and crews of *The Next Generation*, *Deep Space Nine*, *Voyager* and even *Enterprise* in a movie event to end them all? The non-canonical book series certainly dabbled in such crossover events, while the television series all – even *Enterprise*, removed from almost all other *Star Trek* series by the distance of time – found mechanisms to cross characters and sometimes story arcs over to each other. Nevertheless, in the main, each series remained distinct and isolated within their own realms.

In an era beyond the rampant success of comic-book cinema that birthed a new age of the franchise, one built on characters and storylines weaving in and building to gigantic event narratives, *Star Trek* might one day still go where it has never gone before. The age of *Nemesis*, and the original adventures of *The Next Generation*, was too early for such an idea to take flight. Captain Picard and his crew would eventually return but in very different circumstances.

For now, as the Golden Age of *Star Trek* in the 1990s gave way to a new century, a new millennium, Berman and Braga chose a different way to explore the final frontier. Rather than consider endings, their future lay in beginnings . . .

ELEVEN

THE BEGINNING: *ENTERPRISE*

WE HAVE ESTABLISHED that Gene Roddenberry, as far back as the 1960s, enjoyed the idea of a *Star Trek* prequel exploring the origin stories of Kirk and co., a concept that would be fully realised finally as the 21st century and a new era of nostalgia-fuelled storytelling emerged.

What of further back in the mists of the *Star Trek* universe? *First Contact* had depicted the mid-21st century, a world ravaged by a Third World War that finds renewed hope in contact with the Vulcans. As detailed earlier in this book, Captain Robert April had a litany of adventures planned as who Roddenberry considered to be the first commander of the USS *Enterprise*, with *The Animated Series* giving him life, albeit in a semi-canonical context. Yet much of the origins of Starfleet, of the United Federation of Planets, of the world before Kirk, Spock and the original crew, remained shrouded in mystery.

Enterprise, a series that would initially shed the prefix '*Star Trek*', was designed to answer that question, while simultaneously warping the franchise truly where it had never gone before.

Though viewing figures had waned in later seasons, *Voyager* had ended in 2001 and was deemed a success, and UPN desired – against Berman's initial assertions that the franchise might need a rest after over ten years of continuous show production – to create a fourth new series. Rick

Berman contacted Brannon Braga, who following *Voyager* had decided to leave *Star Trek* behind, to help develop the project: "Rick called me and said, 'What do you think about setting it between *First Contact* and Kirk's time?' And I said I thought that was a great idea. We started talking about it and considered what it would give us, and it evolved from there. We never considered another concept. We thought that *First Contact* seemed to be more of a relatable film somehow, because it had characters from the near future versus the distant future, and it allowed a more non-*Star Trek* audience to embrace *Star Trek*. You didn't really have to know much to enjoy that movie."

With fans keen to further explore the 24th century after *Voyager* or even a timeframe beyond that, Berman and Braga were less interested in building on a well-established world and more excited to chart a genuine frontier, as producer Mike Sussman suggests: "You can't go further in the future with communicators getting smaller and our force fields are even more magical. Yeah, go back and let's do *The Right Stuff*. It just sounded so amazing."

Sussman refers to the Oscar-nominated film from 1983, directed by Phillip Kaufman (he of the almost-made 'Planet of the Titans' project), based on the Tom Wolfe about the air force test pilots and their journey to becoming the first American crewmen of a space flight in history, a concept Scott Bakula – who would sit in the captain's chair on the new show, heartily agreed shared DNA with *Enterprise*: "It is *The Right Stuff*. That kind of energy of being the first ones out there and being a little scared sometimes and being a little overwhelmed by the experience, which I think is a great emotion to have to play with. Americans have explored our planet in a variety of different ways. Some successfully, some not. We have a wide history of exploration in this country. Certainly different experiences in Vietnam and places like that where we tried to impose our ideas or philosophies on different cultures, and still are in many places around this planet. Making it more about the experience and less about planting the flag."

Star Trek: Enterprise took place in 2151, over a century before the adventures of Captain Kirk and his crew, at the formation of Starfleet in the mid-22nd century. Captain Jonathan Archer (played by Bakula) commands the *NX-01 Enterprise* in the days before the founding of the United Federation of Planets, as humanity – shepherded closely by the Vulcans – take their first tentative steps of exploration away from Earth. Archer's first officer T'Pol (Jolene Blalock) provides Vulcan temperance, while his chief engineer Lt Cmdr Trip Tucker (Connor Trinneer) adds all-American, energetic brio. Alongside the rest of their crew, this formative *Enterprise* begins to explore a galaxy barely explored, filled with races familiar to us but unfamiliar to them, and behind it a mysterious 'Temporal Cold War' as futuristic aliens seek to undermine and change history around them.

However, despite a genuinely innovative concept, digging into the beginnings of what we know to be the *Star Trek* universe, and even experimenting with standing alone from the loaded prefix and providing a warbling theme tune song (the lambasted 'Faith of the Heart' by Russell Watson), *Enterprise* very quickly copied the dramatic and narrative formula utilised on *The Next Generation* and *Voyager* especially, telling facsimile science-fiction plotlines across the first and second seasons that could have been, and often were, done on those earlier series.

Braga nonetheless had different aspirations initially: "We wanted to do a show that took place in the first season on Earth, we wanted season one to culminate with the launching of the *Enterprise*, and really tell *Star Trek* a little differently. The closest I've seen it done was in J. J. Abrams' first movie; I was really grooving on the Earth part of the movie with the ship being built, because those were images I was hoping to do myself and wasn't permitted to. I thought it was really cool."

Science advisor and writer André Bormanis expanded on this to me: "Brandon originally thought that it would be cool to spend most of the first season of *Enterprise* on Earth, building the starship *Enterprise*, building the NX-01, seeing it in its final stages of construction, and playing stories that basically were about whether or not this ship should ever launch. We wanted to have a contingent of people on Earth. Good people, not bad guys, not villains, but people on Earth who, like the Vulcans, believe that it's too soon for us to get out there in a big way. Like, you would be able to spend some time finding out how Archer assembled his crew instead of everybody being there from the beginning, how T'Pol joined the ship. Wouldn't have happened necessarily, in the first episode, right? Could have been halfway through but I know there was general discussion."

Bormanis continues: "And the Earth was just getting out of this global multigenerational depression, right? I thought that sounded really, really cool. But the studio would not go for that. The studio was, like, 'Nope. *Star Trek* is about a starship going places. You launch the ship in the pilot.' Brannon didn't want to have a transporter. Let's save the transporter for maybe second season or third season. Nah, it's *Star Trek*, you've got to have a starship, you've got to have phasers, you've got to have a transporter. So, there were a lot of constraints placed on the show from the beginning."

Chris Black, a writer on the show, remembers the intentions of the network despite these restraints: "I remember what Rick [Berman] said when he was pitching me the show and saying it was going to be *The Right Stuff* in outer space. Dangerous. Risky. The first guys out there, the test pilots of the program, no one's been out here before. A throwback to good old-fashioned, two-fisted *Star Trek*. An acknowledgment that *Voyager* became too intellectual, sterile, and off-putting. The mandate, as I understood it from the network and from themselves, was to make it fun again."

Manny Coto, a writer on the third and show runner on the fourth and final season, added: "I actually thought it would be more fun to go rougher with it, more *Crimson Tide*, meaning there was no captain sitting in a big chair staring at a big screen. And have the ship a bit more claustrophobic, less comfortable. There wouldn't be big viewscreens, you'd have to look into little monitors. Kind of what *Battlestar Galactica* ultimately did."

Enterprise launched without many of these intentions realised, despite a strong main cast who arrived fully formed. The intention for T'Pol originally was for the female Vulcan presence aboard the *Enterprise* to be T'Pau, a legendary figure in *Star Trek* fandom as the ageing adjudicator in the iconic *Original Series* episode 'Amok Time'. For legal reasons, a new character was devised but T'Pau was eventually used in the fourth season episodes 'Kir'shara' and 'The Awakening', which delved deeply into Vulcan culture. As we will see, she sat well in a season renowned for connectives and tethers to particularly *The Original Series*.

The first season geared into production following the traditional two-part pilot episode, 'Broken Bow', which got the series off to a promising start. Ideas came thick and fast, though as writer Fred Dekker claims across the first season, a great deal were pitched but fell by the wayside: "On *Enterprise*, we staff writers would hear pitches a few times a month, and I came across a couple of ideas that I thought would make terrific episodes. So I would write these up and submit them thinking, 'Yeah, this is going to make for a great episode of *Enterprise*,' only to never hear anything about them again. It was like throwing ideas into a black hole."

An early episode of the show, 'Fortunate Son', added backstory to that of ship's pilot Travis Mayweather (Anthony Montgomery), who was known as a 'Boomer'. In 22nd-century slang, it referred to a human born in space who had spent most of their lives growing up in space on transports or cargo vessels. Braga thought it was a fun concept that the series wasted: "'There are some things that you think are cool when you first create a show, like the space boomer idea. It didn't really go anywhere. I think we did one space boomer episode. But what sounded good on paper, born and raised in space, never been to Earth, what's their perspective? When everyone gets on a ship, week to week, it's kind of like: 'Who cares what the boomer has to say?'"

Plans roughly existed to do a follow-up episode around the 'Boomer' idea but fell by the wayside out of concerns the writers didn't want audiences to feel the *Enterprise* was too close to Earth. "We had another story or two planned with the Boomers, but we decided not to delve too much into meeting Humans all the time." Braga claims, concerned also it would have prevented them finding different ways to explore the Travis character.

One of the series' recurring actors, Vaughn Armstrong, who played erstwhile Admiral Forrest until early in the fourth season, pitched a story in the first season that would have not only connected to the recently ended *Voyager*, 250 years in the future, but given him some additional work. In the final episode of *Voyager*, 'Endgame', Armstrong had played Korath, a wily Klingon scientist from the early 25th century who, in an alternate future where *Voyager* had returned home after decades lost in space, invents a time-travel device called the 'chrono deflector' which is stolen by an alternate, aged Admiral Janeway, who then uses it to change *Voyager*'s history in the past. Armstrong believed there was a means of bringing Korath into *Star Trek*'s history: "An episode I would love to see would show Korath taking the time machine that Janeway stole from him and going back to stop Admiral Forrest from sending people out into space!"

Armstrong believed Korath would steal the device back from Janeway and come back to the events of 'Broken Bow' to stop Forrest giving the order for Archer's crew to explore space. It does not sound like a concept that was ever taken seriously by the writers room, instead more of a flippant story concept to give Armstrong an additional pay cheque, as he quipped: "I'm plugging that because the overtime would be great," It does, however, suggest *Enterprise*'s future, one in which the show would take plenty of opportunities to connect to *Star Trek*'s 'future history' and not feel as isolated as an artefact of the past.

An example of this lies in 'The Andorian Incident', which reintroduced one of *Star Trek*'s oldest creations as semi-antagonists and principally the enjoyable recurring character of Shran (memorably played by *Deep Space Nine* stalwart Jeffrey Combs), would originally have featured the Gorn instead, monosyllabic villains memorably realised in *The Original Series* episode 'Arena'. A Gorn was also meant to feature at Riker and Troi's wedding in *Nemesis*, and eventually did reappear as the main antagonists of the first season of *Strange New Worlds*.

Though it is possible he was joking, Bormanis also commented that the writers pondered many ways to give Archer's pet beagle, Porthos (so named after one of Dumas' Three Musketeers), his own story. Ideas he claims were floated included Porthos communicating with a canine alien, gaining intelligence, and being forced to take command of the *Enterprise*. Bormanis quipped that they didn't want Porthos to steal the show, hence why none of these happened.

Linda Park, who played communications officer Hoshi Sato, wanted the show to produce a musical episode as a means of displaying her ballroom dancing training and give a chance for John Billingsley, who played the quirky Dr Phlox, and Bakula to croon. Musical episodes were often mooted on genre shows of the 1990s and 2000s but rarely came to pass, nor was it the first time such a notion had been floated for *Star Trek*. Park also claims that Trinneer wanted to develop an episode like Quentin Tarantino's *Pulp Fiction*, a key staple of cinematic popular culture in the 1990s, but from the POV of an alien race who only heard the *Enterprise* crew speak gibberish until translated.

These ideas consistently hold true to the notion that quite apart from Braga's initial vision of an edgier, darker series exploring the terror of newly discovered space, *Enterprise* very quickly settled into a familiar *Star Trek* rhythm of how to tell episodic stories that had been honed over the last fifteen years. Andre Jacquemetton, a writer on the series with his wife Marie, refers to Braga's vision: "We were really excited. The way Brannon pitched it was we were going to write our own rules and that space was dangerous and scary. It was really exciting to just be there in the beginning, and it doesn't necessarily have to be the best of the best going out there; we're going to make mistakes. For some reason, we kept on thinking at the end of the season *Enterprise* is going to come back to Earth and dock and, basically, it will be maybe half of the ship."

Marie added: "I remember Brannon said that in his perfect vision of how the season would end, the *Enterprise* would come limping back to port, falling apart and battered by horrors that they had encountered out there. Clearly, that didn't happen."

The second season continued at much the same pace, despite almost the entire writing team departing the series as they steadily either filtered away or were let go, as Braga struggled to communicate the vision he had with Berman and the edicts coming down on him from a studio who did not want *Enterprise* to rock the boat in any way in terms of how *Star Trek* was presented.

An idea during the second season that Bormanis couldn't make work concerned "a completely featureless planet, something that's the size of the Earth but is as smooth as a billiard ball", except he struggled to find a narrative to fit around the intriguing science-fiction concept. Some trace of this idea perhaps filtered down to the Sphere Builders in the Delphic Expanse, the primary antagonists of the very different third season.

Three freelance writers, Jack Treviño, Steve Fratt and Dr Joseph DiLella, pitched an assortment of concepts during the second year which focused on the supporting, less well-utilised characters around the big three – Archer, Trip and T'Pol, who had been designed to mimic the Kirk, Spock, McCoy triumvirate of the 1960s – including a story focusing on Dr Phlox where he ends up creating Frankenstein-style creatures out of six different alien species, including humans. Whether this would have been a horror or a comedy, given Phlox's jovial disposition, remains unknown.

Also pitched was a connection back to the 'The Changeling', the *Original Series* episode about Nomad, a semi-sentient alien probe which gains intelligence with a directive to sterilise imperfect life. Their intention on *Enterprise* was to explore Tan Ru, a probe of unknown origin designed to sterilise soil samples ahead of probable colonisation efforts. Trevino remained convinced that a story about Tan Ru would have been sold but *Enterprise* was cancelled at the point it was floated. It likely would have worked within Coto's vision for the fourth season, given the other 'prequel' tales to threads left over from *The Original Series*.

As the second season closed, *Enterprise* did try and up the ante after another staid run of episodes, and an overarching Temporal Cold War narrative going nowhere fast. Episodes such as 'Judgment' and 'Bounty' introduced an earlier Duras ancestor within the Klingon High Council seeking a vendetta against Archer. 'Regeneration' exploited an ingenious 'pre-destination paradox' allowing them to bring the Borg into the show, in a sequel to *First Contact*, without contradicting existing continuity.

Enterprise remained, nonetheless, listless.

"There was nothing cutting-edge about *Star Trek* anymore in seasons one and two. We were, like, 'Let's do more character-oriented shows.' So we ended up doing some super low-concept shows and the character work we were doing wasn't fun. We were still doing very traditional *Star Trek* character stuff, but getting rid of the cool science-y, high-concept premise, the time travel and such. And we hadn't really replaced it with anything that was bringing us new viewers. We were just alienating the old viewers."

Braga adds: "It wasn't until the end of season two when Jonathan Dolgen, king of all of Paramount, called us in and said, 'You have to do something; the show is being renewed but you have to do something to shake things up.' So we finally got to do what we wanted to do all along, which was a seasonal arc, which at that time was like a big deal. *24* was doing really well, and everyone was saying maybe we can do something serialized, too. I became creatively energized, and season three was actually really fun to do."

'The Expanse', a thrilling second season finale which introduced a new alien threat in the Xindi, saw a devastating attack on Earth, and launched the *Enterprise* on a season-spanning mission into the strange, Bermuda Triangle-esque Delphic Expanse, immediately set what would be rechristened *Star Trek: Enterprise* on a whole new, bold direction for a much stronger third season.

It was, as we will ultimately see, too little, too late.

*

11 September 2001. A date that lives in infamy in the American consciousness for the devastating attacks on the World Trade Center in New York, not to mention the Pentagon. The world changed that day and, for many well-known television shows that launched that month – Kiefer Sutherland thriller *24*, spy-fi adventure *Alias*, and indeed *Enterprise* – the shifting sands of popular culture began to morph around them.

"I say this, and I've never heard from Rick Berman or Brannon Braga if they hate that I say this, but there's a big part of me that feels that 9/11 influenced our show, influenced the writers and their state of mind. When they said, 'We want to go in this darker direction,' I said, 'That feels appropriate to the times.' You look at shows like *JAG*, which was still on then, and *NCIS* and shows that came out of the war . . . it's funny how all the war movies pretty much died, but the TV stuff that touched on it lived on. I felt like it was appropriate. I wish it had been that way from the top."

Scott Bakula's wish that *Enterprise* had embraced the inherent sadness, anger and darkness that pervaded American storytelling in the wake of 9/11, rather than attempting to run back to the unipolar *Star Trek* safety of *The Next Generation* and *Voyager* that had now been shattered, was realised by the nature of a third season instigated by the Xindi attack in 'The Expanse', killing millions of Floridians (including Trip's sister), which was an undisguised refrain on the New York attacks.

Coto, for his money, lamented the move into darker, reactive, serialised territory: "When I met with Brannon, he pitched me the whole Xindi arc. I remember being a little disappointed. I thought the idea was cool, but one of the things I was looking forward to doing on *Star Trek* was coming up with stand-alone episodes; sci-fi concepts that I could explore. When it became a season-long arc, I said, 'Okay, I guess I won't be doing that.' It was kind of a 9/11 allegory in a sense, so I signed on to the idea. Brannon wanted to make the show darker and a little more gritty, because it was perceived as kind of staid, so I was all for that."

Braga denies the 9/11 parallels: "We weren't trying to do 9/11. The show premiered a week or two after 9/11. We didn't do the Xindi arc as a 9/11 metaphor. We did it because an attack on Earth hadn't been done in a while. Let's put Earth at stake so there's a larger purpose."

Although the *Enterprise* was on a singular mission, with many episodes following the same narrative (especially in the rear half of the season), relatively stand-alone plot lines still existed within the framework of the third season and unused pitches, some of which likely would not have worked during the voyage into the Expanse, remained on the table.

Husband and wife team Judith and Garfield Reeves-Stevens – long-held stalwarts of the franchise – wanted to find a way to include an earlier version of the Trill, who had been well featured during *Deep Space Nine* thanks to Jadzia and Ezri Dax. "The idea being what would Archer's reaction to the Trill be? We thought that to [the] first Humans to meet a joined species like the Trill would be something of a horror. It would be like a planet where the body snatchers had won . . . And the Humans would want to separate them."

It sounds like an idea that might have reconceptualised the Trill in a far more alien fashion than *Deep Space Nine* presented them and sadly never materialised, although the Trill of the far distant 32nd-century future would be visited in the third season of *Discovery*, albeit in a different context.

While the third season largely delivered in terms of dramatic stakes and character arcs, numerous writers involved felt their time with *Star Trek* was over, including Braga who had increasingly grown frustrated with what he felt was a network who had little faith in or understanding of the show they were trying to make: "I was pitching a story where our captain and another crew member spend the entire episode stuck on the hull of the ship, which was a daring production challenge, and I was asked 'What's a hull?' by the network. And so we were the only people who understood the show. To be blunt, I don't think they appreciated the show, and at a time when *Star Trek* was at its most vulnerable, it was at a place that was not protecting it or nourishing it, so that didn't help."

As the third season ended, concluding on a time-travelling cliffhanger in 'Zero Hour', Braga passed the baton to Coto, who entered the fourth season with a renewed sense of impetus – although Braga still remained a hovering producing presence, contributing ideas and writing, unable entirely to let his creation go.

Bormanis claims that *Enterprise* had been making a mistake that Coto would soon work to correct: "Where we disappointed the fans was in not really embracing the prequel element. For instance, Fred Dekker very much had to push and fight for the Andorians. "Bring in the Andorians. Let's see how humanity first met these guys with the antennas." And again, Rick and Brannon, not big fans of the original. They're just not that familiar with it. And they were harder to convince to do those explicitly prequel kind of shows. You're never going to please everybody."

The fourth season was commissioned less due to stellar ratings or faith in the series but rather as a means of working toward syndication, for which a series needed to hit a hundred episodes. *The Original Series* had found renewed life in syndication and the network, being aware that *Enterprise* was unlikely to run seven seasons as the previous three sequel series had, had one eye on the greater financial reward in keeping the series on air for even a little longer. Coto picked up the ball and ran with it: "My idea was, let's find cool ideas that have some tie, some relevance with the original series; let's use this as a prequel, let's make a prequel. And let's have fun. We were all huge *Star Trek* fans, André and Sussman and I were all original series fans, so let's have fun and do stories that we'll all really enjoy."

Where the third season had reinvented *Enterprise* as a serialised, 9/11 analogy, pushing the crew into darker, vengeful territory to fit the tenor of American society reeling from the trauma of that event, Coto and his team reinvented *Enterprise* once more as a collection of budgeted fan fiction stories filling in gaps, adding to canon and exploring threads left over from *The Original Series* and other *Star Trek* shows. Brent Spiner played a villainous ancestor of Data's creator Noonien Soong; the history of Vulcan culture and their iconic figure Surak was explored; the season even created an entire storyline to explain why Klingons of the *Next Generation* era looked different from those in *The Original Series*.

Berman, who had to be talked into this approach by Coto, who was convinced it was what fans wanted, added: "Manny is a huge *Star Trek* fan. When I say *Star Trek*, I'm talking mainly the original series. So what he brought to the table was a great love for what was going to be coming in ninety years. He was able to bring to the canon things that the fans loved; things that set up storylines that the fans of the original series knew would be paid off in various episodes of the Kirk and Spock era. He created storylines from many episodes that did tie into the original series, and the fans of the original series enjoyed that."

Coto even had to talk Berman out of setting the entire fourth season in an alternate Second World War as established in the premiere of the fourth season 'Storm Front'. He instead worked on a range of stories within prequel territory, many of which came to pass, some of which never quite made it but could have been fascinating additions to what was already a rich season from a narrative perspective.

An early idea, and one of the boldest, was to remove their main character: "I remember at one point we debated actually killing Scott as a way to inject a dramatic situation into the fourth season, where the characters now have to get used to someone brand-new coming on board. This person would have a totally different way of doing things and have a totally different outlook, and so you would have Trip and the rest of the characters kind of butting heads against this individual, whoever he or she might be, but we decided not to. It's a little like the shift in *M*A*S*H*. I figured you could do the same thing with this; start off with a character nobody liked, butting heads, and they end up respecting him. That was one where Rick said no. It was a radical change, but I probably would have done it if we had known we were going for seven seasons. We didn't have to kill Bakula, he would have just been gone part of the season."

It would have been a bold move from *Enterprise*, with hints of Ronny Cox's acerbic Edward Jellico from *The Next Generation*'s 'Chain of Command' or Todd Stashwick's grumpy Luke Shaw in *Picard*'s third season; the martinet who the crew struggle to respect coming in with a different ethos.

Two of the darkest episodes, from the very end of the season, were 'Terra Prime' and 'Demons', both of which focused on a growing xenophobic movement on Earth against the influence of alien culture since the *Enterprise* voyages and Starfleet had begun, with character actor Peter Weller (who had headlined Coto's one season series *Odyssey-5* previously) as sinister racist John Frederick Paxton. Coto, along with the Reeves-Stevens, wanted Weller to appear earlier as Colonel Philip Green, an infamous character mentioned in *The Original Series*, played eventually in transmissions in the 'Terra Prime' episodes by Steve Rankin.

Green was, essentially, *Star Trek*'s future history version of Adolf Hitler. A despotic militia leader during the Third World War in the early 21st century, not long before *First Contact*, he led a violent faction of eco-terrorists ultimately responsible for the death of 37 million people, as referred to in *The Original Series* episode 'The Savage Garden'. The intended *Enterprise* episode would have revolved around security officer Malcolm Reed (Dominic Keating), in a different manner to how 'Demons' reveals him to be working for the covert intelligence group Section-31 (established in *Deep Space Nine*). He would have found a disturbing connection between his great-grandfather and Green in a story that would have concerned 'the Optimum', a dangerous organisation the writing team devised for their non-canonical *Star Trek* history book, 'Federation', linked to Green. It would also have included *Enterprise*'s sister ship, the *NX-Columbia*, and the opening of the first staircase.

"We'd worked it all out in our office, on cards, and we went in there, and I wish we'd had video of us doing this incredible presentation, where we were smacking those cards on, one after another, so Manny was so excited and said, 'I can't wait to do this episode,'" Judith claimed. Garfield added, "And so, Manny said, 'Yeah, I love this story. Write the outline.' So, we did an entire beat outline, took it to Manny, [he] said, 'Yes, this is great,' and Brannon [Braga] took one look at it and said, 'It's too dark.'"

Aside from displaying the hold Braga still had on development of the fourth season, a reason cited for rejecting the idea was that it would have concerned genetic engineering too soon after the 'Augment trilogy', featuring Spiner and a direct link to Khan Noonien Singh. It was originally intended for Weller as Green to be the main character in that story, until Spiner expressed an interest in appearing. And while many of these ideas filtered into the 'Terra Prime' episode – as did Coto's intention to devise an episode around Martian independence with a Mars equivalent of the Cuban Missile Crisis – perhaps the more intriguing exploration of Green and *Star Trek*'s Third World War was ultimately lost.

One of the biggest missed opportunities during this era, however, was failing to feature William Shatner on *Enterprise*, something that for a while was a genuine possibility.

Before the fourth season was officially commissioned, a board in the writer's room marked the 'Mirror Universe' as a storyline, or story arc, that Coto and the writers wanted to explore, given it had not been seen in the franchise since the final season of *Deep Space Nine*. Coto explained at a 2005 fan convention: "We had talked about doing a mirror universe episode ever since we got into Season 4. But then we had the possibility of getting William Shatner. Coincidentally, the Reeves-Stevens [Judith and Garfield Reeves-Stevens, who had worked with Shatner on several *Star Trek* novels] were a pair of writers whom I desperately wanted to bring on the show. And they, it turned out, had an idea for a mirror universe two-parter which would feature the return of William Shatner."

Garfield explains the idea further: "The idea was that the Tantalus field was not a disintegrator, it was a humane way of dealing with prisoners, by sending them back in time to a sealed penal colony. *Enterprise* (NX-01) comes upon the colony – and Tiberius [mirror-Kirk] is there. Tiberius thinks, 'Finally, a ship with a transporter – I can get back to my own universe, my own time.' He basically goes on the NX-01, gets to the transporter, sets it to go back to the mirror universe – the mirror universe doesn't exist."

Judith added: "It hasn't been created yet," Garfield continues, "So Tiberius and Archer work together to figure out where the division point is between the universes, what point that one split off into the other. And as it turns out, Tiberius and Archer together are responsible for the creation of the mirror universe."

Coto later explained that Shatner himself was keen on the idea: "So we had lunch with Shatner – Rick, Brannon, and myself – and pitched it to him. He thought it was great, too. During that lunch, Brannon and I had to show him how to use his new cell phone. I remember he was having trouble; it was like Kirk trying to figure out how to use a cell phone. He was, like, 'I have to get it to work . . . this is important . . . what am I going to do?' So we finally got it to work and after lunch Bill made one comment, as we were leaving and said, 'You know this is going to cost you?' And Rick was laughing, but ultimately what happened was that Paramount did a study or survey and didn't feel bringing back Shatner would raise ratings enough to warrant the amount of money he wanted, which was considerable. Paramount felt they had already decided this was the last season. 'We're going to move on, so why bother trying to do anything truly exciting?' And that's what happened. The episode would have made a lot of money, but at the time they really didn't give a shit."

Berman also had an alternative idea for how to bring Shatner into the show, which he had worked on with Sussman, which continued his desire to rework *The Prisoner of Zenda* – which he had envisaged for *Insurrection* – as a *Star Trek* tale.

Shatner would have played Chef, an unseen character oft mentioned on the series as providing the characters with delicious food, who was an ancestor of Captain Kirk. Chef and Archer would have time-travelled to the 23rd century, thanks to Temporal Cold War agent and recurring character Daniels, to preserve the timeline after Kirk is kidnapped by temporal agents. In the Zenda-twist, Chef would have to impersonate his iconic descendant during a key historical event. Shatner nonetheless preferred the Reeves-Stevens idea and being part of the Mirror Universe, although negotiations ultimately fell through.

With Shatner out of the picture, attention then turned to the second-biggest legend from *The Original Series* – Leonard Nimoy, who had last appeared on screen in *The Next Generation* two-parter 'Unification', despite rumours he would crop up in *Nemesis* given his heavy involvement with the Romulans. Sussman wanted to do a play on *The Young Indiana Jones Chronicles* episode 'Mystery of the Blues', in which Harrison Ford appeared as an older Indy as part of a framing device for a story about his younger self.

Sussman pitched his concept: "We could find Spock in the 24th century, a distinguished and retired Ambassador, who has a young visitor. Maybe this guy is a Vulcan/Human hybrid like Spock, and needs advice on balancing his two alien halves. This visit could lead Spock into recounting an adventure he had early in his career as a Starfleet cadet. This adventure could involve Young Spock (played by another actor) helping a middle-aged T'Pol (now in her early to mid-100s) on some vitally important mission . . . In the process, Spock could learn some lesson which helped him choose his own path in life. We may learn a lot of new info on Spock . . . Perhaps he was torn between life as a diplomat (like his father) and a career in Starfleet when he was a young man. The flashback adventure should involve Captain Archer (and other members of our cast) in old-age make-up, playing early 23rd century versions of themselves. Maybe their adventure is something of a 'Last Round-Up' for the old crew, whom T'Pol reunites for a secret and possibly illegal TBD mission. I thought it might be fun if our crew have to steal an antiquated NX-class ship from the Starfleet museum for one last adventure together."

Quite apart from the enjoyment of seeing elderly versions of the *Enterprise* crew, and the recasting of a young Spock (which will be made reality a decade later with Ethan Peck's casting in *Discovery* and *Strange New Worlds*), one wonders if this idea wasn't soaked in by Terry Matalas. He will play a bigger part in the *Star Trek* story much later but at this stage he served as an assistant to Brannon Braga during *Enterprise* and, almost twenty years later, would direct *Picard*'s final two episodes where Picard and his crew steal the antiquated *Enterprise-D* for, indeed, one last adventure to save the galaxy. In the world of *Star Trek*, good ideas never truly die.

Though Nimoy would reappear soon after in J. J. Abrams' reboot as an elder Spock, this return for the legend remained just an idea on the drawing board, one of many exciting possibilities Coto and his team had planned not just for the fourth but also a fifth season.

Regarding legends, one of the most intriguing possibilities for the fourth season of *Enterprise* was a crossover with another major science-fiction property – *Doctor Who*.

Under the aegis of writer Russell T. Davies, *Doctor Who* returned after a hiatus of almost two decades (discounting an American-made TV movie) with a buoyant, fun spring in its step and, thanks to Davies and his writers, an American stylistic sensibility in the storytelling. It was an instant hit and renewed itself as a staple of British television, where it remains almost twenty years on, not to mention succeeding internationally. Davies spoke in his diaries about how much he liked the proposition: "I would so love to see the Doctor on board the starship *Enterprise*, puncturing all that Starfleet pomposity with his sheer Doctor-ness. When we began in 2004, *Star Trek: Enterprise* was still on air, and I told Julie (Gardner, *Doctor Who* producer), in all seriousness, that I wanted to do a *Doctor Who/Star Trek* crossover. It was on our list of plans, until *Star Trek: Enterprise* was axed."

Davies claimed subsequently to *The Times* that it almost became a reality: "The very first year, we talked about it. Then *Star Trek* finally went off air. Landing the TARDIS on board the *Enterprise* would have been magnificent. Can you imagine what their script department would have wanted and what I would have wanted? It would have been the biggest battle."

Such a crossover did become a reality in 2012, after Davies' tenure was over, but in a format unencumbered by budget worries – that of the comic book. IDW Publishing had Matt Smith's Eleventh Doctor and his companion Amy Pond visit the *Enterprise-D* as part of a *Next Generation* crossover which brought together the Borg and *Doctor Who*'s Cybermen – that franchise's similar mechanical intelligence – as villains across space, time and dimensions. It was great fun but the idea of a version of the Doctor on the bridge of a starship on television still tantalises.

As of writing, Davies has now resumed control of *Doctor Who* at the beginning of an exciting new era for a franchise with a great deal more money and the backing of a major studio in Disney. If ever there was a moment that Davies could realise his *Star Trek* crossover ambitions, this could well be it . . .

Returning to *Enterprise*, with such iconic popular culture moments fading away, the writing was on the wall. During filming of one of the season's most interesting and innovative episodes, two-part story 'In a Mirror, Darkly', where *Enterprise* did finally revisit the Mirror Universe, the hammer came down. Cancellation. *Enterprise* would not get a fifth season or indeed hit the hundred-episode milestone. It would suffer a similar fate to the series it most cherished and evoked, *The Original Series*.

How to end not just *Enterprise* but, perhaps, the entire *Star Trek* franchise? The answer to that question was not one that anyone expected.

*

'These Are the Voyages', the first *Star Trek* finale since 'Turnabout Intruder' in 1969 to not be a two-part episode, took a unique approach to bringing *Enterprise* to a conclusion.

Set during the seventh season of *The Next Generation*, amidst the events of an episode called 'The Pegasus' where Commander Riker is struggling with learning a former captain of his who he trusted may have been involved in the cover-up of an experimental project, and alongside Deanna Troi uses the holodeck to recreate the final mission of Archer's *Enterprise*, in advance of the signing of the Federation charter, as a means of understanding what he should do about his present-day situation.

Despite the reappearance of the *Enterprise-D*, and seeing Riker and Troi again, 'These Are the Voyages' was lambasted by fans and critics as the worst ending to a *Star Trek* series in history, framed as it was to be less of a goodbye to *Enterprise* but the era of *Star Trek* on television as a whole since 1987, as Braga attests: "The series finale was an hour that's very controversial and I'll take the blame for this with Rick since we wrote it together, but we wanted to end an eighteen-year run that was a huge part of our lives and the audience's with a valentine to this era of *Trek*. Manny had just done a stellar three-part episode, which I considered to be *Enterprise*'s finale in its own right. We wanted the final episode to be a very high-concept idea where we're on Picard's *Enterprise* and Riker's in the holodeck to look at one of his heroes, Captain Archer. What an interesting way to look back at *Enterprise*, through the eyes of a different *Star Trek* character. I thought it was great, but the episode was flat and I don't think it really worked. And killing Trip felt flat and just pissed people off. It certainly pissed the cast off. They hated the script."

By this stage, aware that *Enterprise* had been cancelled, much of the cast and crew were sanguine about a choice many of them – Bakula included – considered a questionable way of ending the series, especially following a fourth season many found had given the show a fresh impetus. Berman claims Trip Tucker's death particularly, which was widely disliked, would have been reworked, as subsequent non-canonical continuation novels did: "We would have been totally shocked if the show had been picked up [for Season 5], and if it had we probably would have made changes to the final episode."

"I really think we could have continued for another two or three years with Manny at the helm. We were already cutting corners, the shows had shifted to high-definition video for the fourth season and I thought it looked like shit, but even with cutting corners, the show could have continued creatively."

Coto and the writers had a number of plans for the prospective fifth season worked out, or at least sketched out, that suggest his tenure running the show would have continued along the lines of both connecting to *Star Trek* lore and establishing the series' place in *Star Trek* history: "I would have loved to have built more toward the Romulan War and explored that and continued to set up the Federation. I loved Jeffrey Combs and I wanted to find a way to bring Combs onto the bridge as a character on our show. I wanted to make him a regular. He was tremendous and he had such a great energy. To have him as an interspecies exchange would have supercharged the season."

As suggested in the pitch for the Colonel Green episode, Coto wanted to explore the building of the first staircase, which ended up being foreshadowed in the fourth season episode 'Bound'. He also hoped to connect an episode back to the second season's well-received Borg tale 'Regeneration', following a pitch from the Reeves-Stevens', as Garfield recounts: "We pitched this story to have Alice Krige back as a Starfleet medical technician who made contact with the Borg from Season 2 and we would see the birth of the Borg Queen."

Krige, after making a mark in *First Contact* as the initial queen, had returned in *Voyager* finale 'Endgame', although Susanna Thompson had played her when she was unavailable in the fifth season two-parter 'Dark Frontier' and set a precedent that the queen could utilise different appearances, indeed that there might be more than one queen out there. Annie Wersching and Alison Pill would play variations of her in *Picard* years later, before Krige herself reprised the role in that show (and in a voice cameo on *Lower Decks*). A story such as this would have cemented her origin more deeply in *Star Trek* canon and possibly struggled to tally with Thompson and later Wersching and Pill's appearances.

Coto also wanted to revisit elements of certain specific *Original Series* episodes, such as 'The Cloud Minders': "I do want to do one or two episodes that take place on the Cloud City of Stratos. I want to see the early stages of that. I think it's a very fertile place for a storyline."

Stratos was a city renowned amongst the Federation as a place of art, culture and prosperity, where the Ardanian elite lived at the expense of the Troglodytes, surface dwellers not allowed in as part of a commentary on class systems. Coto perhaps didn't get far enough in mapping out precisely what his story would have been, but he had hoped to squeeze it into the fourth season, meaning it would almost certainly have been part of Season 5 had the show been recommissioned: "I really wanted to do a two-parter on that location, to see Stratos in its earlier stages . . . That was a wonderful location and wonderful setting for a great two-parter."

He also would have revisited the character of Flint, played by James Daly in 'Requiem for Methuselah', an immortal human who had watched humanity's progress across time and who, at points, had been the true figure beyond some of the most legendary figures in human history – Methuselah, Alexander the Great, Merlin, Leonardo da Vinci and so on.

The idea was never scripted but the intention was for Flint, in the 22nd century, to be using the alias of Abramson, who would have been a famous Earth scientist with connections to likely both Archer's father Henry, who designed the first NX starship, and warp drive inventor Zefram Cochrane. Phlox would have discovered Flint's true nature and established what he called the "disaster of intervention" he describes in 'Requiem for Methuselah' as to why he never discusses his background with anyone.

Coto even wanted to stray into the semi-canonical territory of *The Animated Series* by introducing the villainous Kzinti, seen in 'The Slaver Weapon', a cat-like race who fought wars against pre-Starfleet humanity at the end of the 21st century. An episode reputedly called 'Kilkenny Cats' (though Coto has since denied this) would have served as a prequel to 'The Slaver Weapon' and did get as far as designs being developed by an artist named Jimmy Diggs for a Kzinti vessel called the Dark Stalker.

The Kzinti were canonically established in *Picard*'s first season episode 'Nepenthe' almost fifty years after being seen in *The Animated Series*, and later featured in episode of animated series *Lower Decks*, but an episode directly connecting to events in that show would, at the time, have been an unprecedented step in recognising that series as a fourth year of Kirk's original five-year mission.

Another major story intended for the fifth season would have been another return to the Mirror Universe following the success of 'In a Mirror, Darkly', with Hoshi Sato now as Empress of the Terran Empire. Coto planned to consistently return to the alternate universe four or five times across the season in what he described as a "mini-series within a series". Coto considered it his "big regret" that they never managed to pull the idea off, and later Braga went as far as to suggest plans exceeded even Coto's suggestion: "There was talk among some of us about doing the entire fifth season of *Star Trek Enterprise* as a mirror universe."

While plans such as this would have been unusual for *Star Trek* circa 2005, taking serialisation of the show into an entirely different paradigm, tendrils of these plans for the Mirror Universe worked themselves into the storytelling for *Discovery* just over a decade later, which set the final half of its first season in the Mirror Universe and hinted directly at Empress Phillipa Georgiou (as played by Michelle Yeoh) being a descendant of Empress Hoshi. Plans as radical in terms of serialisation were, for *Enterprise*, perhaps just a little ahead of their time.

Outside of this, Coto also wanted to delve into the *Enterprise* ensemble in places. An episode would have visited Phlox's home planet of Denobula and further explored his culture, while he also intended to introduce the father of T'Pol, thanks to a pitch from Sussman: "I had this sneaky plan to reveal that T'Pol's father was a Romulan, but who knows how that would've played out. I think I could've sold Rick and Brannon on it." He would have been revealed to have posed as a Vulcan before faking his death, in a storytelling move which would have shed more light on T'Pol's willingness to explore her emotions, given the existence of a more fiery Romulan side of her genetic makeup.

Talking of Romulans, their presence would have sizeably increased in the series as *Enterprise* would have built towards depicting Earth's historic war with them, an event that contributed heavily to the establishment of the Federation and created the long-held Neutral Zone, in effect until the explosion of the Romulan star in the late 24th century. Coto planned for the fifth season, in true *Babylon-5* narrative fashion, to "begin whispers of the Romulan War" and chart the "origins of the Federation".

Sussman claims: "The Xindi arc was a lot of fun and we did some great episodes, but if you're going to spend an entire season on one conflict, then just do the Romulan War. That's what season three should've been."

'Future Guy', the shadowy figure who had directed the villainous Suliban agents of the Temporal Cold War since the pilot episode 'Broken Bow', and whose identity remained a mystery at the point *Enterprise* concluded, was according to Coto "probably going to be a Romulan", tying into the upcoming war and being part of a plot to instigate conflict. Coto claimed this was based on comments Berman and Braga had made to him, though Braga later suggested a different and even more intriguing origin for the arch-villain: "For those wondering, Archer as Future Guy was always the idea. Trying to repair a corrupt future by influencing his innocent past self." Responding to fans questioning this, believing he was supposed to be Romulan, Braga suggested the Romulan origin would have been a red herring.

It would be an intriguing experiment to rewatch the appearances of 'Future Guy' across *Enterprise* and try to square his actions with the idea that he could be a darker future version of Archer, in an idea somewhat akin to the haunted future Admiral Janeway of 'Endgame', who compromises all her ethics to change the past. Had this been revealed, it likely would have drawn similar comparisons.

All these plans point to what could have been, had *Enterprise* continued, some of the most thrilling and intriguing seasons of *Star Trek* ever filmed. It was, however, simply too late. *Enterprise* was over and, with it, the franchise seemingly as a whole. *Nemesis* had been the final *Next Generation* movie three years before. No new series of *Star Trek* to replace *Enterprise* was on the drawing board. After 18 years on television consistently, the longest *Star Trek* to date has ever sustained itself, the mission seemed finally to be over.

David A. Goodman points out the unreality of this: "From 1987 to 2005, there was always a new *Star Trek* on. It was great. But there was something to be said about being hungry for it again. I took it for granted that it was always going to be there. And when it wasn't, I was, like, 'Oh wait, there's no *Star Trek*.'"

'These Are the Voyages', for all the mistakes it made, ends this era of *Star Trek* with an openly nostalgic refrain on the classic "Space. The final frontier . . ." speech, featuring the voices of not just Archer but Captain's Kirk and Picard, displaying all three of the iconic *Enterprise* starships flying in space. It was a fitting encapsulation of *Star Trek*'s development from the final *Original Series* movies through to the conclusion of *Enterprise*, which pointed the way toward the 1960s and 1990s era of shows. Had *Star Trek* ended for good right there, it might have felt fitting.

For a time, that is precisely what happened. *Star Trek* was history.

Yet, like the embers of a dimming flame, writers worked on projects with a view to continuing the journey. *Star Trek* might be burned out, but the passion for this world was far from extinguished . . .

TWELVE

UNCHARTED FRONTIERS: THE ANIMATED, VIDEO-GAME AND LIVE-ACTION PITCHES

THUS FAR, MUCH of the unmade story of *Star Trek* lies in the 'what if?' concepts behind many of the movies and television series that were made. The alternate choices for storylines and characters who did and do exist, and how *Star Trek* might have differed had those choices been made.

Since the 1960s, there have also been a litany of *Star Trek* projects that never came into existence, both in live-action, video-game and animated form. Ideas, stories, arcs and characters who either live only in the minds of enterprising writers or in documents on pages that exist online, or on home computers. These are tantalising alternate universes for *Star Trek* where the future of the franchise might look very different than it does today had they been developed and commissioned.

We should start with the animated and video-game projects, a wide variety of unusual and intriguing ideas that have no doubt inspired the bounty of animated and video-game *Star Trek* that exists in the 2020s.

*

In the early 1970s, before the arrival of *The Animated Series*, Gene Roddenberry was given the suggestion of an animated project that saw the crew of the *Enterprise* landing on strange planets and shooting anything deemed different or ugly, in a concept that does not remotely seem to hold true to the principles of *Star Trek* even this early on.

Later, in the 1990s, Paramount approached Rick Berman with a view to developing an animated series that would have combined the crews of *The Original Series* and *The Next Generation*, but he claimed it would have "diluted the franchise" and refused. Given how Leonard Nimoy had needed to challenge the studio producing *The Animated Series* when he learned they did not plan to bring back the entire original cast for voice work, one wonders how difficult corralling both present and past casts back for a project such as this would have been.

At the end of the 1990s, what would have been the most ambitious animated project to date was floated, based on an unreleased *Star Trek* video game called 'Secret of Vulcan's Fury'. The game, from Interplay who held the video-game rights to the franchise and had produced celebrated games such as *Star Trek: 25th Anniversary*, *Star Trek: Starfleet Academy* and *Star Trek: Judgment Rites*, was itself ambitious.

Set in the era of *The Original Series*, it would have comprised eight chapters each set from the perspective of a different male member of the crew. The story concerns the Romulans attempting to make peace with Vulcan after thousands of years of enmity. The game would have delved into a backstory never made explicit canonically, revealing that back in the mists of time, the Vulcans used a space station called 'Fury' to destroy Romulan fleets during a war. The Fury drew power from twin planets, and it would be down to a Vulcan to mind meld with the station to use its weapon. The Romulans fled, establishing their society as they settled a collection of planets and forming, in time, the powerful Star Empire. The USS *Enterprise* is sent as a Federation security measure for the peace talks but Kirk and his crew learn the Romulans are using it as a ruse to secretly find the ancient Fury weapon and use it to destroy the Vulcans.

Quite a large-scale story that does not cast the ancient Vulcans in the greatest of lights, it would have featured in one of the three planned story arcs over eight episodes a tale of strife internally on Vulcan. McCoy would have investigated the murder of a Romulan ambassador in the talks, who the Romulans kill and blame on a Tellarite with a view to starting a war. In a nod perhaps to *The Undiscovered Country*, Kirk and members of his crew are also held by the Vulcans on suspicion of murder. Later chapters would see Sulu and Scotty uncovering secrets about the ancient Romulan/Vulcan conflicts, with Scotty dealing with sabotage on the *Enterprise*. As the game climaxes, the Romulans attack the Federation in a Kirk/Chekov-focused narrative when Starfleet comes to the aid of the Vulcans.

'Secret of Vulcan's Fury' would have gained a level of authenticity thanks to being written by *Original Series* writers D. C. Fontana and John Meredyth Lucas, who had previously collaborated on 'The *Enterprise* Incident' and 'The Ultimate Computer'. Fontana explained her impetus for returning to the world of *The Original Series* after almost three decades: "I've always been a big Spock fan and I saw this as an opportunity to explore his heritage more and to look at how the Vulcans and Romulans became who they are. It's a rich environment for a writer to explore."

Financial problems and technical issues resulted in the game being shut down in 1999, after two years of work and with only an estimated 5% of the game being completed, though certain animated stills and screenshots do exist. Many of the animators working for Interplay moved to work on *Roughnecks: Starship Troopers*, a short-lived series based on the successful Robert Heinlein adaptation by Paul Verhoeven from 1997, and that endeavour led Paramount to strongly consider developing a new animated series based on *The Original Series*. Certain animated tests of Kirk and Spock (including him, strangely, parroting lines from Joe Pesci's gangster character from *Goodfellas*) were developed but the project went nowhere. Whether 'Secret of Vulcan's Fury' might have seen the light of day in such an updated animated series remains open to question.

Speaking of lost *Star Trek* video-game projects, several other intriguing ideas in this vein were lost, often due to similar production factors.

One of the earliest video-game projects was designed to tie in with *The Motion Picture*, albeit four years after the film in 1983, developed by for the Atari 2600 by the Milton Bradley company which promised "exciting and original gameplay" "brilliant color graphics" "realistic sound effects" and "progressive skill levels". It does not appear to have advanced beyond a promotional image. Sega also developed a tie-in game in the same year for *The Wrath of Khan*, again for the Atari 2600 but also for the Atari 5200, but, despite being announced with promotional artwork, the project foundered as a result of the so-called 'Atari shock', a major recession in the video-game industry in the United States between 1983 and 1985, where initial video-game market saturation saw a crash in the value of the industry. The same fate befell a Sega tie-in Atari game for *The Search for Spock*, although curiously artwork exists for a game called 'Star Trek II: In Search of Spock', a mistake on two fronts it seems!

The industry had rallied enough by 1989 when Bandai planned a 2D platform game for the NES (Nintendo Entertainment System) based on *The Final Frontier*. Cancelled and incomplete before the intended release, it reputedly contained many inconsistencies from the finished film, and in 2006 several stills emerged from a leaked prototype version that gave more details. The first two and the final stage saw audiences play a side-to-side shooter, with levels set in Nimbus III's Paradise City and finally the God planet. Later levels saw space combat as players command the *Enterprise* through an asteroid field and battle Klaa's Klingon bird of prey above the God planet. A cut scene also erroneously describes Sybok as "Spock's former classmate at the Valcan (misspelt) School of Thought", rather than his half-brother. It's perhaps a blessing this one did not see the light of day . . .

In the same year that *The Next Generation* ended, Spectrum Holobyte released the memorable *Enterprise-D* adventure *A Final Unity*, where Picard and his crew encountered Romulans, their alien cousins the Garidians and the mysterious Chodak. Ahead of this, the same company planned a game called 'The Next Generation: A World for All Seasons' (presumably a play on *A Man for All Seasons*, Robert Bolt's play about Sir Thomas More, memorably adapted into a 1966 film starring Paul Scofield). It would have featured pre-rendered 3D gaming environments and a 'choose your own adventure' narrative, including space combat for the *Enterprise-D* akin to the popular *Wing Commander* series. Part of why the game failed to materialise is due to it being developed for the 3DO Interactive Multiplayer console, a forerunner of Sega and Sony consoles in the 1990s that have consigned the 3DO to near anonymity.

Around the same time, Paramount Interactive developed for Simon and Schuster for the Mac and MS-DOS a *Deep Space Nine* game called 'The Hunt'. The plot was described as follows: "Somewhere on space station Deep Space Nine is a thief with a stolen treasure of mysterious power. The Cardassians want to retrieve it. The Ferengi's want to steal it. As a Federation Officer, a Klingon, a Ferengi or a Bajoran, you use your wits and personality to interact with *Star Trek: Deep Space Nine* characters, all realistically animated in stereo sound. Your actions will make the difference between success and failure." The characters of those races players could choose to play were named Lieutenant Delgado, a Klingon woman named Garrudan, a Ferengi called Bixtur and a Bajoran called Salu Marn.

Douglas Herring, an art director who worked on the project, claimed completed were "total art design, animation and background key frames and layout for this adventure game based on the TV series. Art was 95% done and I had already moved on when Paramount Interactive put the project on hold."

It is unlikely audiences would have appreciated a *Deep Space Nine* game where they were unable to play as the main characters from the series, though this was frequently the case with games produced and released during this era. The 1990s was a boom time for *Star Trek* games, producing many of the most memorable such as *A Final Unity*, *Elite Force*, *Armada* and *Bridge Commander*, but there remained what could have been lucrative tie-in games that failed to make the cut.

1997 had seen the release of a successful *Deep Space Nine* game, *Harbinger*, and plans were afoot for a *Voyager* tie-in called 'Retribution', also developed by Viacom Home Media. Retribution would have seen players as a 'detached party' in control of the entire *Voyager* crew, allowing the story to take different paths as you solved puzzles and engaged in ground-based and space combat.

Though an overarching story is unclear, 'Retribution' would have contained missions – following a training exercise with the senior staff – that included rescuing an away team abducted by a Kazon sect. Another would have introduced new alien creations, the Gudge and the Ankekket, who would have been key to the broader narrative. Retribution would also have featured Talaxians other than Neelix. All the primary *Voyager* cast had been scanned using motion capture, with every intent on them contributing voice work. Although Harbinger promoted the game, 'Retribution' was cancelled, making way for successful shooter *Elite Force*.

Microprose a year later planned a PC game version of *First Contact*, using the newly designed Unreal engine that would be a feature of many first-person shooter games, with this version designed to place you on the *Enterprise-E* as it tries to prevent the Borg assimilating the ship. They had successfully developed a first-person shooter tie-in for *Generations*, and even packaged promotional material for *First Contact* into that release, given it was released in 1997, by which point *First Contact* had debuted. Microprose struggled financially and later lost the licence to use the *Next Generation* cast to Activision, putting paid to a tie in for what might have been one of the most exciting films to become immersed in.

Activision later attempted their own take on *Star Trek*'s terrifying machines with 'Star Trek: Borg Assimilator', which in 2001 was designed with Cyberlore Studios for the PC as a "world-building simulator" where players would have built empires in the *Star Trek* world through Borg assimilation.

'Borg Assimilator' would have boasted twelve levels with the aim of assimilating enough territory to develop a stable Omega particle (more on that once we return to animated fare), at which point in 'freestyle mode' players could move on and conquer the entire Alpha Quadrant. The project foundered with Activision stating that "the game's design did not reflect the established *Star Trek* universe". Given the terrifying nature of the concept, involving the elimination of as much of the galaxy as possible, one wonders how the idea, intriguing as it was and tapping into a thirst for *Civilisation*-style tie-in games (*Star Wars: Empire at War* being a key example), ever was commissioned.

In many respects, games such as this were a natural forerunner of the MMORPG (Massively Multiplayer-Role Playing Game) evolution born out of the enhancement of the Internet as it became more accessible and faster in the modern home. *Star Trek: Online* was born in 2010 by Cryptic Studios, and continues to this day, as a huge, open-world sandbox for *Star Trek* fans to live in, create, explore, take part in missions etc . . . and to a degree cornered the market for gaming development in this universe.

There were, however, two earlier attempts to make 'Star Trek: Online' a reality, from different production houses. Activision made the first attempt in 2000/2001 but the project was shelved in its infancy, instead working with LucasArts on their *Star Wars: Galaxies* variant. Much more developed was an attempt by Perpetual Entertainment, who in 2008 created much of the baseline material that Cryptic took into their produced version, albeit with very different game mechanics and working off the backstory for the late 24th century provided by the 2009 *Star Trek* movie, which Perpetual at that point did not have.

Though often overlooked, the game world of *Star Trek* contains a trove of albeit non-canonical stories and characters that add richness to the tapestry of this universe, and this glimpse into unrealised material finds equally surprising results.

*

Returning to animation, an unusual project came in around 2000 from the actors Armin Shimerman and Max Grodenchik.

They had played Ferengi brothers Quark and Rom on *Deep Space Nine*, and they developed an idea that focused on the teenage adventures of the characters. "We got pretty far with that, but in the end, when we got to the last pitch session with MTV, they said they didn't want a space cartoon show. But everyone was very happy with the ideas that we had come up with." These ideas, sadly, have never come to light, but while an animated *Star Trek* comedy series might have sounded strange at the time, *Lower Decks* has subsequently proven that comedy in *Star Trek* in this format can work, and work well.

In 2003, Jimmy Diggs – who later developed designs for a potential *Enterprise* fifth season Kzinti episode as earlier discussed – pitched an animated CGI film called 'Star Trek: The Lions of the Night', with the plot described thus: "Captain Sulu takes command of the USS *Enterprise-B* and must stop a Kzinti invasion of Federation Space."

Sulu had of course been promoted to captain of the *Excelsior* during *The Undiscovered Country* so Diggs' film presumably would have taken place after that move, and following the events of *Generations,* which established Alan Ruck's Captain John Harriman as commander of the *Enterprise-B*. Had George Takei agreed to voice the film, he would potentially have been seen interacting with his daughter, Demora, introduced as *Enterprise* helm officer in *Generations*.

Though 'The Lions of the Night' never happened, and Diggs unsuccessfully used some of his designs for the *Enterprise* pitch, an animatic developed as a 'proof of concept' establishes the Kzinti threat as analogous to lions and beasts who hunted primitive man across the savannah, hence the title, as Diggs draws parallels with 23rd-century humanity. His animatic shows a Starfleet ship and crew, circa the *The Original Series* movie era, attacked and boarded by the creatures who is strongly inferred eat the crew. "What if these creatures saw us not as fellow beings but as inferiors? What would it be like to find ourselves knocked down the cosmic food chain? To find ourselves chased across the stars the way we were once chased across the plains?"

In the comments of his animatic, Diggs explains that when he pitched the Kzinti concept, he had the backing of Larry Niven, who created the race for 'The Slaver Weapon'. "Although Larry is still a good friend of mine, he no longer has sole rights to the Kzinti for film and television. Therefore, these creatures are no longer the Kzinti." The video therefore does not label them as such and Diggs explains they would be a new threat called the Rakshasa: "While still felinoid, they have a completely different back story, psychology, and (as you can see) appearance."

Perhaps the most promising and well-developed animated project of this era came in 2006 with 'Star Trek: Final Frontier'.

The brainchild of David Rossi, Doug Mirabello and Jose Munoz, 'Final Frontier' would have been set in 2528, aka the 26th century, at that point the furthest ahead in the *Star Trek* timeline ever focused on. A war with the Romulans in the 25th century has led the Federation to a much darker place, a war instigated after the detonation of dozens of 'Omega particles' across the Federation leading to star systems ships being unable to warp across, isolating half of the Federation from the other. *Voyager* introduced the Omega particle in the fourth season episode of the same name, a molecule so powerfully destructive that nobody in Starfleet below the rank of captain was allowed to know it existed, forcing in that instance Janeway to be very coy around her crew.

The result of the war sees the Klingon homeworld, Q'onos, occupied by the Romulans; the destruction of the planet Andoria; and the secession of the Vulcans from the Federation as they negotiate Romulan reunification after many centuries. Amidst this bleak backdrop, Rossi and the team would have focused on a new starship *Enterprise*, in this iteration a 'Bismarck-class' cruiser that fought in the Federation-Romulan War; an old, blocky ship relegated to border patrol, commanded by intrepid Captain Alexander Chase, a man dedicated to bringing back the old and somewhat forgotten Starfleet creed of exploring new life and new civilisations.

Though in the mid-2000s seemingly at odds with the stylistics of the *Star Trek* shows of the era, the depiction of a darker, somewhat fallen Federation was utilised frequently in the 2017 era onwards, be it the isolationism of the Federation in 2399 during *Picard*, and the after-effects of 'the Burn' which reduce the Federation to almost nothing far ahead in the 32nd century, as explored in *Discovery*.

The team reacted to the cancellation of *Enterprise* with a renewed spirit of keeping the franchise alive, if only in animated form. "We wanted to spark a little life into *Star Trek* and to keep it alive in people's eyes," Rossi claimed. *Enterprise* arguably had pointed the way when it came to a darker palette for *Star Trek* across the third season and Rossi certainly saw the parallels apparent in the world of American military 'shock and awe', that *Star Trek*'s penchant for "couching big social issues in allegories so they are more palatable is kind of passé now. Today shows deal with these issues head on, so we decided to make the entire show an allegory. The premise is an allegory for the post-9/11 world we live in. A world of uncertainty and fear."

Rossi and the team – known as Zero Room collectively – originally pitched to CBS an animated show based on *The Original Series*, an idea seemingly unwilling to disappear, but they were concerned following *Enterprise* about straying too heavily in that era. Rossi received counsel from LeVar Burton, whose advice about *Star Trek* pushing forward encouraged the team to set 'Final Frontier' in a future century, giving them space to invent a whole new creative sandbox. Their plan was to evoke *Star Wars*' popular animated series *The Clone Wars*, the initial Genndy Tarkovsky series of short, six-minute episodes which were critically acclaimed and sported a modern yet nostalgic look to the animation, influenced by the late Darwyn Cooke, with still images of many of the intended main characters rendered. "Although the show is set in the future the designs are founded in TOS, it is a throwback that is also looking forward," Rossi admitted, in a move seemingly designed to allow 'Final Frontier' to evoke *The Original Series* without remaking it.

Zero Room planned for 'Final Frontier' to contain an overarching mystery narrative about who detonated the Omega bursts, revealing it would not have been the Romulans as believed (my money would have been on the Borg), in a plot which does feel akin to mystery of the Burn in *Discovery*'s third season in retrospect. StarTrek.com would have contained a means of audiences catching up with the necessary backstory of 'Final Frontier' with logs and character/world-building descriptions, given the episodes themselves would not have had the scope to cover those aspects. "We won't have long diatribes, we are utilizing a clipped kind of writing and the editing is frenetic," Rossi claimed.

Details of the show and characters had been developed. Chase, square-jawed, white and dark-haired, was an idealist who wanted to make the *Enterprise* akin to the ships that preceded it, though would have faced push back from other members of his Starfleet crew, as Rossi explains: "The Captain is more forward thinking and wants to go out and do some exploring but half the crew will be against that and want to just protect the border." First officer Commander Barric Holden, black and with a profile like Dwayne 'The Rock' Johnson, would have pushed back, an officer seeking his own command and holding resentment toward Chase.

He would have been the second of a planned triumvirate alongside Chase and Lt Kaylen Donal, a female security chief linked with Borg technology to her 'redshirts' with implants called BUGS (Biomechanics Utility Grafts), Rossi adding "they aren't the hapless pajama wearing guys who get vaporized every time . . . these are going to be very thoughtful clever bad-ass soldiers". The main crew also would have included Mr Zero, an alien chief engineer who wears an environmental suit to survive, and a protocol officer named William Preston – one wonders if he might have been a C-3P0 made animate in human form.

"Our target audience was not only existing *Star Trek* fans, but also kids, introducing them to a *Star Trek* that, due to the freedom of animation, had an epic scope to the galaxy and, while peppered with lots of great action, also told a story."

Zero Room were asked by CBS to develop five 'minisode' scripts that Mirabello later claimed was a five-part pilot episode, and subsequent scripts were later made available on a dedicated website which were claimed to be original material.

The untitled 'pilot' saw the *Enterprise* on routine patrol when an automated sentry system destroys a ship seeking asylum in the Federation. The crew rescue the pilot who asks Starfleet for help with his dying breath, as he strangely clutches a *Next Generation*-era communicator. Chase, curious, tracks where the pilot came from, and the *Enterprise* defends a similar ship from an attacking battlecruiser manned by sinister insectoid creatures. They destroy the attackers, but the smaller ship flees into an 'Omega distortion', which the *Enterprise* can't access, but a specially designed shuttle, the Dragonfly, can. Chase leads a team inside and finds a 24th-century Galaxy-class ship (identical to the *Enterprise-D*) inside called the USS *Venture*, which disappeared decades ago.

On the ship they find the aliens who claim to be the Ordrin, sentient beings bred to be food for the Verlicon, the insectoids they encountered earlier. The Ordrin have hidden on the *Venture* but ask for Chase's help to restore engines so they can escape the distortion and the Verlicon. The crew get the ship online but on getting the *Venture* back to normal space, Verlicon ships attack and their leader Kuru Xun demands the aliens be handed over. Chase refuses as Xun sends over 'Harvesters', creatures resembling the Bugs from *Starship Troopers*, to take the ship, and despite Donal's efforts, they kill Preston. Chase manages to destroy the Verlicon ship and the Ordrin are given the *Venture* as theirs to live on. Expecting censure for going off book, Chase is instead given the remit of exploring the frontier and looking for signals akin to the one the *Venture* emitted.

The second script, 'The Empty Eye', begins with Chase and Donal captured on an away mission, fighting off aliens in an arena before being rescued by the *Enterprise*. Zero has discovered a nearby anomaly which turns out to be a gigantic metallic object the size of a moon. Donal and Zero use a Dragonfly to investigate but the moon reacts to scans from the *Enterprise*, which then blips out of existence. The crew find themselves on a strange planet, fighting off insects and struggling to survive. Donal and Zero try to access the sphere, believing the *Enterprise* has travelled inside.

On the planet, Chase and the crew encounter a warrior with four arms called Yara, claiming many ships have been marooned here and are being picked apart by a swarm of squid-like robots trying to prevent their escape. Yara helps them devise a plan to retake the *Enterprise* but upon hearing how isolationist the Federation is, he refuses his offer to take as many of those stranded as he can. They launch an attack on the shipyard and fight off robots trying to access the *Enterprise*, while outside the sphere Donal and Zero regain control of the ship. Chase and the crew escape, thanking Yara, to whom the planet is now home, and Zero ensures the sphere won't trap any future ships again.

These episodes evoke not just the spirit of *The Original Series* but equally *The Animated Series*, designed to tell quick and action-oriented stories appealing across the demographic of fans. The inspirations for the eventual child-friendly animated series *Prodigy* are clear. That too has an alien being in an encounter suit named Zero and a crew who find themselves pulled into sprightly adventures. 'Final Frontier', ultimately, was a victim of timing more than anything else. At the point Zero Room was pitching, CBS and Paramount were putting together a plan to reboot *Star Trek* under the aegis of Bad Robot and director J. J. Abrams, with an entirely new cast appearing as Kirk, Spock and the original *Enterprise* crew. 'Final Frontier' was a casualty of that new direction.

The tide had turned once again back to the past rather than pressing on toward the future.

*

Following the release of *Nemesis*, and the focus on *Enterprise*, the world of *Star Trek* in the 24th century had fallen to non-canonical authors to continue, creating their own 'post-*Nemesis*' future over almost twenty subsequent years, which had a breath-taking depth and scope, one far outweighing the canonical future that *Picard* eventually provided.

After *Enterprise*, several teams of highly talented and experienced writers sought an opportunity to create their own new series as part of the *Star Trek* lexicon, suggesting future directions that ran very contrary to the 'Abramsverse' that came out of the ashes of the Berman era of the franchise.

The biggest pitch arrived in 2006, following the cancellation of *Enterprise*, called 'Star Trek: Federation', spearheaded by a creative team including Robert Meyer Burnett and writer Geoffrey Thorne, under the aegis of Hollywood writer-director heavyweights Bryan Singer – the man behind *The Usual Suspects* and later the *X-Men* franchise – and Christopher McQuarrie – later to make it big with the *Mission: Impossible* series. They put together a twenty-five-page document outlining a concept that went even further than 'Final Frontier's animated 26th-century setting and evoked the future destination of *Discovery* by moving forward to the year 3000, the 31st century.

Their pitch suggested a need for *Star Trek* to move away from the style still apparent in *Enterprise* from the 1990s series, with television evolving into more complex serialised narratives, and that the franchise had to avoid regurgitating old stories or playing in its own sandbox – as *Enterprise* had arguably done in the fourth season – to make *Star Trek* relevant again.

They wanted to establish a far future universe where 'utopia' as Gene Roddenberry had envisaged had failed: "Utopia as a goal is like the fire in a nuclear engine. Utopia in practice is stagnation; it's dry rot; eventually it's death. Which is precisely where we find the United Federation of Planets a few centuries after the last Age of Discovery."

'Federation's changes would have been radical. Humanity was now complacent and "giving up exploration for incremental colonization and focusing more on the rightness of their own cultural view over all others" with many alien races who joined the Federation late now leaving due to a human-focused approach to the organisation. Starfleet is now merely a token force preventing borders wars, with a vastly reduced number of starships due to this decay. These ideas crept into the fear-driven isolationism of Starfleet in *Picard* and the post-Burn decay visible in *Discovery*.

Thorne expands on the thinking behind this: "If you take the history of *Star Trek* as we've been presented with it, the Federation ultimately wins every fight. We either destroy the thing, convince the thing not to destroy us, or absorb the thing into us. So what happens when utopia actually happens? That was actually part of the problem of *Star Trek* as a social phenomena – it started to get church-like for too many people. Even people backstage, which as humans don't have any issues with one another and there wasn't a need for commerce. The only problems came from outside. But that's not how *Star Trek* was when it started; it was very rough and tumble and I wanted to get back to that."

Much as 'Final Frontier' suggested, and *Discovery*'s 32nd century showed to happen canonically, the Vulcans would have moved away from the Federation and reunified with the Romulan Empire, creating a society overseen by a pair of "quasi-religious clerics who rule according to logic and what is best for their unified peoples, combining Romulan Machiavellian politics with Vulcan logic".

Despite plans and overtures by the end of *Deep Space Nine* for Bajor to become a major new entrant to the Federation, they would also have withdrawn to become an insular, religious society "like a planet-sized Tibet", having seceded many of their political concerns over to the Ferengi, who have grown in power and moved away from largely being laughed at for their appearances and avarice. Female equality, even a female Grand Nagus, are "the only concession they have made to progress". They are exploiting a universe leaning more toward capitalism and making huge sums exploiting Bajoran religion and the wormhole to the masses.

Star Trek's most iconic species, the Klingons, have undergone a huge transformation into a "civilization of warrior mystics", maintaining diplomacy while simultaneously expanding their empire by conquest. An equal transformation has been experienced by the Cardassians, from arrogant and brutal overseers to a "society of artists and philosophers" dedicated to a peaceful way of life. The Federation's biggest inversion is taking *Star Trek*'s two most warlike, naturally aggressive species and moving them into an enlightened space.

The pitch team created a new villain to enter the stage known as the Scourge, who confront a ship called the USS *Sojourner* and destroy it plus two colonies, establishing the power of their threat: "Lieutenant Commander Alexander Kirk is the only survivor of the '*Sojourner* Incident', as it's come to be known in the press. And he has no clear memory of the events themselves. Attempts to 'help' him remember cause him to become irrational and violent. All he has is images of carnage and death and a hidden malevolent presence lurking behind it all. When called before his superiors, he paints a picture of the enemy that is scarcely believed and which, if true, might tip the already fracturing Federation Alliance into true collapse."

Thorne continues to expand on the thought process: "My idea was, every episode would start with a video letter home from one of the crew, and that crewman might not necessarily be in the episode, it would just inform what we were about to see. So I said, 'Utopia has occurred and everything has stagnated.' Innovation is driven by necessity, so if you've got everything you need, you've explored everything, you've embraced your enemies, and everything is cool, then you're not making any new stuff. You're not pushing. That's not how evolution works. I pictured a Federation that had hit its plateau and stayed there for three hundred years. Basically using a lot of the same tech from the time of *Next Generation*, and these are old ships. People are pulling out of the Federation because there's no need for a Federation in such a time of peace – but of course it turns out that that's completely wrong. That was the starting point."

Numerous races secede from the Federation as the Scourge threat emerges and, as a result, Starfleet under the aegis of recurring character Admiral Nelscott decide to build a whole new USS *Enterprise* – the first in three centuries – to secretly investigate and combat the looming threat. The pitch establishes the intended main characters for the show, starting with Captain Alden Montgomery, the "perfect Starfleet officer", who they refer to as "The Captain America of the Federation". To add dramatic stakes, he is killed early in the series, to make way for the true intended captain: Alexander Kirk, a descendant of the legendary captain of an earlier *Enterprise*.

He begins as a commander, filled with aggression after events in his past, and thrust into command after Montgomery's death. He copes well though is "total crap at PR aspects of the job". Without realising, thanks no doubt to the *Sojourner* incident, he "possesses information vital to *Enterprise*'s true mission".

Around him is Lt Commander Chel Forlaan, security chief and a member of a new, feline species called the Ektosi (perhaps echoing the aforementioned Kzinti). She has "cat-like" grace and temper, with combat abilities akin to a Klingon or Jem'Hadar. She is described as "mercurial", joining Starfleet for the fun of it, and in line with her cat-features, she has "intense curiosity which sometimes overpowers her".

At communications is Lt Commander Sergei Kenyatta, hailing from Proxima Centauri, who is an enhanced human called an 'Alpha', sporting a perfect physique and higher functioning mental abilities, gifted in linguistics, technology, diplomacy, etc . . . his only drawback being a difficulty with relationships. It is possible he would have served as the Spock/Data/Doctor-style character aboard ship, learning his humanity as the series grappled with his genetically altered nature, given the historic precepts that had caused it to be banned in the Federation.

Much as Zero in 'Final Frontier' was an encounter-suited alien chief engineer, so too would 'Federation' have sported the 76th Distillation of Blue, known as 'Diz', part of a gas-based species from the giant Penumbra who uses a "motion suit" to interact with solid lifeforms. He would, akin to Odo's Changeling abilities, be able to change shape, but he is "not a shape-shifter" and would typically resemble a "slender male humanoid". Again, a character lacking in social skills and happier with technology.

The doctor character, Felicity Chen, would have shared traits with 'Final Frontier''s Donal, being cybernetically advanced thanks to safe Borg technology. She is described essentially as a walking tricorder, with medical abilities and instruments built in. She can use her "nano spines" to heal injuries, but these aspects lead her to constantly grapple with her own humanity. She would no doubt have been an outgrowth and development of Seven of Nine's character arc on *Voyager*.

Finally, in a cute nod to *Star Trek* history, the sentient computer aboard the *Enterprise*, replete with personality and emotions, would have been called M.A.J.E.L. (Multitronic Architecture Junction/Interactive Energetic Library), after Majel Barrett-Roddenberry, and no doubt partly influenced by Marvel's J.A.R.V.I.S., the sentient AI used by Tony Stark's *Iron Man*, who would make his cinematic debut only a few years subsequent to this pitch. The writers suggest interpersonal conflicts would add drama to these main characters, with the series very clearly abandoning the Roddenberry precept of ensuring the crew maintain largely good relationships.

The pitch also describes the *Enterprise* as being "something bigger than *Voyager*, but nowhere near the size of The Battlestar Galactica", replete with features including a 'town square'-style area called the 'Central Core', a 'Landing Envelope' force-field projecting that shoots down to a planet giving away the team's atmosphere to breathe in on hostile planets. This was reputedly considered for *The Next Generation*, though no doubt budgetary considerations preferred the crew travelling largely to similar-looking planets with breathable air.

Enterprise would also have Romulan-style technology, such as a 'Singularity Engine', powered by a microscopic black hole, and a 'Cloaking Device', allowing for covert missions. This would not have been without precedent given *Deep Space Nine*'s USS *Defiant* sported a cloak loaned from the Romulan Empire to help fight the Dominion. There are clear attempts in these technological additions for the Federation to find new avenues as a means of telling *Star Trek* stories than in previous series.

The document also describes a four-part arc to begin the series, with episodic descriptions, which would be an extended longer form 'Pilot' to begin the show.

'The Widening Gyre' begins as "Alden Montgomery encounters another planet where the inhabitants have destroyed themselves in an 'orgy of violence'. Admiral Nelscott orders him to put together his crew for the fast-tracked *Enterprise* project, leading Montgomery on an origin story recruiting mission picking up various staff, including Kirk who is no longer in Starfleet and doesn't want to join, but is the only person who has dealt with The Scourge (forcing Montgomery to 'Shanghai' Kirk)."

This is followed by 'The Blood-Dimmed Tide', as "Kirk and Dr Chen explore a found small alien obelisk and deal with the crew of the *Enterprise* who have become victims of the violent 'Scourge', including the captain", suggesting by this point Montgomery has been killed and Kirk has taken charge. 'Mere Anarchy' begins as "The *Enterprise* chases a larger alien obelisk through space, eventually leading them into hostile Klingon space," and finally in 'The Ceremony of Innocence' "Kirk, now trapped in the obelisk with some Klingons, gets to the bottom of the mystery only to find out the Obelisks are tied to the Preservers (from *The Next Generation*) who had seeded the galaxy with the building blocks of humanoid DNA."

Intriguingly, this connects the Federation back to *The Next Generation*'s sixth season episode 'The Chase', a rather profound story with enormous galactic implications that *Star Trek* chose never to explore further, but which could have sizeable storyline potential. As this opening block of stories concludes, the pitch teases with the following: "So, the riddle of the *Sojourner* Incident is solved and the threat of the obelisks is removed (apparently) but at great cost. Frictions between the Federation and the Klingons have never been worse. The internal fissures are growing wider based largely on the *Enterprise*'s secret mission and Admiral Nelscott's lies to cover up that mission with the council. And, of course, lots and lots of people died. What's next for the survivors of these events? Tune in next week, folks."

Well thought out, with a strong team behind the concept, 'Federation' had a confidence to its presentation. Singer and McQuarrie, who had worked together on *The Usual Suspects* and later *Valkyrie*, planned to write and direct the pilot. Burnett would produce alongside Singer's Bad Hat Harry production firm. They had the concept planned to present to Paramount in 2006, once Singer had completed post-production on *Superman Returns*.

Thorne explains why this alternate future never happened: "Everyone seemed very happy with the pitch and were about to present it when J. J. Abrams came in and said, 'I want to make these movies.' The new *Star Trek* films destroyed the possibility for Federation to get off the ground, and that was the end of it."

It would be a similar story for an earlier pitch which leaned toward a similar concept to the one Abrams would eventually provide.

'Star Trek: Reboot the Universe' was pitched in 2004 by J. Michael Stracynzski and Bryce Zabel. The former a science-fiction heavyweight, creator, and almost principal writer on *Babylon-5*, still to date one of the most brilliantly constructed science-fiction 'novels for television' ever committed to screen, not to mention a successful screenwriter, author and comic-book writer in his own regard. The latter with less credentials, though had achieved brief acclaim developing *Dark Skies*, a promising inheritor of *The X-Files* unfortunately cancelled after one season.

Zabel recalls how the combination of forces came to be: "Joe [Straczynski] and I were working on a network pitch for a limited series called *Cult*, and we started talking about the state of the *Trek* universe. Before we could stop ourselves, we banged out a fourteen-page treatment ... We wanted to do what they would do in the world of comics: create a separate universe for all the past TV and film *Trek* continuity in order to free ourselves creatively so we could embrace the good stuff, banish the bad, and try some new things."

The 'Reboot the Universe' pitch begins with a polemical summation of the creative lack of ambition and waning fan interest for *Star Trek* before suggesting the answer of how to fix the problem: "What we propose is not *Star Trek*: Another Generation, or *Star Trek*: A New Ship, or even

Star Trek: The Search for Plots. In other words, not a copy of a copy, or a distillation of a variation. We want to re-boot *Star Trek*. The original. Pure and simple. The characters, universe and situations that have attracted, and continue to attract, a worldwide audience. Re-set . . . re-imagined . . . re-invigorated . . . Imagine taking those characters, and using what we know now about the universe, and combining it with the kind of storytelling that audiences of 2004 are used to seeing in modern prime-time television. Hard-hitting. Exciting. Character-driven. Innovative. And armed with the very latest EFX in support of our stories."

Their plan was to remake *The Original Series* and the five-year mission with Kirk, Spock and McCoy front and centre. "Before we go any further, let's answer the obvious question: Will the fans of the original series (call it *Star Trek*: Classic) accept a new cast and series under the original *Star Trek* banner? The answer, we believe, is a firm and unequivocal 'yes'. Remember, for a moment, that the final episode of *Star Trek*: Classic aired less than six weeks before humans first set foot on the moon. More than enough time has passed to allow fans the luxury of considering new faces in familiar roles."

This belief presaged the reality of the 2009 movie which did, indeed, reboot the universe, albeit in less of a stripped back manner than this pitch desires to do. J. Michael Straczynski (JMS) and Zabel were correct in their assertion that *Star Trek* fans, or at least many of them, would embrace new actors in such iconic roles. They make the point that Marvel and DC heroes and even classical characters not protected by copyright have been recast and reinterpreted for generations, and they consider *Star Trek* to be no less durable in such a manner.

JMS and Zabel explain their starting point: "We will start with a two-hour pilot that tells the story no one has ever seen: the circumstances that lead Kirk and McCoy (friends before this) to meet Spock for the first time. It will involve their discovery of a lost city on an uncharted world, nearly a million years old, and their encounter with the race that built it, a race long sought after by every civilized world for the tremendous advantages they could provide. Along the way, we'll learn how Kirk – the youngest starship captain in the Federation – won command of the *Enterprise* in the course of a battle with another race in pursuit of that ancient mystery. By the end of this pilot, Kirk, Spock and McCoy will be aboard the Federation's *Enterprise*, poised at the edge of known space, poised to explore the billions of stars inside our galaxy. We will embrace, truly, the famous Captain's Log from nearly four-decades ago."

Their pledge is to find ways to develop new technologies, as exciting as communicators and tricorders were to audiences before the age of smart phones that evoked them, for audiences to become lost in as audiences were in the 1960s. They aim for the relationships between the main cast to be modern and mature. And, perhaps evoking the prevalence of serialised, 'mystery box' storytelling to come, they pledge to place a core enigma at the heart of their *Star Trek*: "Had Kirk, Spock and McCoy stumbled upon something that could have a profound effect on human history? Had they caught a glimpse of a new and previously unknown race a million years ahead of mankind . . . a race whose secrets could elevate humanity to unparalleled levels . . . a race that left its footprints on a hundred worlds where its touch had changed evolution and led to civilization as we know it? A race, long thought dead, but which our characters know is still out there somewhere . . . waiting for us . . . waiting to see if its children can come and find it, there in the darkness between the stars . . . And there are others out there, also searching for this race . . . forces of darkness who may view our activities with more than a little hostility."

This idea feels like an outgrowth of JMS' alien villains on *Babylon 5*, the Shadows, who themselves were steadily unveiled and contained a connection to ancient human history. They plan to take this one step further, extending an idea – much as Federation had planned to do – already tackled to some degree in *The Next Generation*'s sixth season episode, 'The Chase': "One thing we will discover is that buried deep within the DNA of humans, Vulcans (even Klingons) and other intelligent bi-pedal races is a mathematical code, something buried so deep and of such complexity that it could not possibly have occurred by chance. Someone or something put it there . . . an 'artist's signature' perhaps . . . In the re-booted *Star Trek* universe, there is a 'Prime Directive' but it is not about non-interference in the matters of other races. This Prime Directive states simply that it is the mission of the starship *Enterprise* to do whatever is necessary to find this long-lost race, and discover the truth about the common origin of all life forms everywhere, the truth that will unite a galaxy. Who are we? Why are we here? Are we special? Are we tools? Cannon fodder? Or are we being prepped for something . . . amazing? Over the next five years, we'll offer up the answers."

Their means of reconceptualising the 'Prime Directive' would have been quite revolutionary for *Star Trek*, and whether it would have been well-received by fans is highly questionable. It does speak to their ambition for 'Reboot the Universe' to be a fusion of old precepts and striking, new, almost heretical ideas.

They also planned not to over-utilise the technological constructs that *The Next Generation*-era often fell back on: "Note that the original *Enterprise* never needed a holo-deck so that the characters could have exciting adventures because there were more than enough adventures, more than enough excitement to be found in the real world they occupied every day. If you need a holo-deck to make an interstellar starship on the bleeding edge of the unknown interesting, something is seriously amiss."

Many fans would likely agree that the holodeck allowed for some of the more inventive storytelling possibilities in the 1990s era of *Star Trek*, but JMS' sensibility in how he developed *Babylon 5* shines through for a pitch designed to ground *Star Trek*, make it earthier in a similar fashion, not to mention hold true to a very simple, clear narrative plan: there will be a beginning, middle and end to this series. "It will be exactly five seasons, with each season equalling one year of their five-year mission. The crew of the *Enterprise* will leave in our pilot episode, and they will return five years later from their scientific and security mission. If the studio or network wishes the series to continue after that, the chronology of our story will note that they have completed their mission, then move the franchise into new territory, or a new series."

JMS and Zabel also planned to go where the series had not gone for several decades when it came to developing stories for the series: "We can also do something that the original *Star Trek* did to great success: purchase and adapt short stories by leading SF writers. The original *Trek* made use of the creative work of Richard Matheson, Robert Bloch, Harlan Ellison, Jerome Bixby, Fredric Brown, Norman Spinrad and Theodore Sturgeon. They provided the stories behind some of *Trek*'s most original, innovative episodes. Now imagine a new *Star Trek* calling upon the talents of writers like Neil Gaiman, Stephen King, Ray Bradbury, Dean Koontz, Michael Crichton, Anne Rice, Kurt Vonnegut, Anne McCaffrey, and others. Finding stories by these writers that would fit in the *Star Trek* universe and adapting them would not only result in some terrific episodes, but would be excellent publicity for the series."

One wonders if the financial factor of this goal would have somewhat turned Paramount off the pitch, as exciting a prospect as stories from many of these modern genre masters in the *Star Trek* universe would have been. It could also have given the series more of an anthological bent, a concept that will come into play during early development later of *Discovery*.

JMS and Zabel sought to clearly delineate this version of *Star Trek* from the previous series and films by designating those as 'Universe A' and this as 'Universe B', making the point that comic-book continuity has for decades operated in such a fashion and fans have grown used to varying 'universes' depicting alternate versions of the same characters and stories. In this approach, JMS and Zabel place themselves decades ahead of the curve, with the 2020s now heavily embracing 'multiverse' narratives and constant reimagining of classic franchises.

Nonetheless, they liked the idea of putting a fresh spin on 'Universe A' material and from *The Original Series*, which they named as '*Star Trek*: Classic': "We know that a planet-eater was rampaging through space in *Star Trek*: Classic . . . but what if we discover that the device was a left-over piece of warfare tech from the race our characters are pursuing? Do they allow the planet-sized weapon to destroy a sparsely-populated colony world if in doing so, they gain the time to get information that could save billions of lives elsewhere? We know that the *Enterprise* was once infested with tiny cute Tribbles piled three feet high in some places . . . but what if they came equipped with an agenda, an attitude . . . and teeth? We know that Scotty was constantly called upon to perform technical miracles and ably did so...but what if Scotty was a female character (just an example!), proof positive that in the future women equally excel in science and math? Our point is simply this: the fun, the excitement and the passion of the re-boot is in the imagining of the alternative."

They go on to map out specific rough plans for what would be the first season: "In our pilot, we deliver the story the fans never saw, the coming-together of Kirk, Spock and McCoy . . . the handing-over of the *Enterprise* . . . the mystery behind the mission . . . the launch into history. Four or five episodes that build on this mystery, each with a stand-alone main plot but with a B-plot that lays out the clues like bread-crumbs. These would be the equivalent to the so-called 'mythology' episodes which drove the '*X-Files*' series. Four or five episodes where the source material comes from stories by major writers in the science fiction and fantasy genre, adapted to teleplay by our writing staff. Four or five episodes that re-imagine specific stories or events from the original series, adapting teleplays from the original writers. Filled-out by stand-alone episodes that place Kirk, Spock and McCoy in new adventures filled with action, humor, strong characterization and dynamic storytelling. A season finale which drops a huge clue into play, and forces the *Enterprise* to take a stand putting its very existence on the line."

This plan sees the Reboot pitch combine a multitude of styles that pre-existed in television at the time. *The X-Files*, and indeed *Babylon 5* to a different extent, propagated the combination of 'mythology' tales that forward the broader narrative with stand-alone stories that would sometimes contain breadcrumbs, sometimes not. This, combined with plans to adapt stories from celebrated writers and to 'cover' *Original Series* stories, would have been quite the break from *Enterprise*'s recent shifting style – moving from sedate, *Voyager*-style storytelling to darker and breakneck serialisation, through finally to clusters of popular, fan service multi-part stories exploring established canon.

JMS and Zabel conclude their pitch with a renewed belief that *Star Trek*'s light has dimmed and a call to arms for how exciting the prospect of a new Kirk, Spock and McCoy would be to popular culture: "This new series will re-capture the chemistry which existed between these historic characters, as it appeared on-screen, and as it translated to members of the viewing audience. It will give the fans what they've always dreamed of. A chance to see those wonderful, original characters done with the state-of-the-art talents available today. Remember how thrilling it was to first hear the Captain's Log and to let your mind wander to what wonderful things would happen in that 'five-year mission'? It can happen again."

And indeed, it did, but not in this incarnation. "It was, admittedly, pretty audacious." Zabel would later admit.

Nonetheless, in a different form, rebooting the universe did happen five years later, just on a bigger cinematic canvas. In many respects, JMS and Zabel had imagined the future of *Star Trek* heading into the 2010s in advance of Paramount agreeing that revisiting the original crew, the iconic assortment of characters, was the way to revitalise the brand.

Before the advent of *Star Trek 2009*, however, a plan existed to place one toe in both worlds. To continue the exploration of the *Star Trek* universe after *Enterprise* and before *The Original Series* while exploring the legend of Kirk in a manner nobody would have imagined . . .

THIRTEEN

THE MOTION PICTURES: PART III

AFTER THE SLOW death of *Enterprise*, and the end of *Star Trek* on television after so many years, few fans had a great deal of hope for the future of a franchise that had fallen so swiftly in such a short space of time.

Rick Berman was not yet ready to concede defeat and rather looked instead back to the big screen with a project that became known as '*Star Trek*: The Beginning', on which he worked with producers Kerry McCluggage and Jordan Kerner, who recruited Eric Jendresen, a writer of some renown thanks to working on HBO's celebrated mini-series *Band of Brothers*, to pen the script, which was delivered in August of 2006.

"Shortly after *Band of Brothers*, I got a call from my agent, who said, 'Would you be interested in getting into *Star Trek*?' And I said, 'No.' First of all, because I don't really like science fiction. I'm kind of an odd purist that way. If it's not Jules Verne or H. G. Wells or Edgar Allen Poe or Arthur Conan Doyle, I'm not that interested. The space opera genre of science fiction is just something that has never held any interest for me. But they didn't take no for an answer. [Producer] Jordan Kerner really wanted to have a conversation, so they called me back and said, 'Would you come consult with us?' And I said, 'Sure.' And I was very honest with them. I loved two things about *Star Trek*. The first was this sort of Horatio Hornblower aspect to Kirk. All of that boldness. It's sort of a throwback to a great kind of literary figure and hero. Second, I realized

I loved the fact that the stories were always, at the time, of political or social relevance. There was a message behind them all. And it was kind of lovely. I really respected that."

'The Beginning' was set in 2159, four years after the events of *Enterprise* episodes 'Demons' and 'Terra Prime', and two before the foundation of the Federation as witnessed in 'These Are the Voyages'. Jendresen's script focuses on a group of daring pilots in training including Gardner Jr, the son of Starfleet commander in chief Admiral Gardner; smart-talking Jaxx; female pioneer Rixxen and Tiberius Chase, an ancestor of James T. Kirk, the son of a radical xenophobic extremist on the verge of being blacklisted from joining Starfleet, as they prepare, in the wake of the Coalition of Planets being formed, to launch a new, faster warp-capable ship the *NX-Omega*. As Chase falls in love with Admiral Gardner's daughter, Penelope, Earth is attacked in a shock move by the sinister, unseen Romulans, who send an armada to obliterate the planet as part of an intended ethnic cleansing throughout the galaxy of their Vulcan cousins. Chase, flying in the face of Starfleet rules and regulations, prepares to use old Earth technology to stage an attack on the Romulans as Starfleet prepares for the first, devastating stage of what will become a major conflict in *Star Trek*'s future history.

"I said, 'Imagine this baby as a trilogy. It should be something that fills that missing place in the canon. 'It was sort of like having an encyclopaedia. This encyclopaedia is missing the letter T. There's a gap. And interestingly enough, at least for the original series, an inciting incident that's referred to but we've never seen is the Earth-Romulan War that started the whole thing."

Jendresen makes passing references to the canonical *Enterprise* series that would have covered this war had the series continued – mentions of the Xindi conflict leading to increased defences on Earth, including vast subterranean bunkers given the orbital attack seen in 'The Expanse'; the reappearance of Jeffrey Combs' Commander Shran as a cameo aiding the Coalition's defence; and a reference to Archer and his *Enterprise*, conveniently too far away on the pleasure planet Risa to be involved in the conflict. Overall, though, Jendresen manages to craft 'The Beginning' into a defiantly cinematic, earthy combination of *Enterprise*, *Top Gun* and a Second World War movie. Chase's father even lives in a secret Nazi Antarctic base, cementing UFOs in *Star Trek* lore as Nazi flying saucers, one of the great occult conspiracy theories of the 20th century.

He admits the reaction from Paramount was positive, etching out what he imagined the story beyond 'The Beginning' would look like. "I said, 'I'd ever so loosely fashion the first one on *The Iliad*. And the sequel would be ever so loosely based on *The Odyssey*. I would love to leave the hero and his crew stranded and having to make their way slowly back to Earth having no idea whether Earth exists or not. It's going to take them years to get back on this crippled ship. And that journey in the sequel to the prequel would also involve some of the interesting moments that harken back to the original series. But it happened decades before. It would be a tremendous trek on the way back.' Then I added, 'And then the third one, I have no idea what it will be.' And they loved it!"

Jendresen's script very much establishes Chase in the Kirk mould without any direct, coded reference to his descendant, and fuses his heroic, space cowboy nature with a sense of Greek mythology underpinning the *Star Trek* world. Chase romances Penelope by outlining the ancient Greek mythological heroes and titans – figures such as Arcturus and Atlas – in the stars. In a manner perhaps not seen since the 1960s and Roddenberry's vision of *Star Trek*, he imagines a philosophical grandness to the franchise while simultaneously delivering pulp thrills, action spectacle and the cold, alien nature of space and exploration that *Enterprise* quickly drifted away from.

Equally writing in the wake of 9/11, clearly already well-worn territory in *Enterprise*, Jendresen rather deliberately explores a recent real-world parallel: "This is all happening during the Serbian-Croatian conflict. So the whole notion was of this interstellar ethnic cleansing going on. It was really about something. And the fact that the Earth stands up against the Romulans [in defense of the Vulcans, whom they've had a strained relationship with since *Enterprise*] and says, 'No.' The needs of the few outweighs the needs of the many. That is the moment when the Earth stands up and says no."

Despite a great deal of positives around the script, which remains vibrant and feels akin to a natural successor to *Enterprise* on a bigger, broader scale, Jendresen found that interest waned, despite Kerner and McCluggage joining the project. Berman, tangentially involved, seemed disinterested as Jendresen worked on presenting the idea to Paramount: "We went in to pitch it to the head of the studio, Donald De Line. We sat down and started telling the story. I've been in a lot of rooms in Hollywood. I've pitched a lot of projects. I've never been in a more preternaturally dead room than this one. It was like being in a sensory deprivation tank. There was not a sound, and in the middle of the pitch I thought, 'This is really odd.'"

Sensing the writing was on the wall, Jendresen decided to go for broke: "So, I think, to hell with it, I'm going to go take a really big swing here and I told the whole story. I took forty-five minutes to do the entire thing. And I was just riffing and also sort of discovering and creating things as I sort of started embellishing on my story. I get to the end. Dead silence. And then De Line clears his throat and he says, 'Umm, how long would it take you to write this?' I said, 'Eight to ten weeks.' And then he sticks his hand out and just shakes my hand and says, 'Write it fast.' He bought it in the room. And so we walk out and all the producers are just falling all over themselves. They're so thrilled. 'We're doing the next *Star Trek*! This is unbelievable!'"

One of the key factors of 'The Beginning' was the conflict, inherent in *Star Trek*, between the boldness of exploration and the rigorous strictures of Starfleet itself: "By the time I was finished writing it, I was quite shocked about the whole thing. I really enjoyed the process. I was also very well aware of the fact that because of the agnostic feeling I had toward the genre, and I wasn't a die-hard fan, I was able to serve it better, because I wasn't precious. My own feelings about a story or a canon of material are as strong as most Trekkies are for the Arthur Conan Doyle books. That was something I was crazed about as a kid. To this day, I still am. So, I thought, well, I have to think of this legion of folks who hold this so dearly and try to serve that. It really served canon. And I went deep in my research and tried to make sure that this entry didn't in any way defy the canon. Having to come up with some kind of clever way to be able to have a human encounter a Romulan and deal with the notion that no one lives to tell of it. And it was really fun to try to tackle the idea of Kirk's progenitor. Who is this guy that he was named after? Where did his spirit originate from? I really embraced it."

Chase wonders, in voice-over letters to Penelope that are dotted throughout the script, akin to Civil War-style missives dispatched to family rather than the traditional 'Captain's Log': "I will still, and forever, wonder how one can go boldly and follow at the same time?" Built into the DNA of *Star Trek* lies that contradiction which had led to every single captain across five series, and over ten movies, frequently betraying orders in the purpose of 'boldly going' and the greater good. Chase, as the template for Kirk and in essence every *Star Trek* protagonist since 1966, is designed to interrogate that idea. In that respect, 'The Beginning' would have truly lived up to its title.

"I was well aware of the fact that this story was a departure from that intention Roddenberry had always held close [for *Star Trek*]. I was trying to be respectful of it. And those issues are sort of addressed in the story. But, I had them also face the simple fact that Starfleet came out of a conflict, that sort of wonderful swords-to-plowshares thing that ultimately happened can't happen without the swords part."

Jendresen would have also held true to lore embedded within *The Original Series*, where Spock describes the war with the Romulans as using "primitive atomic weapons", which feels at odds with the technology introduced in *Enterprise* that had much in common with later (or rather earlier) *Star Trek* series. The Vulcan Ambassador, Skon – here a supporting character – is the biological father of Sarek, Spock's father. Then, as mentioned, there are the direct Kirk connections, regarding one character who Jendresen had even started considering casting: "I did have one person in mind when I wrote it. But it's a tertiary character. Tiberius is Kirk's great-grandfather. So his great-great-grandfather is Tiberius' father, Otto Chase, who leads this group of xenophobes, and I was just absolutely convinced there was only one guy to play him. And that was Christopher Walken. I would have brought him back in the sequel. He was such a colorful character. The idea of Walken in this subterranean cavern with all of these ancient rotting Nazi UFOs would've been great."

Had 'The Beginning' been made, it would have perhaps been as radical a franchise reinvention as *Casino Royale* to James Bond or *Batman Begins* to the Caped Crusader were in the mid-2000s – both of which responded to the edgier palette adopted by Hollywood filmmaking in the wake of 9/11 with grittier, grounded approaches to larger-than-life heroes. In a much different, and more directly canonically tethered respect to 2009's *Star Trek* reboot, 'The Beginning' could have invigorated *Star Trek* stylistically and, for the first time since 1987, moved deliberately away from how the franchise had portrayed itself in decades gone by.

Jendresen remains sanguine about why the project failed to materialise: "To this day I don't know and will never know if it would've worked. But, of course, I went ahead and wrote it and turned the script in and on Wednesday of that week, the head of the studio [Donald De Line] was fired. It's a tried and true, honored tradition of Hollywood that regime change is a slate-wiper. Any new regime coming in, even if a film is going to be a success, it's bad news for them because they had nothing to do with it. So they can't really risk it. It was just so unlucky."

Whether the proposed 'Final Frontier' animated series, also with a protagonist named Chase, took a cue from 'The Beginning' or was simply a coincidence is open to question. Numerous teams of writers, on various pitched projects across film and television, all seemed to believe *Star Trek*'s evolution lay, however, in a return to a Kirk-style captain figure who could command the same combination of brio, adventure and swagger William Shatner immortalised in the 1960s.

Though Jendresen never successfully managed to place his stamp on the *Star Trek* world, thanks to the ever-shifting vicissitudes of the corporate landscape, he understood the core nature of the universe and what it could still offer to a world that was, potentially, moving beyond it. "I read an interesting piece online about the relevance of *Star Trek*. It posed the idea that maybe it's not relevant anymore. It was an impressive argument, but a fine story is always relevant, and I think solid storytelling that's rooted in the absolute spirit of the *Original Series* is what it was all about to begin with."

An almost prophetic statement given the filmmaker who would not just revive *Star Trek*, give it a whole new relevance, but catapult it into a critical and commercial space it had long since drifted away from, would return to the heart of *Star Trek*'s foundational text as his means of doing so.

J. J. Abrams was about to boldly return to an entirely different beginning.

*

In the wake of the cancellation of *Enterprise,* and the success of previously mentioned franchise reboots *Casino Royale* and *Batman Begins* in 2005/2006, Paramount awakened to the idea that *Star Trek* might be given similar treatment on the big screen as a valuable, globally recognised intellectual property.

Consigning the Berman era, and those involved, resolutely to the past, they approached a team about to work together on the latest, third iteration of *Mission Impossible* for the same studio, a film itself that would turn out to be a soft reboot of a franchise that would sail on into much more successful waters. The trio were Abrams, Alex Kurtzman and Roberto Orci, who recalls the time: "It was Marc Evans who was an executive over there, and it was prior to *Mission: Impossible III* [released in 2006], it was before we did that with [director] J. J. [Abrams]. He knew we were *Star Trek* fans and said, 'Do you have any ideas of what it could be?' And we said yes. We would go back to the youth. We didn't have the whole idea, but we had an inkling of how it should feel and going back to the original characters. We didn't know yet how to figure out an in-canon reboot."

Manny Coto recalls the feeling in the air at the time: "The end of *Enterprise* was all ratings and the fact that the last movie had underperformed, so there was a sense that the franchise was waning and needed a creative boost – and, by, the way, I predicted what was going to happen. When they were talking about whether to bring *Star Trek* back, I said they were going to find a hotshot filmmaker to revamp the series. And that's exactly what happened. By the way, that's what I would do if I were Paramount. I would look for someone who was big, powerful, and had made successful properties and is a *Star Trek* fan."

Abrams, in truth, was always far more of a *Star Wars* than *Star Trek* fan, as he would display on helming the iconic return of the legendary space opera in 2015 with *Star Wars: The Force Awakens*, and he would candidly admit he came to the franchise without the pre-existing detailed knowledge and awareness of the lore and history. That was where his writers came in. Orci and Kurtzman both retained that knowledge and were able to construct with him a framework for what they believed a new starting point would be. "It felt to me that if you were going to do a version of *Star Trek*, you would have to do it in such a way that it would bring it to life in a way that never had been done before. What I realized was that in my mind Kirk and Spock were the key, the heart, of *Trek*. Approaching this movie, [screenwriters] Alex Kurtzman and Roberto Orci, [producers] Damon Lindelof and Bryan Burk, and I discovered that's what we wanted to examine and explore: what Kirk and Spock were all about."

Star Trek, as the 2009 film is simply known with a stripped back title, begins with the birth of James T. Kirk as a strange alien ship destroys the USS *Kelvin* and kills his father, George. As Kirk grows up fatherless and falls into Starfleet after reluctantly being recruited by mentor and *Enterprise* captain Christopher Pike, Spock meanwhile rejects Vulcan learning to join Starfleet and as he and Kirk move through the Academy, the same alien ship, commanded by a Romulan named Nero, destroys Vulcan. As Kirk, Spock, McCoy and the rest of the crew clash on Pike's *Enterprise*, they discover, thanks to an elder, time-travelling Spock, that Nero hails from a future where Romulus was destroyed by an exploding supernova and is seeking vengeance. Kirk and Spock must put aside their differences as Pike is captured and Nero makes to destroy Earth with a powerful super-weapon.

Orci claims the initial plan went back to the same field ploughed by David Loughery and Harve Bennett two decades earlier, that of the long-mooted 'Starfleet Academy' concept, one that Orci confirmed would have featured both a young Kirk and Spock: "We developed a version of it which was just the Academy, very much inspired by one of the *Next Generation* episodes where Wesley is in the Academy and he goes through that whole tribunal where his ship was part of a disaster. That story inspired us to develop a complete 'Academy Days' story. But then as we got further into it and started to realize they were going to hand us the keys to the kingdom and the idea that we could get to Leonard Nimoy, that made us expand our scope."

The Academy concept was of course realised in the eventual movie during the first act, telling the story of Kirk and Spock's individual journeys to Starfleet and ultimately the *Enterprise*, but it forms only a component of Abrams' much larger narrative construction and reboot. As Orci states, the involvement of Nimoy, portraying a much older Spock after the events of 'Unification' in *The Next Generation*, served as the foundation text for the story ultimately pitched and greenly, one the writer has always maintained to be as much a sequel than reboot. Nimoy and Spock, in exploring his younger self, was critical. "Originally, we had it so the original Nimoy Spock would show up very much at the beginning of the story in the teaser as this mysterious character. You didn't know who it was. They were chasing this potentially trouble-making time traveler as a fake villain, who would be revealed to be Mr Spock. And he would reveal why he had gone back in time, because of this whole problem. He was a MacGuffin Darth Vader figure who was mucking around in time. And then it turns into what was the reveal we have for Mr Spock in the '09 movie."

Presenting Spock initially as a shadowy villain figure would have cast the movie in an entirely different light, but the idea of retaining mystery around his presence is intriguing. We might as an audience have lost the enjoyable anticipation, early on, that Nero seeks the 'Ambassador Spock' that we know. Yet Orci admits they considered an even more eyebrow-raising, fascinating possibility for Spock: "The other blind alley we had was that he was disguising himself as Robert April or something like that and that he was the origin of the character of Robert April. We also explored doing that in *Star Trek Into Darkness* as well, but decided it was too inside *Star Trek*."

This was probably a wise decision, given April – as we have seen, Roddenberry's first *Enterprise* captain creation – was a 'deep cut' *Star Trek* character reference. The reveal could well have been lost on the new, vibrant and younger audiences *Star Trek* 2009 sought to covet. Kurtzman also claimed that scenes were written that would have involved Kirk becoming aware, from elder Spock, of the character of the elder versions of his *Enterprise* crewmates: "Kirk points out that it is incredibly odd that they all sort of turned as they would have. Nimoy Spock tells Kirk 'I knew this character as this person and that character as that person' and Kirk says 'wow, those characters are exactly the same ones that I know' and Spock says something like, 'Fascinating, that must be the timestream's way of trying to mend itself.'"

The closest the *Kelvin* pictures would get to realising this lies in young Spock, in *Star Trek Beyond*, being left a picture in the deceased elder Spock's effects which showed the *Original Series* crew in a bridge shot during *The Undiscovered Country*, giving him an insight into the alternate future, and serving as an emotional audience beat to celebrate the franchise's 50th anniversary.

In the vein of attempting to engage younger audiences, Orci admits they cut the addition of a familiar love interest for Chris Pine's Kirk: "Also, in the original pitch I had Carol Marcus in the story as a love interest for Kirk, and to set her up for sequels. But it turned out to be a little bit too unwieldy for what we were trying to do. We already had a kind of bromance with Kirk and Spock and the whole crew, and that felt like something more important."

Ultimately, Carol – the mother of Kirk's son David as established in *The Wrath of Khan* – would appear in the guise of Alice Eve during *Star Trek Into Darkness*, though she never truly blossoms into the same relationship as Kirk had with Carol in the original timeline. An early draft also included Nurse Christine Chapel, played by Majel Barrett in the 1960s and in 1980s movie cameo appearances, before being revived as a main character in *Strange New Worlds*.

Early drafts also included George Samuel Kirk, Kirk's elder brother as established in the *Original Series* episode 'Operation – Annihilate!', and who would later appear as a recurring player in *Strange New Worlds* during the original timeline, but his absence opens a question mark on his existence in the *Kelvin* timeline. Also intended to feature was Captain Garrovick, Kirk's first commander on the USS *Farragut* as established in the *Original Series* episode 'Obsession', but as Kirk's connection that ship changed, Garrovick was excised.

In advance of the much-anticipated film, an enormous amount of casting rumours circled around who might portray these iconic characters, before Chris Pine, Zachary Quinto, Karl Urban etc were set in stone. Though Mike Vogel, best known for his role in the recent Abrams-producer *Cloverfield*, was the runner up for Kirk, Matt Damon was heavily mooted for the part and Abrams reputedly discussed it with him. He also briefly spoke to Adrien Brody for the role of Spock, though Gary Sinise denied he was in contention for McCoy, as did James McAvoy for the role of Scotty. Keri Russell, who featured in Abrams' first TV series *Felicity* and later starred briefly in *Mission Impossible III*, almost played a Klingon but this sadly never came to pass.

Speaking of Klingons, they featured in the most significant deleted sequence of *Star Trek* 2009. Following Nero's ship, the *Narada*, being disabled by the *Kelvin*'s destruction in the opening sequence, the drifting vessel would have been surrounded by Klingon ships and the crew of Romulans taken to Rura Penthe, the Klingon prison planet Kirk and McCoy visited in *The Undiscovered Country*, as a means of explaining why Nero took decades to eventually resume his plan of destruction. The masked Klingons realise Nero and his crew are from the future and torture him using a Centauran slug – as Nero ultimately does to Pike in the final act – in the hopes of learning more about his 'Red Matter' weapon of destruction. Nero and his henchman Ayel eventually escape with their crew, having devised their plan of destruction during captivity. The lead Klingon interrogator, in another Abrams call back, was one of his *Alias* stars Victor Garber, in scenes that were filmed and now only exist as DVD extras: "Well, it didn't destroy my relationship with J. J. [Abrams], but pretty close [laughs]. No, it was something where he said, 'I got a fun idea,' and whenever any director says that to you, [you go], 'Fun for who, exactly,' and then I had to learn Klingon. I was disappointed because it would've been fun to be a part of it, and it was hard work. And learning

Klingon was something I'll never, never do again. It wasn't fun. It was a labor of love because I would do anything J. J. asked."

Abrams added: "It's one of those things I hated to cut for a number of reasons. One of them was I loved the design, I love the world, I love the story – in that moment it was really cool, and I'm excited for people to see this scene."

A major reason the Klingon scenes were excised, much to Abrams' chagrin, was in not wanting to provide an on-screen explanation for whether the Klingons had forehead ridges or not, a disparity between *The Original Series* and *The Next Generation* so often mentioned by fans that *Enterprise* devised an entire story arc to resolve it. When Klingons did appear briefly in *Into Darkness*, they wear masked helmets containing ridges, despite sporting a slightly alternate look. Losing the Rura Penthe scenes for Nero are disappointing but understandable, but we get a blink-and-you'll-miss-it image of Nero toiling there during elder Spock's mind meld with young Kirk, perhaps lightly confirming these events did indeed take place.

Other deleted or planned scenes include Spock's birth with Sarek and Amanda Grayson at the beginning of the film; an early sequence before child Kirk steals his uncle's Corvette, which would have established the presence of his brother George; a very different conclusion to the Nero and Ayel relationship as the former kills the latter when he dares to suggest they should abandon the attack on the Federation and return to their Romulan homeworld (in the completed film, Ayel dies during Kirk and Spock boarding the *Narada* and fighting); and an additional moment at the end where elder Spock passes his younger father Sarek, who looks at him with bewilderment and perhaps an uncanny moment of recognition.

One of the biggest and most profound lost additions to *Star Trek* 2009 was the presence of the original Kirk, William Shatner himself. In the climactic moments of the film, as Zachary Quinto's younger Spock meets Nimoy's elder self, now intended to found a new Vulcan colony and live quietly in this alternate past, there was an original scene written – though not reputedly presented to Shatner – which would have included the original Kirk in a holographic recording, made before Kirk's death in *Generations*. The moment would have seen Shatner's Kirk sending elder Spock a happy birthday recording and congratulating him on becoming an ambassador that segues into Kirk philosophising on their place in the universe, their destiny exploring the stars, framed as a voice-over during concluding scenes including young Kirk being made captain in a ceremony, all while young Spock emotionally watches the elder version of his new best friend.

"Who's to say we can't go one more round? By the last tally, only twenty-five percent of the galaxy's been chartered . . . I'd call that negligent. Criminal even – an invitation. You once said being a starship captain was my first, best destiny . . . if that's true, then yours is to be by my side. If there's any true logic to the universe . . . we'll end up on that bridge again someday."

By all accounts, Shatner was never directly asked, and he often stated that he refused cameo appearances and would perhaps have been unsatisfied with such a small role – as opposed to Nimoy's presence – but Orci claims Abrams was at one point serious about including the scene: "Ultimately J.J. nixed it because he felt it was too inside baseball. I personally stand by it and we subsequently had a conversation about it where he sort of said maybe we should have done it. He was not sure. But, ultimately it was his call and if you were to ask him I think he would honestly say he was ambivalent about it to this day. I certainly loved that ending but I also love giving Nimoy his due as we end it now. But, I liked that scene a lot and it felt very natural."

The scene as written, hearing the dialogue in Shatner's voice as best possible, could well have been a very stirring means of proving symmetry alongside Nimoy's Spock and given Shatner as Kirk a touching coda to a role for years he had teased us – such as in *Enterprise* – about returning to, in one form or another. It will perhaps stand as one of the biggest, lost moments in *Star Trek* lore, given it remains unlikely that Shatner – in his 90s but still going at the time of writing – will reappear as Kirk in the future.

Star Trek 2009 even flirted with the idea of a post-credits sequence, arriving as it did in the wake of *Iron Man* and the nascent MCU, which reinvigorated the concept of the teasing additional sequence at the end of the film to entice viewers into a sequel. Orci expands: "We considered finding the Botany Bay as a post-credits sequence. But, it felt like it would have locked us into a sequel we weren't ready to commit to. Again, I don't think that would have meant anything to non-fans and I think that is why we ultimately nixed it. We wanted to make one movie that was completely self-contained before we started counting our chickens before they hatched."

Orci refers of course to the SS *Botany Bay*, the 20th-century space vessel launched containing supervillain Khan Noonien Singh and his Augmented followers after being banished from Earth, which would have committed the writers into a sequel featuring Khan before *Into Darkness* was decided upon and a plan was devised to bring back *Star Trek*'s most iconic and memorable villain.

Even without these additions, *Star Trek* 2009 cruised to both rampant commercial success and largely strong critical praise. It remains the second most successful *Star Trek* film to date, eclipsed only by its sequel, and in the main brought together *Star Trek* fans both of the *Next Generation* era and *The Original Series*, fusing the styles of those series into that of a bold, visually spectacular blockbuster of the like the franchise had never before seen.

The sky, or the stars perhaps, were surely the limit as *Star Trek*, for a time seemingly dead in the water by 2005, was back in business.

*

The result of *Star Trek* 2009's success, however, was an enormous amount of expectation on what would become *Star Trek Into Darkness*, a sequel that took four years to reach cinema screens.

Aware they had created in Abrams' reboot a relatively stand-alone reintroduction to the iconic franchise, the returning writing team of Orci, Kurtzman, Damon Lindelof and producer Bryan Burk – as well as Abrams as director once again – took time in developing a narrative that would logically continue everything established in the previous picture and both extend and enhance the scale of the storytelling in play, as Abrams commented: "For the story to move forward, this had to be a more ambitious movie than the first. The action and the scale were light-years ahead. Bringing in IMAX and 3D technology gave audiences yet another kind of excitement and fun to be had. But at the same time, no matter the scale or the format, the thing that still mattered most to everyone was to tell the most exciting and emotional story yet."

Ideas included centering the story around the after-effects of Vulcan's destruction in *Star Trek* 2009, given the enormous reverberations such a choice had on the *Star Trek* universe. Abrams stated that they spent a great deal of time figuring out where to take the narrative: "I can't tell you how many story meetings we had. We were constantly collaborating, making adjustments, figuring out what needed to be set up."

Star Trek Into Darkness sees the *Enterprise* return from a mission to a native civilisation where Kirk deliberately breaks the Prime Directive to save Spock's life to find a furious Starfleet brass – including now Admiral Christopher Pike – considering whether Kirk should be in command. As hawkish Admiral Marcus plans for impending war against the Klingons, a terrorist named John Harrison kills Pike, attacks Starfleet Headquarters, and leads the *Enterprise* into a deadly mission to the Klingon homeworld to stop him gaining weapons of mass destruction. Little do they know he and Marcus are in league as part of a conspiracy hiding Harrison's true identity – that he is legendary Earth supervillain Khan Noonien Singh, plotting Starfleet's downfall, and perhaps only Kirk betraying orders once again can stop them.

The true nature of 'John Harrison', as played by celebrated British character actor Benedict Cumberbatch – at this point best known for the BBC's hugely successful series *Sherlock* as the eponymous super sleuth – was a hotly debated online question. Almost everyone believed the name, shared by the 18th-century clockmaker who invented the marine chronometer, was a pseudonym. Many were convinced Cumberbatch was portraying Gary Mitchell, a Starfleet officer turned cosmic super-being in the *Original Series* episode 'Where No Man Has Gone Before'. Karl Urban even groggily stepped off a long flight and told a reporter of Cumberbatch's casting: "He's awesome, he's a great addition, and I think his Gary Mitchell is going to be exemplary." Other cast members, including Simon Pegg, consistently suggested Khan's involvement was just a myth, despite trade publications consistently reporting casting announcements for the character for almost two years in advance of the film arriving.

The presence of Khan was heavily debated by the writing team, with Lindelof lobbying for him as the villain while Orci lobbied against it. Kurtzman states: "We knew going in that we were biting off an enormous amount by taking on Khan, and it took us literally a year of debate about how to proceed, whether or not it was the right thing to do, and what it would mean to do that. And what the expectation would be by taking that on."

Cumberbatch was not the first choice, with Benicio del Toro initially offered the role, a deal that fell apart due to financial concerns, but it does suggest the original intention for Khan's portrayal would have been closer to the Ricardo Montalban incarnation thirty years earlier, especially as Spanish actors Edgar Ramirez and Jordi Molla later also tested for the part. Cumberbatch plays Khan as an ethnically white, British-accented psychopath, entirely at odds with the initial presentation of Khan in 'Space Seed', and another example of how Abrams' alternate universe was prepared to directly alter canonical aspects of *Star Trek*'s history to either serve casting or narrative purposes.

Leonard Nimoy returned for the last time before his death in 2014 as Spock for a small but crucial cameo, providing a tether to the original timeline, despite denying that he would earlier be in the film. Michael Dorn, who played Worf and also featured as Worf's grandfather in *The Undiscovered Country*, also claims he almost appeared in *Into Darkness*: "I don't know what the role was. They called in November or December of last year and said, 'Hey, we would like to know if Michael is interested in playing a part of an officer – a soldier.' And we said 'Yes.' Then time went by and we finally talked to them at maybe the end of January or February and they said they had changed their mind and that's as far as it went."

One can only speculate that Abrams intended to cast Dorn as one of the Klingon warriors who Kirk, Spock and Uhura face on Kronos, in a fan-pleasing tether to *The Next Generation*. This is just speculation, ultimately, but a Dorn cameo would have been a delightful nod and wink to *Star Trek*'s most celebrated Klingon.

One aspect of the original pitch for *Into Darkness* was the fate of the *Enterprise*, as Orci explains: "In the first movie we were pitching that the *Enterprise* should totally be destroyed. It was actually (then-Paramount president) Gail Berman who said, 'No, please don't do that.' She was right, and we realized, 'OK, destroying the *Enterprise* is sort of a cliché.' So we changed our minds and didn't destroy the *Enterprise*."

Though the *Enterprise* is heavily given a beating by the *Vengeance* during the film, *Into Darkness* avoided inevitable comparisons to *The Search for Spock* by not destroying the ship, although the famous vessel would ultimately meet such a fate in the next film.

Numerous tweaks and alterations occurred during the process of developing *Into Darkness*, be it additions to scenes or sequences or alterations, even ADR, as a means of generating emotional resonance or context to the narrative. Lindelof claims a sub-plot, alongside Khan's attack on Starfleet, was planned: "There were earlier story iterations where the Klingon Fleet was simultaneously heading for Earth to get retribution, only to be turned around via diplomatic intervention by Uhura. We dropped it pretty early on, as it didn't feel intimate, cool, or earned."

The climax wasn't originally intended to be set on Earth, as indeed partly the end of *Star Trek* 2009 also was, until Abrams saw the potential of crashing the *Vengeance* into San Francisco. His original plan was to have the ship destroy Alcatraz, the iconic island-prison, which had been the name of a science-fiction mystery series Abrams' production house Bad Robot developed that had recently been cancelled. He also developed the climactic Spock/Khan chase sequence to better evoke a Saturday-morning serial nature of derring do: "The fight was originally conceived as a fight between two guys on a street, essentially. To make it into a fight on the garbage barge traveling through the city upped the stakes of the whole thing. It gave the thing a kind of an energy that it wouldn't have had otherwise."

There was a determination to lose the colon that previous eras of *Star Trek* films, even after they stopped including numbers after *The Undiscovered Country*, still utilised. Abrams considered 'Star Trek Vengeance' as a possible title, so named after Marcus' powerful, sinister Starfleet attack vessel, but this was decided against thanks to the release of *Ghost Rider* sequel, *Spirit of Vengeance*, though that title was used for the Russian release of the film. Nevertheless, they wanted a title that best represented the nature of where the tone of the sequel was heading, as Orci explains: "When people heard the title, the first thing they thought was, 'Oh, they're trying to be *The Dark Knight*.' Our point of view is that the optimism that Gene Roddenberry created is still there, and *Into Darkness* is indicative of the obstacle that comes in to threaten this optimistic utopia."

With reported intentions that Orci and Kurtzman originally intended the story of *Into Darkness* to span two films, the scope of Abrams' sequel was certainly broader than the 2009 reboot, and the relatively successful box-office return continued to suggest audiences retained a thirst for *Star Trek*. Nonetheless, many both in the audience and involved in the project came away with the sense that *Into Darkness* had failed to match the promise of the movie that preceded it.

Abrams admits as much in hindsight: "*Into Darkness* was in some ways a harder film to make. I'm not sure we ever fully realized the story, and I take full responsibility for that. I think we leaned too much on the series' past in telling that story."

It is hard to argue against that given sequences such as the 'death' of Kirk, witnessed by Spock in a precise, role-reversed copy of Spock's iconic demise in *The Wrath of Khan* – even to the point the same dialogue is used in places – which immediately tethered *Into Darkness* to what many consider the greatest cinematic example of *Star Trek*. Much like *Nemesis* a decade earlier, Abrams' film had a hard act to follow and ran afoul of trying to do so.

Three years later, the next *Star Trek* movie – despite having a much rockier journey to the screen – would be, in places, a lighter affair designed to reflect a reason *Star Trek* was justified in looking back to its own past.

The franchise was about to celebrate a very special birthday by going *Beyond*.

*

2016 was the vaunted 50th anniversary of *Star Trek*, the next major milestone for the franchise after *The Undiscovered Country* marked 25 years and TV series *Deep Space Nine* and *Voyager* dedicated episodes to mark the 30th. The 40th had sadly gone unmarked thanks to the cancellation of *Enterprise* just a year earlier.

Everyone wanted the film that became *Star Trek Beyond* to truly do justice to a franchise that remained, a decade after it had last featured on television, durable and indefatigable. Simon Pegg, who ended up one of the two credited writers on the eventual picture, made this point: "It was so important to us that *Star Trek Beyond* be out in time for the fiftieth anniversary. Even more since Leonard Nimoy passed away. We wanted to sort of tie all of that in together. I don't mean having Leonard in the movie, but just acknowledging *Star Trek*'s legacy and Leonard's legacy and everyone that's been involved with it from the beginning. It feels right that it be the fiftieth-anniversary year. We wouldn't have wanted to miss that."

Star Trek Beyond sees the *Enterprise* amid its historic five-year mission as Kirk deals with anxiety about his role as captain and Spock mourns the passing of his elder self. They are sent from the Yorktown, a vast Federation starbase, to respond to a distress signal inside a nebula and are attacked by a swarm of ships led by a vicious alien named Krall, who destroys the *Enterprise* and takes prisoner the escaped crew on a planet called Altamid. With the crew separated, Kirk, Spock and the rest must uncover Krall's identity and why he wants to destroy the Federation while rescuing the crew and, for Kirk, rediscovering who he is as captain of the *Enterprise*.

After the commercial if not entirely critical success of *Into Darkness*, everyone expected Abrams to remain at the helm of a third *Star Trek* picture, however in 2012 Disney announced to the world – in perhaps the cultural shock of the decade – that they had purchased LucasFilm and intended to make a new *Star Wars* sequel trilogy, set after the original, legendary George Lucas pictures. Abrams very quickly was announced as director of what would become *The Force Awakens* and, consequently, he stepped away from directing what was known then as 'Star Trek 3', moving purely into a producing role.

Though in 2014, Roberto Orci was named as director of the film, numerous writers and directors previously began circling the project after Abrams' departure. Zach Stentz and his writing partner Ashley Edward Miller claim they pitched in August 2013 when Orci was still directing an idea: "My recollection was that our antagonist was more a 'noble adversary' à la 'Balance of Terror' than another Khan. There was also Dyson Sphere and an ancient, Lovecraftian menace to the galaxy."

This take suggests more of a specific fusion of elements seen in *The Original Series* and *The Next Generation*, as the Dyson Sphere concept had memorably been seen in 'Relics', the story that saw the return of James Doohan's original Scotty. Lovecraftian influences would certainly later creep into *Star Trek*'s return to television, especially in the first season of *Picard*.

Abrams publicly endorsed rumoured directors such as Rupert Wyatt, who had successfully steered *Rise of the Planet of the Apes* to the screen, and Joe Cornish, former comedic sketch writer turned director whose British science-fiction picture *Attack the Block* had gone down a storm. It seemed like, barring Orci, *Star Trek* was breaking from those who had steered it back to the screen. Kurtzman stepped away, as did Lindelof – not before openly suggesting the third film would bring Khan back and see a Klingon-Federation war – which was the reputed plan for the second film in the supposed 'two-part' story *Into Darkness* to lead into, creating a cliffhanger where Earth was under Klingon occupation.

Though Paramount prevaricated somewhat on offering Orci the role thanks to his lack of directorial experience, he nonetheless was recruited and began penning the script with writing team Patrick McKay and J. D. Payne – who several years later would successfully revive *The Lord of the Rings* for Amazon on television with *The Rings of Power*. After a year developing the project, Orci stepped down as director after Paramount rejected his script, which by all accounts intentionally steered away from *Into Darkness*' attempts to make *Star Trek* edgier and veered back toward the tone of *The Original Series*, the plot rumoured to echo 'Who Mourns for Adonais' and contain a super-powered alien being – similar to the rumours of Gary Mitchell. Pegg elaborated: "They had a script for *Star Trek* that wasn't really working for them. I think the studio was worried that it might have been a little bit too *Star Trek-y*."

This statement intrigues as it suggests Paramount were jittery about *Star Trek* moving too closely back to the light, playful tone of certain of its television output, and previous *Next Generation* pictures such as *Insurrection*. Audiences turned out for *Into Darkness*, despite how often it didn't hue close to Roddenberry's initial vision for the franchise, and Paramount encouraged Pegg – and his eventual co-writer Doug Jung – to develop a stylistic adventure, a heist or Western, and port *Star Trek*'s characters and trappings around that: "When Doug Jung and I began writing, it was apparent to us that the crew would be out on the mission that made the show popular in the first place – a deep space mission for five years. The first two films were spent with us really getting to know each other, and in the case of the last film, having an adventure which stayed within our own solar system. Doug and I felt, let's get them out there now and get onto that wagon train in space and start boldly going where no one has gone before."

Paramount openly wanted the latest *Star Trek* film to evoke the fun, frothy nature of Marvel's hugely successful *Guardians of the Galaxy*, which opened the potential of pure science fiction within that uber-successful franchise. To wit, in 2015 they hired Justin Lin as director, best known for helming more than one highly successful, blockbuster film in the *Fast and Furious* franchise, and someone they believed would bring the requisite 'whizz bang' to *Star Trek* as it warped swiftly toward that 50-year anniversary deadline.

"Let's face it, the *Star Trek* of 2016 has to be different. We can't make those kinds of small, thoughtful little plays like the episodes used to be now. In terms of a cinematic sense, the studios just wouldn't bankroll it, and it's not what the larger audiences who have now gone to see *Star*

Trek – and who have as much right to it as the fans – want. We have to make something that people are going to come in and see so we can keep making it. It doesn't mean we can't keep what made the show special and try and invigorate what *Star Trek* 2016 means with what *Star Trek* 1966 meant as well."

The turnaround was fast, with filming only beginning in 2016 with the intention of hitting a summer deadline, and Lin hired Pegg – recognised as a huge popular culture geek and *Star Trek* fan before a successful comedian and actor – and Jung to quickly turn around a script for what was now known as *Star Trek Beyond*. Given Paramount had rejected Orci's intended script, Pegg and Jung had to work around the clock to make the deadline, as Lin himself worked faster than typically expected, certainly in comparison to the malaise that had prefigured *Into Darkness*' development.

Their eventual plot attempted to both capture the scale of *Star Trek* adventures of the past – with elements of this, perhaps fittingly, echoing the original third *Star Trek* movie, *The Search for Spock*, such as the destruction of the *Enterprise* – and encapsulating the stand-alone feeling of *The Original Series* with a pulpier aesthetic. Jung admits he and Pegg theoretically could have gone in a very different direction during the development process: "We did have some ideas that were just physically out there for science-fiction, depictions of worlds and what they might be. We had other ideas that were deep sci-fi, a little bit more along the lines of *The Motion Picture*, extrapolating from what we know to be the near future."

Pegg and Jung also attempted to give certain of the additional characters beyond Kirk, Spock and Uhura – who all arguably had benefited from the greatest screen time in the previous two films – more to do, with plenty of enjoyable Spock/McCoy interplay and a sub-plot for Sulu which confirmed long-suspected speculation that he might be gay – Jung even plays his husband briefly, named Ben. One moment was cut, as described by John Cho, that would have added even more flesh to the bones of Sulu's family dynamic: "There was a scene that is not in the film but was written which is very revealing, where Sulu makes a confession to Uhura and says that his husband didn't want to move out to [Starbase] Yorktown, which is this remote outpost, but he made that sacrifice for Sulu's career. Sulu felt a very heavy sense of guilt about having made that move and now had inadvertently endangered is family, and then Uhura comforts him. You know, that was a color that wouldn't have come out if we hadn't been paired off, and I thought that was cool."

Beyond the current crop of characters, as part of celebrating *Star Trek*'s half a century milestone, reports suggested there would be connections back to the earlier eras of the franchise. The film itself had Spock discover the photo of the *Original Series* crew but, once again, as with *Star Trek* 2009, there were strong rumours that William Shatner might somehow make an appearance as the original James T. Kirk. Shatner claimed that, in advance of Nimoy's death, Abrams had called him while shooting *The Force Awakens* claiming that 'the director' of *Beyond* had an idea of how he could be featured. Shatner said, in principle, he would be delighted. "It's all over the Internet that the director had held an interview and said they want Shatner and Nimoy to be in the next movie. I'll bet you J. J.'s frothing at the mouth at this point. So the news is out that they have an idea that they want Leonard and myself . . . they might want Leonard and myself in it. But I would love to do it. But how do you get me fifty years later into the movie? I mean how do you rationalize it. I know it's science fiction, but even I couldn't come up with an idea. So that's the news on that."

One suspects the idea to involve Shatner pre-dated Justin Lin's involvement and 'the director' Shatner mentioned here was Roberto Orci, given Nimoy died in 2014 and that was while Orci was attached and developing the script with McKay and Payne. Lin had also made comments suggesting he wanted to move past any historic villains or characters from *Star Trek*'s history. Ultimately, Shatner once again never materialised in a *Star Trek* movie beyond *Generations*, despite theoretically the 50th anniversary being a timely mechanism for him to do so.

After an appropriately fast and furious production, *Star Trek Beyond* successfully arrived ready for the 50th anniversary celebrations, and while fans and critics certainly seemed to appreciate the picture more than *Into Darkness*, it failed to generate anywhere near the same expectation or excitement of *Star Trek* 2009 and the box-office performance was the worst of the Abrams-rebooted films by some distance. Indeed, with marketing costs factored in, *Star Trek Beyond* lost money. If not back in the doldrums of *Nemesis* in 2002, *Beyond*'s underperformance signalled that audiences were not chomping at the bit for more adventures from Kirk, Spock and company.

Pegg, ultimately, was frustrated with how *Beyond* was marketed: "It was a big year for *Star Trek*, and I felt it was never embraced. I feel sometimes people get scared of the *Star Trek* fanbase as being a kind of closed shop. If we were to mention *Star Trek* in some way, it would turn all the other people who hadn't seen *Star Trek* off. It felt an odd thing to do."

He also claimed the first trailer for the movie ruined the inclusion of 'Sabotage' by the Beastie Boys in the eventual climax of the film: "It was supposed to be a very fun and heightened twist, and something that was a big surprise and they blew it in the first trailer, which really annoyed me. They also made the film look like a boneheaded action film. And they were scared, I think, of mentioning the 50th Anniversary. It was fumbled as a thing; they didn't know what to do with it and it's a real shame."

Though Paramount had faltered cinematically, the success of the Abrams rebooted films arguably contributed to the more championed direction of *Star Trek*'s future that, as *Beyond* emerged, was readily in development: the franchise's return to television via CBS All Access, which would premiere in 2017. We will tell that story in the next chapter.

On the big screen, however, though years on, as of writing the fourth *Star Trek* film has not arrived, the story of the franchise on the big screen has nonetheless been far from over.

*

Even though *Star Trek Beyond* did not set the box office alight, Paramount have maintained plans to develop another film ever since 2016, and in many cases with the Abrams-created ensemble of Pine, Quinto, Saldana et al returning to their roles.

Abrams, still in his producing capacity, claimed around the time of *Beyond*'s release that a story was very much in place for 'Star Trek IV' based around the return of Chris Hemsworth to the series, reprising the role of Kirk's father George, last seen being blown up on the USS *Kelvin* at the very beginning of *Star Trek* 2009 as Kirk was born. With Hemsworth subsequently, thanks to playing Thor in the MCU, rising to A-list stardom, the announcement of his casting was considered a coup, and one that would lean heavily toward time travel once again featuring in a *Star Trek* movie story.

Some years later, McKay and Payne – hired to develop 'Star Trek IV' in the wake of their contributions to *Beyond* – revealed more details. McKay: "The conceit was that through a cosmic quirk in the Star Trek world, they were the same age. It was going to be a grandfather-son space adventure – think *Indiana Jones and the Last Crusade* in space. We were really thrilled about it. We had an original villain and a really cool *2001: A Space Odyssey*-esque sci-fi idea at the core. We worked on it for two and half years with Lindsey Weber, our non-writing executive producer on *Rings of Power*, and an amazing director, S. J. Clarkson. The movie eventually fell apart and it really was a heartbreak for us."

Clarkson, a British television director who also helmed the cancelled *Game of Thrones* prequel pilot, 'The Long Night', for HBO, was one of numerous directors attached to developing '*Star Trek* IV' since 2016 and by all accounts shepherded the Hemsworth/Pine team-up that the writers developed. Payne gives more details: "There's an episode of *Star Trek: The Next Generation* called 'Relics' where they find Scotty, who's been trapped in a transporter for a couple of decades, and they're able to have a cool adventure with him. Our concept was, 'What if right before the *Kelvin* impacted with that huge mining ship, George Kirk had tried to beam himself over to his wife's shuttle where his son, Jim Kirk, had just been born? And what if the ship hadn't completely exploded – what if it left some space junk?' Think about when you send a text message and you've typed it out, but you haven't quite hit send. On the other side, they see those three little dots that someone has typed. It's like the transporter had absorbed his pattern up into the pattern buffer, but hadn't spit him out on the other side. It was actually a saved copy of him that was in the computer."

This idea would, perhaps unintentionally, survive into the first season of *Strange New Worlds* and the sub-plot of Dr M'Benga's daughter, kept in suspended transporter animation for years. McKay added: "So the adventure is that Chris Pine and the crew of the *Enterprise* have to seek out the wreckage of the ship that his father died on because of a mystery and a new villain. In the ship, they stumble across his father's pattern. They beam him out and he has no idea that no time has passed at all, and that he's looking at his son. Then the adventure goes from there."

A script was developed at the point Clarkson arrived on the project, with Abrams producing, and his and Paramount's intention was to find a female director for the project, given no woman had ever previously helmed a *Star Trek* movie. With Pine and Quinto signed back on as Kirk and Spock, during 2018 the project appeared to be developing well, until in August of that year contract negotiations with Pine and Hemsworth broke down as Paramount sought – following *Beyond*'s underperformance – to reduce costs on '*Star Trek* IV'. The film fell apart in early 2019 and

Clarkson left the project. Hemsworth subsequently commented that he walked away because he didn't love the script: "I didn't feel like we landed on a reason to revisit that yet. I didn't want to be underwhelmed by what I was going to bring to the table."

While '*Star Trek* IV' was in development, however, an enormously intriguing possibility was rearing its head during 2017: Quentin Tarantino started to aspire to direct the next *Star Trek* movie.

As early as late 2015, before *Beyond* was released, Tarantino made noises on The *Nerdist* podcast that he would entertain the idea, much as he had earlier expressed interest during the 2000s in developing an adaptation of Ian Fleming's *Casino Royale* to revitalise the James Bond franchise, believing that many classic episodes of *The Original Series* could be utilised. "The only thing that limited them was their '60s budget and eight-day shooting schedule. You could take some of the classic *Star Trek* episodes and easily expand them to 90 minutes or more and really do some amazing, amazing stuff."

In December of 2017, Tarantino actively approached Paramount and Abrams with an idea for what could be the next *Star Trek* movie, by all accounts retaining the Pine and co. cast, and Paramount started to develop the concept alongside '*Star Trek* IV'.

Despite Paramount's determination to make *Star Trek* appeal cinematically to the Marvel-style crowd, they agreed to Tarantino's demand that his *Star Trek* movie would be 'R-rated', therefore giving him scope to include darker, more profane material. "The thing is, when I talked to JJ about it, it's not that radical. We're just not worrying about stuff like that. JJ said, 'Quentin, I love this idea because I think with *Star Trek* we can go any way we want to.' Look, I've got a situation. As long as Paramount likes the idea and the script they almost got nothing to lose right now when it comes to *Star Trek*. *Deadpool* showed that you can rethink these things, do them in a different way. So really, even before JJ knew what the idea was, his feeling was, if it wants to be an R rating, fine. If it wants to be the *Wild Bunch* in space, fine."

A writer's room to develop ideas was assembled with Tarantino and Mark R. Smith, best known for adapting *The Revenant* for Alejandro Gonzalez Inarritu in 2015, was given the job of penning a script based on Tarantino's concept. The idea, fittingly for the director, revolved around adapting to some extent 'A Piece of the Action', the *Original Series* episode involving a parallel Earth culture based on 1930s gangster America.

Smith discussed in 2021 the process of working on the project: "It was through J. J. Abrams, through Bad Robot. I've done a few things with them. And so they always bring me stuff . . . But Tarantino, he wanted to do this. And so we all gathered in a room and we talked about the ways in. After that, they just called me and said, 'Hey, are you up for it? Do you want to go? Quentin wants to hook up.' And I said, 'Yeah.' And that was the first day I met Quentin, in the room and he's reading a scene that he wrote and it was this awesome cool gangster scene, and he's acting it out and back and forth. I told him, I was so mad I didn't record it on my phone. It would be so valuable. It was amazing. Then just we started working. I would go hang out at his house one night and we would watch old gangster films. We were there for hours . . . We were just kicking back watching gangster films, laughing at the bad dialogue, but talking about how it would bleed into what we wanted to do."

He also added nuggets around the content of the script: "Kirk's in it, we've got him. All the characters are there. It would be those guys. I guess you would look at it like all the episodes of the show didn't really connect. So this would be almost its own episode. A very cool episode. There's a little time travel stuff going on. There's all this other . . . it's really wild."

Tarantino stated in the middle of 2019, amidst press for his ninth film *Once Upon a Time in Hollywood*: "I don't know if I'll do it or not. I've got to figure it out, but Mark wrote a really cool script. I like it a lot. There's some things I need to work on but I really, really liked it. I get annoyed at Simon Pegg. He doesn't know anything about what's going on and he keeps making all these comments as if he knows about stuff. One of the comments he said, he's like, 'Well, look, it's not going to be *Pulp Fiction* in space.' Yes, it is! [laughs hard]. If I do it, that's exactly what it'll be. It'll be *Pulp Fiction* in space. That *Pulp Fiction*-y aspect, when I read the script, I felt, I have never read a science fiction movie that has this sh*t in it, ever. There's no science fiction movie that has this in it. And they said, I know, that's why we want to make it. It's, at the very least, unique in that regard."

There remained some confusion about just who might appear in the Tarantino-helmed movie, and indeed whether it would strictly be set in the same timeline as the Abrams films. Tarantino admitted in an interview with the *Happy Sad Confused* podcast that he neither understood nor liked the time-travel gambit of the 2009 movie, and that he perhaps wanted some kind of 'halfway house' approach to the muddied waters of the *Star Trek* timeline: "I want the whole series to have happened, it just hasn't happened yet. No, Benedict Cumberbatch or whatever his name is, is not Khan. Khan is Khan. I told J. J. I don't understand this, I don't like it. And he went: 'Ignore it! Nobody likes it! I don't understand it. Do whatever you want. If you want it to happen in the exact way it happened on the series, it can.'"

By 2020, however, perhaps due to a certain level of conflict with his long-asserted (and factually questionable) intention to retire after making ten movies, Tarantino had begun to distance himself from the idea of himself directing a *Star Trek* movie. "I think they might make that movie, but I just don't think I'm going to direct it. It's a good idea. They should definitely do it and I'll be happy to come in and give them some notes on the first rough cut."

That, by all accounts for now, is that for the Tarantino film. He has since announced he will develop his tenth and seemingly final film known as 'The Movie Critic', set in the 1970s in Los Angeles and very much on terra firma. And while the suggestion of a Tarantino-directed *Star Trek* movie divided new and established fans down the middle, given all the preconceptions and baggage arguably the most iconic filmmaker of his generation carries, the idea of his footprint on *Star Trek* history will, even if he never makes his idea, remain a tantalising possibility.

Smith, at least, remains open to the idea it could still happen: "Guys like Quentin can do stuff that the rest of us can't. So they are going to trust him because they know what they're going to get is going to be something that's going to be talked about for years. And it was. The script, it is so Tarantino, and it's hard-R [rated] and it's violent. It's got all these great elements. And I guess Paramount has done different things and kind of veered back on *Star Trek*. They probably feel like Tarantino is worth being able to veer off path and always come back."

Paramount, aware that the initial '*Star Trek* IV' was dead in the water and Tarantino was distancing from his idea, in late 2019 brought on a new writer-director in the form of Noah Hawley to develop a film project. Hawley is best known as the creative force behind the highly successful adaptation of the Coen Brothers crime drama *Fargo* to the small screen, in multiple series of entertaining anthologies, not to mention shepherding Fox's surreal *X-Men* adjacent comic adaptation *Legion*.

Though, initially, it was believed Hawley's film would feature the Abrams cast, Hawley put paid to this idea and claimed his approach would feature new characters and new material: "To call it *Star Trek* IV is kind of a misnomer. I have my own take on the franchise as a lifelong fan." He claimed that the idea would, nevertheless, have a specific canonical connection that fans would pick up on: "We're not doing Kirk and we're not doing Picard. It's a start from scratch that then allows us to do what we did with *Fargo*, where for the first three hours you go, 'Oh, it really has nothing to do with the movie,' and then you find the money. So you reward the audience with a thing that they love."

Hawley's arrival and approach to the material coincided with two major factors that affected Paramount's approach to *Star Trek* – the arrival of executive Emma Watts, tasked with deciding which approach from the multiple possibilities for *Star Trek* to move forward on; and the devastating reality of the COVID-19 pandemic. Hawley's *Star Trek* movie script reputedly featured, as well as the economically risky reality of a new cast and setting, a deadly virus as part of the narrative, which immediately considering the pandemic gave Watts pause in terms of Hawley's approach.

As of late 2020, Hawley recognised that his *Star Trek* film was likely a thing of the past, despite almost coming to fruition: "I think when Emma came in, she took a look at the franchise and wanted to go in a different direction with it. But you know, life is long, we were very close to production but in this business that doesn't mean much. You got to get out of the gate to be in the race if you know what I mean."

Intriguingly, and perhaps coincidentally, during the same period two old hands and former *Star Trek* producing partners who had a key role in *The Wrath of Khan*, and thereby the entire construction of *Star Trek*'s future, both were in the process of pitching movie ideas to Paramount.

The first was Robert Sallin, who pitched an idea, but this coincided with Hawley's take and he was told that no decisions would be made while that script remained in contention: "I don't have it completely written, but I have a lot of it written. I have a concept for another *Star Trek* feature that I've had discussions with Paramount about – at least on the phone. This one I guarantee you is unlike anything that has been done in *Star Trek*, and it will be part of the canon."

Second was Nicholas Meyer – who will play a key role in the re-establishment of *Star Trek* on television as we shall see – who with producing partner Steven Charles-Jaffe seem to be treading along similar lines in attempting to write a *Star Trek* movie concept that honours canon and has the scope to lead to more films or even TV series down the road: "This was an independent piece of the *Star Trek* universe based on holes in the chronology, which would allow for the insertion of original material."

Neither of these approaches from older hands seem to have been adopted by Abrams, the man responsible for the TV era of *Star Trek* in the 2020s, Alex Kurtzman or Emma Watts at the studio, but they represent the continued interest in a multitude of possible approaches to a future *Star Trek* film that both honour continuity and seek original approaches at the same time. A new writer around the same time, early 2021, entered the frame, Kalinda Vasquez, not only a writer on *Discovery*'s third season but also named after a character in *The Original Series* episode 'By Any Other Name', just to add a sense of manifest destiny to her involvement in the franchise. Vasquez had her own concept for a film set to premiere in the summer of 2023, but her approach does not seem to have taken flight.

In the middle of 2021, Watts managed to attach the first significant director to the project in some time, Matt Shakman, fresh from making a directorial mark on Marvel's *WandaVision* series for Disney+. The project was coming full circle as Paramount had conducted research on whether audiences were still enthusiastic for the Abrams cast and it appeared they were, making their return a viable option for the studio, when it felt in recent years that all signs were moving away from their return. Abrams announced early in 2022 with Shakman aboard: "We are thrilled to say that we are hard at work on a new 'Star Trek' film that will be shooting by the end of the year that will be featuring our original cast and some new characters that I think are going to be really fun and exciting and help take 'Star Trek' into areas that you've just never seen before. We're thrilled about this film, we have a bunch of other stories that we're talking about that we think will be really exciting, so can't wait for you to see what we're cooking up. But until then, live long and prosper."

Abrams had declared years before that following the tragic death of Anton Yelchin, his character Pavel Chekov would not be recast, but the rest of the main cast – including Pine after previous contract negotiations – appeared to be returning. Then . . . Shakman became the next director to leave the project, having agreed to make the highly anticipated *Fantastic Four* movie for the MCU and unable to make both projects align. He refused to discuss the story that Abrams alluded to that had been worked on, believing the concept remains one in active development, suggesting a story with the Abrams cast is ready to go. Abrams claimed in early 2023 that: "I will say it's the first time [since the original reboot] that we have a story that feels as compelling as the first one."

Following reports that the revival of '*Star Trek* IV' had been announced before making the cast aware, Pine – as of 2023 – is somewhat jaded about the whole experience, claiming actors are the last to know of developments around the project. When asked how he feels about this, he said: "I would say it's frustrating. It doesn't really foster the greatest sense of partnership, but it's how it's always been. I love the character. I love the people. I love the franchise. But to try to change the system in which things are created – I just can't do it. I don't have the energy."

As of writing, in mid-2023, '*Star Trek* IV' remains in development, almost seven years since the last *Star Trek* movie to grace the big screen. It will, by the end of the year, beat the record between *Nemesis* and *Star Trek* 2009 for the longest gap between *Star Trek* movies since *The Motion Picture* kickstarted Gene Roddenberry's cinematic ambitions in 1979. Quite what form a future *Star Trek* movie will take, who will feature and how fans will respond to it in the 2020s, remains unknown. There is now a strong chance that as *Beyond* celebrated 50 years of *Star Trek*, we might next see a big screen adventure to mark 60.

If *Star Trek*'s success on the big screen continues to remain elusive, the same cannot be said for the small. Since 2017, the beginning of a new era has resulted in *Star Trek* thriving to a degree unrivalled since the middle of the 1990s, with no end in sight.

Our story now moves to a new frontier, and a voyage of discovery . . .

FOURTEEN

STRANGE NEW SHOWS: THE AGE OF *DISCOVERY*

THOUGH *STAR TREK BEYOND* had been the primary avenue for celebrating fifty years of the franchise, the announcement a year earlier that CBS would develop, for their brand-new streaming service All Access, a new *Star Trek* series for the first time since 2005, generated just as much excitement around the anniversary: "There is no better time to give *Star Trek* fans a new series than on the heels of the original show's 50th anniversary celebration," David Stapf, president of CBS at the time, stated.

CBS turned to Alex Kurtzman, who last worked on the franchise for *Into Darkness*, to produce the new series alongside Heather Kadin, as they fended off attempts by various big players in the blooming era of streaming – Netflix, Amazon, Showtime – for the chance to put a new *Star Trek* series on their platform in the United States. The question remained over who would take the helm in the manner Rick Berman, Brannon Braga, Jeri Taylor, Michael Piller or Ira Steven Behr had on previous series after Gene Roddenberry's original.

One man stood out as the front-runner: Bryan Fuller.

"I told my agent and told the people of J. J. Abrams' team I want to create another *Star Trek* series and have an idea that I'm kicking around. I would love to return to the spirit of the old series with the colours and attitude . . . [of] the '60s fun and I would love to take it back to its origin . . . *Star Trek* has to recreate itself."

And in February 2016, it became official. "When we began discussions about the series returning to television, we immediately knew that Bryan Fuller would be the ideal person to work alongside Alex Kurtzman to create a fresh and authentic take on this classic and timeless series. Bryan is not only an extremely gifted writer, but a genuine fan of *Star Trek*. Having someone at the helm with his gravitas who also understands and appreciates the significance of the franchise, and the worldwide fan base was essential to us."

Fuller had, of course, worked on *Star Trek* during the 1990s and early 2000s era, contributing episodes of *Deep Space Nine* and *Voyager*, and subsequently had emerged as one of television's most innovative show runners thanks to quirky, well-loved series such as *Pushing Daisies*, or cult favourites such as *Hannibal*. One thing that plagued him, however, was the inability to keep a series on the air for a long period of time, with many of his expensive, thoughtful, high concept series being cancelled in the late era of network television. Had he come of age in the streaming era, chances are many of the shows he developed would have found greater success.

At the time of joining *Discovery*, Fuller was also developing alongside Michael Green the adaptation of Neil Gaiman's huge, vivid tome *American Gods* for Starz, which would last for three seasons and achieve a moderate level of success. This would eventually lead him and CBS into problems, but not before Fuller tabled a fascinating roadmap for what the series which became *Discovery* could be: an anthology show: "The original pitch was to do for science-fiction what *American Horror Story* had done for horror. It would platform a universe of *Star Trek* shows."

American Horror Story, from creator Ryan Murphy, revolutionised the anthology tale for television, crafting season-long arcs across different eras of American history, telling camp, heightened-reality, blood-soaked stories across ten episodes, often featuring a retinue of returning actors. Though Charlie Brooker's *Black Mirror* had proven the interest in anthological episodes within shows, à la *The Twilight Zone* or *The Outer Limits*, Murphy's creation – which soon extended into sister series *American Crime Story* and *American Horror Stories*, an episodic series – sparked a trend which spread to hits such as FX's *Fargo*, returning anthology storytelling to the mainstream.

Fuller's idea for the revived *Star Trek* series was to pull the same trick, begin with what likely became the first half of *Discovery*'s first season – a prequel to *The Original Series* and the unseen Klingon-Federation war – and move to seasons that covered the post-*Original Series* space, *The Next Generation* era, and eventually to the 'post-*Nemesis*' timeline not canonically charted beyond Abrams' 2009 film. This would have allowed Fuller and Kurtzman to have their cake and eat it, depicting stories within a variety of *Star Trek* eras and each season rebooting with new and almost certainly reappearing characters. One wonders if a variation of what *Picard*'s third season ended up being might have served as one of these future anthological seasons.

CBS, however, baulked on this approach. They asked Fuller and Kurtzman to develop a single show with recurring characters. The result was *Discovery*, a series Fuller eventually departed from at the urging of CBS when he objected to certain casting and directorial choices, budgetary issues and the reality of trying to run *American Gods* at the same time, plus as he was intending to reboot another anthology series that would eventually appear on Apple TV, *Amazing Stories*.

He nonetheless did leave a stamp on the series – from the *Original Series*-era timeline to the presence of a black female commander of the ship, a role he offered to Angela Bassett initially, who turned it down due to other commitments. One wonders if she might have played the Georgiou character, killed off in the pilot episode, rather than the Burnham we ultimately had – the big movie star unexpectedly removed at the outset.

Star Trek: Discovery ultimately was set in 2155 and introduces Michael Burnham, first officer on the USS *Shenzhou*, who commits mutiny during a Klingon attack which leads to her captain and mentor, Phillipa Georgiou, being killed, is arrested, and transferred to the USS *Discovery* under the aegis of captain Gabriel Lorca, who seeks her counsel in battling an extremist Klingon threat targeting the Federation. Burnham must gain the trust of her new Captain and crew, especially when they are thrown into the sinister Mirror Universe, ran by a genocidal version of Georgiou and where Lorca conceals a dark secret.

Fuller has been reticent to talk a great deal about the *Discovery* experience subsequently: "I got to dream big. I was sad for a week and then I salute the ship and compartmentalize my experience."

Though he did several years later, on the *Robservations* podcast, reveal details of what his ideas were for *Discovery*'s Mirror plot line, given he had parted ways with the series well before the mid-season move from the Prime timeline into the Mirror timeline for *Star Trek*'s most extensive arc in that era. Intriguingly, Fuller wanted to move away from recreating the

Terran Empire pomp seen from 'Mirror, Mirror' through to *Deep Space Nine* and *Enterprise*'s versions of the dark flipside: "There was something in the mistakes made by Burnham in 'Battle of the Binary Stars' that had this ripple, but the Mirror Universe was always meant to be an exploration of a small step in a different direction. So, it wasn't necessarily the Mirror Universe we know from all of the other series. It was something that was closer to our timeline and experience, so you can still recognize the human being and go, 'What did I do? How did that seem like a good decision for me in that moment and how do I continue with my life forward?' And everything was a sort of an extrapolation out on that. So, there were things that I wanted the Mirror Universe to function in a narrative exploration of like, 'Oh fuck, if I just didn't do that one thing, everything would be better.' As opposed to, 'I don't recognize that person, I don't know who that person is, because they are a diametric opposite of who I am.'"

While it would have perhaps resulted in a disjunction between the canonical *Enterprise* and *Original Series*-era Mirror universe portrayals, Fuller's grounded approach to the concept might have best fitted the tone of *Discovery* as presented in the early few episodes he did retain creative control over, which aesthetically worked to bridge the gap between *Enterprise* and *The Original Series*. Fuller's impact on *Discovery* and the newest era, as of writing, of *Star Trek* will remain a key touchstone, even as the storytelling and style have subsequently leaned closer to Kurtzman's approach.

Under his aegis, and several show runners he has delegated responsibility to including Aaron Herbert's and Gretchen J. Berg (who left during the second season under something of a cloud) and Michelle Paradise, who has steered the ship from the third through the upcoming fifth and final season, several intended concepts for *Discovery* episodes have remained unproduced.

David Mack, a long-time *Star Trek* novel author and consultant on the franchise, told the *Literary Treks* podcast of a clash between both TV and novelisation media: "I can't name names, but I know there was at least one member of the [DIS writers'] room who was extremely frustrated by it because it means I took the idea he wanted to do for an episode."

Mack is referring to his tie-in *Discovery* novel, *Desperate Hours*, released around the point the first season aired and which serves as a prequel character story for Burnham, set a year before the events of *Discovery* premiere 'The Vulcan Hello'. Serving on the *Shenzhou* under Georgiou as acting first officer, Burnham must prove her mettle when the ship investigates a Federation colony under attack from an ancient, alien vessel called the *Juggernaut* that has emerged from within the planet, a vessel Burnham infiltrates to save the colony as Starfleet deem those on the planet expendable. They are assisted by the USS *Enterprise* under the command of Christopher Pike and Burnham's stepbrother Spock, who she infiltrates the vessel alongside.

Mack's story prefigures the second season of *Discovery* in which the *Enterprise*, Pike and Spock play major roles, in part establishing the cast and crew for eventual spin-off series *Strange New Worlds*, and it is possible during the first season writers were looking for mechanisms to explore Burnham's relationship to Spock, as established in her relationship with a younger Sarek. What is unfortunate is that we only ever see Pike and Georgiou interact as fellow captains in the novel rather than on screen.

Plans also existed to feature a tardigrade named Ephraim as part of *Discovery*'s main crew, interacting with human characters. Harberts explains: "There were full-on scenes. We have the scripts with scenes between Ephraim and Burnham where he's talking to her about the meaning of life, and spores and the beauty of mushrooms."

A major part of *Discovery*'s storytelling, the tardigrades were genetic cousins to humans who also served as multi-dimensional creatures that live in space and can navigate the 'mycelial network', a biological undercurrent to the fabric of space that allows for travel across vast distances. *Discovery*'s initial innovation was a 'spore drive' that uses a trapped tardigrade to travel across space in the blink of an eye, with Lorca exploiting the creatures to help win conflicts against the Klingons and, ultimately, return to his original Mirror Universe.

The reason Ephraim never manifested was down to budgetary concerns and the amount of visual effects necessary, though the concept both morphed into 'Ripper', a tardigrade central to the spore drive, and an animated episode of *Short Treks* – a tie-in of minisode stories connected to various *Star Trek* shows, principally *Discovery* – called 'Ephraim and Dot', written and directed by *Star Trek* movie composer Michael Giacchino, where we eventually see Ephraim as a tardigrade who forms a sweet relationship with a repair drone named Dot.

One of the crucial first season episodes, 'Si Vis Pacem, Para Bellum', sees *Discovery* make first contact with the Pahvans, peace-loving natives of the planet Pahvo, who are in harmony with their environment and use crystal 'music' as a means of trying to unite the Federation and the

Klingons. Kirsten Beyer, one of the writers on the series, hoped to return to Pahvo for a subsequent *Discovery* episode, but instead passed it over to a different form of *Star Trek* media – *Star Trek Online*: "Kirsten Byer [sic] had a story of Pahvo that she wanted to do on the show but didn't have time . . . she gave it to us. So we'll be exploring that in the game."

Pahvo featured in four missions of *Online*'s 'Age of Discovery' campaign, set over 150 years after the *Discovery* episode, which sees a time-displaced Mirror Universe crew of the ISS *Discovery* – commanded by a sinister version of *Discovery* crew member Sylvia Tilly – attempt to take control of Pahvo, leading to a conflict with Klingon forces.

Discovery has since sailed into uncharted waters, transporting the crew and many of the main characters from the very beginning into the far distant future, the 32nd century, allowing them a whole new sandbox to play in. It will chiefly be remembered for issuing a new age of discovery for *Star Trek*, the show that launched potentially a thousand ships.

There have been other concepts, however, outside of *Discovery* and the series that canonically followed it, all of them different, all of them looking to approach *Star Trek* through all new – and in many cases old – eyes.

*

Outside of fan hopes for a 'Captain Sulu' project during the *Next Generation*-era, as earlier documented, few other concepts for new *Star Trek* series created as much interest as the possibility of a 'Captain Worf' series featuring Michael Dorn.

In the interim following his last appearance as Worf in *Nemesis*, and the end of *Enterprise*, Dorn repeatedly voiced his interest in playing *Star Trek*'s favourite Klingon in his own series. He had reputedly been asked to appear as an ancestor of Worf (perhaps even the father of the character he had portrayed in *The Undiscovered Country*) during early episodes of *Discovery* featuring Klingons – presumably in scenes concerning the extremist villain T'Kuvma and his followers – but he turned the offer down due to his pay being lower than in previous *Star Trek* series.

Dorn, focused on his own Worf idea, suggested it could be a lower budget production around 2012, at the point *Star Trek* was not a going concern on television, and felt a movie would be the better outlet: "I think there is a place for it. Straight to DVD or straight to cable. Who wouldn't want to have this kind of thing going on? It is going to help their movie. The fans aren't going 'we are going to see this movie, but we aren't going to go see the big movie in the theater.'"

Dorn envisaged Worf as having graduated, following *Nemesis* and the events of *Deep Space Nine*, to being captain of a Federation ship on the front lines "chasing terrorists", framed with a darker aesthetic perhaps matching plans for *Into Darkness* currently in development: "I think we will have some of our *Star Trek* people in it, but mostly new characters. It will be interwoven into the fabric of *Star Trek*. And also what we [are] going through right now?"

Before taking the idea to CBS, Dorn planned to get his ducks in a row via several meetings beforehand: "First with Rick Berman, who produced all of our shows, just to see what he thinks. Then my manager. And I know people at SyFy. And I'll just start gathering information. If anything happens it is going to be next year because I have a bunch of stuff to do this year. I have already started writing the script and excuse my language, but it f – ing great."

Nothing came of the idea but in 2021, as *Discovery* had instigated the newest era of *Star Trek*, including the post-*Nemesis* adventures of *Picard*, Dorn claimed he did indeed meet with CBS about the idea: "And, interestingly enough, it seems to rise and fall. There's interest and then there's not. Then there's interest and then there's not. And I guess it was two years ago I thought they would take it a little further. But that did not happen. So I don't know if the whole idea is dead – not in my mind. [laughs] I believe that they are missing a great opportunity to insert something into *Star Trek* that's always been part of the *Star Trek* lexicon, which is the Klingons."

Having spent longer fleshing the concept out, Dorn gave more details on what 'Captain Worf' might look like: "Instead of looking at the Klingon Empire from Starfleet, we look at Starfleet from the Klingon Empire. And it has been going on for decades, the Klingon Empire just can't go on. It's the Russians, basically. And they decide that they have to either die with a sword in their hands and go extinct, or change with the times and become something different. And Worf is the guy that says, 'We have to change with the times, that is the mark of a warrior.'"

This approach feels like an extension of efforts in *Deep Space Nine*, such as Worf-centric episodes like 'Soldiers of the Empire', to flesh out Klingon life and ritual, fused with a latent echo of *The Undiscovered*

Country and how, in the wake of the Cold War and a Chernobyl-like event, the Klingon Empire needed to change their mindset or face extinction. Dorn continued: "And so two things happen. They start letting other races into the Klingon world. And the only way they can do that is by letting in Starfleet officers. That's sort of the way it's done. 'We'll let in other people, but first Starfleet offers because we understand Starfleet. They're soldiers, we're soldiers.' The second thing they have to do is their resources are limited and dwindling, because the Klingon universe is just like the Federation. They have planets and worlds and societies that they own, but they do it in a brutal way. And so they have to go out to every one of these worlds and either give them their freedom, or try to work with them, which is something that's anathema to Klingons."

Dorn reveals, in this approach, that Worf would captain not a Starfleet ship but a Klingon one, visiting worlds in Klingon space as part of their efforts to modernise as a culture: "And since Worf opened his big mouth and said, 'This is what we have to do,' then they say, 'Okay, then you're the guy that has to go out to all these worlds.' And every world is different. Some worlds are rebelling. Some worlds want to be part of the Klingon Empire. Some worlds want to be independent. And so every episode is that."

One suspects J. G. Herztler's Chancellor Martok, last seen in the *Deep Space Nine* series finale would have featured in some capacity, and perhaps Worf's Klingon-born son Alexander Rozhenko, with whom he has always had a difficult relationship. It is also possible Dorn might have featured a means of including *Deep Space Nine* and *The Next Generation* characters Worf had a significant dynamic with, such as Ezri Dax or Deanna Troi. The possibilities for a series that explored the post-*Nemesis* world from a different side of the galactic fence, anchored by a beloved *Star Trek* character, remain tantalising.

"What I wrote, it's claustrophobic. It's Shakespearean in its scope. There's assassinations and coups and behind-the-scenes politics going on. It's such a great fit and it doesn't feel like anything else that's on All Access. It's funny because it's like they are looking for something and they've totally ignored this easy path. But we'll see what happens. I don't know if it's dead or not."

Dorn has since returned to play Worf in the final season of *Picard*, in which show runner Terry Matalas reinvented him as a Klingon 'ronin'; a somewhat enigmatic modern, sword-wielding mercenary samurai, albeit still Worf with his penchant for humour and deadpan asides. Dorn has suggested the approach taken for an early 25th-century Worf is rather different from what he imagined, but *Picard* does strongly suggest that Worf served on the *Enterprise-E* after most of the *Next Generation* crew moved on. Una McCormack's non-canonical prequel *Picard* novel, 'The Last Best Hope', also names Worf as captain of the ship, succeeding Picard seemingly, and *Picard* (albeit jokingly) hints Worf might have been responsible for the ship going out of commission.

Matalas adds more detail about whether it means Worf was captain: "It does. But I wanted to leave its exact fate open for someone to tell that story. It's more fun that way. Better left to the audience's imagination. What do you mean it wasn't his fault? Was it an accident? A mission gone wrong?! The possibilities are endless!"

Dorn isn't convinced any of this was set in stone but crafted his own idea of what Worf might have done in the interim years: "The only thing I had in my backstory is that he went to – and this is something that they didn't really write, but I think it was in our heads as they were writing these things – is that Worf went back to this planet, Boreth, which is like a monastery. He went back there to study because he learns that there are other things besides trying to slice people up. And he is learning about the spirituality of the journey. And I think that was the only thing that I clued them in on, and that was it. And I think it was great because they didn't write anything about that, but they kept that in their lexicon, I guess."

He, arguably, steals the show across *Picard*'s final season and given Dorn looks remarkable given his advanced years as a white-haired Worf, there seems little reason the character could not feature in his own series.

Indeed, there is nothing to say that Dorn's own concept itself could not be revived for the post-*Picard* landscape, although Dorn seems sceptical about what he previously developed: "I don't think that my script lends itself now because it's totally different than what they've written, but I think what they've written could easily be translated into a Worf show. But all of those decisions are above my pay grade, so I'll let them do all that stuff. And if it happens, great. If it doesn't, I think that I've had a great career."

Time will tell. What seems certain is that whether 'Captain Worf' ever materialises or not, *Star Trek* is unlikely to have seen the last of Dorn's Klingon.

*

In first developing what became *Discovery*, Fuller recruited to his development staff an iconic figure in *Star Trek* history: Nicholas Meyer, director and writer of *The Wrath of Khan*, parts of *The Voyage Home* (as writer only) and *The Undiscovered Country*.

His tenure on *Discovery* did not last very long, moving on it seems roughly around the time Fuller parted ways, but his involvement in *Star Trek* seems to have creatively fired him up to find ways of further exploring ideas within this universe. We have discussed the movie pitch he has worked on for Paramount, but he has also been busy developing series ideas that could work within the Kurtzman-era approach of different *Star Trek* concepts across multiple time zones.

Meyer announced in the middle of 2017 he was working on a series project that was later revealed to be known as 'Ceti Alpha V', a three-part limited series which would tell the story of Khan Noonien Singh's exile to the doomed planet between the events of 'Space Seed' and the USS *Reliant* finding he and his people in *The Wrath of Khan*. Already the subject of a (very good) non-canonical novel by Greg Cox, the series would serve as an extension of Meyer's seminal *Star Trek* work in the early 1980s.

The series had not materialised by the middle of 2019 when Meyer suggested that a conflict between rights to the cinematic *Star Trek* adventures and TV production, resolved following a merger between Viacom in CBS that year, was part of the reason why 'Ceti Alpha V' had not entered production: "I think what happened, or up to a point what happened, was that the business model for streaming was changing really fast. And what was originally commissioned as a three-hour or three-night event, by the time I finished writing it, three hours was not enough. They wanted longer stuff. And somewhere between those two imperatives, the thing sort of fell between two stools. And I still don't know why they're not doing it, even if it's to say, 'Give us ten episodes instead of three or whatever.' I don't know why."

Given Meyer also claimed that Kurtzman approached him with the idea of a limited series featuring Khan in this way, it feels a strong possibility that the concept might yet emerge. Meyer believes it doesn't have legs beyond a contained three-part story: "I think if it went on and on and on about Khan and Ceti Alpha V it risks becoming a kind of

Gilligan's Island. Which I think is a wrong idea . . . It was commissioned as a three-hour thing and there were certain parameters that were put down, to which I adhered. And they're all fungible."

However, since Meyer discussed this, the parameters have begun to change as to how *Star Trek* tells stories. Kurtzman has deliberately stated he wishes to move away from the CBS plan to feature *Star Trek* on air every week of the year and craft projects that either work as stand-alone movie events – such as the Michelle Yeoh-fronted *Section-31* film destined for Paramount+ revolving around Emperor Georgiou – and limited series, leaving only certain projects to exist as longer-running properties. 'Ceti Alpha V' sounds, in theory, the perfect kind of project for this approach.

Nonetheless, the project seems destined to be arriving in a different and more modern medium than Meyer would have imagined when he first considered the project: as *Star Trek*'s first narrative podcast. In 2022, it was announced that *Star Trek: Khan – Ceti Alpha V* would debut in audio format, presumably allowing them to tell Meyer's story in a manner that may not have meshed with their creative aspirations on television.

Kurtzman stated: "Nick made the definitive *Trek* movie when he made *Wrath*, and we've all been standing in its shadow since. Forty years have offered him a lot of perspective on these extraordinary characters and the way they've impacted generations of fans. Now he's come up with something as surprising, gripping and emotional as the original, and it's a real honor to be able to let him tell the next chapter in this story exactly the way he wants to."

Will there be appetite amongst audiences outside of *Star Trek* fandom for a series about the franchise's greatest supervillain, and exactly how he became the unhinged figure immortalised for generations of fans?

Time will tell.

*

For a long, long time, Patrick Stewart said no. No to playing Captain Jean-Luc Picard again after 2002's final *Next Generation* film, *Nemesis*.

"I'd done everything I could with Picard and *Star Trek*," he explained.

Then, at San Diego Comic Con in 2018, everything changed. Kurtzman surprised the crowd by introducing Stewart, who confirmed a new series – the second new *Star Trek* series of the era following *Discovery* – was in development around his iconic *Enterprise* captain. *Star Trek:*

Picard became the first series directly built around a veteran character as opposed to a series concept.

Stewart had taken some convincing to return, asking Kurtzman along with Kirsten Beyer, Akira Goldman and Pulitzer prize-winning author Michael Chabon to create a document outlining what they imagined for the series. Stewart claims he "took a look at the names, and there were Academy award and Pulitzer prize winners. So I thought the most courteous thing to do would be to have a meeting to tell them face to face why I was going to turn them down."

Kurtzman added. "It turned into a 34-page document – with no way to shorten it. We were going on all in and he was going to read it or not read it, love it or hate it. It was our best attempt at trying to get him to say yes."

What they subsequently developed, with Stewart heavily a presence in the writer's room to a degree he never would have been during production of *The Next Generation*, convinced him that the approach intended was different enough from what came before to make his return worth it.

Picard begins in 2399, the end of the 24th century, with now-retired Starfleet Admiral Jean-Luc Picard living on his French vineyard without a lust for life. Following the death of a mysterious young woman called Daaj who seeks out his help, Picard is drawn out on an adventure to expose a dark conspiracy involving an extremist faction of the former Romulan Empire, the Zhat Vash, one that connects back to forces within an isolationist Federation and the legacy of his old friend, Data. Along the way, Picard assembles around him a crew of exiles and outsiders, including one or two old faces from 1990s *Star Trek* history.

Though *Picard* very quickly moves into the space of a science-fiction conspiracy thriller adventure across the first season, Chabon flippantly imagined an alternate path the tone of *Picard* might have taken: "You know, personally speaking, my own tastes and inclination, I always said when we were in the earliest versions of the room for this show, if we could have just done a whole show about Picard and the dog on the vineyard in France, with no starships, no phasers, the only Romulans would be those two Romulans who work for him on the vineyard, and no politics – just, like, there's a funfair down in the village and they all go, and maybe Picard solves a very low stakes mystery in the village, like, someone has stolen the antique bell out of the bell tower, or something like that? I would have loved to write that show. Um. I don't think the world's quite ready for a '*Star Trek*' show like that, and there's probably maybe not that big of an audience for a '*Star Trek*' show like that."

This does speak to something of a conflict over quite what form *Picard* would take, a conflict that leads the show to morph into alternate forms across three very different seasons. The first detaches largely from the lore of the *Next Generation* era, surrounding Picard with new characters such as grumpy ex-Starfleet officer Cristobal Rios, Picard's paranoid post-*Enterprise* confidante Raffi Musiker, and morally complicated Dr Agnes Jurati. The second season engages in high-concept, time-travel, alternate-timeline storytelling which creeps in well-trodden elements from *The Next Generation* – the Borg Queen, Guinan, Q, and presents Starfleet more in the vein of the institution we know well. The third and final season serves finally as a ten-part 'reunion movie' for the entire *Next Generation* cast, climaxing with them literally dragging the *Enterprise-D* out of mothballs to save the galaxy from the Borg.

One character who grew in stature after appearing in several episodes of the first season was Seven of Nine, played again by Jeri Ryan, and reconceived as a 'Fenris Ranger', essentially a mercenary patrolling what was Romulan space and trying to protect innocent people. Seven steadily moved closer to Starfleet in becoming a regular across the next two seasons, realising the ambition of Captain Janeway in *Voyager* for her to become an officer. Matalas claims a story during *Picard* they broke would have not only linked back to the Rangers but introduced a minor 'legacy' character from the *Voyager* era: "We broke an episode where Naomi Wildman was a Fenris Ranger, following in the footsteps of Seven of Nine – and maybe was a bit more aggressive in her style than Seven. The crew this season certainly gets into some trouble, and Seven might have needed to go to somebody for help, and that person would have been Naomi Wildman. Ultimately, there just wasn't the real estate for it this season."

Production and cast changes affected the trajectory of the series. Chabon stepped away after the first season, leaving the role of show runner predominantly to Goldsman for the second alongside Matalas, who himself after a couple of episodes moved to sole show running duties for the third season, which was filmed back to back with the second. The COVID-19 pandemic, which hit just at the point the first season premiered, forced delays and inevitable production changes.

Goldsman even proffered, in a piece for *Vulture* about pandemic episodes of well-known television shows, what he would do with a pandemic-set *Picard* episode: "Admiral's Log. The quarantine stretches on. Essential systems continue to fail. And though many of us are used to long periods of isolation, the prohibition on physical contact, not to mention our inability to leave the ship, is beginning to wear on even the most seasoned members of the crew. Remote communication flourishes — still I am reminded there is no substitute for a direct gaze or the reassurance of a friendly touch. I am emboldened by the crew's resilience. Despite the hardship, they continue to work their stations; productivity and routine can be an excellent balm on fear. And fear they do, how could they otherwise? The threat we face is real with no immediate end in sight. But that does not make it endless. On the contrary, this period of darkness will end, as surely as it began. Fear will fade to memory. We will survive, stronger, perhaps more aware of the profound connections we have always shared. And a time will come when we once again right this ship and sail forward together into the future, that bright unknown."

Arguably, the final season of *Picard* was both the most anticipated and the most celebrated by *Star Trek* fandom, perhaps to a degree unseen since the franchise returned to television in 2017. The reunion of the entire *Next Generation* cast — including characters such as Beverly Crusher or Geordi la Forge who had not been seen on screen for twenty years — was a singular moment in popular culture's current fascination for nostalgia and revisiting beloved characters across the last forty to fifty years. Having them haul the *Enterprise-D*, last seen half destroyed in the movie *Generations*, added a deeper layer of excitement. The crew had finally come home.

Matalas admits, however, that not every ambition for *Picard*'s climax came to bear: "In the original finale script, it was a giant movie that we were building on a television time schedule. The fact that we saw what we saw was miraculous that we pulled it off. Like, it nearly killed us all. But there was a scene with Soji and Data that we could not afford to do and bring back another actor. There is a scene in which they found Ro Laren in the dungeons of the *Intrepid* with Tuvok and that she had survived and we weren't able to pull off. Harry Kim had appeared at one point. We wanted Kate Mulgrew to be part of Seven of Nine's promotion. These are all things that are all in the first script and then your line producer says, 'Are you out of your f***ing mind? You can't afford these things. You are not *Avengers: Endgame*.'"

The final season largely jettisoned much of the initial cast of *Picard* to focus on the return of the older crew, but a Soji and Data meeting would have added a sense of continuity to the earlier seasons that the third is missing. The return of Ro Laren, long since desired by fans after Michelle Forbes turned down the chance to become a main character in *Deep Space Nine*, was memorable but brief and her demise comes largely thanks to production realities. The absence of Admiral Janeway is particularly disappointing, given her connection to Seven historically and Kate Mulgrew's strong connection to *Star Trek* currently thanks to her voice role as a holographic version of the character in *Prodigy*.

Matalas adds that Harry Kim would have received the same promotion we saw him gain in *Voyager*'s future-set episode 'Timeless': "He was Captain, actually. I talked to Garrett [Wang] about it. He was very, very disappointed. He was Captain and yeah, that's all I can say about it. Again, it's time, it's money." Wang remains connected to *Star Trek* thanks to his successful podcast *The Delta Flyers*, recapping *Voyager* with co-star Robert Duncan McNeill (himself recently having voiced Tom Paris on *Lower Decks*), and one wonders if 'Captain' Kim might have featured as part of Seven's promotion to captain of the *Enterprise-G*.

The final episode also features the voice of Walter Koenig, one of the surviving members of *The Original Series*, as the Federation president, who also happens to be the son of his character Pavel Chekov, Anton, with Matalas claiming he had even bigger ambitions for the actor: "I really wanted one of the original series' actors to appear. Initially, I wanted to get him on camera, and I ran out of time and money to do that. There's a lot of things – we could talk about that too. But we were able, luckily, to do this great voiceover warning not-to-approach-Earth moment with him, and he was so wonderful."

Though come the end of the final season of *Picard*, concluding with an echo of the final moments of *The Next Generation* finale 'All Good Things . . .', Stewart has suggested he is truly hanging up his captain's uniform for the last time, and *Star Trek*'s future appears to be heading further and further into the past.

To conclude, we turn our vision to the undiscovered country of *Star Trek*, of what comes next, of the legacy that *Star Trek* continues to provide . . .

EPILOGUE

WHERE NO FRANCHISE HAS GONE BEFORE

ACROSS EIGHTEEN YEARS, from 1987 to 2005, *Star Trek* had an unbroken period on television across four different series. Aside from the natural breaks between network television seasons, *Star Trek* was never off the air in that time, bringing audiences a total of 624 episodes across that span. It remains the undisputed 'Golden Age' of *Star Trek* as a franchise.

Nevertheless, since 2017, that dominance has been challenged. While *Star Trek* is unlikely to produce a similar number of stories as those heady days, thanks to the production model of network television morphing into that of streaming, with fewer episodes but often greater production value, the ambition of CBS and later Paramount to air *Star Trek* every week, fifty-two weeks a year speaks to how central the franchise has become to their corporate brand, even if as of writing in 2023 these ambitions have slightly scaled back in light of economic realities.

The point remains – a thirst for *Star Trek* still strongly exists, as it has done now for generations. D. C. Fontana makes this point: "I don't know why people keep coming back to it, but I have had so many people, whether they're in my business, or whether they are outside – civilians, if you will – coming in to say, '*Star Trek* still talks to me. But I like the original series.' They always come back to the original series. We were talking to an audience that was listening. We were trying to tell intelligent stories with good actors and good messages, and I think we succeeded.

The goal on any show is to tell the best stories you can. We succeeded admirably, especially in the first two seasons of *Star Trek*."

Brannon Braga adds: "Anything you can think of you can really and truly do on *Star Trek*; any idea you want to explore, you can explore. It's an open book. It's kind of like when I think about it, I'm, like, 'God, I miss this show.' I could write for the show again, it never really got old. Every episode had its own challenges, but different sensibilities come and go, and I think the J. J. Abrams movies definitely infuse a new energy and budget into the whole thing."

As indeed has the newest iteration of *Star Trek*, from the arrival of *Discovery* to *Picard* and via animated forays such as *Lower Decks* – a well-meaning and often highly successful lampoon of *The Next Generation*-era, in the ironic style of a *Family Guy* or *Rick and Morty*. Or *Prodigy* – a Nickelodeon-fronted adventure story aimed at a younger market with a rag-tag assortment of youthful aliens who voyage in a lost Starfleet ship, stewarded by a returning Kate Mulgrew as a holographic Captain Janeway, circa the era of *Voyager* – through to *Strange New Worlds*, the series closest to *The Original Series* since the 1960s, telling the story as it does of Christopher Pike, the captain who preceded James T. Kirk and who featured in the original pilot, 'The Cage'.

Star Trek has circled back to where it all began.

We have seen across this book the many ways *Star Trek*'s story could have taken a different turn. What if the five-year mission of *The Original Series* had played out across five seasons? Would there have been the same sense of letter-writing, fan injustice that carried *Star Trek* through the 1970s and toward a cinematic rebirth? If *Phase II* had been produced, would there later have been a need for *The Next Generation* and would we have seen the aforementioned 'Golden Age' of the franchise at all? Would there have even been a movie franchise? And had *Enterprise* been a greater success, continuing the series on television, would J. J. Abrams reboot had been necessary, a reboot that texturally and creatively informed the *Discovery*-led era of *Star Trek*?

These are hypotheticals that would make even the Department of Temporal Corrections' heads spin. Forks in the road. Creative choices. Corporate decisions. Simple luck, good or bad, which informed the path *Star Trek* took over decades, surviving and reinventing itself, even against a tide of fan opprobrium in places. Nobody initially wanted Captain Picard and his crew, yet *Picard* saw them gain their iconic send-off as legends equally powerful to that of Kirk and company. *Deep Space Nine* was considered the curious stepchild yet now retains a critical place as, for many, the finest *Star Trek* series of all time.

Nobody ever quite knows what they want from *Star Trek* until it arrives, and even then it takes the passage of time for audiences to accept the place it holds in our collective culture.

Rod Roddenberry, son of creator Gene, has a somewhat pessimistic view on the outlook of the franchise: "Does the world still want *Star Trek*? I know the answer, yeah, everyone still wants *Star Trek*. I am curious, though, as we all get older, are the people who are brought up with the current movies going to care? *Star Trek* will be more of a historical footnote than something that's really affecting people."

Nobody, truly, knows the answer to this question. Nobody knows what popular culture will survive not just decades but centuries. *Star Trek*, however, has the potential for the same kind of durability as Sherlock Holmes, who continues to dazzle storytellers a century and a half on. The world Roddenberry created, and many subsequent writers and producers have shepherded onwards into the present day, still maintains the capacity for dramatic excitement and social commentary. The pilot episode of *Strange New Worlds* toed a line between allegory and commentary in depicting the 6 January Capitol Hill insurrection of 2021 as one of the triggers for an eventual Third World War, but it spoke to a continued determination to maintain *Star Trek*'s cultural relevance.

The franchise, equally, has no plans to disappear into the stars. Aside from the ongoing development of a fourth Abramsverse film, and despite the end of *Picard* and soon, as of writing, *Discovery*, the animated series continue apace with the potential of many future series to come. *Section-31*, starring Michelle Yeoh and revolving around the sinister human intelligence agency, could trigger a new series of TV movies or short event series on Paramount Plus. A series called *Starfleet Academy*, the genesis of which goes back decades as we have seen, will be the next major series in 2024. Fans too have backed the hashtag #StarTrekLegacy, with calls for a post-*Picard*, 25th-century-set follow-up combining old and new characters from *The Next Generation*-era.

What appears certain is that *Star Trek*'s future looks bright, on television at least and hopefully one day once again on the big screen. That too means a future history of the 'unmade', the ideas and concepts that future writers, actors and creatives will dream up, and will never come to be.

Unmade, unproduced stories and character arcs that will again offer an alternate history to *Star Trek*'s continuing mission to explore strange new worlds, seek out new life and new civilisation. They will, perhaps, be more consistently chronicled in years to come than many of the lost tales this book has covered.

Whatever path *Star Trek*'s future takes, know there will always be another. As Kirk says to Saavik in *The Wrath of Khan*, trapped in the Genesis cave, quoting his lost friend. "I like to think there always are . . . possibilities." That is what this book is. A book of possibilities.

Star Trek has always been about imagination. Let us imagine, and cherish, all these roads not taken that could have steered *Star Trek* where no franchise had gone before . . .

BIBLIOGRAPHY

After Trek. Star Trek: Discovery: 'Choose Your Pain' aftershow. CBS. 2017.

Alexander, David. *Star Trek Creator: The Authorized Biography of Gene Roddenberry*. Penguin. 1994.

Alter, Ethan. 'Walter Koenig Reveals Favorite *Star Trek* Movies, Salutes Anton Yelchin, and Approves Continuing Films Without Chekov'. Yahoo. September 1, 2016.

Altman, Mark. A. and and Gross, Edward. *Captains' Logs: The Unauthorized Complete Trek Voyages*. Little Brown & Co. 1995

Altman, Mark. A. *Charting the Undiscovered Country: The Making of Trek VI*. Image Pub of New York. 1992

Altman, Mark. A. and Gross, Edward. *Lost Voyages of Trek and The Next Generation*. Boxtree Ltd. 1995.

Altman, Mark. A. and Gross, Edward. *The Fifty-Year Mission: The Complete, Uncensored, Unauthorised Oral History of Star Trek: The First 25 Years*. Thomas Dunne Books. 2016.

Altman, Mark. A. and Gross, Edward. *The Fifty-Year Mission: The Next 25 Years: From The Next Generation to J. J. Abrams*. Thomas Dunne Books. 2016.

Arnold, Richard. Interview with Tim Lynch. 1991.

Asherman, Allan. *The Star Trek Interview Book*. Pocket Books. 1988.

Berkmann, Marcus. *Set Phasers to Stun: 50 Years of Star Trek*. Abacus. 2017.

Blackmon, Joe. 'William Shatner Confirms He Was Contacted About *Star Trek 3* And He Would Love To Do It.' Comicbook.com. June 30, 2015.

Block, Paula. M. *Star Trek: Deep Space Nine Companion*. Star Trek. 2000.

Bormanis, Andre. Author's interview, 2023.

Buck, Jerry. "*Star Trek* Engenders Cult in U.S., England." Youngstown Vindicator. March 14, 1972.

Bulletproof Screenwriting Podcast. 'BPS 116: From Horror Indies to *The Revenant* with Mark L. Smith.' April 14, 2021.

Burnett, Robert Meyer. Robservations podcast: Bryan Fuller. August 12, 2020.

Braga, Brannon; Lay, Roger. Jr; Moore, Ronald. D. 'All Good Things' BluRay commentary. 2014.

'Braving the Unknown' feature. *Star Trek: Voyager* Season 1 DVD. 2004.

Brian, B. 'Erik Jendresen talks about the 11th *Star Trek* film.' Movieweb. Mar 10, 2005.

Brown, Scott. 'Star Script Doctor Damon Lindelof Explains the New Rules of Blockbuster Screenwriting'. *Vulture*. Aug 4, 2013.

Caldwell, Sarah. '8 Star Trek Spec Scripts That Never Saw the Light of Day'. *Vulture*. September 27, 2017.

Connelly, Sherilyn. *The First Star Trek Movie: Bringing the Franchise to the Big Screen, 1969-1980*. McFarland. 2019.

Couch, Aaron. '*Star Trek* Boss: Picard Leads "Radically Altered" Life in CBS All Access Series.' *The Hollywood Reporter*. January 8, 2019.

'Crew Dossier: Kira Nerys' feature. *Star Trek: Deep Space Nine* Season 1 DVD. 2003.

Cult Times magazine. August 2005.

Cushman, Marc. *These Are The Voyages – TOS: Season One*. Jacobs Brown Press. 2014

Cushman, Marc. *These Are The Voyages – TOS: Season Two*. Jacobs Brown Press. 2014.

Cushman, Marc. *These Are The Voyages – TOS: Season Three*. Jacobs Brown Press. 2014.

D'Alessandro, Anthony. '*Fargo* Season 4 Finale: Creator Noah Hawley On Tonight's Gangland Outcome; The Future Of 'Cat's Cradle' & Those 'Alien' TV Series Rumors.' *Deadline*. November 29, 2020.

Davies, Russell. T. 'The Writers Tale: The Final Chapter'. BBC Digital. 2013.

Detroit Free Press, The. September 6, 2016.

Devega, Chauncey. 'Remembering *Star Trek: Deep Space Nine*: A controversial sci-fi landmark.' *Salon*. May 12, 2019.

Di Lella, Joseph. D. 'Writing For *Star Trek Part IX*: How To Pitch (Part Two)'. IFeb 3, 2003.

Diggs, Jimmy. '"Star Trek: The Lions of the Night" Animatic.' YouTube. January 31, 2009.

East, Michael. 'The time *Doctor Who* tried to cross over with *Star Trek: Enterprise*'. Winterscoming. 2021.

Epsicokhan, Jamahl. 'Jammer Goes to L.A.: Seeing the Franchise from Another Perspective'. *Jammers Reviews*. April 26, 2000.

Erdmann, Terry. *Star Trek: Action!* Prentice Hall & IBD. 1998.

Erdmann, Terry. *Star Trek: Deep Space Nine Companion*. Star Trek. 2000.

Fenwick, James. *Unproduction Studies and the American Film Industry*. Routledge. 2021.
Fernandez, Maria Elena. 'If I Wrote a Coronavirus Episode.' *Vulture*. April 2, 2020.

Fleming, Jr. Mike. 'Quentin Tarantino *On Once Upon A Time*, His Vision of *Star Trek* As *Pulp Fiction* in Space, and Hopes to Turn Leo DiCaprio '50s Western 'Bounty Law' into Series.' *Deadline*. July 17, 2019.

Franich, Darren. 'Doug Jung talks Sulu's husband and the *Zero Dark Thirty* of *Star Trek*.' *Entertainment Weekly*. November 1, 2016.

'The 10 unbelievable (or awful) *Star Trek* episodes that never got made.' Games Radar. September 8, 2016.

Goldberg, Lesley. '*Star Trek* Boss: Picard Leads "Radically Altered" Life in CBS All Access Series.' *The Hollywood Reporter*. January 8, 2019.

Green, Jeff. 'The Classic *Star Trek* As You've Never Seen It Before'. *Computer Gaming World*. May 1998.

Green, Michelle Erika. 'Harve Bennett'. *TrekToday*. February 28, 2006.

Hardwick, Chris. Nerdist podcast: Quentin Tarantino, Dec 18, 2015

Harvey, Aaron. 'INTERVIEW: John Cho Talks Sulu's Journey, Cut Scene in *Star Trek Beyond*.' Trekmovie. July 19, 2016.

Hibberd, James. 'Bryan Fuller on his *Star Trek: Discovery* exit: "I got to dream big"' *Entertainment Weekly*. July 28, 2017.

Holloway, Daniel. 'Noah Hawley on *Fargo* Season 4, His *Star Trek* Film and *Lucy in the Sky* Variety. 2020.

Horowicz, Josh. 'Happy Sad Confused: Tom Hanks' podcast. September 7, 2022.

Horowicz, Josh. 'Happy Sad Confused: Quentin Tarantino' podcast. December 28, 2015.

Hughes, Aaron. 'Neglected Masters: Book Review'. October 9, 2010.

Hughes, David. *The Greatest Sci-Fi Movies Never Made*. Titan Books. 2008.

Iacovino, Kayla. 'JJ Abrams to Direct *Star Trek: Excelsior* Starring George Takei as Capt. Sulu + Cameron Mackintosh Announces *Star Trek: The Musical* [April Fools]'. Trekmovie. April 1, 2012

'In Conversation: Rick Berman and Brannon Braga' feature. *Star Trek: Enterprise* Season 1 Blu-ray. 2013.

Joest, Mick. 'Victor Garber Reflects On J.J. Abrams Cutting His Klingon Role From 2009's *Star Trek*.' Cinema Blend. July 4, 2022.

Kaplan, Anna. L. '*Star Trek: Deep Space Nine*'. *Cinefantastique*, Vol. 29, No. 6/7. 1997.

Kaplan, Anna. L. 'Special Visual Effects'. *Cinefantastique*, Vol. 31, No. 11. 2000.

Kaplan, Anna. L. 'Armin Shimerman'. *Cinefantastique*, Vol. 32, No. 4/5. 2000.

Kaplan, Anna. L. 'Ron D. Moore Q&A Pt 1". Lcars.com. March 30, 2020.

Kaye, Don. '*The Wrath of Khan* Producer Hints at New Potential *Star Trek* Movie.' Den of Geek. July 9, 2020.

Kutzera, Dale. 'All Our Yesterdays'. *Cinefantastique*, Vol. 25/26, No. 6/1. 1994.

Kutzera, Dale. 'Time Travel Epic'. *Cinefantastique*, Vol. 27, No. 4/5. 1996.

Kutzera, Dale. '*Voyager* Episode Guide'. *Cinefantastique*, Vol. 28, No. 4/5. 1996.

Lawson, Mark. 'Interview: Patrick Stewart: "I'd go straight home and drink until I passed out"'. *The Guardian*. March 2, 2022.

Lovett, Jamie. '*Star Trek*: Ronald D. Moore Talks *Deep Space Nine* Season 8, Possibility of Returning to the Franchise'. Comicbook. Nov 23, 2019.

Lovett, Jamie. '*Star Trek: Picard* Season 3: Michael Dorn on Worf's Series, Son, and Captaincy'. Comicbook. March 6, 2023.

Lovett, Jamie. '*Star Trek* Officially Announces Nicholas Meyer's Khan - Ceti Alpha V.' Comicbook. September 8, 2022.

Lovitt, Maggie. '*Picard* Season 3 Showrunner Terry Matalas Breaks Down Episode 10, Fatherhood, and That 45-Minute Poker Game.' *Collider*. April 21, 2023.

Mack, David. Literary Treks #335 podcast. TrekFM. December 9, 2021.

McLean, Craig. 'Simon Pegg on rewriting *Star Trek 3*, "geekdom" and playing a romantic lead.' *Radio Times*. May 29, 2015.

Mooney, Darren. '*Assignment: Earth*'. Them0vieblog.com. May 1, 2015.

Moore, Ronald. D. Author's interview, 2023.

Neal Jones, Preston. *Cinefantastique*, Vol. 9, No. 2. 1979.

Nimoy, Leonard. *I Am Not Spock*. Celestial Arts. 1975.

"Ask TV Scout". *Palm Beach Post, The*. July 18, 1969.

Pappademas, Alex. 'It's Chris Pine Time!'. *Esquire*. March 1, 2023.

Parkin, Lance. *The Impossible Has Happened: The Life and Work of Gene Roddenberry*. Aurum Press Ltd. 2016.

Pascale, Anthony. 'CBS Considering New Animated *Trek* Series For The Web.' Trekmovie. December 13, 2006.

Pascale, Anthony. 'Interview With Leonard Nimoy – Part 1'. *Trekmovie*. Aug 1, 2007.

Pascale, Anthony. 'Interview: Reeves-Stevenses Talk Mars and *Enterprise*.' *Trekmovie*. September 22, 2007.

Pascale, Anthony. 'The Reeves-Stevens Talk Books With TrekMovie.com.' *Trekmovie*. Oct 16, 2007.

Pascale, Anthony. 'INTERVIEW: Star Trek Writers Alex Kurtzman & Roberto Orci.' *Trekmovie*. April 30, 2009.

Pascale, Anthony. 'VegasCon09: Braga & Coto Talk *Enterprise* Season 5 + Star Trek 2009 & more'. *Trekmovie*. August 10, 2009.

Pascale, Anthony. 'Exclusive: Read The Star Trek 2009 Scene Written For William Shatner.' *Trekmovie*. November 23, 2009.

Pascale, Anthony. 'George Takei "Baffled" Paramount Never Made Sulu Series'. *Trekmovie*. June 11, 2010.

Pascale, Anthony. 'Exclusive Details & Excerpts From 'Star Trek: Federation' Series Proposal.' *Trekmovie*. April 16, 2011.

Pascale, Anthony. 'EXCLUSIVE: Michael Dorn On (Almost) Part In Star Trek Sequel + Plans To Pitch Capt. Worf TV Movie + More'. *Trekmovie*. May 26, 2012.

Pascale, Anthony. 'Karl Urban Reveals Cumberbatch *Star Trek* Sequel Character?'. *Trekmovie*. July 9, 2012.

Pascale, Anthony. 'Interview: Roberto Orci Talks Writing 2009's *Star Trek* And The Roads Not Taken.' *Trekmovie*. May 9, 2019.

Pascale, Anthony. 'Interview: Michael Dorn Pitches *Captain Worf* Show; Explains What It Would Take To Do *Star Trek: Picard*'. *Trekmovie*. January 22, 2021.

Pascale, Anthony. 'Exclusive: Nicholas Meyer On What's Holding Back His 'Ceti Alpha V' *Star Trek* Mini-Series.' *Trekmovie*. March 13, 2021.

Pascale, Anthony. 'Exclusive: 'Wrath Of Khan' Director Nicholas Meyer Has Pitched A New *Star Trek* Movie To Paramount.' *Trekmovie*. March 20, 2021.

Petrakovitz, Caitlin. 'Victor Garber Will Make All Your Klingon Dreams Come True'. *Gizmodo*. October 13, 2009.

Piller, Michael. *Fade In: The Making of Star Trek Insurrection*. Posthumously published by family, 2016.

Pirrello, Phil. '*Star Trek: First Contact* Co-Writer Ron Moore Recalls Story Clash With Patrick Stewart'. *The Hollywood Reporter*. Nov 22, 2021.

Poe, Stephen Edward. *A Vision of the Future: Star Trek: Voyager*. Pocket Books. 1998.

'Observer Effect' audio commentary. *Star Trek: Enterprise* Season 4 Blu-ray. 2014.

Orquiola, John. '*Star Trek Picard* Showrunner On Season 3's Shocking Twists.' *Screenrant*. April 13, 2023.

Orquiola, John. 'Terry Matalas Breaks Down The *Star Trek Picard* Season 3 Finale.' *Screenrant*. April 20, 2023.

Reilly, Ken. 'INTERVIEW — Terry Matalas on Keeping the TNG Reunion on *STAR TREK: PICARD* a Secret, and the Almost-Return of Naomi Wildman.' *TrekCore*. February 15, 2023.

Reeves-Stevens, Garfield & Judith. *The Lost Years: The Making of Star Trek: Phase II*. Star Trek. 1997.

Roddenberry, Gene. 'The Questor Tapes' pilot script. 1973.

Sackett, Susan. *The Making of Star Trek: The Motion Picture*. Pocket Books. 1980.

Sackett, Susan. *Inside Trek: My Secret Life with Star Trek Creator Gene Roddenberry*. Self-published. 2013.

Sci Fi Universe, September 1994 issue.

Sci-Fi Universe, Vol. 1, issue 1.

Setoodeh, Ramin. 'How Chris Hemsworth Found His Way as a Movie Star With Thor and *The Avengers*'. *Variety*. May 28, 2019.

Shatner, William. *Star Trek Movie Memories*. Harper & Row Ltd. 1994.

Sharf, Zach. 'Quentin Tarantino Hints at *Star Trek* Exit: "I Don't Think I'm Going to Direct It."' *Indiewire*. January 14, 2020.

Starburst. Special #29. October 1996.

Starburst #256. December 1999.

Starlog #106. 'Leonard Nimoy: A View From the Bridge: The Actor/Director Looks Back at the Drama of *Star Trek III*.' May 1986.

Starlog #119. 'Beyond "The Naked Time": *Star Trek* Writer Brings a Unique Form of "Justice" to *The Next Generation*.' June 1987.

Starlog #127. 'In Memory Yet Mudd: Playing *Star Trek* Con Games Was a Special Joy For the Late Roger Carmel. February 1988.

Star Trek Magazine #118. December 2004/January 2005.

Star Trek Magazine #131. 'Quark Express'. March/April 2007.

Star Trek Magazine #180. April 2015.

Star Trek Monthly #39. May 1998.

StarTrek.com. 'Interview with Harve Bennett #2.' August 24, 2010.

StarTrek.com. 'Catching Up with *Star Trek* Writer Mike Sussman'. September 30, 2010.

StarTrek.com. 'Sir Patrick Stewart Interview'. Oct 4, 2010.

StarTrek.com. '*Trek* Writer David Gerrold Looks Back - Part 2'. January 24, 2011.

StarTrek.com. 'Recalling "Yesterday's *Enterprise*" with Eric Stillwell - Part 2'. Feb 17, 2011.

StarTrek.com. 'David R. George III On *Trek* Novels, His Career, Part 2'. May 28, 2012.

StarTrek.com. EXCLUSIVE: Orci Opens Up About *Star Trek Into Darkness*, Part 2.' May 24, 2013.

StarTrek.com. 'New *Star Trek* Series Premieres January 2017'. November 2, 2015.

StarTrek.com. 'Bryan Fuller Named Co-Creator of New *Star Trek* TV Series.' February 9, 2016.

Star Trek: Communicator #108. August/September 1996.

Star Trek: Communicator #121. 'The 34th Rule: A Novel Approach With a Familiar Name'. February/March 1999.

Star Trek: Communicator #139. August/September 2002.

Star Trek Online. Twitter.com. August 5, 2018.

Star Trek: The Magazine Volume 1, Issue 2. June 1999.

Star Trek: The Magazine Volume 1, Issue 5. September 1999.

Star Trek: The Magazine Volume 1, Issue 20. December 2000.

Star Trek: The Magazine Volume 2, Issue 9. January 2002.

Stentz, Zack. Twitter.com. Jul 13, 2020.

Straczynski, J. Michael. '*Star Trek*: Re-boot the Universe' pitch. 2004.

Sussman, Mike. 'We're Gonna Edit Out All This Klingon Stuff, Right?'. The Ready Room podcast. September 26, 2015.

T'Bonz. 'Takei Supports IFT In *Voyages* Interview'. *TrekToday*. June 9, 2010.

'The Longest Trek: Writing the Motion Picture' feature. *Star Trek: The Motion Picture* Blu-Ray. 2009.

The Official Star Trek: Deep Space Nine Magazine #8. 1994.

The Official Star Trek: Voyager Magazine #6. April 1996.

The Official Star Trek: Voyager Magazine #9. November 1996.

'Ron Moore & Ira Steven Behr Interview, Part II'. *TrekCore*. May 17, 2013.

Trekdocs. Twitter.com. June 3, 2017.

Trekdocs. Twitter.com. October 5, 2016.

Trekdocs. Twitter.com. May 24, 2016.

Trekdocs. Twitter.com. August 27, 2016.

Trekdocs. Twitter.com. April 23, 2017.

'Simon Pegg Reflects On 'Star Trek Beyond' – Talks "Maddening" Process, Critiques Marketing And More.' Trekmovie. April 4, 2018.

TV Zone #62. January 2005

TV's Top 5 podcast. 'Fargo' creator Noah Hawley on season 4'. September 25, 2020.

Westenfeld, Adrienne. 'For the Rings of Power Showrunners, the Road Goes Ever On.' *Esquire*. October 14, 2022.

Van Hise, James. *The Man Who Created Star Trek: Gene Roddenberry*. Pioneer Books. 1992.

Vary, Adam. B. '*Star Trek* Cast, Including Chris Pine and Zachary Quinto, Returning for Fourth Film.' *Variety*. February 15, 2022.

Vary, Adam. B. '*Star Trek: Picard* Is Divisive — and Showrunner Michael Chabon Doesn't Mind at All.' *Variety*. Mar 25, 2020.

Ayers, Jeff. *Voyages of Imagination: The Star Trek Fiction Companion*. Pocket Books. 2016.

Zabel, Bryce. '*Star Trek*: Re-boot the Universe' pitch. 2004.